Open Systems Interconnection Handbook

Open Systems Interconnection Handbook

Gary R. McClain, Ph.D.

**Intertext Publications
McGraw-Hill Book Company**

New York St. Louis San Francisco Auckland Bogotá
Hamburg London Madrid Mexico Milan Montreal
New Delhi Panama Paris São Paolo
Singapore Sydney Tokyo Toronto

All product names mentioned in this book are trademarks of their respective companies. AmLink3 and Am29000 are trademarks of Advanced Micro Devices, Inc.

Chapter 5 copyright © 1990 Eastman Kodak Company. Chapters 8 and 10 copyright © 1990 Westwood Technology Management. All rights reserved.

Library of Congress Catalog Card Number 90-85587

Copyright © 1991 by Multiscience Press, Inc. All rights reserved. Printed in the United States of America. Except as permitted under the United States Copyright Act of 1976, no part of this book may be reproduced or distributed in any form or by any means, or stored in a database or retrieval system without the prior written permission of the publisher.

10 9 8 7 6 5 4 3 2 1

ISBN 0-07-044969-4

Intertext Publications/Multiscience Press, Inc.
One Lincoln Plaza
New York, NY 10023

McGraw-Hill Book Company
1221 Avenue of the Americas
New York, NY 10020

Composed in Ventura Publisher by High Text Corp., Colleyville, TX.

Foreword

Open Systems Interconnection Handbook is meant to be a collection of viewpoints, suggested guidelines, and implementation examples, compiled with the goal of broadening the reader's awareness of the potential of the OSI model. The chapters included in the book reflect the diversity of the issues surrounding the OSI model, as well as the unique concerns and approaches of individuals active in the field.

I owe a special debt of gratitude to those who contributed chapters to this book. Each contributor took time out of a hectic schedule in order to do so. They are all actively involved in OSI and are dedicated to seeing that the standards and protocols become the foundation for day-to-day network connectivity.

The MAP/TOP Users Groups were especially helpful in providing me with information, and many of the members of the group's steering committee either suggested potential contributors, or wrote chapters themselves.

I would also like to thank Alan Rose of Intertext Publications for his support, as well as Bruce Sherwin for his patience and encouragement as he managed the book's production.

Contents

	Foreword	v
	Preface	xiii
	Introduction	xv
Section A	**Standards and Protocols**	1
Chapter 1	**An Overview of Standards and Protocols**	3
	Introduction	3
	ISO/CCITT OSI Model	3
	Standards-Based Protocol Specifications	14
	TCP/IP Protocol Suite	21
	Proprietary Protocols	28
	DECnet	28
	SNA	30
	NETEX	31
	Summary	33
	About the Author	33
Chapter 2	**U.S. GOSIP: Not Just for Government Procurement**	35
	Creation of the OSI Protocols	36
	User Profiles	37
	Creation of U.S. GOSIP	37
	The NIST Implementor's Agreements	38
	U.S. GOSIP Profile	39
	Physical Layer	40
	Data-Link Layer	40
	Network Layer	40
	Transport Layer	41

	Session Layer	41
	Presentation Layer	42
	Application Layer	42
	Conformance and Interoperability Testing	43
	Comparison of U.S. GOSIP to Other Profiles	44
	What U.S. GOSIP Doesn't Provide	44
	Questions to Ask Vendors	48
	Conclusion	49
	About the Author	50
Chapter 3	**Moving Toward Standards:** **The Rapid Growth of OSI in Europe**	**51**
	OSI Profiles	52
	The Government Sector	54
	OSI in Industry	60
	An OSI Deployment Strategy	62
	Using International Standards	63
	The Benefits of OSI	65
	Conclusion	67
	About the Author	67
Chapter 4	**ISDN and the Global Network**	**69**
	What's in a Name?	69
	Rebuilding the Network	70
	Software Structure	76
	Open Standards Issues	80
	Terminal Equipment and Terminal Adaptors	80
	About the Author	89
Section B	**Networks and Architectures**	**91**
Chapter 5	**An Architectural Vision** **Based on Standards**	**93**
	Abstract	93
	The "Integrated" State	93
	Capabilities Common to More Than One Application	96
	Network Basics	99
	Standards in Support of Networking Capabilities	100

	An Architectural Vision Based on Standards	104
	Getting There from Here (Migration to a Future State)	105
	About the Author	106
Chapter 6	**Concepts and Protocols of the OSI Network Layer**	**107**
	Overview of OSI Network Layer Functions	107
	Network Addresses	108
	Data Transfer Services	108
	Routing and Relaying	116
	Network Layer Addressing	116
	Network Entity Titles (NETs)	125
	SubNetwork Point of Attachment (SNPA) Addresses	125
	Internal Network Layer Architecture	126
	Network Layer Data Transfer Protocols	127
	Protocols to Provide the Connection-Oriented Network Service (CONS)	128
	Protocol to Provide the CLNS	139
	Network Layer Routing	156
	Static Configuration of Routing Information	156
	Algorithmic Determination of Routing Information	158
	Routing Protocols at the Network Layer	158
	Acknowledgments	185
	About the Author	185
Chapter 7	**Using the OSI Model for Network Architecture Analysis**	**187**
	Introduction	187
	Foundation	188
	Development of a Network Architecture	192
	Summary	204
	About the Author	206
Section C	**X.400 and X.500**	**207**
Chapter 8	**Successful OSI Migration Strategies**	**209**
	Introduction	209
	Interconnect Alternatives	210

x Open Systems Interconnection Handbook

	Case 1	212
	Case 2	215
	Case 3	217
	Key Implementation Strategies	219
	Summary	220
	About the Author	221
Chapter 9	**X.400 and Xerox Network Systems Mail**	**223**
	Introduction	223
	The Grapevine System at PARC	224
	The Development of Xerox 8000 Network Systems	226
	The Incorporation of the X.400 Mail Gateway	227
	Xerox's Early Influence on X.400	229
	Comparison of XNS and OSI Stacks	230
	Architecture of XNS Mail	233
	Conclusion and Lessons	238
	References	240
	About the Author	243
Chapter 10	**An X.500 Overview**	**245**
	Introduction	245
	Directory Information	248
	User Access to the Directory Information	252
	Internal Operations of the Directory	254
	Directory Applications and Future Directions	257
	Appendix A. Glossary of Selected X.500 Terminology	261
	Appendix B. Summary of X.500 Recommendations	263
	About the Author	263
Chapter 11	**The Distributed Computing Environment**	**265**
	Section 1. The Role of a Distributed Computing Environment	265
	Summary	277
	Section 2. Distributed Name Services	279
	Section 3. The OSF DCE Name Service	288
	Summary	294
	Sources	295
	About the Author	295

Section D	**Implementation Considerations**	**297**
Chapter 12	**How to Justify an OSI-Based Network**	**299**
	Introduction	299
	LAN Selection Overview	300
	Prerequisite Information	300
	Network Selection Parameters	303
	Network Selection Goals	305
	Network Guideline Procedure	307
	Phase I: Guideline Prerequisites	307
	Phase II: Interview Process	307
	Phase III: Comparison and Analysis	313
	Phase IV: Management Report	323
	Case Study — Tank Car Project	325
	Case Study — Prerequisites	326
	Case Study — Interview Process	327
	Case Study — Comparison and Analysis	336
	Case Study — Final Recommendations	346
	Summary	347
	About the Author	347
Chapter 13	**OSI Transition Strategies:**	
	How to Get There from Here	**349**
	Introduction	349
	The Historical Context — Network Evolution	350
	Benefits — The Advantages of Evolving to OSI	351
	The Transition Process — An Overview	352
	About the Authors	373
	Glossary	**375**
	Index	**385**

Preface

The overall purpose of *The OSI Handbook* is to provide a much needed perspective on the "real world" technical and business issues surrounding the implementation of the Open Systems Interconnection (OSI) model. The standard documents themselves are not particularly easy, or even interesting, to read, save for those that are both technically adept and determined. There are a number of excellent books that clarify and illustrate the OSI model. This book is aimed at rounding out the available references in the field by serving as a single reference source for those who are, or expect to be, dealing with OSI issues on a daily basis. Contributors are all extensively involved in the practical implementation of OSI.

The audience for *The OSI Handbook* is really twofold. It is for technical professionals, individuals with systems and networking concerns, who need more information about specific OSI-related topics. MIS managers and users with a technical orientation will also find the information useful.

The chapters in *The OSI Handbook* are arranged in four sections. The first section, "Standards and Protocols," includes a more indepth look at the OSI model and related standards, including ISDN, and serves as a foundation for the rest of the book. The second section, "Networks and Architectures," focuses on technical issues related to the network layer of the model, as well as cooperative processing. The third section, "X.400 and X.500," takes a closer look at distributed computing, X.400 and X.500 considerations, and an electronic mail implementation. The fourth section, "Implementation Considerations," explores the development of the OSI business case, and specific migration concerns. The chapters in the book present not only a discussion of the technical issues but also practical solutions.

The Open Systems Interconnection model holds the promise of bringing together the diverse hardware and software resources that exist in most organizations. The foremost goal in the development of this book is to clarify, and promote, the potential of OSI.

– Gary R. McClain, Ph.D.

Introduction

As organizations grow and develop, and their information management needs expand accordingly, it is not uncommon to reach for the quickest solution. As a result, "islands of information" sprout up, with departments unable to communicate or share information with one another. Proprietary solutions are in abundance — computers, terminals, workstations, databases, and application packages — but outside of their own work groups, users can't share information, or communicate electronically.

The next frontier in the development of information technology is the ability to share information and applications across the organization. The Open Systems Interconnection model, or OSI, has the potential of creating bridges between the islands of information through connectivity international standards.

In its purest form, OSI is basically a set of technical standards (*pages* and *pages* of technical standards) that provide a basis for data communications, such that computers from a multitude of different manufacturers can share data, and even applications, with one another. The OSI model does not imply that all the hardware vendors get together, share their proprietary secrets, and come up with one master computer. The OSI model provides standards that simply permit communication between different architectures so that, for example, an electronic mail message can be sent from a user on an IBM machine to a user on a DEC or NCR machine. OSI allows users in an organization to communicate and share data as necessary, while the organization's hardware and software investments are both protected and maximized.

Since 1984, a key to OSI has been peer-to-peer communication, as opposed to the more traditional master–slave relationship. In other words, each communications unit in the system has equal status, rather than one overriding the other during the process of communication across the network. Equipment from different vendors can truly be treated as equals. Is the much-discussed seamless operation finally a reality with OSI standardization? Again, the answer is yes, no, and maybe. This question can only be answered on an organization by organization basis, because each implementation of OSI has its own nuances.

As hardware and software vendors recognize the potential of OSI standardization, users will in turn benefit through greater availability and efficiency. Adoption of OSI has been a gradual process, however, due both to the slow evolution of the standards, as well as the proprietary traditions of vendors.

The Seven Layers

One of the unique aspects of the OSI model is its organization. The standards are arranged into seven layers, each representing one of the major functions required to effectively send data through a network. The layers are organized as a stack, so that, for example, a message going through a network would pass through the stack of seven layers. There are specifications in each layer. Thus, a vendor who is implementing OSI in the product development process must select specifications from each level (though not *all* the specifications at each level may be necessary) if the product is to fully conform with OSI standards. The relationship between the seven layers is in a sense hierarchical. In transferring a message, for example, certain actions are expected before, and after, the message passes a specific layer.

The focus of the *physical layer* is on the actual physical attachment to the network, for example, the means of connecting two nodes (or links) in the network. Cables, modems, and other connections are regulated at this level.

The *data link layer* focuses on the control of communication between the two nodes, checking for errors and "packaging" the message for the rest of the trip through the network.

At the *network layer,* a path is set up for the trip through the network, and the communication is routed to its destination, for example, from one node in the network to another.

The first three layers thus serve to package the communication and get it off to wherever its destination is in the network. From here, it passes through the fourth layer, called the *transport layer,* which essentially acts as a buffer between the beginning point of the trip and the destination. The transport layer handles the control of the flow of data in the network, making sure that the data is not lost and that the destination is not inundated with incoming data.

The top three layers, the services layers, focus on the actual destination of the communication and operate in reverse of the bottom three layers. It is in these layers that the communication is recompiled as necessary and passed on for processing or storage. As the communication reaches the *session layer*, it is passed to its appropriate destination, and the communication session is ended.

At the *presentation layer*, the communication, now that it has arrived, is translated into the appropriate syntax, so that the recipient can understand it. If the communication being sent is in the form of data, for example, it might be translated into a machine-readable language, appropriate to the destination, or even into a foreign language, understandable to a human.

The *application layer*, as the name implies, focuses on specific applications unique to the organization. At this layer, communications are matched with the specific user-applications to which they are appropriate, such as electronic mail, or an accounting package.

Standards: By Committee

Think about all the pieces that might make up a computer network: connections, channels, cable, mainframes, monitors, as well as other considerations, such as values, syntax, encoding, virtual versus real, context, . . . And then think of all of these pieces as they relate to the hardware and software of competing vendors. In addition to being an end user's nightmare, it is good material for a list of "designed by committee" jokes. But this describes the dilemma of developing OSI standards.

OSI is the responsibility of the International Standards Organization, but this is not to imply that a small group of technical gurus in Geneva, Switzerland, sat down and wrote a book of standards. OSI is more than protocols designed by a committee — they are actually designed by numerous committees (international, no less) meeting every six or nine months. Those involved must make competent technical decisions, as fair as possible considering the multiple vendors involved, yet realistic at the same time. This is no easy task, and certainly explains why the standards represent an evolutionary process.

In fact, probably the only thing the committee members fully agree on is the objectives. What finally becomes a standard might be the result of five years of meetings, representing an interim standard that was subsequently implemented and tested. It is important to remember that just as technology is changing and evolving, so is the

OSI model. This is not to imply that the OSI model is languishing. In fact, it was recently given a boost from the U.S. government, which has developed its own government OSI program, referred to as GOSIP. The U.S. government has mandated that within the near future, all new federal systems will comply with OSI. This means that information system vendors selling to the federal government must build OSI standards into their products.

The Major Forces

In addition to the International Standards Organizations, other organizations and companies have been formed to assist in the push towards OSI. Additionally, major vendors have made announcements indicating that they too are taking OSI seriously.

The Corporation for Open Systems is one of the more visible proponents of open systems. A non-profit organization founded in 1986, it is composed of members representing the federal government, academia, hardware and software companies, and various industries including communication, engineering, and manufacturing. The basic goal of the Corporation for Open Systems is to provide impartial verification of OSI, as well as ISDN products, to ensure that these products are truly in compliance with OSI standards. Those products judged to meet the OSI standards are given a "COS Mark," meaning that they will work with other OSI-compliant products in a multivendor environment.

MAP/TOP Users Group is composed of companies from around the world who have joined together to work to establish communications standards for factory automation (Manufacturing Automation Protocol) and engineering and office automation (Technical and Office Protocol). The specifications developed by MAP/TOP are based on the OSI model.

An important benefit of the MAP/TOP standards is that they provide a means of integrating various business functions, including factory floor control and office systems. Integration of the various functions in an organization is often missing, and seemingly impossible, as a result of the island approach to information management. The MAP/TOP standards seek to operationalize the OSI model to make this integration a reality.

In addition to non-profit and membership organizations, various hardware and software companies are also considering the OSI model in their product development activities.

Why Try to Agree?

A common question about the development of the OSI model concerns the need to come to an agreement at all. For example, why don't all vendors simply choose the architecture of a major vendor, such as IBM, and make that *the* standard for all vendors. Logically, this makes some sense, considering the installed base of large organizations using IBM's Systems Network Architecture (SNA).

First of all, the International Standards Organization is truly an international organization, and members seek to protect the free market interests of countries around the world. Second, a major goal of those adapting the OSI model is to gain maximum use of existing hardware and software, regardless of vendor, and the standards are designed to interconnect these diverse architectures.

Each hardware vendor offers unique strengths that make sense, depending on the specific needs of an organization. The OSI model, in effect, offers a new level of freedom of choice, allowing organizations to choose the best solutions without sacrificing overall connectivity. In large, medium, and small companies, the multivendor shop is here to stay.

Preparing for a Global Role

The world is shrinking, and even the most insular industries are finding themselves thrust into a much more competitive and multicultural environment. Companies in one country are being bought by larger companies based in another country and international monetary standards, as well as languages, must be considered. To prepare for this expanded role, effective sharing of information and resources within the organization is critical, so that necessary resources are available at a moment's notice.

Efficient communication in the global marketplace must begin within the organization. OSI essentially provides a basis for maintaining a central, coordinated focus on information resources, rather than compartmentalizing resources with no means of sharing the information. It is the foundation for the "controlled diversity" of information management in the dynamic organization. And as the communication barriers within the organization are surmounted, those outside can be approached from a position of strength.

Section A

Standards and Protocols

Chapter

1

An Overview of Standards and Protocols

by James F. Doar

Introduction

This chapter describes the Open Systems Interconnection model, beginning with a brief history of the development of the model. OSI is best understood in relation to other standards and protocols, some of which are based on OSI, others of which coexist with it, and still others of which are proprietary. Standards-based protocol specifications are also described, including the MAP/TOP protocols, GOSIP, and TCP/IP. Additionally, overviews of major proprietary protocols, DECnet, SNA and NETEX, are presented (Figures 1-1 and 1-2).

ISO/CCITT OSI Model

The International Standards Organization (ISO) is an international agency for the development of standards on a wide range of subjects. It is a voluntary, nontreaty organization whose members are designated standards bodies of participating nations and nonvoting observer organizations. Although ISO is a nongovernmental organization, more than 70 percent of ISO member bodies are governmen-

4   Open Systems Interconnection Handbook

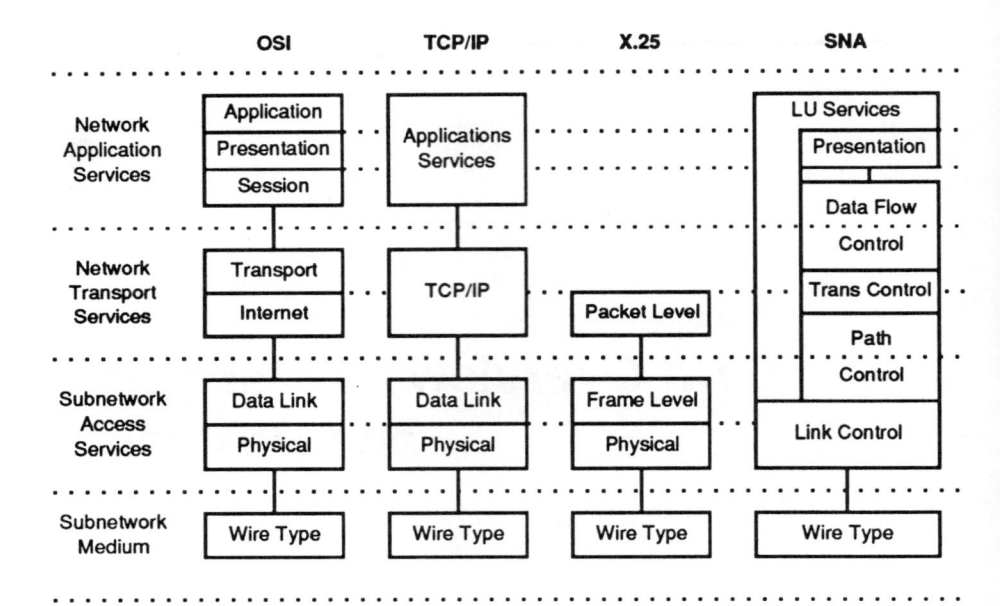

	OSI	TCP/IP	X.25	SNA
Network Application Services	Application / Presentation / Session	Applications Services		LU Services / Presentation / Data Flow Control
Network Transport Services	Transport / Internet	TCP/IP	Packet Level	Trans Control / Path Control
Subnetwork Access Services	Data Link / Physical	Data Link / Physical	Frame Level / Physical	Link Control
Subnetwork Medium	Wire Type	Wire Type	Wire Type	Wire Type

Figure 1-1 OSI and its relationship to other standards and protocols.

tal standards institutions or organizations incorporated by public law. Most of the remainder have close links with the public administrations in their own countries. The United States' member body is the American National Standards Institute (ANSI).

The International Consultative Committee on Telephony and Telegraphy (CCITT) is an international treaty organization of government agencies concerned with developing standards for information technology and communications. The United States' member body in CCITT is the U.S. State Department. Where ISO and CCITT standards developments overlap, the two agencies either form joint technical committees or maintain an official, close liaison through the use of designated *rapporteurs* who attend both committees' meetings. OSI standards are generally accepted and published by both bodies in essentially identical form.

ISO was founded in 1946 and has issued more than 5000 standards on a broad range of areas. Its purpose is to promote the development of standardization and related activities to facilitate international exchange of goods and services, and to develop cooperation in the spheres of intellectual, scientific, technological, and economic activity. Standards have been issued to cover everything from screw threads to solar energy. ISO is organized as a group of technical

An Overview of Standards and Protocols 5

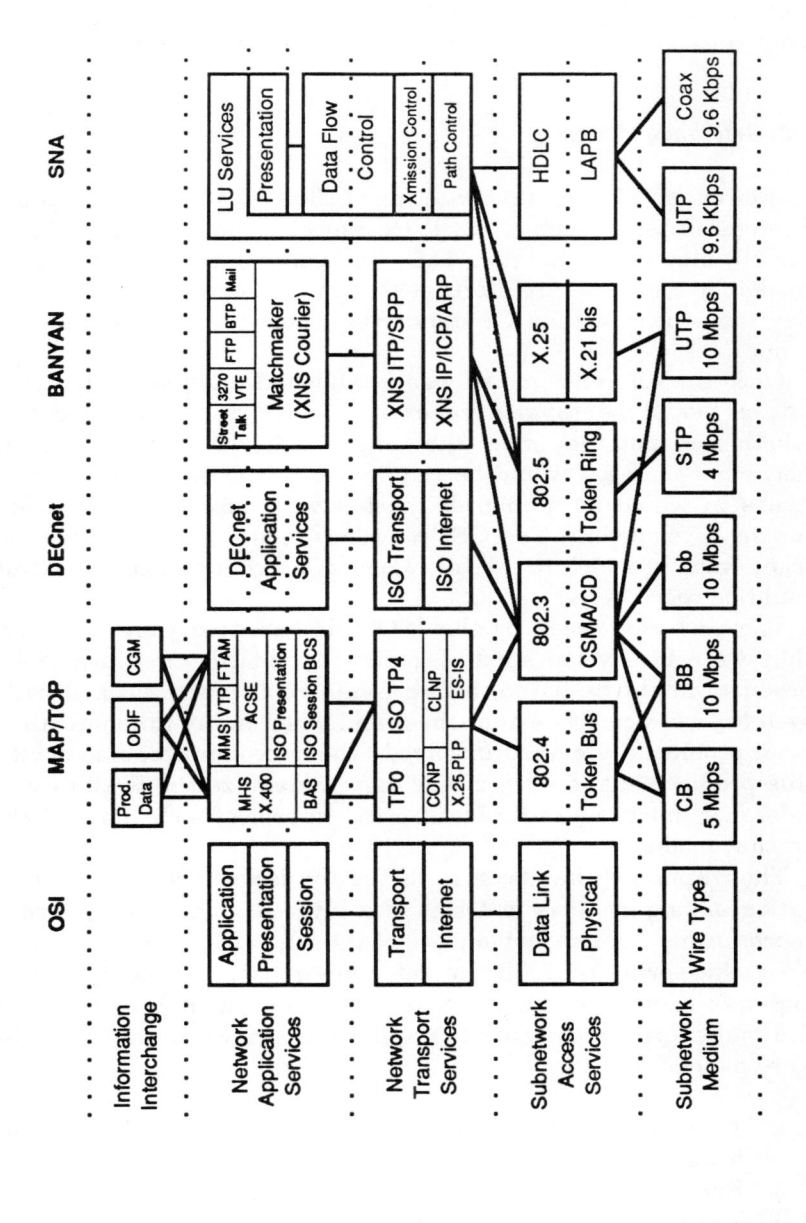

Figure 1-2 OSI and its relationship to other standards and protocols.

committees chartered to produce standards in various areas. Each committee is in turn organized into subcommittees and working groups that actually do the work of producing the standards.

OSI Reference Model

In March of 1978 the first meeting of the ISO subcommittee on Open Systems Interconnection (OSI) (technical committee 97, subcommittee 16) met in Washington, D.C. Its task was to develop a reference model for a general architecture that might serve as a context for the development of worldwide standards for distributed information systems.

Once the reference model was established, the task of the subcommittee would be to analyze existing ISO standards to determine whether or not they meet the general criteria of the model, and if not, what changes would be required to bring them into alignment. Areas in which no standards existed were also to be identified for future development. The OSI reference model was therefore to be a framework in which the development of all communication standards could be coordinated.

The problems faced by the ISO subcommittee were considerable: they were to develop a set of general standards on which emerging products might be based, before commercial practices in distributed systems were clearly established, and when many fundamental technical problems remained unsolved. The subcommittee has dealt with this predicament in such a way as to maximize the flexibility of the reference model and to minimize the impact of technological change on that model.

Their approach has been to define the issues related to communication among systems in terms of a layered architecture, each layer representing a manageable piece of the whole.

By the spring of 1983 the reference model had been formulated and was adopted as an international standard. It has seven layers; the major principles that ISO applied to arrive at the seven layers were as follows:

1. A layer should be created when, and only when, a different level of abstraction is needed.
2. Each layer should perform a well-defined function.
3. The function of each layer should be chosen with an eye toward defining internationally standardized protocols.

4. Communications between identical layers in cooperating end systems should occur on a logical peer-to-peer basis (i.e., no master–slave relationship should be required).
5. The layer boundaries should be chosen to minimize the information flow across the interfaces.
6. The number of layers should be large enough that distinct functions need not be thrown together in the same layer out of necessity, and small enough that the architecture does not become unwieldy.

Layer 1: Physical Layer

The physical layer is concerned with transmitting row bits over a communication channel. Its purpose is to provide a physical connection for the transmission of data among network entities and a means by which to activate and deactivate a physical connection.

The design issues are concerned with making sure that when 1 bit is sent, it is received by the other side as a 1 bit, not as a 0 bit. Typical questions here are:

1. How many volts should be used to represent a 1 and how many a 0?
2. How many microseconds does a bit occupy?
3. May transmission proceed simultaneously in both directions?
4. How is the initial connection is established, and how is it torn down when both sides are finished?
5. How many pins does the network connector have, and what is each pin used for?

In some cases a transmission facility consists of multiple physical channels, in which case the physical layer can make them look like a single channel. Higher layers can also perform this function.

Layer 2: Data Link Layer

The primary purpose of the data link layer is to provide a reliable means of transmitting data across a physical link. It breaks the input data up into data frames, transmits the frames sequentially, and processes the acknowledge frames sent back by the receiver. Since layer 1 merely accepts and transmits a stream of bits without any regard to meaning or structure, it is up to the data link layer to create and recognize frame boundaries. This can be accomplished by attaching special bit patterns to the beginning and end of the frame. Since these bit patterns can occur accidentally in the data, special care must be taken to avoid confusion.

A noise burst on the line can destroy a frame completely. In this case, the data link layer software on the source machine must retransmit the frame. However, multiple transmissions of the same frame introduce the possibility of duplicate frames. A duplicate frame could be present, for example, if the acknowledge frame from the receiver back to the sender was destroyed. It is up to this layer to resolve the problems caused by damaged, lost, and duplicate frames, so that the network layer can assume it is working with an error-free line.

Another issue that arises at the data link layer (and most of the higher layer as well) is how to keep a fast transmitter from drowning a slow receiver in data. Some mechanism must be employed to let the transmitter know how much buffer space the receiver has at the moment. Typically, this mechanism and the error handling are integrated together.

If the line can be used to transmit data in both directions, this introduces a new complication that the data link layer software must deal with. The problem is that the acknowledge frames for A to B traffic compete for the use of the line with data frames for the B to A traffic.

The data link layer is divided into two sublayers in the IEEE 802 LAN standards project, namely, the Media Access Control (MAC) sublayer and the Logical Link Control (LLC) sublayer.

Layer 3: Network Layer

The network layer routes information from one network computer to another. These computers may be physically located on the same network or on another network that is connected in some fashion. Like a street map, the network layer defines all the possible avenues that a message could travel to get from one network to another.

What this layer of software does, basically, is accept messages from the source host, convert them to packets, the units of information exchanged in layer 3, and see to it that the packets get directed toward the destination.

A key design issue is how the route is determined. It could be based on static tables that are built into the network and rarely changed. It could also be determined at the start of each conversation, for example, at the start of a terminal session. Finally, it could be highly dynamic, being determined anew for each packet to reflect the current network load.

If too many packets are present in the network at the same time, they will get in each other's way, forming bottlenecks. The control of such congestion also belongs to the network layer.

The network layer is divided into four sublayers:

1. The access sublayer
2. The intranetwork sublayer
3. The harmonizing sublayer
4. The internetwork sublayer

The access sublayer provides a link service access interface to the data link layer. It is an interface sublayer, and it does not perform any routing function. It provides the necessary logical interface between adjacent sublayers.

The intranetwork sublayer provides message routing within networks of one type. It performs all intranetwork routing functions to, from, and through a node within the immediate local network. This could be a vendor proprietary LAN.

The harmonizing sublayer provides harmonization of internetwork and intranetwork sublayers. It is an interface sublayer. It does not perform any routing function but provides the necessary logical interfaces between adjacent sublayers.

The internetwork sublayer provides global message routing. It performs all internetwork routing functions.

Layer 4: Transport Layer

The purpose of the transport layer is to provide a network-independent transport service to the session layer. The basic function of the transport layer is to accept data from the session layer, split it up into smaller units, if need be, pass these to the network layer, and ensure that the pieces all arrive correctly at the other end. Furthermore, all this must be done in the most efficient way and in a way that isolates the session layer from the inevitable changes in the hardware technology.

Under normal conditions, the transport layer creates a distinct network layer connection for each transport layer connection required by the session layer. If the transport layer connection requires a high throughput, however, the transport layer might create multiple network layer connections, dividing data among the network layer connections to improve throughput. On the other hand, if creating or maintaining a network layer connection is expensive, the transport layer might multiplex several transport layer connections onto the same network layer connection to reduce the cost. In all cases, the transport layer is required to make the multiplexing transparent to the session layer.

The transport layer also determines what type of service to provide the session layer and, ultimately, the users of the network. The most popular type of transport layer connection is an error-free point-to-point channel that delivers messages in the order in which they were sent. However, other possible kinds of transport service include transport of isolated messages with no guarantee about the order of delivery and broadcasting of messages to multiple destinations. The type of service is determined when the connection is established. At the lower layers, the protocols are carried out by each machine and its immediate neighbors.

Many hosts are multiprogrammed, which means that multiple connections will be entering and leaving each host. There needs to be some way to tell which message belongs to which connection. The transport layer must also take care of establishing and deleting connections across the network. This implies some kind of naming mechanism, so that a process on one machine has a way of describing with whom it wishes to converse. There must also be a mechanism to regulate the flow of information so that a fast host cannot overrun a slow one.

The transport layer is a true source-to-destination or end-to-end layer. In other words, a program on the source machine carries on a conversation with a similar program on the destination machine, using the message headers and control messages.

The transport layer is often implemented by a part of the host operating system. In contrast, the network layer is typically implemented in the host by an input/output driver. The data link and physical layers are normally implemented in hardware.

The services of the transport layer protocol can be thought of as fitting into two general types: connection management and data transfer services. Connection management services allow a transport layer user to create and maintain the data path to a correspondent transport layer user. Four specific services are provided:

1. Establishment service, which provides for the establishment of transport layer connections.

2. Close (abort) service, which provides for the orderly termination of a transport layer connection.
3. Disconnect service, which also provides for the termination of a connection but with the possible loss of data.
4. Status service, which informs the user about the attributes and status of a transport layer connection.

Data transfer services provide the means to exchange data between a pair of transport layer users. Three specific services are provided:

1. Data (normal) service, which allows a user to transfer data to a correspondent user on a transport layer connection.
2. Expedited (urgent) service, which allows for the transfer of a limited amount of data outside the normal data stream.
3. Unit service, which allows for the transfer of data to a correspondent user without the need to first establish and terminate a transport layer service.

Layer 5: Session Layer

The session layer is the user's interface into the network. It is with this layer that the user must negotiate to establish a connection with a process on another machine. Once the connection has been established, the session layer can manage the dialogue in an orderly manner, if the user has requested that service.

A connection between users (technically speaking, between two presentation layer processes) is usually called a session. A session might be used to allow a user to log into a remote time-sharing system or to transfer a file between two machines. The operation of setting up a session between two processes is often called *binding*.

A session layer connection may be structured so that interactions between users occur as:

1. Half-duplex, which is two-way alternate
2. Simplex, which is one-way interactive
3. Full-duplex, which is two-way simultaneous

To establish a session, the user must provide the remote address he wants to connect to. Session addresses are different from transport addresses in that session addresses are intended for use by users or their programs, whereas transport addresses are intended for establishing transport layer connections. To request that a transport connection be set up, the session layer must be able to convert a session address to its transport address.

Another function of the session layer is management of the session once it has been set up. For example, if transport layer connections are unreliable, the session layer may be required to attempt to transparently recover from broken transport layer connections. As another example, in many database management systems, it is crucial that a complicated transaction in a database never be aborted halfway, since doing so would leave the database in an inconsistent state. The session layer often provides a facility by which a group of messages can be bracketed, so that none of them is delivered to the remote user until all of them have arrived. The session layer can also provide for ordering of messages when the transport service does not. In short, the session layer takes the bare-bones, bit-for-bit communication service offered by the transport layer and adds application-oriented functions to it.

In some networks, the session and transport layers are merged into a single layer, or the session layer is absent altogether, if all the users want is raw communication service.

Layer 6: Presentation Layer

The presentation layer provides for the negotiation and establishment of the transfer syntax, which represents the encoding of values for the purposes of transferring structured data types. A data type may have more than one possible transfer syntax, providing greater or lesser degrees of compression or security.

A set of data-type notations, using a well-defined notation, constitutes what is called an abstract syntax for the information that is contained in values of any of the data types.

The functions of the presentation layer fall into two categories: those dealing with the session layer and those dealing with syntax. Each presentation connection is mapped one-to-one onto a session connection. Before a presentation connection can be used to exchange data, the two presentation protocol entities must agree on a transfer syntax. Since each entity knows the abstract syntax of its user, and each has available one or more transfer syntaxes that are suitable for encoding, it is simply a matter of the two entities agreeing on a particular transfer syntax to use.

The ISO standards make no assumptions about the way in which abstract or transfer syntaxes are specified. The presentation service is general-purpose and is intended to support all application protocols and any appropriate syntaxes.

Layer 7: Application Layer

At the top layer of the OSI model, the application layer exhibits some differences from the other layers. Specifically, the application layer does not provide services to a higher layer. The application layer does provide services, but these services are provided to application processes that lie outside the seven-layer architecture. Application processes can be manual, computerized, or physical. Examples of application processes are:

1. A person operating a banking terminal is a manual application process.
2. A COBOL program executing in a computer center and accessing a remote database is a computerized application process. The remote database management systems server is also an application process.
3. A process control program executing in a dedicated computer attached to some industrial equipment and linked into a plant control system is a physical process.

Application processes in different open systems that wish to exchange information do so by accessing the application layer. The application layer contains application entities that employ application protocols and presentation services to exchange information. It is these application entities that provide the means for application processes to access the OSI environment.

The application entities can be thought of as providing useful services relevant to one or more application processes. It is true that when two application processes on different machines communicate, they alone can determine the set of allowed messages and the action taken upon receipt of each. Nevertheless, there are many issues that occur here that are quite general. For example, the whole question of network transparency, hiding the physical distribution of resources from the user, occurs in many applications. Another issue is problem partitioning: how can the problem be divided up among the various machines, preferably automatically, to take maximum advantage of the network? Distributed databases also give rise to many interesting problems in the application layer. Industry-specific protocols, such as for banking and airline reservation, allow computers from different companies to access each other's databases, when needed.

Standards-Based Protocol Specifications

MAP Protocol Suite

Development of the MAP (Manufacturing Automation Protocol) specification was initiated by General Motors in an effort to force standardization of its own factory floor communications. The development and maintenance of the MAP specification is now the responsibility of the North American MAP/TOP Users Group, under the auspices of the Information Technology Requirements Council (ITRC), which provides permanent staffing for the (mostly) volunteer activities of the Users Group. The objective of MAP is to define a LAN and associated communication architecture for terminals, computing resources, programmable devices, and robots within a plant or complex. It sets standards for procurement and provides a specification for use by vendors who want to build networking products for factory use that are acceptable to MAP participants.

History of MAP

In late 1979, the Advanced Product Manufacturing and Engineering Staff (APMES) at GM Tech Center created a MAP task force. The charter of the task force was to identify a set of communication standards for a factory LAN. These standards were meant to provide multivendor data communications between computers and other intelligent devices, such as numerical control units and graphics systems. The task force was composed of representatives from approximately 15 GM divisions and a number of factory automation vendors in order to address as wide a range of manufacturing communication requirements as possible. The participating divisions represented many diverse activities, from foundry operations to final vehicle assembly, in an effort to ensure that the appropriate computer and control of vendors' products were involved.

Soon after its formation, the GM MAP task force identified the OSI model as the basis for the MAP communication network. The OSI model, however, only specifies how its seven layers should function. Compliance to the model does not assure multivendor communication compatibility. The solution of the GM MAP task force was to specify a selected protocol and its implementation at each of the seven layers.

GM formally adopted the initial MAP specification on October 23, 1982, and issued an ultimatum. Any vendor wishing to do business with GM in the future must implement networking with MAP.

The response by computer vendors was underwhelming. GM wanted generally available, competitively priced multivendor networking. What they got instead was high-priced, custom implemented specials developed just for bidding on GM contracts. Even the world's largest corporation did not have the clout to move mainstream vendors from business as usual with proprietary networks.

MAP 1.0

MAP 1.0 actually refers to the second version of the original MAP specification. It was released on April 18, 1984, and was a major rewrite of the original 1982 specification. Several appendices were added to explain how it was supposed to work. MAP 1.0 was installed in a very limited number of GM plants and was demonstrated at the 1984 National Computer Conference (NCC). The conference demonstration is often credited with changing the perception of MAP as an onerous MAP procurement specification to its current status as the foundation of computer-integrated manufacturing.

MAP 2.0

MAP 2.0, published on February 2, 1985, moved MAP over to standard protocols for all the lower layers. Installed in a few GM pilot installations, it is known today simply as the starting point for the 2.X compatibility class. Like MAP 1.0, it has never been commercially available as a full seven-layer implementation, although several vendors did offer conforming products for the physical and data link layer specifications.

MAP 2.1

MAP 2.1 marks the first "real" MAP specifications. Consisting of compatible extensions to 2.0, this version of MAP added the missing pieces of directory service and network management that allowed the implementation of a useful network. The 1985 demonstration at AUTOFACT was implemented to the MAP 2.1 specification, allowing additional problems to be discovered and ironed out before any major vendors had nonconforming products in the marketplace.

The MAP 2.1 errata, about 200 pages long, documents all the fixes required to get the AUTOFACT demonstration to work. Considered a correction and clarification of the original printing, MAP 2.1 is not known to contain any technical changes except for clarification of ambiguities and matching what was actually implemented at AUTOFACT in 1985. The MAP 2.1 errata have since been published as the MAP 2.1A specification and incorporated in a combined release as part of the MAP 2.2 specification document.

MAP 2.2

Designed to provide a compatible growth for MAP 2.1 networks, MAP 2.2 adds several key cost and performance enhancements to MAP 2.1. Originally scheduled for publication in early 1986, it suffered multiple delays as one bug after another needed to be fixed before release. While frustrating, most of the delays were caused by conservatism on the part of the developers as they tried out different parts of the specifications before committing to them. Since there was not to be a major multivendor demonstration for 2.2 as there was for 2.1 and for 3.0, this conservatism was justified even though it delayed release until fall of 1986.

The major changes in MAP 2.2 were the carrierband alternative to broadband and Enhanced Performance Architecture (EPA). Carrierband has the potential to reduce the cost of connecting to a small segment by 50 percent. The EPA provides for real-time network response. The miniMAP extension to EPA allows a network connection requiring minimal memory and hardware for very low-end controllers, sensors, and the like.

MAP 2.2 also included a new appendix on application-level naming and addressing and more details on bridges and their use in MAP. Other items originally planned for MAP 2.2 were postponed until the release of MAP 3.0.

MAP 3.0

MAP 3.0 marks the incompatible leap from the draft proposal protocol subsets used in MAP 2.X to international standard protocols for all seven layers. Progression through a series of 3.X releases can be foreseen as capabilities such as security, concurrency control, and database are developed, refined, standardized, and added to the specification.

Delays in the development of stable international standards directly affected the availability of MAP 3.0, which was demonstrated at the Enterprise Networking Event International '88 (ENE88i or ENTERPRISE) in Baltimore in June 1988. The final version of the 3.0 specification was completed in August 1988 and published by the North American MAP/TOP Users Group.

While many users were disappointed by the delays affecting MAP 3.0 availability, most will find the services provided well worth the wait. The MAP 3.0 service selection is superior, even when compared to many proprietary networks. The experience of early pioneers with MAP 2.1 has been put to good use. Their experience has not only affected what services were selected but also how they are provided. Included in version 3.0 are standard programming interfaces to services so that user applications implemented on one machine can be easily moved to others.

All services in MAP 2.1 are available in MAP 3.0. FTAM (File Transfer and Access Management) is enhanced with remote file access features and improved file management. The interface to ACSE (Application Control Services Element) is extended to allow access to more of its capabilities. Network management and directory services are also expanded, but not as much as desired because the international standards for them are still under development. The only major incompatibility from the user application perspective is the move from the GM-developed MMFS specification for manufacturing messaging to MMS (Manufacturing Messaging Service), an ISO Draft Proposal at the time, which is now an IS.

Major new application services for MAP 3.0 are Computer Graphics Metafile (CGM) and Initial Graphics Exchange Specification (IGES) for graphics data exchange. Inside the network layer there are improvements to the routing specifications and more efficient use of X.25 links. In addition, a broadband cable plant planning, installation, and maintenance guide has been published as a companion volume to the 3.0 specification.

MAP Strategy

The MAP strategy has three parts:

1. For cases in which international standards exist, select those alternatives and options that best suit the needs of the MAP participants.

2. For standards currently under development, participate in the standards-making process to represent the requirements of the MAP participants.
3. In those cases where no appropriate standard exists, recommend interim standards until the international standards are developed.

Thus, MAP is intended to specify standards, and options within such standards, that are appropriate for factory environments. This guarantees a large market for products that conform to those standards. To date, hundreds of companies have participated in the MAP effort.

MAP Product Certification

The goal of MAP is to provide a recognized open network architecture. This architecture eliminates many of the problems associated with proprietary solutions. For a vendor to achieve true MAP compatibility, their products must be certified by an approved testing agency. MAP/TOP 3.0 conformance tests were jointly developed by the Corporation for Open Systems (COS) and a European conformance test development consortium, the Standards Promotion and Applications Group — Communications Network for Manufacturing Applications Conformance Testing (SPAG-CCT), with significant contributions from the Japanese MAP Users Group (JMUG) and the Industrial Technology Institute (ITI) in Ann Arbor, Michigan. COS and SPAG-CCT are providing conformance test services to ensure that a MAP-compatible product does, in fact, conform to published MAP standards and to provide the customers of these products with a wide choice of compatible and certified vendors.

TOP Protocol Suite

TOP (Technical and Office Protocol) was developed by Boeing Computer Services for much the same reason as MAP. The target environment was the office, not the factory floor. Because the environments have different network communication requirements, TOP differs in specific ways from MAP. Following GM's lead with MAP, Boeing insisted that the TOP specification conform to the OSI model. TOP is a direct subset of the full OSI model.

TOP 1.0

The original TOP specification was sponsored by Boeing Computer Services and was first published in November 1985 in conjunction with the MAP/TOP demonstration at AUTOFACT in Detroit. TOP 1.0 was designed to allow access to MAP networks from office and technical computers, an early deficiency in MAP recognized at the 1984 NCC demonstration. TOP 1.0 provided file transfer to and from MAP 2.1 systems connected via bridges or intermediate systems. A guiding principle in the development of the TOP specifications was to maintain compatibility and interoperability between MAP- and TOP-conformant systems. This was recognized by the formation of a single MAP/TOP Users Group with a joint MAP/TOP Steering Committee early in 1985.

TOP 3.0

The TOP partner for MAP 3.0 is TOP 3.0. Though TOP 3.0 is actually the second TOP release, it has been designated TOP 3.0 to emphasize the partnership of MAP/TOP 3.0. Like TOP 1.0, TOP 3.0 differs from its MAP partner only where absolutely necessary to meet the unique needs of office workers and engineers. For example, supported cable plants are IEEE 802.3 and 802.5 as well as 802.4, and the factory-floor-only Manufacturing Messaging protocol is not included. Common MAP/TOP 3.0 protocol specifications ensure smooth communications between office and manufacturing floor. MAP 3.0 application layer services included in TOP 3.0 are FTAM, CGM, IGES, network management, and directory service.

TOP 3.0 is the first release of TOP that can effectively implement fundamental office services. Unlike TOP 1.0, TOP 3.0 includes services not found in MAP that are of interest in the development of integrated engineering and office applications. Basic Class Virtual Terminal (VT-B) allows interactive remote computer access. X.400 Message Handling Systems (MHS) provides electronic mail service. Office Document Architectures (ODA) for characters, graphics, and facsimile in processible, formatted, and processible formatted form allow complex documents to be generated, shared, and modified by multiple users.

Network connectivity is enhanced by the addition of media alternatives to 10base5 IEEE 802.3, including broadband IEEE 802.3 and token ring IEEE 802.5 User application portability is provided by specification of the Graphical Kernel System (GKS) for two-dimensional graphics. TOP 3.0 elevates TOP from its original status as a subordinate of MAP to a full-capability office network that justifies its own existence. Outside the manufacturing world, it meets the needs of service and retail industry users ranging from government agencies to insurance agencies and banks. Inside or outside the manufacturing world, it provides an OSI alternative to the proprietary and de facto multivendor networks currently required for office automation.

GOSIP Protocol Suite

In 1985, the federal government began the development of a protocol specification based on OSI standards as part of a drive to allow federal agencies to procure computing and communication equipment from standard components in place of custom-developed products to meet government standards. Following the recommendation of the National Research Council, the government, under the leadership of the National Institute of Standards and Technology (NIST), began investigating appropriate OSI profiles. The MAP/TOP Users Group and the Government OSI Profile (GOSIP) developers worked closely together to ensure that vendors would be able to build one product that would satisfy the needs of both industry and government. As a result, the GOSIP specification is a proper subset of the TOP specification, and TOP- and GOSIP-conformant end systems can interoperate with one another. In August 1988 GOSIP 1.0 was published as a Federal Information Processing Standard (FIPS) and can now be used by federal agencies for procurements. In August 1990 GOSIP became mandatory for all federal agencies as the sole procurement standard for new acquisitions.

GOSIP 1.0

GOSIP 1.0 is a subset of the TOP 3.0 specification, leaving out the protocol specifications for protocols that had not yet been included in the December 1987 Stable Agreements Document of the NIST OSI Implementor's Workshop. In particular, it does not include a specification for network management, but recommends the use of the MAP/TOP 3.0 specification for agencies that wish to procure a network management function.

GOSIP 2.0

GOSIP 2.0 was released in 1989, based on the NIST OSI Implementor's Workshop December 1988 Stable Agreements Document. It incorporated several items that were in the TOP 3.0 specification, e.g., the TOP 3.0 ODA/ODIF profile, as well as compatible enhancements that do not affect interoperability, e.g., the Computer-aided Acquisitions and Logistics Systems (CALS) Standardized Generalized Mark-up Language (SGML) profile for technical publishing. GOSIP 2.0 and MAP/TOP 3.0 end systems will still be able to interoperate and it is the intent of both organizations to maintain that capability.

TCP/IP Protocol Suite

TCP/IP (Transmission Control Protocol/Internet Protocol) is an efficient, widely implemented set of networking protocols that grew out of the ARPANet Project of what is now the Defense Advanced Research Projects Agency (DARPA) of the U.S. Department of Defense (DoD).

ARPANet

Starting in the late 1960s, the ARPA office began stimulating research on the subject of computer networks by providing grants to computer science departments at many U.S. universities as well as to a few private corporations, including MIT, UCLA, UCSB, Stanford University, University of Utah, University of Hawaii, SRI International, the Institute for Advanced Computation, and Bolt, Beranek and Newman (BBN). This research led to an experimental four-node network that went on the air in December 1969.

The ARPANet was publicly demonstrated in 1972 at the First International Conference on Computers and Communications to prove the feasibility of long-distance packet-switching technology. The network included many universities and research sites whose host computers had all implemented a number of experimental machine-to-machine communication protocols. Since then, ARPANet has been used extensively to support computer science and military research projects of many kinds. Much of our present knowledge about networking is a direct result of the ARPANet project.

The year the ARPANet was demonstrated, work began on a second generation of protocols designed to use the knowledge gained from the original experiment. By 1982, a family (or suite) of new protocols had been specified, implemented, and subjected to extensive experimentation, including four complete cycles or versions. The two oldest of these protocols are the TCP and the IP. The term TCP/IP now typically refers to the entire family of protocols.

In 1983, TCP/IP became the standard protocol suite used on the DoD Internet, including the ARPANet. During this time, a second network, MILNET, was split off the ARPANet to carry out the military research section of the original ARPANet. MILNET and the ARPANet, along with a number of classified networks, are known as the Defense Data Network (DDN). Gateways exist between the ARPANet and MILNET to facilitate information flow between the two.

In 1988, the DoD adopted the Government Open Systems Interconnection Profile (GOSIP 1.0), a Federal Information Processing Standard (FIPS) published in August 1988 as a costandard with TCP/IP. In August, 1990 GOSIP became mandatory for all new government procurements, thus becoming the sole procurement standard for all defense agencies for new acquisitions. To ease the transition from TCP/IP to GOSIP, the government has developed specifications for gateways between the two.

TCP/IP Overview

The services of the two main protocols, TCP and IP, are augmented by other services provided in the higher layers. These services include remote login, file transfer, and electronic mail as well as a number of miscellaneous services such as clock setting, listing active users, etc. Below is a description of some of the core protocols and their services. (Note that the TCP/IP protocols are not conformant to the OSI model, although they are layered in a similar way and are discussed below in terms of where their principal functions fit into the OSI model.)

Layer 3 (Network Layer)

1. IP (Internet Protocol) provides internet transaction services for layer 4 clients. It is generally thought of as providing host-to-host datagram delivery. The word "internet" is used to refer to any interconnected set of networks.

An Overview of Standards and Protocols 23

2. ICMP (Internet Control Message Protocol) is used by gateways and host in an internet to apprise other hosts of conditions related to their IP services.
3. ARP (Address Resolution Protocol) maps an IP address into an associated Ethernet address.
4. RARP (Reverse ARP) maps an Ethernet address to an associated IP address.

Layer 4 (Transport Layer)

1. TCP (Transmission Control Protocol) is a connection-oriented, reliable byte-stream protocol.
2. UDP (User Datagram Protocol) is an unacknowledged, transaction oriented protocol parallel to TCP.
3. NVP (Network Voice Protocol) provides real-time, transaction-based service for carrying digitized, compressed voice.

Layers 5–7 (Session, Presentation, and Application Layers)

1. FTP (File Transfer Protocol) permits exchange of complete files between computers. This is the standard program used to get and send files to remote and arbitrary brand hosts. It is a combination application/presentation layer protocol. It will convert test files into the proper character set and line termination scheme for the user's host system.
2. SMTP (Simple Mail Transfer Protocol) facilitates composing, sending, and receiving messages across various hosts, transport facilities, and media.
3. TELNET (Telecommunications Network) provides virtual terminal services for interactive access to hosts. It allows the user to log into a remote host as if the user were logging in via a directly connected terminal.
4. DNS (Domain Name Service) provides directory services. It is a complex, distributed service for mapping a name to an address.

TCP/IP Usage

As users realize they need multivendor connectivity, the TCP/IP solution has become extremely popular. The TCP/IP protocol family is currently on over 50,000 computers and is supported by over 150 vendors in more than 100 implementations. TCP/IP is widely recognized as the most available semistandardized method for interconnecting different computers, operating systems, and network technologies.

TCP/IP Services

The services offered by TCP/IP are discussed in more detail below. They include FTP, TELNET, SMTP, and session layer interface.

File Transfer Program (FTP)

FTP is a protocol, or set of agreements on procedures, that specifies how information organized as files should be transferred from one computer to another over a data network. FTP is intended to support implementations on computers from different manufacturers and makes few assumptions about the details of the operating systems. FTP is a specification for the behavior of a computer, as seen by another computer, and is not concerned too much with the details of the implementation on a particular machine.

The way that files are stored, accessed, and protected differs among different types of computers. In fact, it is difficult even to find a single definition of a file that would satisfy all systems. Instead, FTP presumes some basic properties, such as data type, file organization, and file ownership, that are common to files on most systems and provides a means by which one computer can manipulate these properties of files on another computer without knowing much detail about that other system.

Files on a remote system are manipulated by means of a set of commands and responses that are defined by FTP and are exchanged by the two machines. Examples of manipulation are: get a file from, and send a file to, a remote system.

FTP does not attempt to translate files from one computer type to another, or establish a *network virtual file*. Rather, it provides three dimensions, data types, file types, and transmission modes that can be used by two computers to establish a common ground.

There are four defined data types. Of these, two are most suitable for representing text files: ASCII and EBCDIC. For exchanging data between machines of the same type, the IMAGE data type is used. The final data type is Logical Byte Size, which is used when the data unit size must be preserved. FTP is a fairly low-level standard and is

An Overview of Standards and Protocols 25

not involved with the higher level structure of a file beyond these four defined data types.

FTP allows the user to transfer files to and from other hosts on the network. It converts automatically for the user to and from different character sets where appropriate. For example, to edit on VAX 8530 a file stored on an IBM 4381, a user can first transfer the file from IBM to VAX by:

1. Logging into the IBM from the VAX with FTP.
2. Using the GET command in FTP to bring the file over.
3. Logging out of FTP.

The file is now on the VAX, stored in the ASCII character set, and can be edited using any editor available on VAX. When the editing is done, the file can be sent back to IBM via the following steps:

1. Log into the IBM from the VAX with FTP.
2. Use the PUT command in FTP to send the file over.
3. Log out of FTP.

The file, including changes, will now be back at the IBM stored in the EBCDIC character set.

FTP provides all of the basic file perusing and manipulation commands, such as change directory, multiple gets, multiple puts, list directory, and several others.

FTP has matured into a reliable standard, widely available on many of the types of computers that are used in modern communication-oriented systems. Essentially all of the machines accessible on TCP/IP and similar networks have working FTPs. As with all complex standards, however, implementations of FTP vary in supported features. Most implementations support those data types and transfer modes of use in communicating with like systems. Moving simple text files and some kinds of numerical data works fairly well. More complicated applications, involving moving executable program images and perhaps storing such images in intermediate systems as distribution points, can be troublesome.

From another point of view, FTP provides a fairly low level of functionality. The user process must interact with a lot of the details of establishing the transfer path and managing the transfer. A customized file system can shield the user process from knowledge of most of the intermachine transfer, and this can help to greatly reduce application system complexity.

Virtual Terminal Protocol (TELNET)

An early motivation for data networks like the ARPANet was providing remote access to interactive hosts across the network; that is, allowing a user to log into a remote host over the network as if he or she were using a terminal directly connected to that host. Remote terminal access is particularly useful within an organization in which users require access to many hosts.

Consider, for example, two departments: a data processing department and an engineering department. The data processing department has a host and terminals for doing resource inventory. The engineering department has another host and terminals for developing applications. Now, assume that the data processing host has an interactive database program for collecting resource information, and the engineering department is required to use that program. Instead of having a separate terminal directly connected to the data processing host, the engineering department could use a remote terminal access protocol such as Telnet from its host over a network to the data processing host. This reduces the number of physical terminals required to access host resources in the organization and provides two of the benefits of a network (low cost, higher reliability) between sites that are geographically separate.

Telnet is a protocol used to link terminals to applications. It can be characterized as follows:

1. It specifies a network standard terminal. Thus, characteristics of specific terminals are mapped into the standard. This allows terminals from a variety of vendors to be connected to a variety of hosts.
2. It specifies the protocol between terminal and host. This allows certain terminal characteristics to be negotiated. Examples are line width, page size, full-duplex versus half-duplex, remote versus local echo.
3. It provides reliable data exchange by means of TCP.
4. It allows a user at a terminal to interact with an application in a remote host as if the user were a local user of that host.

Telnet is implemented in two modules: User Telnet and Server Telnet. User Telnet interacts with the terminal input/output module on the system. It converts the characteristics of real terminals to the network standard and vice versa. Server Telnet interacts with process and applications. It acts as a surrogate terminal handler so that remote terminals appear as local to the process or application.

An Overview of Standards and Protocols 27

While Telneting between a Prime and HP or VAX is easy and unremarkable, Telneting to an IBM is not. Users Telneting to an IBM from a non-IBM host will get line-at-a-time service only, which is of very limited use. One remedy is to install a 3270 emulation package on the IBM to provide full-duplex ASCII terminal emulation (virtual terminal). This provides an IBM 3270 emulation, complete with PF keys. This allows someone using either an IBM PC or a VT100 terminal to run IBM applications that require a 3270 style half-duplex, screen-at-a-time terminal. The user would follow these steps:

1. Log into the IBM from a non-IBM host with Telnet.
2. The 3270 emulation module installed in the IBM will show a menu for ASCII terminal selections.
3. After an ASCII terminal is selected (say, a VT100), the IBM will send the proper VT100 codes to simulate a 3270 on a VT100 terminal. Carry out work as if on a 3270 connected to IBM.
4. Terminate the Telnet session by typing the proper escape sequence.

Printing

The TCP/IP suite with the Berkeley remote commands such as rlogin, rsh, rexec, and the remote line printer command "lpr" is available among some of the TCP/IP software vendor offerings. The lpr command requires the existence of a Berkeley style printer spooler server somewhere on the network.

E-Mail, Simple Mail Transfer Protocol (SMTP)

SMTP provides a standard way to send electronic mail. It is frontended by host mail programs such as the VMS mailer on VAX systems and PROFS on IBM/VM systems, among others. The Berkeley mailer "mail" is provided with some TCP/IP software vendor offerings.

The user uses the local mailer to format and send a message, which causes SMTP to send a message to another host. The other host has an SMTP server that listens for incoming messages and forwards them on to the destination user or relays them to the next host.

Session Layer Interface

The most widely known and implemented session layer interface to TCP/IP is known as the Berkeley socket interface. Several network vendors have implemented this interface; the others provide the means to implement it or at least interface to it with their own session layer library (or system) calls.

Proprietary Protocols

Proprietary architectures are nonstandard and do not conform to any formally agreed-upon methods or criteria. Proprietary architectures are sometimes developed by companies in response to their own data processing needs or occasionally are the results of hasty product development efforts.

Choosing a proprietary approach usually locks the buyer into support from a single source company. Where a product has developed a strong market share, third-party support is sometimes available. This places a consumer in a precarious position should the primary vendor fail or refuse to continue to support a certain product line.

There are several networking companies whose products currently enjoy major successes in the marketplace. These products are considered de facto standards due to the market share they control. They enjoy a wide user following and third-party software support. Choosing one of these de facto standards is a proper choice for a company looking for short-term solutions to data communication problems.

The presence of these de facto standards should continue to be a force in the local area networking market for the next two to four years. It is important to note, however, that immediate and short-term solutions to data communication needs do not guarantee long-term migration of equipment and software.

Unfortunately, since these proprietary solutions are not agreed to by the development community at large, source code or customer modifiable code usually does not exist. Companies who buy proprietary solutions can also run the risk of losing upward compatibility for new releases of software.

The following subsections evaluate three major proprietary network protocols: DECnet, SNA, and NETEX.

DECnet

This is Digital Equipment Corporation's proprietary network. DEC first released some DNA (Digital Network Architecture) products back in 1976 for its RSX-11M and PDP-11S systems. Now they have

An Overview of Standards and Protocols 29

a sophisticated set of network utilities and capabilities that extend not only across their current product line but into the IBM world as well.

The Digital Network Architecture is the framework for all Digital communication products (DECnet, DECnet/SNA Gateway, communication servers, and so on). DNA, like many other network architectures, is loosely based on the ISO/OSI model. Major DECnet product capabilities are discussed below.

Program-to-Program Communication

Cooperating programs running under different operating systems and written in different languages can exchange data. Different operating systems that DECnet can interface to are IBM's MVS and VM and PC or MS-DOS. Operating systems that DECnet cannot interface to are Primos, Banyan Vines, and Hewlett-Packard's MPE operating system.

Network Virtual Terminal Capability

This allows a terminal user to establish a logical connection to other systems in the network. It is essentially the same as the Telnet functionality, but only to other DECnet hosts.

File Transfer

This is the capability to exchange files among systems in a network. The File Transfer Program in the TCP/IP or Internet suite also provides this capability.

Remote Command/Batch File Submission and Execution

A user at a source node can request that a destination node execute a command file. The command file can already be at the destination node, or the source node can send it along with the request.

Remote Resource Access

This allows the sharing of resources such as expensive peripheral devices and massive database files for reasons of economy and convenience. This capability is sometimes referred to as "remote file access" when programs access file-structured devices remotely. DECnet offers both remote file and record access.

Electronic Mail — MAILbus Electronic Mail Interchange

MAILbus is a set of application software that links multivendor electronic mail systems and electronic mail applications into an enterprise-wide electronic messaging system. MAILbus allows a company to tie all of its mail systems together in a corporate-wide electronic mail backbone and enables electronic mail exchange with public electronic mail systems. Support exists for the CCITT X.400 Message Handling System Standard, IBM SNADS, and an interface to MCI Mail, called MAILGATE. An interface to the Internet mail standard of SMTP however is not available from DEC, except through third-party software suppliers of TCP/IP for DEC machines.

SNA

This is the proprietary IBM networking architecture. It connects all of the IBM mainframes. Many non-IBM computer vendors have implemented some kind of IBM SNA compatibility. SNA has layers, as do all modern networking schemes. They are discussed below.

Data Link Control

This layer is responsible for transmission of data over a particular physical link. A primary function is to detect and recover from transmission errors.

Path Control

This layer routes data from one node in the network to the next. In a complex network this path often passes over many separate data links through several nodes and may cross several domains.

Transmission Control

Keeps track of the status of sessions that are in progress, controls the passing of data flow within a session, and sees that the units of data that make up a message are sent and received in the proper sequence. It also provides an optional data encryption/decryption facility.

Data Flow Control

Concerns the overall integrity of the flow of data during a session between two network-addressable units. This can involve determining the mode of sending and receiving, managing groups of related messages, and determining what type of response mode to use.

Function Management

- *Data Services* — Coordinate the interface between the network user and the network and the presentation of information to the user. Control and coordinate the activities of the network as a whole and of all active sessions.
- *NAU (Network-Addressable Units) Services Manager* — Provides services to the function management data services sublayer below it and also to the data flow control and transmission control layers below the function management layer.

Application Layer

Application programs that interface with the SNA network.

NETEX

Formed in 1974, Network Systems Corporation (NSC) of Minneapolis, Minnesota, was the first company to develop multiple-vendor interconnect technology. Its HYPERchannel product provides high-speed data transmission not only among different brands of computers, but also over varying distances. The HYPERchannel capability is further broadened with a family of software called NETEX (NETwork EXecutive), which was designed specifically for the network environment. NETEX provides a simplified, high-level access to the network. It serves as a language translator among more than thirty different computer operating systems.

HYPERchannel Network

The NSC's HYPERchannel is a high-performance networking facility that provides channel-speed interconnection between mainframes, minicomputers, and peripherals of mixed manufacture. Computer systems are connected to a HYPERchannel network via appropriate HYPERchannel adapters.

The HYPERchannel is available in two series, Series A and Series B. These two series differ mainly in their data transmission speeds. The A Series can transmit 50 million bits per second (Mbps), while Series B can transmit only 10 Mbps. Nevertheless, the slower HYPERchannel Series B is easier to reconfigure if the interconnected computer systems are relocated. For an evolving network, it is therefore more desirable to establish it first as a HYPERchannel B Series network. As the locations of the computer systems on the network are stabilized, a B Series network can be migrated easily to an A Series network if a much higher data transfer speed is needed.

NETEX Software

NETEX is the NSC's software product family that provides a universal access method for computer systems interconnected by a HYPERchannel network. NETEX allows any two application programs in separate hosts to communicate with one another without regard to the actual network configuration. It facilitates such applications as file transfer, job transfer, and transaction processing in either a single- or multivendor environment at or near native channel speeds and on a real-time demand basis.

A version of NETEX is designed to operate with a specific operating system. It requires that each computer run the proper version of NETEX module. NETEX receives all requests for services and prepares the requests for transfer onto the HYPERchannel network via the HYPERchannel adapter. These requests are received in turn by the addressed HYPERchannel adapter and passed through to the receiving host's NETEX module.

NSC has standardized the versions of NETEX that exist for different operating systems, allowing application programs running on computers of different manufacture to communicate with each other. In addition, NETEX has a standard high-level language interface that allows high-level language programs (such as FORTRAN or Pascal) to be moved from one host to another without changing the logic used to call and function with NETEX.

NETEX has been designed along the lines of the OSI model, although it does not strictly follow the model's functional definitions. It does have service calls at the session and transport layers that are consistent with emerging network communication standards.

The NETEX session layer interface allows applications to address others by a symbolic name and conduct communications; the transport layer interface allows direct addressing of applications that know the destination's physical address. A third (driver) level interface within NETEX (but not part of OSI model) allows selected users to interface the HYPERchannel network messages.

Summary

The OSI Model is really an ongoing set of standards, continually being developed with the goal of making interconnected computing a reality. However, the OSI Model must presently coexist with related standards and protocols, both public and private.

About the Author

James F. Doar is Vice President, Integration Technology, Geibel Systems Integration Services, Inc., 13180 South Carus Road, Oregon City, OR 97045; Telephone: 503-263-6240; Fax: 503-263-6239. Dr. Doar has over thirty years of scientific and technical experience in industry and academia. His last sixteen years have been in interactive computer systems, CAI, CAE, CAD, CAM, CIM, Factory Automation, MAP and TOP Local Area Networks, and standards-based strategic computing architecture development. In his role at Geibel, Dr. Doar is responsible for all technology-related aspects in providing for the integration of computer and automated systems, particularly the development of computing and communication architectures and the design and installation of integrated plant-wide computing networks.

Dr. Doar was one of the founding members of the MAP (now MAP/TOP) Users Group Steering Committee, founded in 1984. He was Executive Chair of the Users Group for several years and is currently Chair of the Users Group Corporate Affiliates. Dr. Doar is also active in the Computer and Automated Systems Association of the Society of Manufacturing Engineers and is a past Chair of the Seattle chapter.

Chapter 2

U.S. GOSIP: Not Just for Government Procurement

by Bob D. Tausworthe

The United States Government Open Systems Interconnect Profile (U.S. GOSIP) was created to facilitate the use of the International Standards Organization (ISO) OSI protocols by federal agencies. The reason for GOSIP is simple. Federal agencies do not, under normal circumstances, have the ability to contract with a specific vendor to solve their procurement needs. They procure computer systems on a bid-by-bid basis. The government procurement process requires these agencies to make decisions based solely upon functionality and cost. This policy has left the government with (arguably) the world's largest multivendor network. Since the purpose of the OSI protocols is to allow for interoperation of computer networks in a multivendor environment, it is natural for the U.S. government to satisfy their multivendor networking needs by moving toward this set of protocols.

Companies in the private sector are also finding themselves with multivendor networking problems. There are several reasons for this. In the past, many companies did not have a unified procurement strategy. Entities within an organization would often make computer purchasing decisions independent of the other entities. This resulted in companies having incompatible computer systems. Similarly, some companies merged with or bought other companies, and along with them their computers and networks, which were more often than not incompatible with their own.

Even companies that provided strategies for purchasing computer systems found themselves with a need to solve the multivendor networking problem. Companies wanted a "mix and match" approach toward purchasing these systems. They wanted to take advantage of vendors' strengths, while not locking themselves into a single vendor's product line. These companies moved away from their previous dependencies on large mainframes and terminals and equipped their employees with workstations and personal computers often made by several different vendors. This approach to computer purchasing can only be successful if multivendor networking is a reality.

Although companies have arrived at their networking problems for different reasons than the U.S. government, the desired solution is the same: multivendor networking. Wouldn't it be great for customers and vendors alike if the solution the government is pursuing would work for private industry as well? This paper attempts to show that it does — that the guidelines specified by U.S. GOSIP can be used by businesses as a base to solve their multivendor networking problems.

Creation of the OSI Protocols

Every major vendor has products that provide, to one degree or another, data communications between its computer systems. Many have created proprietary network architectures that allow communication only between systems sold by that vendor. Other vendors who want their computer systems supported on networks of this type must implement the proprietary solutions as well as maintain their own network development. IBM's Systems Network Architecture (SNA) and DEC's DECnet Phase IV are examples of solutions of this type. Many vendors, such as SUN and Hewlett-Packard, provide products that allow their computers to communicate on these networks, but at a large development cost to the vendors, and with only limited functionality for their customers.

To satisfy the multivendor networking needs of federal agencies as well as private companies, systems must be capable of communicating with one another in a normal and predictable manner. In 1976 the International Standards Organization (ISO) began work on a communication architecture that would allow all systems to communicate in this manner. This effort resulted in the definition of the "OSI Reference Model." This model is defined in International Standard 7498, Information Processing Systems — Open Systems

Interconnection — Basic Reference Model, and in Recommendation X.200, Reference Model of Open Systems Interconnection for CCITT Applications, which is published by the International Telegraph and Telephone Consultative Committee (CCITT). The reference model was defined in such a way as to be independent of hardware and software requirements; it can be implemented on any vendor's systems.

The OSI Reference Model provides a framework by which systems can communicate. It does not define the protocols necessary for actual communication to be accomplished. The definition of these protocols is an ongoing process. Many have already been adopted by ISO and more are currently under development.

User Profiles

The protocols alone, however, are not sufficient for effective interoperation in a multivendor environment. Many of the protocols are incompletely specified, leaving the definition of field values or functionality as "local matters," or "for further study." Some protocols have several equivalent modes of operation and do not specify which one to use. Also, a protocol is sometimes found to have errors after it has been adopted.

Because of these problems, it became necessary for groups requiring interoperable systems to produce guidelines called "operational profiles" or simply "profiles." The purpose of a profile is to specify a set of protocols to be used for data communication and to define any ambiguities that the protocol specifications may have. When vendors implement a set of protocols using a profile as the guideline, the chance that their implementations will interoperate with other systems is greatly increased. Examples of groups that have defined profiles are the National Institute of Standards and Technology Implementor's Workshop (NIST Implementor's Agreements), the Manufacturing Automation Protocol and Technical Office Protocol (MAP/TOP Profiles), and the ENV profiles created by the European standards bodies CEN/CENELEC. The United States Government OSI Profile (U.S. GOSIP) is also a profile. It is the profile that federal agencies must specify conformance to in their procurement requests that include OSI protocols.

Creation of U.S. GOSIP

Version 1 of U.S. GOSIP was published as "Federal Information Processing Standard 146" (FIPS 146) in August 1988 by the National

Bureau of Standards (which later became the National Institute of Standards and Technology, [NIST]). On August 15, 1990, use of FIPS 146 became mandatory for all government procurements that specify computer networking compatible with the functionality specified by U.S. GOSIP.

Three separate groups of sources were used to create U.S. GOSIP. FIPS 146 classifies these as primary, secondary, and tertiary. The sole primary source was the "Stable Implementation Agreements for Open Systems Interconnection Protocols," created and maintained by the NIST Workshop for Implementation Agreements for Open Systems Interconnection Protocols. This document is commonly called the "NIST Implementor's Agreements." Except for the few differences listed in FIPS 146, U.S. GOSIP conforms to the NIST Implementor's Agreements profile.

Secondary sources were used to create a complete set of functionality when the NIST Implementor's Agreements did not suffice. Secondary sources for U.S. GOSIP include: International Standards and Recommendations, Draft and Proposed Draft International Standards, and working papers within the international standards bodies. The key phrase is "international standards." U.S. GOSIP is not to be based upon any standard, however mature, that is not part of the international standards process.

Tertiary sources, however, are used to supply functionality not derived from the international standards process. They are interim solutions permitted only when international standards do not provide the necessary functionality. All functionality derived from tertiary sources will be replaced with suitable primary or secondary substitutes when they become available.

The NIST Implementor's Agreements

Because the NIST Implementor's Agreements are the primary source for functionality in U.S. GOSIP, this document deserves a closer look. The NIST Implementor's Agreements were created by a consortium of vendors, users, and national and international standards bodies with the intent of producing a profile that provides functionality to meet the requirements of most OSI users. Virtually every group that has produced, or is in the process of producing, a profile has used the Implementor's Workshop as a forum to discuss the OSI protocols and their uses. MAP/TOP, ANSI, and CEN/CENELEC have all participated in the workshop. Because of this, most of the profiles they have generated are, for the most part, compatible with the Implementor's Agreements.

Work in the Implementor's Workshop is an ongoing process. The workshop meets several times a year to discuss the evolution of OSI technology. It produces "ongoing agreements" at these meetings that are distributed for review. Once these agreements have been deemed stable, they are used to amend the Stable Implementor's Agreements. Therefore, as the OSI protocols evolve, so too do the Implementor's Agreements.

U.S. GOSIP Profile

U.S. GOSIP specifies compliance requirements or recommendations for all layers of the OSI Reference Model. This is done by specifying amendments to the NIST Implementor's Agreements profile. The complete suite of protocols supported by U.S. GOSIP, and the functionality defined, is shown below in Figure 2-1.

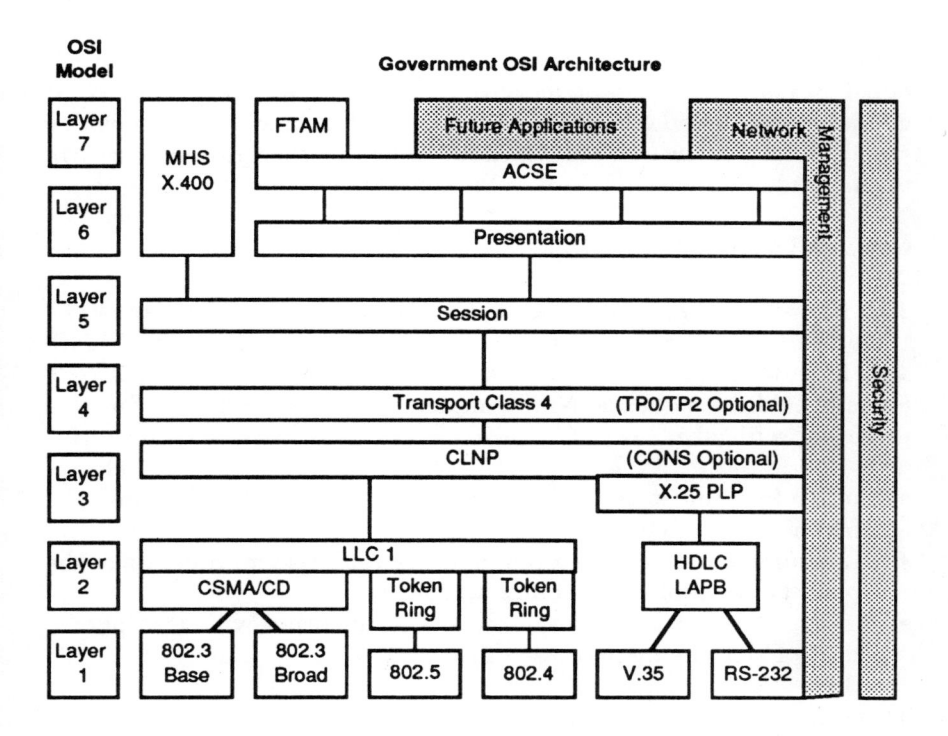

Figure 2-1 The OSI model and U.S. GOSIP.

Physical Layer

U.S. GOSIP does not require any specific physical layer standards. It allows vendors to use the nonproprietary interfaces that best suit the transmission medium line speed, modem type, and transmission distance. U.S. GOSIP does, however, recommend the use of EIA RS-232-C for line speeds up to 19.2 kilobits/second, and CCITT V.35 for line speeds above 19.2 kbit/second when using X.25 as the data-link protocol.

Data-Link Layer

The data-link protocols that can be used in conjunction with X.25 are High Level Data-Link Control (HDLC) and Link Access Procedure B (LAP B). The data-link protocols that can be used in conjunction with ISO 8802/2 (IEEE 802.2) are ISO 8802/3 (IEEE 802.3), ISO 8802/4 (IEEE 802.4), and ISO 8802/5 (IEEE 802.5).

No one data-link protocol is required by U.S. GOSIP. Instead, it specifies a set of standards that vendors may implement, any one being sufficient to claim compliance with U.S. GOSIP. So, for instance, a vendor who creates a product that operates using IEEE 802.3 is just as compliant as a vendor who creates a product that operates over X.25/LAP B. It is up to the purchaser to specify which standards it requires. Whatever data links are chosen must conform to the guidelines specified in the Workshop Agreements.

Network Layer

The Network Layer for all U.S. GOSIP implementations must be ISO 8348/AD1, the Connectionless Mode Network Service (CLNS) and ISO 8473, the Connectionless Mode Network Protocol (CLNP). Specific additions to the NIST Implementor's Agreements for this protocol profile are:

- End Systems must be able to control the value of the Lifetime Parameter for the PDU's they originate.
- Checksums must be supported, and the End System must have the capability of enabling/disabling its use.
- The use of the priority option must be supported with the highest priority PDU's being processed first.

These additions complement the Implementor's Agreements Profile. They do not make the two incompatible.

In addition to CLNP and ISO 8348, the Connection-Oriented Network Service (CONS) operating over X.25 as per ISO 8878 may also be used in conjunction with X.400 MHS when it's operating over public data networks. However, every U.S. GOSIP compliant implementation must support CLNP over at least one data-link protocol.

ISO 9542, the End System to Intermediate System Routing Exchange Protocol (ES-IS), is not part of version 1 of U.S. GOSIP. However, since it is part of the NIST Implementor's Agreements, most vendors' GOSIP compliant products also include it in their Network Layer implementations.

Transport Layer

The Transport Layer must be ISO 8073, the Connection-Oriented Transport Protocol, class 4 operation. The recommended length for the transport selector is two octets, although selector lengths up to 32 octets should be supported.

Transport class 0 operation may also be used in conjunction with CONS for the purposes of operating X.400 MHS over public data networks.

There are no specific requirements for an Application Programmatic Interface to the Transport Layer. U.S. GOSIP leaves this requirement for the purchaser to determine.

Session Layer

ISO 8327, Basic Connection-Oriented Session Protocol must be used as the Session Layer. Both Session version 1 and Session version 2 are allowed. Session version 2 is limited to 10240 octets of user data. The recommended length for session selectors is two octets, although selector lengths of up 16 octets should be supported.

The following session functional units are allowed: Kernel, Duplex, Expedited Data, Resynchronize, Exceptions, Activity Management, Half-duplex, Minor Synchronize, Major Synchronize, and Typed Data. The specific set of functional units required is dependent upon the Applications Layer services supported and the Session Application Programmatic Interface requirements defined by the purchaser.

There are no specific requirements for an Application Programmatic Interface to the Session Layer. U.S. GOSIP leaves this requirement for the purchaser to determine.

Presentation Layer

ISO 8823, Connection-Oriented Presentation Protocol will be used as the Presentation Layer. The recommended length for presentation selectors is two octets, although selector lengths of up to four octets should be supported.

Application Layer

ISO 8650, Protocol for the Association Control Service Element, must be supported for all applications except X.400.

Version 1 of U.S. GOSIP specifies two Application Layer protocols: FTAM and X.400 MHS. The support of the File Transfer, Access, and Management (FTAM) protocol has been divided into two categories: full-purpose systems and limited-purpose systems. A full-purpose implementation provides positional file transfer, simple file access, and management. This means it can transfer simple text, binary, record-oriented, and indexed sequential files. These file types may also be accessed remotely without the entire file being transferred.

A limited-purpose implementation of FTAM provides simple file transfer and management. This means that it must support at least the transfer of simple text and binary file types. A limited-purpose FTAM must be able to interoperate with a full-purpose FTAM where the two implementations have common capabilities.

A U.S. GOSIP compliant implementation of the X.400 Message Handling Service (MHS) will have the Message Transfer Service and the Interpersonal Messaging Services as they are specified in the NIST Implementor's Agreements.

Currently, X.400 is the only application that can operate over Transport class 0 and CONS. To be truly compliant with U.S. GOSIP, this is only allowed when the communication between two Message Transfer Agents occurs when at least one of the agents resides entirely and exclusively inside a public message domain that is under the administration of a public data network. All agents residing in private management domains must operate over Transport class 4, and therefore, CLNP. If a system is connected to both a public and a private domain it must adhere to the above guidelines. An agent in such a configuration is often used as an "application gateway" for forwarding messages from a private to a public domain. An application gateway is the only supported method for relaying between CONS and CLNS networks. Interworking units such as transport relays and MSDSG gateways are not supported.

Companies not under government acquisition control are not limited by the above restrictions for operating X.400 MHS. A company can choose to use Transport class 0 and CONS when performing message transfer within private domains. Many vendors allow their FTAM service as well as their X.400 to be used over Transport class 0 and CONS.

Conformance and Interoperability Testing

NIST has been given the responsibility of providing a conformance testing program for version 1 of U.S. GOSIP. NIST has contracted with the Corporation for Open Systems (COS) to provide the test program for verifying vendors' compliance.

COS operates the U.S. GOSIP testing program in much the same way it manages its own conformance accreditation program. Independent sites are allowed to go through a certification program and become COS-accredited test sites. These sites have the ability to run the tests on a vendor's OSI product and determine their conformance to the U.S. GOSIP protocols suite. Vendors themselves have the ability to become accredited test sites. Hewlett-Packard, for example, has become an accredited test site and has the right to verify conformance for its products as well as the products of other vendors who contract with HP to perform the testing.

Once the test site has passed a vendor's implementation, the vendor may then apply to the National Computer Systems Laboratory for a Certificate of Conformance Testing. Once conformance testing has been passed, the vendor's product may undergo interoperability testing.

Presently, NIST does not have an interoperability test suite. Instead, NIST has created the OSINET network, which is a network available to vendors to facilitate the performance of interoperability testing. Vendors who wish to perform this testing subscribe to the OSINET network. They contact the vendors they wish to test against and access their implementations over OSINET. Although informal, the OSINET testing process does provide a common network over which many products can be accessed. By subscribing to OSINET vendors can test against many implementations instead of having to negotiate with each vendor separately, or buy the vendor's product and test in-house. Vendors can also test their U.S. GOSIP conformant products with other vendors' products that may conform to OSI profiles other than U.S. GOSIP.

U.S. GOSIP requires conformance products for federal agency procurement. Companies, however, are not under this restriction. It is important for companies to know the conformance status of a vendor's product, or the strategy for achieving conformance. However, it is more important for a company to know how well a vendor's implementation interoperates with other vendors' products. Companies should be sure to verify that the products they wish to purchase interoperate with one another.

Comparison of U.S. GOSIP to Other Profiles

The following table (Figure 2-2) is a comparison of the U.S. GOSIP profile to four other major profile families: U.K. GOSIP version 3.0, the MAP/TOP family of profiles version 3.0, the NIST Implementor's Workshop Agreements version 3.0, and the CEN/CENELEC ENV profiles. These families of profiles were chosen because they cover the major OSI user groups in both the United States and Europe.

The purpose of this table is simply to give the reader some idea of the functional breadth of the various profiles and to show how U.S. GOSIP fits into the profile scheme. It should give companies a relative measure of how well the U.S. GOSIP profile interoperates with other user profiles.

The table is only a qualitative comparison since some of these profile families include up to seven separate profiles (e.g., CEN/CENELEC). Also, the profiles have their own way of defining each layer's requirements. For instance, the U.K. GOSIP and CEN/CENELEC profiles define layers 1 to 4 in "transport profiles" and include layers 5 to 7 in each individual "application profile."

NOTES:

1. Only 1984 X.25 is allowed
2. To be used only by X.400 MHS over public data networks
3. 802.2 Type I service shall be used
4. 802.2 Type II service shall be used

All of the above profile families specify X.400 MHS 1984 operation. They allow communication between User Agents and Message Transfer Agents and between adjacent Message Transfer Agents.

What U.S. GOSIP Doesn't Provide

Although U.S. GOSIP provides a stable base for performing intervendor networking, it does not provide some functionality that many companies deem necessary for systems to do real work. Also, U.S.

U.S. GOSIP: Not Just for Government Procurement

Layer	USG	NIST	UKG	MAP	TOP	ENV
Physical/Link						
802.3	X	X	X		X	X
802.4	X	X		X	X	
802.5	X	X	X		X	X
X.21	X	X	X		X	X
X.21 bis	X	X	X		X	X
HDLC	X	X	X		X	X
LAP B	X	X	X		X	X
Network						
CLNP/X.25	X(1)	X			X	
CLNP/802.2	X	X	X	X	X	X
CONS/X.25	X(1,2)	X	X			X
CONS/802.2		X(3)	X(4)			X
ES-IS		X	X	X	X	X
Transport						
TP4/CLNP	X	X	X	X	X	X
TP4/CONS		X	X			
TP0/CONS	X(1)	X	X			X
TP0,2/CONS		X	X			X
Session						
Version 1	X	X	X	X	X	X
Version 2	X	X	X	X	X	X
Pres/Application						
ACSE	X	X	X	X	X	X
FTAM File Transfer						
Simple	X	X	X	X	X	X
Positional	X	X	X	X	X	X
Hierarchical	X	X	X	X	X	X
FTAM File Access						
Positional	X	X	X	X	X	X
Full	X	X	X	X	X	X
FTAM Management	X	X	X	X	X	X

Figure 2-2 U.S. GOSIP compared to other major profile families.

GOSIP imposes certain restrictions on the functionality it does define, thereby making it less attractive to nongovernment companies. This section discusses these shortcomings and attempts to provide solutions for these deficiencies.

Probably the largest deficiency in version 1 of U.S. GOSIP is its omission of the ES-IS protocol. This is rectified in version 2 of U.S.

GOSIP, but it does make systems that implement only version 1 limited in their effectiveness on local area networks (LAN's). However, most vendors understand this. They also understand that version 1 of U.S. GOSIP is the only profile which does not require its use. MAP/TOP, NIST Implementor's Agreements, and U.K. GOSIP all require the use of ES-IS protocol over LAN's. Therefore, vendors usually add support of the ES-IS protocol to their OSI implementations. HP, DEC, SUN, and AT&T all provide ES-IS in their OSI products.

U.S. GOSIP does not define the specific application programmatic interfaces (API's) that should be used to access the various layer services. It says only that API's should be provided and it is up to the purchaser to specify which services are required. All vendors provide API's to some layers in the protocol suite, but there is little standardization among them. Few profiles specify API's. Except for MAP 3.0, which specifies an API for FTAM, API definitions are nonexistent. Various users groups are now trying to tackle this problem, but it will be several years before all vendors offer consistent interfaces. AT&T, along with DEC, IBM, HP, and other vendors, is working on creating consistent API's for use with ACSE/Presentation, Transport, and CONS. The Network Management forum is doing the same thing for X.400. Other groups, such as POSIX and X/OPEN, are also working along similar lines. Companies should be sure to ask vendors to specify what API's they support and at what layers.

Similarly, U.S. GOSIP does not specify interactive interfaces for its FTAM and X.400 services. This is not unusual. Most profiles do not specify these. However, it is important to know how these services are to be used. This is especially true for X.400. Of particular importance is whether the vendor's MHS implementation acts only as a gateway (Message Transfer Agent), or whether it can be used in a user agent configuration as well. If the latter is true, the interactive interface to the user agent is very important.

U.S. GOSIP is somewhat different from other profiles in that it has specific requirements concerning the use of addresses at all layers in its protocol profile. It defines a family of NSAP addresses that federal agencies must use, and it defines default selector values for the FTAM and X.400 MHS services. Companies cannot use these NSAP's as they are reserved for the government and the selectors defined may not fit into a company's addressing strategy.

U.S. GOSIP does, however, allow communication with nongovernment networks and therefore requires that U.S. GOSIP compliant implementations support any valid NSAP address format. Valid format means that the NSAP conforms to ISO 8348/AD2, Addendum to the Network Service Definition Covering Addressing. So even though

U.S. GOSIP defines a specific NSAP address space, companies can use their own NSAP address structures in U.S. GOSIP compliant products.

The selector value specifications are only guidelines. U.S. GOSIP requires compliant implementations to accept any valid selector value within the constraints previously listed. Since the constraints listed in the protocol section are in line with all other major profiles (except MAP/TOP 3.0, which allows presentation selector values of up to 16 octets; U.S. GOSIP/NIST only allow up to four octets for a presentation selector), virtually any profile-compliant address can be used with U.S. GOSIP.

Version 1 of U.S. GOSIP does not have any directory service specifications. This is because X.500, the CCITT directory service standard, was not stable when U.S. GOSIP was written. Instead, U.S. GOSIP suggests the use of well-known addresses or the registration of addresses with a central authority, namely NIST. Almost all vendors supply some form of directory service product, whether it is X.500 or a proprietary solution. Companies wishing to use directory services will need to evaluate individual vendor's solutions to see if they meet their directory service needs. Companies should also verify what the vendor's plans are for changing their directory service product to an X.500-based solution.

U.S. GOSIP allows interworking between CONS and CLNP networks only at the Application Layer by way of application gateways. This is insufficient for many companies, especially those who operate both in the United States and in Europe. Companies who need this functionality should be sure to query the vendor about its strategies to solve this problem.

U.S. GOSIP only supports Transport class 4 over CLNP (TP4/CLNP). Although it does allow limited use of Transport class 0 over CONS (TP0/CONS), there are other Transport class/Network Layer combinations that customers may want to use. The most important one is Transport class 2 over CONS (TP2,0/CONS). Transport class 2 has many advantages over Transport class 0. It allows the use of expedited data and the ability to multiplex several transport connections over a single X.25 virtual circuit. Another possibility is Transport class 4 over CONS (TP4/CONS). This is less popular, but it does have advantages when interworking between CONS and CLNP networks.

U.S. GOSIP does not support the use of CONS and X.25 over 802.2 networks. This profile is gaining popularity mainly in Europe where most networks are X.25 based. U.K. GOSIP and CEN/CENELEC both support this profile. The NIST Implementor's Agreements support this as well, but in a slightly different way. As there are very few vendors who actually offer this profile in a product today, companies who need this functionality should evaluate vendors' products very carefully. U.S. GOSIP is an evolving profile. New versions of U.S. GOSIP are being created by NIST to address the limitations of the current version. New versions become the mandated profile 18 months after publication. Figure 2-3 is a list of functionality that is planned for future versions of U.S. GOSIP. These services and the versions listed for release are not final. NIST should be contacted to obtain revised schedules and dates for release.

Questions to Ask Vendors

Here is a list of questions companies should ask vendors about their U.S. GOSIP compliant implementations. The answers to these questions will give companies a good idea about how well a vendor's product will suit their needs. It will also tell the company how robust the product is and how committed to OSI the vendor is.

- What Link Layer standards does the product support?
- What versions of X.25 does the product support? 1980, 1984?
- What layers have supported Application Programmatic Interfaces? What are the interfaces? What is the vendor's strategy for moving toward standardized interfaces?
- What is the vendor's strategy for obtaining U.S. GOSIP conformance marks? Is the vendor an accredited test center?
- Has the vendor performed interoperability testing? What other vendors can the product interoperate with?
- Does the product support the ES-IS protocol?
- Can the product support any valid NSAP address format?
- Can the product support TP0/CONS over private X.25 networks?
- Can FTAM operate over TP0/CONS?
- Is TP2,0/CONS supported? Is TP4/CONS supported?
- What is the vendor's strategy for providing directory services?
- Can the X.400 MHS act as an application gateway between TP4/CLNP and TP0/CONS networks?
- Does the vendor support Interworking Units such as MSDSG or Transport Relays?
- What functionality does the FTAM have — full-purpose or limited-purpose? Does the vendor have an interactive interface?
- What other user profiles does the product support?

U.S. GOSIP: Not Just for Government Procurement   49

GOSIP 1
Pub Feb 89 / Req'd Aug 90

FTAM NBS 2 subset
— Positional File Transfer (T2)
— Management (M1)
— [Simple File Access (A1)]

MHS/X.400'84

Transport Classes 0 and 4

TP0 only for X.400 public messaging domains

Connectionless Network Service (CLNS)

X.25, 802.3, 802.4, 802.5

GOSIP 2
Est. Pub Oct 90 / Req'd Jun 92

VTP
— telnet profile
— forms profile

ODA/ODIF

ES-IS routing protocol
* Connectionless Transport Protocol (CLTP)
* Connection Oriented Network Service (CONS)

ISDN

GOSIP 3
Est. Pub Oct 91 / Req'd Jun 93

FTAM NBS 3 subset

MHS/X.400'88/EDI

VTP
— X3, page, and scroll profiles

X.500 Directory Services

MMS Manuf. Message Spec.

CGM/SGML

Network Management
* Security Enhancements

IS-IS Routing (Intra-domain)
* TP2

FDDI

GOSIP 4
(Date undetermined)

DTP (Distributed Transaction Processing)

RDA (Remote Database Access)

IS-IS Routing (Inter-domain)
* Additional Security Enhancements
* Additional Network Management Functions

Source: NIST

Figure 2-3 Planned U.S. GOSIP functionality.

Conclusion

Companies are looking at the OSI protocols as the solution to their intervendor networking problems. However, the protocols themselves do not guarantee interoperability between vendors' implementations. Consortiums of users and vendors have been created to write profiles of the protocols to help ensure interoperability between OSI implementations. Choosing which profile, or profiles, to use may be one of the most important decisions a company will make in the next few years. U.S. GOSIP is a profile that companies should evaluate.

U.S. GOSIP is a profile that has many benefits for companies. Since it is based upon the work of the NIST OSI Implementor's Workshop, companies are assured that U.S. GOSIP complies with the most popular user profiles. Also, since U.S. GOSIP is an evolving profile, a company's OSI network may evolve with it, thereby ensuring a smooth transition toward full OSI.

Copies of U.S. GOSIP and additional information about the U.S. GOSIP program may be obtained at the following address:

Order Number: FIPS PUB 146
U.S. Department of Commerce
National Technical Information Service
Springfield, Virginia 22161

The NIST Implementor's Agreements may be obtained at the following address:

National Institute of Standards and Technology
NIST Workshop for Implementors of OSI
Building 225, Room B-217
Gaithersburg, Maryland 20899

About the Author

Bob D. Tausworthe graduated from the New Mexico Institute of Mining and Technology in 1980 with degrees in mathematics and computer science. He is currently employed by Hewlett-Packard as a software engineer in its Information Networks Division. He has been working as an OSI protocol specialist for the past four years and most recently architected the addressing and routing portions of HP's United States GOSIP-compliant OSI Transport Services (OTS/9000) product.

Chapter

3

Moving Toward Standards: The Rapid Growth of OSI in Europe

by Mikael Johansson

In major European organizations today, multivendor networking is already a reality. Communications among computer systems from vendors like IBM, Digital Equipment, and Hewlett-Packard, as well as among local European makers' equipment, has been possible for a number of years through the use of gateways, black boxes, custom software, and to some extent through the use of de facto standards like TCP/IP and SNA.

But these standards no longer suffice. Today, international de jure standards increasingly are being perceived as the key to multivendor networking, and OSI is becoming a viable alternative to costly developments of custom communication software.

Why is this happening? And why now? There are several explanations:

- OSI is now seen as more than just another set of communication protocols. It is perceived as the only feasible networking base for a multitude of multivendor applications, primarily in the areas of information exchange and distributed processing.

- Current growth of these standardized applications ranges from around 20 percent annually for order entry and database inquiry to 60 percent annually for Electronic Data Interchange applications, in certain geographical markets.
- While often used today on top of proprietary or de facto networks, standardized multivendor applications like the Office Document Architecture (ODA) or the Electronic Data Interchange (EDI) will, in the near future, operate over a standardized networking base. Only then can a truly open system be created. As we move into the 1990s, the networking focus will more and more be on the application side. In other words, the focus will be on how to use an OSI networking base, rather than on how to implement it.

Today, preparing for this future by putting the building blocks in place is the key to future competitiveness and success.

OSI Profiles

The seven-layer OSI model can most easily be divided into three distinct areas of functionality. At the bottom are the network links and access methods. These media options and access methods were the first sets of protocols to become international standards. Today, terms like X.25, 802.3, CSMA/CD, and others are familiar. These protocols constitute the foundation (Figure 3-1).

Above the familiar links reside the transport protocols and services. These also have been standardized for some time. OSI Transport and Session protocols were developed during the early 1980s and are well-known international standards throughout industry and government.

The application layer has been the critical area of development. But even this area is now part of the international standards domain. Application level functions such as file transfer and messaging have now reached a state of maturity in the FTAM and MHS specifications.

This has not been an easy process. A large number of organizations have contributed to the final ISO specifications; IEEE specified the LAN link protocols (802.X), CCITT the WAN protocols, to name two key organizations. Various bodies ratified and added functionality. It has taken some 15 years for the OSI model to be turned into a specification for Open Systems Interconnections.

Today, the ISO protocols available span a wide range of networking needs. They also allow implementors to choose among an ever-

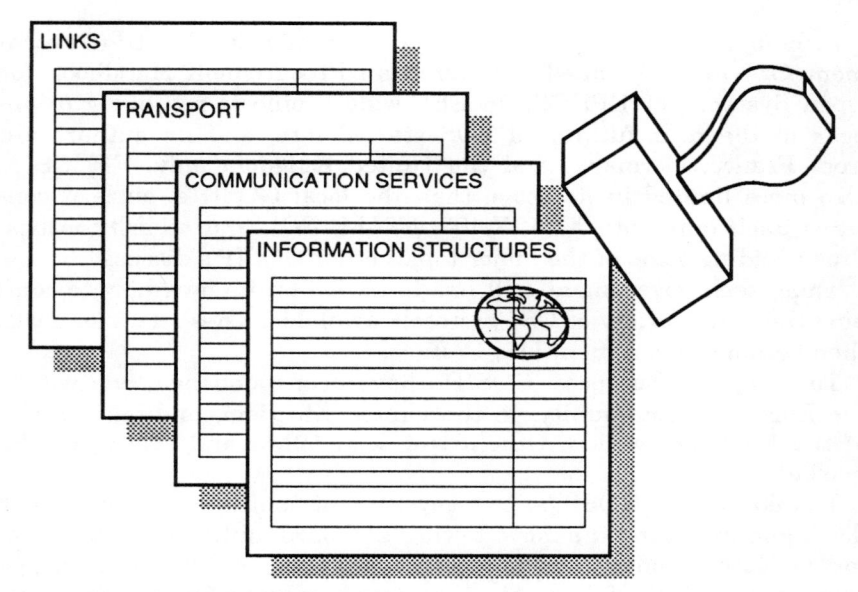

Figure 3-1 OSI standard protocols.

expanding set of options. To overcome some of the standards confusion, OSI profiles are being created. These profiles combine a given set of OSI protocols into recommended sets, optimized for specific environments.

Profiles like the Manufacturing Automation Protocol (MAP) specify the use of certain links and services ideally suited for manufacturing applications at the shop floor level. Yet others, like the Technical and Office Protocol profile (TOP) are adapted to more commercially oriented environments.

Government OSI profiles specify certain combinations of links, transport services, and application services to be used in areas like ministries, the health care sector, and defense, to name just a few. Once published, the profiles become the purchasing recommendations for their respective environments, in some cases mandating functionality to be provided by the networking products' vendors.

The basis for European government OSI profiles is an EEC Council decision (EEC/87/95) made in 1987. The Council decided to recommend to its member states to use International Standards, based on the OSI model, wherever and whenever possible. This decision is valid for central and local government authorities across Europe for information technology contracts valued above 100,000 European Currency Units (ECU).

Although work is in progress on a common EEC GOSIP (Government OSI Profile), called the European Procurement Handbook for Open Systems, or EPHOS, an EEC-wide profile is not likely to appear in the near future. EPHOS started late, and its authors are from France, Germany, and the United Kingdom only. EPHOS is also more limited in its scope than the local GOSIP's, since it concerns itself only with X.25, X.400, FTAM, EDI, and security issues, thus avoiding some of the major topics other GOSIP's discuss.

Thus, each government still has to decide on its own how to combine the wide variety of OSI protocols available. These decisions will then become Government OSI Profiles.

To date, two European GOSIP's have been published; one within the European Community, in the United Kingdom, and one outside of the EEC, in Sweden. Others will soon follow and evolve, as the market evolves.

Thanks to the GOSIP's, the government markets are the major driving force behind the move toward standard multivendor networking in Europe today. Taken together, the EEC governments represent around 27 to 28 percent of the total amount of money spent on information technology (IT) across Europe. In 1989, this amounted to some $11.2 billion. Over the following three years, the growth rate is expected to be around 8 percent annually, totaling close to $15 billion by 1992.

European government markets today are typically dominated by IBM and a local player. In France, IBM and Bull hold 80 percent of the government markets. In Germany, IBM and Siemens hold a similar position. In Italy, the main players are Olivetti and IBM.

Only in the United Kingdom is the situation different; there IBM commands less than 5 percent of the central government market. This, plus the recent privatization of British Telecom, is the main reason for the very strong drive toward OSI standards in the United Kingdom. A similar situation could soon occur in the Netherlands, based on similar market trends. Others might follow.

The Government Sector

Any European government can be divided into three distinctly different areas of responsibility: central government authorities, local government authorities, and government-related authorities.

The central government typically consists of ministries and various dependent bodies. In most cases, the skills and knowledge levels are high, and implementations of information technology usually involves a high level of customization. Personnel from ministries often participate actively in standards groups and organizations. They hire consultants, fund pilot projects, and develop specialized applications. Based on their findings, reports are published and recommendations to other government bodies are issued. Often, an IT project at this level of government can span more than one fiscal year.

A simple breakdown of the costs involved in a typical project at the central government level shows that some 60 percent can be related to applications development, another 30 percent to the hardware purchased, and 10 percent to communications. With the price erosion currently occurring on the hardware side and bearing in mind the increased use of standardized applications mentioned above, the communication cost is fast becoming the critical factor in IT purchasing plans.

Without standardized communication protocols and products, central government spending on communications will increase far above the hardware and applications software cost levels. Standardizing on single-vendor protocols will only delay this process, although it may bring some relief in the short term. Hence the current emphasis on OSI.

At the local level, in city administrations and related environments, standardizing on a single vendor has long been the key to success. Lacking the skills found at higher levels in the administrative hierarchy and being restricted by budget allocations limited to a single fiscal year, local governments have often sought turnkey solutions. Although tenders were often solicited from several sources, the predominant vendor usually succeeded in maintaining and expanding his influence.

With the new recommendations coming from the central authorities, this picture is changing. The degree of uncertainty associated with new and unfamiliar vendors and technology is being minimized by adherence to centrally issued profiles. Local governments are falling in line behind their ministerial counterparts.

There is also a highly diverse group of government-related organizations, ranging from power utility companies to waste disposal administrations, from post and telecommunications giants to the local tax collector, and from airports to harbors, whose computer communication needs and skills vary greatly. In general, government related authorities behave like their public equivalents with one major exception: they are often bound by ministerial directives.

More and more decisions regarding the purchase of communication equipment are being based on the local GOSIP. In many cases, as in the various arms of the defense forces, the GOSIP's extend to outside contractors as well. It is becoming increasingly difficult to underestimate the influence of the GOSIP's.

Potentially, the local GOSIP's will bring several benefits to governments as well as to the OSI vendors. GOSIP's already generate a great deal of public awareness and visibility for OSI standards. They are also instrumental in pushing the standards toward completion much faster than the industry would have done on its own.

In addition to being a testing ground for OSI products through their conformance and interoperability demands, governments will also become a significant market for OSI products, a market with great reference potential for OSI vendors.

But today each European government is likely to have its own interpretation of what "flavor" of OSI should be implemented, creating unwanted uncertainty in the marketplace and slowing development efforts in the computer industry.

Each GOSIP is divided into four sections, the T-, A-, F-, and C-subprofiles (Figure 3-2). The T- or Transport subprofile defines the available choices at the link through the transport level. The A- or Application subprofile defines functionality at the Session through

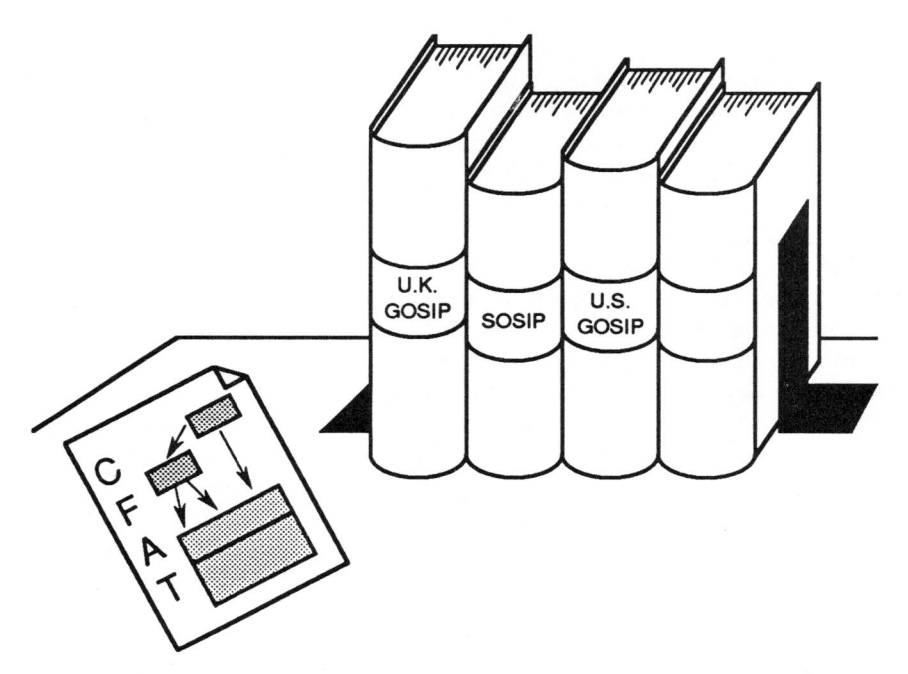

Figure 3-2 Government OSI profiles.

Application levels. The F- or Format subprofile deals with the various document interchange formats available. Finally, the C- or Character subprofile deals with the character repertoires deemed necessary in the local marketplace. An additional profile, the Y-subprofile, dealing with terminal interfaces, may be added to future revisions of the GOSIP's.

Depending on local preferences and realities, differing priorities have been made in the profiles published to date. Although it is possible to identify several common traits, there are some important differences that need to be taken into account.

The U.K. Government OSI Profile

The U.K. GOSIP is produced by the U.K. Central Communications and Telecommunications Authority, CCTA, a part of the Treasury Department of the British Government. The U.K. GOSIP is primarily intended as a purchasing aid for U.K. government departments. Due to the purchasing power and influence of the government authorities, however, it is hoped that the possible audience will extend widely outside of the U.K. government itself. The U.K. GOSIP is applicable to U.K. government purchases as of February 1989.

Although the CCTA has made considerable efforts to align itself with other standards bodies, this aim has only been achieved at the very lowest levels of the model, within the T-subprofile. Even there, however, there are significant differences from other profiles. The higher in the protocol stack we look, the greater the divergence from other local profiles.

Some major items to be considered:

- For local area network (LAN) connections, the U.K. GOSIP views connection-oriented protocols as the strategic direction. While accepting CSMA/CD CLNS and Token Ring CLNS as intermediate solutions, CSMA/CD CONS and Token Ring CONS are the strategic choices. Token Bus CLNS is totally excluded from the T-subprofile.
- For wide area networks (WAN's), the U.K. GOSIP specifies the use of X.25 (1984) using Transport level specifications class 0 and 2, as well as the normally optional class 4.
- Linking LAN's to WAN's should be made possible through the use of CONS profiles on both sides. LAN (CLNS) to WAN (CONS) to LAN (CLNS) is not accepted.

- At the A-subprofile level, the U.K. GOSIP is clearly an OSI purist. Very few intermediate solutions are accepted while waiting for finalized standards. Thus, non-OSI terminal support, such as Telnet, is not accepted. Neither is the current interim solution for OSI Network Management, ISO DIS 9596, CMIP. Likewise, the FTAM A/112 profile (1988) is not accepted. For message handling systems, several U.K. options have been added to the X.400 (1984) spec.
- At the F-subprofile level, the U.K. GOSIP does not accept the ODA/ODIF Q/113 and has added a set of mandatory, U.K.-specific options to the ODA/ODIF Q/111 specification.

Ultimately, the U.K. GOSIP will have to (and is intending to) converge with international profiles. By international profiles, we mean the International Standards Organization's International Standardized Profiles, or ISO ISP's. There is currently no time frame given for this development.

The Swedish OSI Profile

In Sweden, an equivalent procurement profile has been produced by the Swedish Agency for Administrative Development, a section of Statskontoret, the Swedish Government Procurement Office.

The Swedish OSI Profile, SOSIP version 1.0, is valid from April 1989, although a general application of OSI communications according to SOSIP was not available until January 1, 1990. This means that all work with government requirement specifications commenced in 1989 and expected to be installed in 1990 or thereafter referred to SOSIP in relevant parts.

The approach is similar to the U.K. GOSIP's, but with more consideration of market realities. Products not expected to be available in the market for some time are not included in SOSIP. Instead, interim solutions are recommended.

Main items to be considered include:

- At the T-subprofile level for LAN's, SOSIP specifies connectionless communications only. The token bus specification is included, although with a lower priority than CSMA/CD (CLNS) and token ring (CLNS).
- For WAN's, SOSIP is identical to the U.K. GOSIP, with the addition of the X.21 (CONS) specification to be used with the Swedish public data network, DATEX. This is ranked, however, as a lower priority than the X.25 standards.

- Relay profiles allow combinations of CONS and CLNS communications. What was deemed a strategic direction in the U.K. GOSIP, LAN (CONS) to LAN (CONS) and LAN (CONS) to WAN (CONS), is not allowed in SOSIP.
- At the A-subprofile level, SOSIP includes the Telnet profile, while waiting for OSI VTP to become accepted in the marketplace. Likewise, OSI Network Management, the CMIP specification, is included in its draft format.
- For message handling, MHS, the U.K. specific options are not included. At the F-subprofile level, the same situation occurs. U.K. specific options are not accepted additions to the ODA/ODIF specification.

A German OSI Profile

In Germany, there is no federal OSI profile, or German GOSIP. Instead, each of the 11 German states will define its own OSI requirements and then publish profiles. To date, only one state has completed this work, Nordrhein-Westfalen, NRW. This state has for the past eight years implemented OSI-like protocols for communications among its computer systems, currently consisting of 14 different brands.

Today, multivendor communication systems in Nordrhein-Westfalen are primarily OSI-based at the link level. At the transport level, an intermediate solution called Common Higher Communications Protocols, or CHCP, has been applied. Gradually, this is being replaced by ISO OSI TP 4, class 2 and 3, for transport services, and by other ISO protocols at the higher levels. Since applications above are written for CHCP4, migration tools are necessary. The preferred migration tool is the X/Open recommended transport level interface, ISO/XTI.

Ultimately, NRW will ask all suppliers to conform to its recently published OSI profile. An outline of the profile follows:

- Link level options are CSMA/CD 802.3 for LAN, X.25 for WAN. Level three is CCITT X.25 only. No ISO IP is included. The transport level specification at the moment specifies only ISO 8073 class 0.
- At the higher levels, a considerable number of specifications have been included, adding to the complexity of the NRW profile. These include ACSE, CCR, RTSE, and ROSE, directly above the session level, and MHS, FTAM, and Distributed Transaction Processing on top of the previously mentioned specifications.
- At the equivalent of the F-subprofile level, ODA/ODIF and EDIFACT are specified.

The NRW does not give a time frame for when the profile will become mandatory, nor does it prioritize among the various options available, which will undoubtedly be a cause of concern for potential vendors.

OSI in Industry

How will OSI impact IT procurement outside of the government markets, within the European industry? Today, public companies represent just over 70 percent of the total IT market. Those 70 percent, however, are split into some highly diverse and regionalized market segments, some with conflicting needs and wants. One segment in particular stands out: the major global industrial corporations of Europe.

Although heavy users of de facto standards, these European corporations view OSI as the key to future communications. By a margin of nearly two to one, they rank their computer vendors' support of OSI as more important than improved multivendor connectivity in general. They also consider the support of OSI nearly six times more important than improved network management facilities for their existing networks. OSI is clearly the issue of the day.

One in every three European corporations is implementing OSI networking products today. Close to another third is committed to the idea of OSI. Interestingly enough, these opinions are independent of the current suppliers' OSI commitments. Customers of a supplier with a weak OSI commitment implement and support OSI only fractionally less than do customers in general.

Given that industry is committed to implementing OSI, what functionality does a typical corporation look for? This all depends on the industry, and the size of company we are looking at. In general, large multinational companies have a high level of understanding of OSI. They also have the people and the skills to implement the functionality they require.

Within these companies, there are two clearly different environments looking toward OSI. The first is the Management Information Systems, or MIS, departments. Here, centralized computing power is slowly being replaced by decentralized applications environments. The role of the MIS department is now changing, and MIS managers looking to the future see two trends affecting their work. The first trend is the distribution of computing power to the users and the subsequent linking of cooperating applications. This trend causes the demand for standardization of the three key IT items: operating systems, applications, and networks. The other trend is related to the increased demand for control and maintenance of these environments. This results in a strong demand for OSI-standard, multivendor, network management facilities centrally located and controlled by the MIS department.

The second environment is the shop floor of the manufacturing companies. While changes in production techniques based on the use of information technology have, until recently, been most prominent in the discrete manufacturing companies, the process industries are rapidly following suit. The previously mentioned trends toward cooperating applications environments is as strong here as it is in the MIS department, though based on a different reality.

In the MIS environment, the five top priorities are:

1. Message handling (X.400 and X.500)
2. Security (C2 moving toward B1)
3. File transfer (FTAM)
4. Document architecture (ODA)
5. Communication management (CMIS/CMIP)

In the manufacturing environment, the main multivendor issue is on the factory floor itself. The proliferation of equipment is not so much at the computer levels as at the device levels. Most major corporations have many different brands of PLC's, CNC's, and NC's.

A major food products manufacturer mentions some 80 brands in 20 plants across Europe. A packaged goods specialist lists more than 50 brands of PLC's. Automotive companies typically have 5 to 10 different brands on the factory floor, each with its own type of proprietary messaging protocol.

Priorities in the manufacturing environment are:

1. Messaging systems (MMS and its companion standards)
2. Migration tools (API's)
3. Data base access (No current OSI standard)
4. File transfer (FTAM)
5. Virtual terminal (VTP)

Although strongly interested in OSI, most corporations as well as government procurement offices can easily explain why they have not adopted full-scale OSI. Apart from the obvious lack of products from some major vendors, other factors play a great role. An external factor often mentioned is the local PTT. If not privatized (and even if privatized), the monopoly status of the PTT can seriously stall implementation plans if the PTT is not fully committed or is implementing OSI according to its own plans. Another external factor often mentioned is the lack of conformance certifications and clear performance and reliability data from vendors.

Often-cited internal barriers to OSI include a skills shortage, a lack of cost justifications, and the often missing migration strategy.

These barriers can be overcome. The first step is to have a clear commitment to OSI standards at the top management level. This should be based on financial justifications, whereby OSI is shown to provide major long-term productivity gains. This step is the key to successful OSI implementations.

Second, a knowledge and skills build-up has to take place at lower levels in the organization. If the migration strategies (outlined below) are followed, it should be possible to accomplish this at a comparatively low cost level. A sensible approach must be based on "think big, start small" principles, moving step by step to full-scale OSI utilization.

An OSI Deployment Strategy

Although demonstrations have been major stepping stones toward the actual implementation of OSI in industry and government, large-scale installations and market acceptance do not happen overnight. A phased approach to actual implementations is necessary to handle the build-up of knowledge, the technology diffusion, and the migration from existing ways of multivendor networking.

There are four distinct steps toward the eventual market dominance of OSI networks: initial OSI pilot installations, the creation of OSI subnets, a long coexistence phase, and finally, the OSI dominance phase (see Figure 3-3).

During the pilot phase, the requirements from the marketplace are primarily concerned with experimentation. OSI networks are installed in isolated environments, in controlled circumstances, and serve the purpose of familiarization with a new technology. These networks contribute to the knowledge build-up necessary to enter the second stage.

In the second phase, OSI subnets, the requirements are primarily related to the creation of OSI applications and the need to integrate the OSI network with existing multivendor networks. These OSI networks are no longer isolated in controlled environments, but are becoming fully integrated into the organization's communication structure. While the de facto standards continue to be supported, proprietary networking products are being replaced by OSI products to the

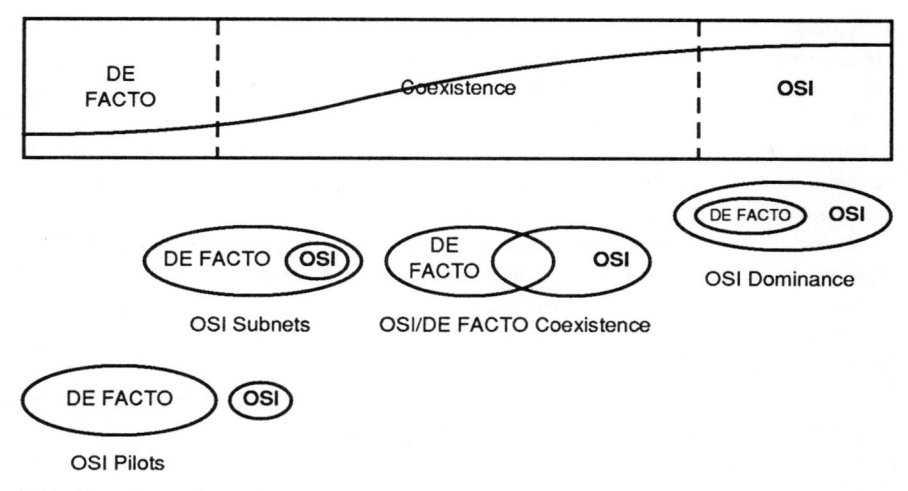

Figure 3-3 OSI deployment strategy.

extent that technology implementations will allow. Applications layer gateways provide the vital links between de facto standards-based applications and the newly added OSI-based applications.

In the third stage, organizations create OSI-only networks, providing functionality that previously only de facto standards-based networks could. Compatibility with older networks is assured, while the de facto standard TCP/IP is being replaced by OSI Transport protocols. The use of multiprotocol routers, or encapsulation techniques, ensures that existing cabling plants can be utilized by both de facto and OSI-based networks.

The final stage of the OSI evolution is the eventual dominance of OSI networks. Here, OSI replaces de facto standards networking as the industry accepted means of multivendor communication. Older TCP/IP-based networks become subnets to the OSI backbone, connected through transport layer gateways.

According to a recent Gartner Group report, by 1995 some 80 percent of all new multivendor networks will be OSI-based. Clearly, this is a mark of the final stage of the OSI evolution.

Using International Standards

How, then, can OSI networking be used today? To what purpose and in what context will OSI be useful as a communication media and service provider?

Consider the following example: A northern European manufacturing company has business dealings across the continent. Its supplier of raw materials is based in the eastern part of Europe, its distributor of final products has its home somewhere in the center of Europe, and its primary market lies in the south, where stores are selling its goods. Financial dealings between the manufacturer and its supplier are handled through its primary bank in the south of Europe.

Information processing needs among the companies are of four types: price information, stock information, order information, and financial transaction information. How can open standards communications best be used to provide multivendor intercompany communication services?

The business proceedings, as seen by the manufacturer, begin with a request for price information from the outlet in southern Europe. This information is stored in a regularly updated database at the manufacturing site. The manufacturer, used to this type of request, transmits a file that updates the local database in the store. Here the FTAM OSI protocol, used over a public X.25 WAN link, will provide the service needed.

The manufacturer, notified of an interest in its products, then wants to make sure its distributor has adequate supplies of the products in question. A request for stock status is sent to the distributor and a reply received. This communication uses an X.25 link with X.400 messaging services on top, since there is only a simple message that needs to be transferred.

Based on this reply, the manufacturer decides to produce more material to meet the expected demand. He sends an order to the raw materials supplier; the supplier responds with an acknowledgment of the order, delivery of the material, and an invoice for the amount due. This process uses not only the X.25 links and the X.400 services, but also an application level service called EDIFACT. This service helps reduce the amount of documentation necessary and significantly increases the speed of the transaction. The manufacturer can thus truly adjust his production for just-in-time manufacturing and capitalize on the reduced levels of stock related to work in progress in his plant.

Seen from the distributor's point of view, the messaging services of his X.25/X.400 system provide all the information necessary. The store regularly checks the stock status, and the manufacturer does the same. In both cases, X.400 messages convey the information, timely and accurately.

Seen from the supplier's point of view, all transactions are handled by the EDIFACT application on top of the X.25/X.400 links and services. The supplier receives an order from the manufacturer in the agreed-upon standard format, containing part numbers, quantities, addresses, and other descriptors such as color and price. The same information is then used for invoicing the manufacturer.

To handle the financial data needed to complete the transaction, a copy is dispatched to the supplier's bank contact. The bank extracts the information necessary and finalizes the transaction between the two companies.

All this is possible through the use of current X.400 networking solutions, if EDIFACT translation is added to the basic store and forward mechanisms.

Through a PC or terminal on an in-house LAN, a stock request is generated. It is transmitted via an electronic mail application, through an X.25 link, into the recipient's environment. If this is a single-vendor environment, the process is repeated in reverse. If the corresponding environment is a multivendor OSI environment, the recipient will utilize its implementation of the relevant OSI protocols in a similar manner. Of course, this will be transparent to the end user.

Through the use of Application Programming Interfaces (X.400 API's) additional services can be added to the basic messaging used in the previous example. Fax messages can be created on a PC screen and dispatched to a receiving Fax machine. Teletex is an alternative media, and of course, EDI is recommended for use on top of the X.400 Application Interface.

To handle this traffic, 802.3 protocols are used internally; X.25 protocols are used for external traffic. Multivendor addressing is made possible through the use of the X.500 Directory Services protocols.

Various corporate entities have applications that require communications with external bodies. Local financial applications, used in the order entry department or the accounting department, are transmitted in their local application format to a translator. The translator will convert the message into ANSI X.12 or EDIFACT format and pass it on to a gateway. The gateway is attached to a value-added network, VAN, as are the trading partners at the receiving end. This is identical to the case presented before. In the model, this is also true for the shipping department and the manufacturing operation.

The Benefits of OSI

Given the technology described above, how will OSI benefit its users? First of all, it gives a user the possibility to choose the right system for the right job. In a small organization with limited communication requirements, a small Unix machine can act as the X.400 server. In larger organizations, multiple machines or machines with greater processing power can be used. Irrespective of the brand name, OSI protocols provide the functionality needed.

Second, the information flow can be increased and better directed using OSI networks. More timely information will reach those concerned and provide a sound basis for decision making. OSI also reduces expenses since it is a more efficient way of communication, and it reduces the investment in multiple networking technologies since only one, OSI, is needed. Complete network transparency across multivendor systems is provided by OSI.

A case for the financial benefits of Open Systems Interconnection can easily be made:

- OSI reduces system complexity and the number of protocol converters needed. When OSI protocols are used throughout the environment, costly investments in "black box" technologies can be avoided.
- The number of gateways can likewise be reduced, as can the installation times for networked systems. With a single type of interface being used, only a small number of gateways will be needed. Since these gateways would be used primarily for backward compatibility with older types of networks, a planned phase-out can be accomplished, with overall system complexity subsequently reduced.
- Few validations are needed, and the maintenance costs will subsequently fall. With a unified approach to multivendor networking, only one type of network training, documentation, and software will be necessary.

Taken together, all of this translates to a significant reduction of the direct communication costs compared to the costs involved in designing, installing, and maintaining proprietary systems.

OSI can also make a difference in the area of application costs:

- OSI requires fewer types of interfaces. It does not need converters. It reduces both implementation and installation times. And it reduces the number of validations to only one.
- Since a single technology is used, technicians can be moved from one application area to another without having to relearn the networking technology. Highly specialized knowledge of "black boxes" and customized software becomes obsolete. No longer will the knowledge leave the organization when the technician leaves.

Conclusion

The rapid growth of OSI networks in Europe is likely to continue over the coming years. By the mid-1990s, OSI is very likely to have become *the* multivendor networking standard. Today, the driving forces behind the move toward OSI are the various European governments, through their purchasing profiles, or GOSIP's, and the main global manufacturers within the EEC. The barriers to implementation are successively being overcome through individual and concerted efforts throughout Europe. OSI has arrived.

About the Author

Mikael Johansson is currently the OSI Program Manager for Hewlett-Packard Information Networks Division, based in Cupertino, California. As such, he is responsible for the marketing of a wide range of OSI products across a variety of computer platforms, on a worldwide basis. Prior to his current assignment, he was Hewlett-Packard's European OSI Program Manager, based in Grenoble, France. He joined the company in 1987.

Previous to Hewlett-Packard, Johansson held the positions of Marketing Manager, Continental Operations, for Allen-Bradley Europa, based in Amsterdam, the Netherlands; Product Manager, Interactive Systems, for 3M Sweden, based in Stockholm, Sweden; and various marketing positions with ASEA Electronics, also in Sweden.

Johansson graduated in 1979 from the University of Uppsala, Sweden, with a degree in Business Administration, specializing in Industrial and International Marketing.

Chapter

4

ISDN and the Global Network

by Dale Gulick

The emerging Integrated Services Digital Network (ISDN) is the logical next step in the evolution of the world telephone network. Essentially, ISDN is the conversion of the existing network from an analog to a digital infrastructure. The result is a network that combines the global interconnection capabilities of today's voice telephone network with universal, standardized data transmission.

In this chapter we will investigate the structure of ISDN as an environment for user applications, not as the end applications themselves. We will look at the organization of the network, the functions performed at each layer of the ISO model, the structure of the required software, and the various types and classifications of terminal devices.

What's in a Name?

Integrated services represents the combination of voice and data on a single, all-digital network. This means more than voice and data communications sharing the same wire; it implies a synergistic relationship between voice and data information. Two examples of this synergy are: digitized voice stored on the hard drive of a personal computer, providing voice store and forward capability as well as voice-annotated e-mail; and automatic file call up, which would, for example, provide an insurance agent with the ability to automatically call up a customer's policy data file whenever the customer calls. In the latter case, the agent's terminal is connected to the host computer via the same telephone line that is used for the voice call. The calling party's telephone number is automatically used to access the data file.

The key to ISDN is that it is totally digital from end to end. The present telephone network utilizes analog lines to transmit both voice and data (via a modem) between the user's site (customer premise) and the telephone switching network. These analog lines have a restricted bandwidth of about 3 kHz. While it is true that the portion of the telephone network that connects one central office to another is primarily digital, the connection between the customer premise and the central office is analog. This is called the *analog subscriber loop*. To oversimplify things, ISDN replaces this analog subscriber loop with a totally digital path, providing two 64-kbps voice and/or data connections and a 16-kbps signaling/data channel, which is referred to as the ISDN Basic Rate Interface (BRI). To be sure, there is more to ISDN than this (we will go into detail later), but the totally digital nature of ISDN is the key.

Rebuilding the Network

ISDN as an Environment

From a system integrator's standpoint, ISDN is the environment in which the system exists, as opposed to being part of the system. ISDN provides a worldwide, standardized, virtually seamless interconnection capability, but it does not specify how this capability is to be used. The designer of the computer network/system is free to take advantage of ISDN's global interconnectivity and voice/data synergy, without being hampered by incompatible protocol standards. Nor is the designer constrained by preconceived notions of how the network is to be used.

The universal nature of the network extends beyond the physical layer of voltage levels and connector pinouts to data transmission protocols and software standards. ISDN is based on CCITT standards, conforming to the ISO/OSI seven-layer model. That the international standards precede the existence of the network is what leads to its seamlessness.

The ISDN Landscape

The digital portions of the present telephone network are based on a 64-kbit-per-second channel (voice is digitized as 8000 eight-bit words per second). In general, ISDN retains this basic 64k rate, but allows it to be used for either voice or data.

ISDN service is divided into two classes: basic rate and primary rate. As mentioned above, basic rate service provides two 64-kbit-per-second channels for either voice or data (referred to as bearer or B channels) and a 16-kbit-per-second signaling/data channel (labeled the D channel) for call control and low-speed (up to 9600 bits per second) packet data. This "2B plus D" capability is the standard service provided to the user; i.e., the telephone jack on the wall in an office provides the basic rate interface. Primary rate service provides a combination of 23 B channels and one 64-kbit-per-second D channel. (In Europe, primary rate service is 30 B channels plus one D channel because the European interoffice trunk network is based on a 2.048-megabit-per-second data rate instead of the 1.544-megabit-per-second rate used in North America.) This "23B plus D" service is used primarily to connect PBX's to central offices and mainframe (or mini) computers. The general idea is that the B channels from all of the basic rate interfaces are gathered by the switch, PBX or central office (Centrex service), and routed within the switch to other local basic rate interfaces or to distant basic rate interfaces via other switches and primary rate interswitch trunk lines, or concentrated and routed to a local or remote computing facility via primary rate lines. There are other options, such as providing primary rate service all the way to the user's desk, but these are the predominant configurations.

The bandwidth of the primary rate interface can be partitioned in ways other than 23B plus D. For instance, one D channel can support its associated 23 B channels, plus 24 B channels from each of an additional three primary rate interfaces. Alternatively, the bandwidth of the primary rate channel can be partitioned into four 384-kbit-per-second "H0" channels or one 1.536-megabit-per-second "H11" channel (1.92-megabit-per-second "H12" in Europe). H0 channels can be used in combination with 64-kbit-per-second B channels on the same primary rate line.

Independent of whether basic or primary rate service is provided, the network topography from the desktop to the switch is the same. Figure 4-1 shows this topography, identifying specific classes of equipment that make up the network. In addition, certain "reference points" are defined that represent various interfaces. At each of

72 Open Systems Interconnection Handbook

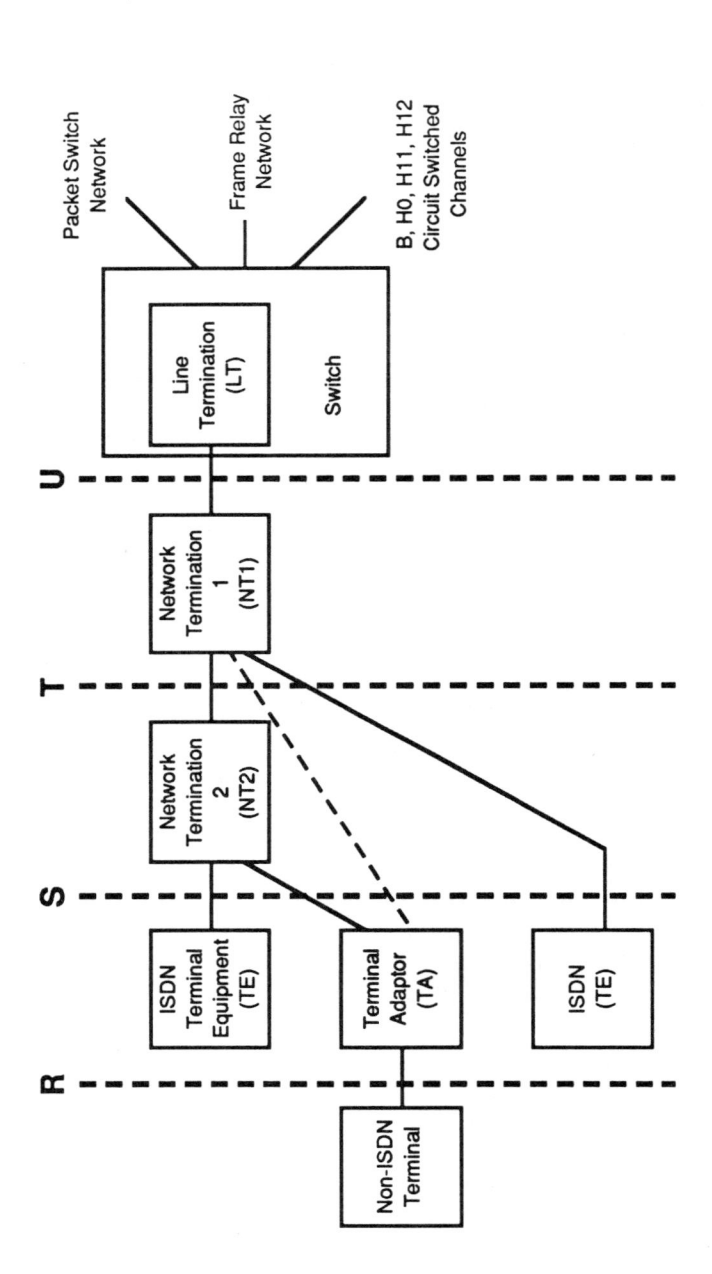

Figure 4-1 ISDN Network Topography. The physical connection between a piece of terminal equipment and the public network is divided into segments. These segments, shown here by vertical dashed lines, are call reference points (R, S, T, and U). The various international standards that define ISDN describe the operation of the network at each of these reference points. Separate standards (referred to officially as recommendations) exist for each of the appropriate layers of the ISO model at each reference point. For example, CCITT Recommendation I.430 defines the layer 1 operation of the basic rate S interface.

these reference points, the CCITT has established, or is in the process of establishing, standards for both hardware and software.

Equipment Classification

The equipment comprising the network is classified based on function and location within the network. Starting from the network and moving toward the user there is first the Line Termination (LT), which is located in the telephone company's switch, often at the central office. Directly downstream of the LT is the Network Termination (NT). There are two types of NT's, NT1 and NT2. The NT1 performs such functions as line length extension (repeaters) and two-wire to four-wire conversion (U-to-S interface). A key characteristic of NT1 devices is that they deal only with layer 1 of the OSI seven-layer model. NT2's are intelligent and actively participate in the call routing/control process. PBX's and line concentrators are examples of NT2 devices (a PBX actually contains both an NT1 and an NT2, with the T reference point being internal to the switch). Additionally, NT2 devices can be connected to multiple types of ISDN lines simultaneously. Further downstream is the Terminal Equipment (TE). TE's represent computers, telephones, data terminals, etc., which are directly compatible with the ISDN. The last class of equipment is the Terminal Adaptor (TA). TA's are the "box modems" of the ISDN world. They provide for the connection of non-ISDN-compatible equipment to the network, i.e., to existing equipment.

R Reference Point

The R reference point establishes the boundary between non-ISDN-compatible equipment and the network. Terminal adaptors (TA) are used to convert the communication protocol used by the non-ISDN-compatible terminal to the desired basic rate or primary rate protocol. It should be mentioned at this point that the network does not specify the data protocol used on either the B or H channels; all the network sees is a stream of bits. As a practical matter, however, standard protocols such as V.110, V.120, and X.25 are used.

S Reference Point

The S reference point provides the connection between the NT2 equipment and the terminal equipment (TE) or terminal adaptor (TA). If no NT2 is present, there is no S reference point. In this case, the TE or TA is connected directly to an NT1 device, and the interface is designated as a T reference point. Both primary rate and basic rate services can be provided at the S reference point.

It should be noted that it is common to refer to the four-wire basic rate service specified by CCITT recommendation I.430 as S interface service. While it is true that the S reference point is most often implemented this way, a two-wire basic rate interface or a primary rate interface can also be used at the S reference point. In addition, the four-wire interface can be used to provide the U reference point. To keep the ISDN alphabet soup straight, it is important to remember that the various reference points identify the connection points between equipment classes, and not the specific implementation or protocol of the interconnection.

T Reference Point

In addition to the connection of TA's and TE's to NT1 equipment, the T reference point provides the connection between an NT1 and an NT2. In a PBX, for example, the line circuit that connects to the network in the upstream direction (U reference point) provides the NT1 function, and the line circuit that connects to the TE or TA equipment (S reference point) provides the NT2 function. The T reference point in this case is internal to the PBX.

U Reference Point

The U reference point connects the LT to the NT1. Normally, a two-wire basic rate interface or a primary rate line is used, but the four-wire basic rate interface can also be used.

Protocols and Standards

ISDN is structured around the ISO-OSI seven-layer model. Layers 1, 2, and 3 provide the basic network infrastructure, while the higher layers provide services that are more specific to the user's system environment and application. For example, layers 3 and below are not dependent on the specific operating system, user interface, or application used in a TE, while layers 4 and above are. We will, for the most part, concern ourselves with the first three layers.

Layer 1

Layer 1 is the physical layer and is concerned with wire types, connector pinouts, encoding schemes, voltage levels, and the like. There are several layer 1 standards used in ISDN, including the I.430 four-wire basic rate interface, the 2B1Q (2 binary — 1 quaternary) and 4B3T (4 binary — 3 ternary) two-wire basic rate interface standards, and the G.703 primary rate standard. The four-wire basic rate interface is used primarily, but not exclusively, on the customer's premises to provide either the S or T connections.

One of the key characteristics of the I.430 interface is that it provides for multi-dropping of several terminals on a single line; this is referred to as a passive bus configuration. A typical office application would have a four-wire interface running to the desk where an ISDN telephone and an ISDN-equipped PC would share the same line (recall that the basic rate interface provides two independent 64k channels that can be used for either voice or data).

The two-wire interfaces are primarily used for longer distance connections from the telephone company to the customer premises (U reference point). The two-wire standards are designed to use the existing wire pairs currently providing the analog subscriber loop. While the two-wire schemes provide greater distance capabilities and use fewer wires, the electronics costs significantly more and does not provide multi-drop capability.

The primary rate interface is designed to use the existing T1 (CEPT in Europe) transmission facilities and for the most part are compatible with T1 at layer 1.

Layer 2

Layer 2 is the link layer of the seven-layer OSI model, and is responsible for the transmission of data from point to point. On the D channel, all data is sent as HDLC-like packets using the Link Access Protocol — D channel (LAPD). LAPD is an expansion of its LAPB predecessor used in X.25. The key new capability added to LAPD is the ability to support multiple logical connections on a single physical channel. On the B channel, there is no single protocol specified; it is a 64-kbps clear channel. There are, however, several common layer 2 protocol standards, including LAPB and LAPD for X.25, LAPD (slightly modified) for V.120, SDLC for SNA, and a bit replication-based rate adaptation protocol for V.110. Of these, V.120 is perhaps of the most interest since it is the first real international standard for statistical multiplexing.

Layer 3

Layer 3 is the network layer of the seven-layer model. On the D channel, layer 3 provides the call control functions (call setup/teardown, etc.), as well as packet-data-handling functions. CCITT Q.931

and Q.932 are used for call control. The X.25 packet layer protocol and layer 3 of V.120 are most often used for packet data.

Software Structure

As mentioned before, ISDN is built along the lines of the ISO/OSI seven-layer model. This is of greater importance from a software standpoint than from a hardware point of view. Figure 4-2 shows the structure of the AmLink3™ ISDN code stack, supporting layers 3 and below. The AmLink3 software, which is commercially available from Advanced Micro Devices, is representative of practical ISDN software implementations.

Layer 1

Layer 1 of the code stack is responsible for interacting with and supporting the establishment of the physical channel. Tasks include the activation of the S, T, or U interface, support of network maintenance functions such as loop backs, establishment and support of the R interface, and more. In general, the actual implementation of the layer 1 functions is hardware-specific, meaning that this piece of code is not portable between hardware implementations using different IC's. As a consequence, the AmLink3 code partitions these functions into low-level driver (LLD) modules that are IC-specific. This allows the higher layer software to be completely hardware independent.

Layer 2–

There are a number of tasks that are hardware-dependent, such as the movement of B and D channel data between the actual IC and memory-resident buffers, address recognition, and packet status reporting. These functions are a part of layer 2, but are not directly part of the LAPB or LAPD layer 2+ protocol (LAPB and LAPD just assume that these functions are taken care of). It is desirable to create a separation between these hardware-dependent tasks and the formal LAPB and LAPD software. Collectively, we will refer to these tasks as the layer 2 minus (or layer 2–) sublayer and the LAPB and LAPD functions as layer 2 plus (or layer 2+). In the AmLink3 software implementation, layer 2– is part of the LLD module. The layer

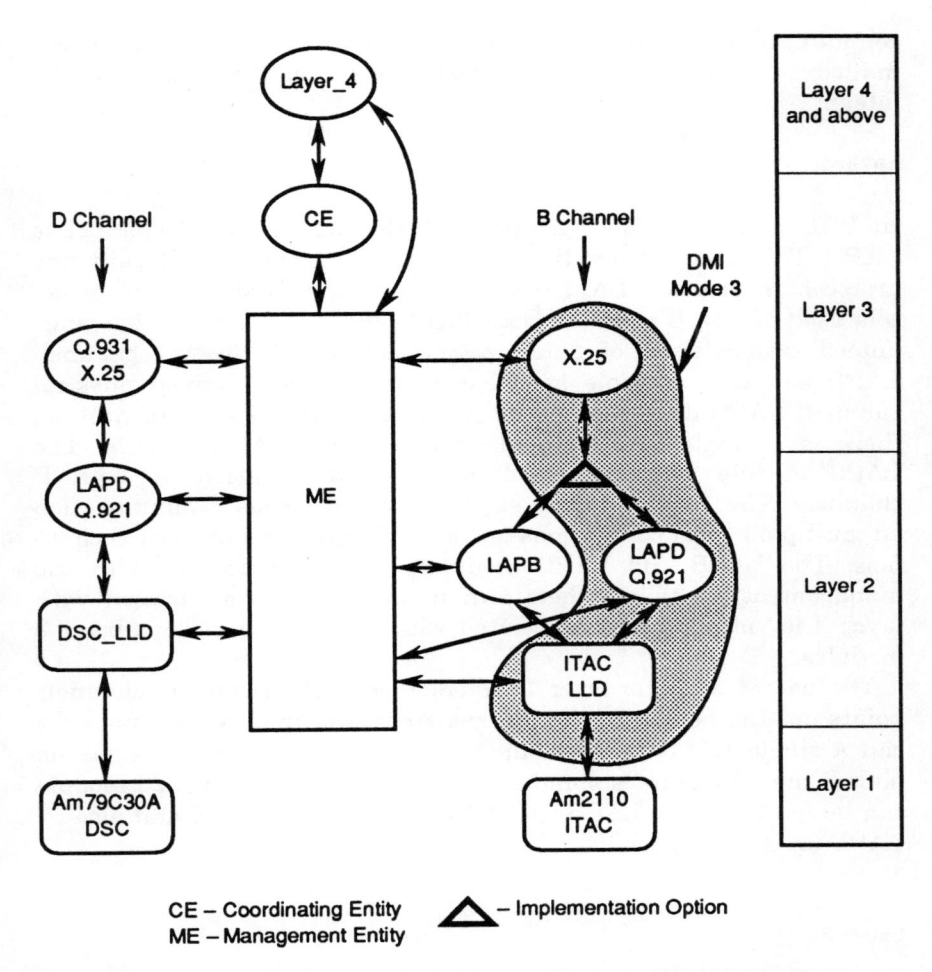

Figure 4-2 AmLink3™ ISDN Software Block Diagram. ISDN software is divided into modules that perform specific B or D channel functions at each of the ISO layers. The arrows indicate the communication flow among the modules.

2– code sits directly on top of the hardware, communicating directly with the ICs' physical registers (and physical addresses). The interface between the layer 2– and LAPB or LAPD layer 2+ software is via command and event mailboxes, with "commands" going from the higher layer to the lower layer and "events" being reported to the higher layer from the lower layer. The layer 2– software also communicates with the management entity via command and event mailboxes (we will discuss the management entity in more detail later).

Layer 2+

In ISDN, the only layer 2+ protocol allowed on the D channel is LAPD. This is not true of the B channel, which can use virtually any protocol. In practice, LAPB and LAPD are the most common protocols used on the B channel. Both LAPB and LAPD provide for guaranteed transmission of data packets across the layer 1 channel. LAPD supports multiple logical connections over a given physical channel; LAPB does not. In the AmLink3 software implementation, there is a single LAPB module and a single LAPD module. The LAPB module supports simultaneous communication on both B channels. The LAPD module supports simultaneous communication on multiple logical connections on the D channel and on both B channels. The LAPB and LAPD modules each communicate with the management entity via their own mailboxes. Communication with layer 3 is via mailboxes associated with each of the various layer 3 modules.

The use of a single layer 2+ module for both B and D channels points out the benefit of the layered structure. In this case, not only can a single LAPD module support multiple logical connections on both B and D channels simultaneously, but the layer 3 X.25 module can be fed by either LAPB or LAPD from the B channel and also by LAPD on the D channel.

Layer 3

The D channel supports both call control functions and packet-data services, while the B channel need be concerned only with packet data. The D-channel call control, or network-signaling, functions are specified by the CCITT Q.931 and Q.932 standards. Virtually any packet-based layer 3 protocol can be used for the data service (the AmLink3 package provides an X.25 module for layer 3 data service). The result is that layer 2 provides two types of data to layer 3, either signaling (D channel) or packet (B- or D-channel) data. This information, either signaling or packet data, is communicated among peer layer 3 entities; for example, the layer 3 entity in an ISDN terminal communicates with the layer 3 entity in a mainframe computer. To do this, each end of the conversation utilizes the services of its respective layer 2 and layer 1 entities.

Each of the two layer 3 entities, signaling and packet data, have their own mailboxes to the management entity and to the LAPB and LAPD layer 2 entities. The interface with layer 4 is a bit more complex since layer 4 does not know about B and D channels. To solve this problem, a coordinating entity (CE) is used between the layer 3 and 4 entities.

Coordinating Entity (CE)

The software entity at layer 4 knows very little about ISDN. The details are hidden from it by the layered nature of the protocol — after all, this is the purpose of the seven-layer model. This creates a problem, though, since layer 3 is made up of separate B and D channel entities (network signaling and user data) and layer 4 sees layer 3 as a single entity. A layer 4 to 3 conversation might go something like this: "Here is some data to send to so and so; I don't care how you send it, just tell me when he has acknowledged receipt of the data." Something must exist at the layer 3 to 4 boundary that can understand this message and translate it into specific instructions to the layer 3 B and D channel entities. This something is called the coordinating entity, or CE. The CE communicates with the management entity, network-signaling entity, and the packet-data entity via separate mailboxes.

The CE to layer 4 communication is also via command and event mailboxes. This is particularly important in applications such as a PC add-on board, where two processors are often utilized. In the AmLink3 code, this is where the line is drawn between what is run on the communication processor (layers 1–3) and tasks left for the system processor (layers 4–7). The actual mailbox structure is usually constructed using a shared memory arrangement such as dual-port RAM.

Management Entity (ME)

Cleanly layered software is very nice in textbook applications, but the real world is rarely so accommodating. Such is the case with practical ISDN implementations. The problem is not any shortcoming of either the concept of layering in general or of the ISDN model specifically. The problem is one of global services that are required by all layers. Examples of these services are timers, buffer allocation, and message exchange (mailbox support) mechanisms. These services are provided by the system and cannot be partitioned into any one of the layers. To get around this problem, a new entity is required, the management entity, or ME. Each of the various layer entities passes requests for support to the ME via its mailbox mechanism. In return, the ME performs the required function (e.g., the allocation of a memory buffer to the layer 2– D-channel handler), passing the response back through the mailbox.

One other note before we leave the discussion of software structure. ISDN software, by its nature, operates in a real-time multitasking environment. This implies the support of a real-time multitasking operating system kernel. The layers 1 through 3 code stack and the ME both sit on top of the real-time OS, relying on it for task-scheduling functions.

Open Standards Issues

With respect to the D channel, layer 2 (CCITT Q.921, LAPD) is essentially complete, while layer 3 is still being worked on. Q.931, which specifies the basic call setup and teardown procedures, is stable, but Q.932 (supplementary services such as placing a call on hold) is still being finalized. At present, each switch manufacturer has its own variation of layer 3 software that works only on its switch. As the standards are completed, more and more of the incompatibilities will be eliminated, but it will be some time before there is a single layer 3 software package that works with all switches. Most commercially available software packages, such as AmLink3, support the majority of ISDN switches via compile-time options. It is important to keep in mind that compatibility is a fundamental goal of ISDN, partly due to significant pressure from the purchasers of ISDN switches requiring portability of terminal equipment.

On the B channel, V.110 and DMI (AT&T's Digital Multiplexed Interface, which uses LAPD at layer 2 and X.25 at layer 3) are stable. V.120 is still evolving, but due to the significant interest in its statistical multiplexing capability, work is progressing very rapidly in the standards committees.

Terminal Equipment and Terminal Adaptors

Having looked at the structure of the network and the organization of the software, it is time to take a look at ISDN terminal equipment. The variety of possible types of terminals and terminal adaptors is nearly unlimited. Some of these are of particular interest, specifically telephones, PC add-on boards, integrated voice/data terminals, adaptors for async and SDLC video data terminals, D-channel-only terminals, and LAN gateways.

Telephones

From the user's perspective, an ISDN telephone is not much different from its analog or proprietary digital (PBX and key system) counterparts. The difference is that the ISDN telephone can take advantage of the global digital signaling environment provided by the ISDN D channel. While many of the "ISDN features," such as displaying the number of an incoming call, are offered today by non-ISDN PBX's, the features work only at a local level. The features offered by an ISDN telephone are an evolutionary extension of those offered by modern PBX's. The revolutionary aspect of ISDN is that these features/services can now be standardized across the entire network, independent of the equipment vendor.

The ISDN telephone itself differs from its analog predecessors in that the voice signal is converted to digital form inside the telephone, not at the central office. This eliminates any voice quality degradation caused by the analog connection between the telephone and the central office. The cost of this improved quality is complexity — digital telephones require significantly more hardware than their analog counterparts. In return, additional features are possible, and the interface to those features can be made more friendly (displays, etc.). ISDN telephones are somewhat more complex even than proprietary digital telephones since they must conform to the ISDN software protocols — the benefits of standardization are not without cost.

PC/Workstation ISDN Boards

These boards provide ISDN connectivity to a personal computer or workstation, supporting either data or voice and data. This also allows PC's to be networked without the cost of additional cabling, since the existing telephone lines can be used for both voice and data. Figure 4-3 shows a block diagram of a typical implementation. There are three major issues concerning the incorporation of ISDN into a PC or workstation:

1. Does the main microprocessor in the PC or workstation run the ISDN software below layer 4, or is there a dedicated processor on the add-on board?
2. What data protocols does the board support?
3. How are the voice telephone functions handled?

82 Open Systems Interconnection Handbook

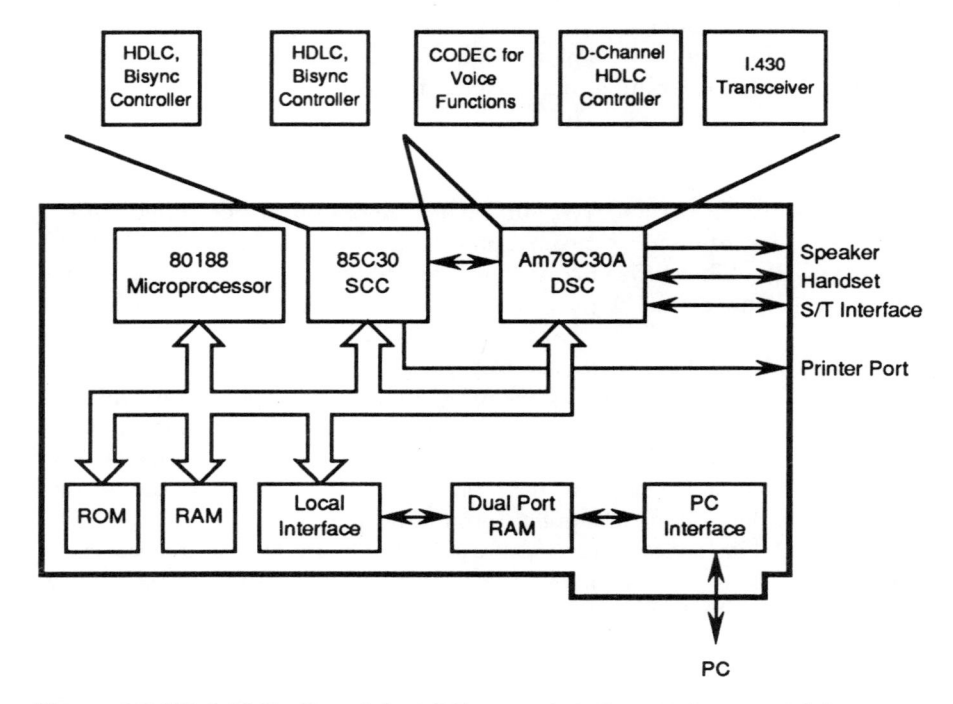

Figure 4-3 PC Add-On Board. In a PC or workstation environment it is common to use a dedicated microprocessor to handle the tasks at and below layer 3. The 85C30 dual serial communication controller provides protocol support for both B channels. The Am79C30A device provides the voice codec functions, the D channel LAPD hardware, and the layer 1 S/T interface transceiver. Communication between the ISDN board and the PC is via dual-port RAM.

The question of one or two processors depends on how the ISDN services are to be used. In applications in which data communication via the ISDN is infrequent, such as printing, the PC or workstation's microprocessor is sufficient. In applications that involve fairly heavy data traffic that must run in the background, an intelligent ISDN add-on board is required. The ISDN software protocol stack is fairly processor-intensive, involving a fair amount of real-time processing. If the PC's or workstation's microprocessor is used to run this code, there is little extra processing power available for other tasks. If an intelligent add-on board is used, the PC's or workstation's microprocessor need only run the layers 4 through 7 functions, leaving it free to run other user applications.

The issue of protocol support is driven by the application. For the most part, X.25 and V.120 protocols will be used at the lower layers, but this is dictated by the protocol used by the computer/network that the PC/workstation is communicating with. The key point is that ISDN provides low-error-rate 64-kbps data pipes (basic rate). These pipes are transparent and do not impose any specific protocol on the user.

A network that provides for the integration of voice and data creates the opportunity for many interesting applications, such as voice-annotated e-mail, PC/workstation-based voice mail (complete with a clean graphical user interface — if you have ever used a voice mail system, you know that the telephone-based user interface is less than optimum), speech recognition/response, etc. The problem is how to merge the PC/workstation with the telephone. One option is to build the telephone functions into the computer. Attempts to market such products in the past have met with little success for a number of reasons, but principally because such a combination restricts the user's freedom to choose computer and telephone vendors, and it does not allow the computer to be placed on a table with the telephone on the user's desk. A second option is to connect the telephone to the ISDN board in the computer. This allows the use of a separate telephone, while still providing a connection between the voice path and the ISDN board, enabling the voice information to be processed or stored in the computer. This is the approach most prevalent today. The only consideration with this approach is the nature of the interface to the telephone. If the ISDN board provides a traditional analog telephone interface, any existing standard telephone can be used, but the user will not have access to all of the interesting telephone services provided by the ISDN. If an ISDN S interface connection is provided, a standard ISDN telephone can be used, providing full ISDN capability. The restriction is that the existing analog telephone must be replaced.

Integrated Voice/Data Terminal

This is a native-mode, ISDN-based terminal that provides both voice and data capabilities. Terminals of this type are generally used in applications in which data entry/retrieval occurs in combination with a phone call. For example, a client's insurance or medical file could be called up automatically whenever the client calls the agent or doctor; this is possible since the terminal has access to the calling party's telephone number, which could then be used to access the file. Figure 4-4 shows an example of an IV/D terminal.

84 Open Systems Interconnection Handbook

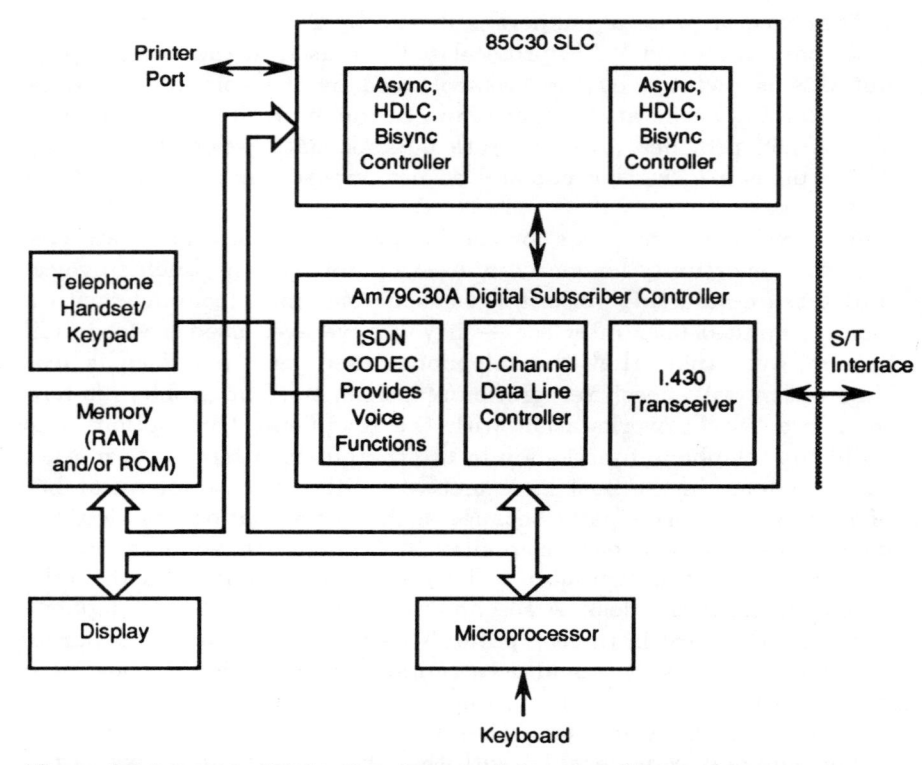

Figure 4-4 Integrated Voice/Data Terminal. In a terminal designed to use ISDN as its serial communication link with the host computer, a single processor is usually sufficient for both communication and terminal operations tasks. The 85C30 dual serial communication controller provides protocol support for one channel and a printer port. The Am79C30A device provides the voice codec functions, the D channel LAPD hardware, and the layer 1 S/T interface transceiver.

Integrated voice/data terminals generally are based on a single processor architecture. This is practical since the processor overhead of the terminal functions is typically less than the overhead in a PC or workstation, and communications is a fundamental task for the terminal. This holds true even in a higher end environment, such as an X Windows terminal.

Adaptors for Non-ISDN Terminals

These adaptors are used to convert the serial communication channel of a non-ISDN terminal into an ISDN-compatible format. In effect, terminal adaptors are modem replacements. In a typical application, the PBX or Centrex provides a local area network/concentrator for connecting computer terminals to one or more mainframe computers. Basic rate service is used for the terminal interface, and primary rate lines are usually used for the switch-to-mainframe link. Figure 4-5 shows the block diagram of a terminal adaptor utilizing the V.120 standard.

Three different sets of protocols are required for any terminal adaptor, one for interfacing to the terminal, one for interfacing with the network, and one for establishing the connection across the network. The terminal interface protocol is determined by the protocol

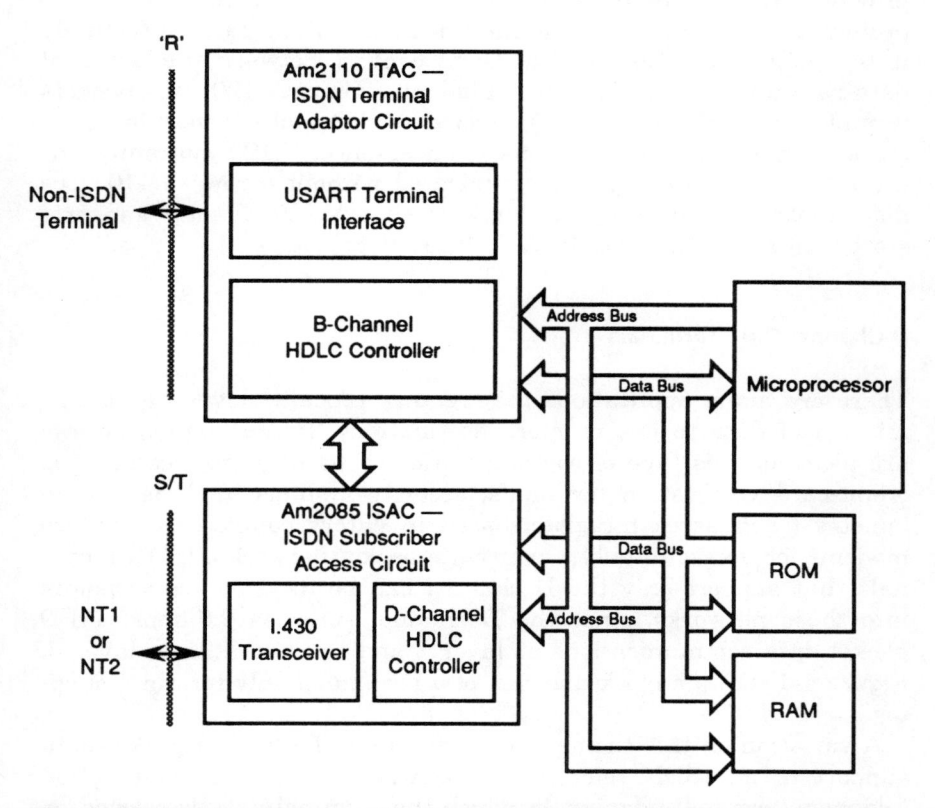

Figure 4-5 Terminal Adaptor. The terminal adaptor performs a translation function, allowing the connection of non-ISDN-compatible terminals to the network. The terminal connects to the Am2110 IC in the terminal adaptor using the terminal's normal serial protocol. The Am2110, with the help of the microprocessor, converts the data rate to 64 kbps and the data format to the protocol being used on the network. The Am2085 provides the D channel LAPD hardware and the layer 1 S/T interface transceiver.

supported by the terminal (RS-232, SDLC, etc.). The network protocol can theoretically be any 64 kbps synchronous mechanism, but in practice is one of a small set of standards, such as V.110, or V.120. The network access protocol is the ISDN D-channel-based call Q.921 (LAPD) and Q.931 layer 2 and 3 protocol stack.

V.110 and V.120 are quite different in their approach to the problem. V.110 is based on a bit replication scheme that converts a slow-speed terminal, say 9.6 kbps, to the 64-kbps B-channel rate by sending the data bits multiple times. The advantage of this is simplicity, which translates directly into lower cost. The drawback is that V.110 is wasteful of the B-channel bandwidth. In addition, V.110 does not provide any error detection/recovery at layer 2 (V.110 is a layer 2 protocol). V.120, on the other hand, utilizes HDLC packets (actually it is a slight variation on LAPD) to convert between the terminal data rate and the 64-kbps B-channel rate. Since V.120 uses packets (complete with CRC checking), error detection and recovery is an integral part of the layer 2 protocol. In essence, V.120 guarantees at layer 2 that the data get communicated without errors; V.110 does not. Another significant difference is that V.120 directly supports statistical multiplexing at layer 2; V.110 does not.

D-Channel-Only Terminals

There are many applications that require repeated low-speed transmission of data to one or more destinations. Packet-data networks are ideal for this type of communication. Presently, devices such as credit-card verification terminals, security systems, and remote telemetry (such as cash-register-based inventory control) use dial-up modems for access to public or private packet networks. ISDN terminals that support only the D channel can be used as access points into these networks, since the D channel supports 9.6-kbps LAPD packet-data communications at layer 2 and can use X.25 at layer 3. Figure 4-6 shows a block diagram of a D-channel-only terminal adaptor.

A variation on this theme is the addition of D-channel packet-data support to an ISDN telephone. Essentially, this is a combination telephone/terminal adaptor, in which the terminal data is carried on the D channel. The telephone typically has an RS-232 connector for interfacing to the serial port of a terminal or PC. Data received from the RS-232 interface is packetized using the same hardware and layer 2 software that the telephone uses for call control over the D channel.

ISDN and the Global Network   87

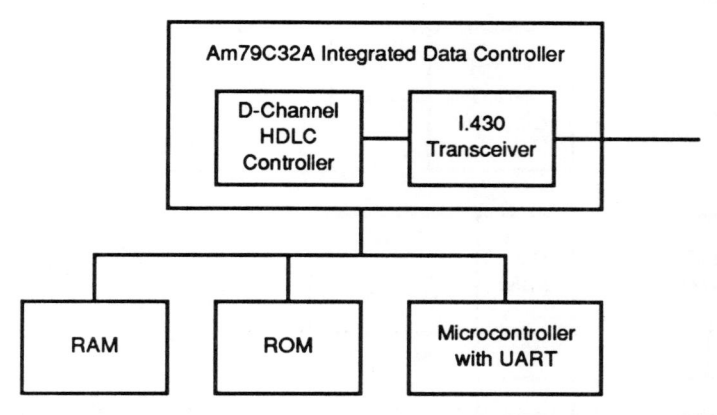

```
┌─────────────────────────────────────────┐
│  Am79C32A Integrated Data Controller    │
│   ┌──────────┐      ┌──────────┐       │
│   │ D-Channel│      │  I.430   │       │
│   │   HDLC   │──────│Transceiver│──────
│   │Controller│      │          │       │
│   └──────────┘      └──────────┘       │
└─────────────────────────────────────────┘

   ┌────────┐   ┌────────┐   ┌──────────────┐
   │  RAM   │   │  ROM   │   │Microcontroller│
   │        │   │        │   │  with UART    │
   └────────┘   └────────┘   └──────────────┘
```

Figure 4-6 D-Channel-Only Terminal. In some applications, only low-speed data (9.6 kbps) is required. A terminal that utilizes the ISDN D-channel packet-data capability can provide this function without using the B channels. The Am79C32A device provides the D-channel LAPD hardware and the layer 1 S/T interface transceiver. Voice support can be added by using the Am79C30A device instead of the Am79C32A.

LAN Gateways

ISDN will not replace high-speed LAN's. Instead, gateways between the LAN and the ISDN will provide global communication capabilities to the LAN environment. The trick is to make the new system as seamless as possible. As a rule, the more seamless an internetworking environment, the higher the required processing power in the gateway. Fortunately, the new generation of RISC-based processors, such as the Am29000™ microprocessor from Advanced Micro Devices, provides the level of processing required to do the job. Figure 4-7 shows a block diagram of an Ethernet-to-ISDN gateway.

New Capabilities

The most interesting aspect of ISDN is the integration of voice and data on the same network. Traditionally, voice and data functions have belonged in their own separate worlds. There have been numerous attempts to market integrated voice/data workstations, without much success. The problem was that there was no way to create a synergistic relationship between the voice and data. ISDN changes this situation. Because the voice is digitized at the terminal and because a common digital signaling channel is used for network control

88 Open Systems Interconnection Handbook

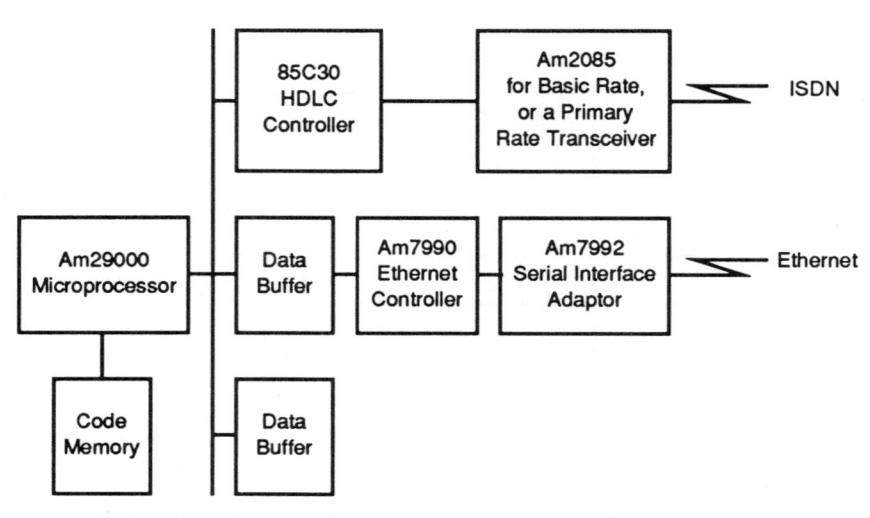

Figure 4-7 ISDN/Ethernet Gateway. ISDN allows LAN's in separate cities to be interconnected. The 85C30 dual serial communication controller provides protocol support for both B channels. The Am2085 provides the D-channel LAPD hardware and the layer 1 S/T interface transceiver. The Am7990/7992 pair provide the Ethernet interface. An Am29000 RISC-embedded processor controls the gateway.

(the D channel), voice and data operations can now be linked. Earlier we discussed a scenario in which a client's files could be automatically called up on a terminal by his doctor, insurance agent, or stockbroker. This is but one example of the new services made possible by integrating voice and data on one network. Another example is PC/workstation-based voice store and forward. Since voice is digitized in the ISDN terminal, an ISDN-equipped computer can be used for this purpose, with the voice being stored on the PC's hard disk. The advantage of this is that the PC can be used to provide a user-friendly interface, for example, by displaying on the screen the list of received messages, allowing random selection of messages. Voice annotated e-mail is an extension of this concept, whereby digitized voice is stored along with an e-mail message. It works like this: Person A sends person B the text of an upcoming press release via e-mail, asking for comments. Person B reviews the text, inserting verbal comments much like making notes in the margin of a hard copy of the text. Person B then e-mails the press release with comments back to person A who can listen to the comments and edit the press release as required.

About the Author

Dale Gulick has twelve years of experience in defining and designing data communications, telecommunications, and computer products. He is currently Senior Member of the Technical Staff at Advanced Micro Devices, where he has been employed since 1985, and is involved in product planning for ISDN and digital cellular products. Prior to this, he was with Datapoint Corporation. Gulick is a 1978 graduate of Texas A & M University.

Section B

Networks and Architectures

8

Networks and Architectures

Chapter 5

An Architectural Vision Based on Standards

by Chris Williams

Abstract

This chapter will link an architectural vision of open systems in manufacturing with the efforts planned or in progress in the International Standards community.

The "Integrated" State

Much discussion has been devoted lately to the topic of "integration," yet to date the definitions of the "integrated" state have been working definitions at best. Recently, some thought about the attributes or descriptors of the integrated state resulted in the following statements.

The integrated state:

- uses an "open" architecture, which is
  — (although capable of implementation in a single vendor environment) vendor independent with respect to hardware, application software, and network services. There are compelling reasons,

even when the integrated state has been achieved, to implement all or substantial parts of applications within a single vendor's environment. A classic example is the desire to reduce the diversity and extent of hardware spares which must be maintained on site. Conversely, there should be no compelling reason to restrict an application or functions within an application, to a single vendor environment. This is clearly not the case today, where dissimilar operating environments and dissimilar/incompatible networks mandate functional placement based in part on the compatibility of the development environment with the production environment. Therefore, an open architecture is also

— independent with respect to function placement (where a "function" represents a discrete, identifiable element of an application, such as the inventory update function of an inventory management application). This statement is not meant to imply that functions should be scattered about willy nilly. On the other hand, there should be no physical constraints to mandate that a function must reside on a specific hardware platform, or within a specific software environment.

- is capable of using a distributed architecture, which is
  — implemented on more than one hardware platform. Again, this is not meant to imply that the application should be distributed for the sake of leveraging the latest and greatest in technology. Conversely, physical separation of application components should not be a barrier to effective application operation.
  — optimized for placement of data, processing power, and application functions where they are used most frequently. This particular attribute will certainly cause spirited debate. As will be discussed later, the directions taken by emerging international standards, as well as stated directions by some of the other large users participating in the standardization work, indicate that the central processor or cluster in manufacturing will continue to have a future, but decreasingly as a place for users to interact with processing power, and increasingly as a robust and secure data archive, accessible for inquiry and update, but not extensively used for operation of application programs that are compute or display intensive. Issues that come to mind immediately are the changes (and incurred costs) which will be encountered as the IS organization evolves to meet this architecture. How, for example, will a centralized program maintenance function be implemented if the application users are relying on distributed workstation "front ends" linked to a common "back

end"? (It should be noted that this problem has been successfully solved within personal computer networks.)
- implements a data driven environment, in which
  — every application is built to a fully attributed and normalized data model.
  — application data models are proper subsets of the "enterprise" data model.
  — Common data meanings and representations (encodings) have been established for each attribute identified by name.
  — data is "owned."
  — data is managed by the "owner" (or "steward").
  — a "data management" function exists to coordinate and arbitrate proposed differences between application data models and the enterprise data model.
- is based on appropriate standards, which
  — are discussed later in this chapter.
  — facilitate a consistent look, feel, and behavior within an application environment, and ideally across and between applications. The "look and feel" issue will also be the cause of ongoing debates. The current thrust into 4GL programming is expected to yield great benefits in productivity. However, the choice of a particular 4GL package is also implicitly a choice of a particular look and feel regarding the way in which the application will appear to the end user. If the 4GL package cannot meet the presentation requirements of the user, then the alternatives are to use another 4GL package with the proper look and feel, rewrite the application in a 3GL so that the fit is "perfect" (until the next change request), or force the user to recognize the impracticality of the request. (As a totally unrelated but completely relevant side issue, corporate IS departments appear to be in constant turmoil as to how to balance the needs of the user with the optimization of the systems development "business.")
- supports the concept of open access/data transparency, where
  — user access to data and functions is transparent with respect to the architecture. In other words, there is geographic location independence of users and/or function. Again, this is absolutely not meant to imply that users, functions, and data should be arbitrarily scattered to the corners of the universe. On the other hand, if the principles of open, distributed architecture have been adhered to, any barriers to data access become administrative, as opposed to physical. Clearly, some barriers are a practical necessity. Also clearly, administrative changes that result in the repositioning of barriers are easier to deal with than physical changes, and thus less costly.

It is interesting to note that the current architectural view of 3, 4, or more "levels" of computers is derived from what has historically been clearly distinct technologies, each with its own development and operating environment, and interconnected by communications that have been surpassed for efficiency and reliability. Current thinking about distribution of function holds that there are multiple functional "managers" or "controllers" within a manufacturing hierarchy. To illustrate, one possible hierarchy includes the

- device, which performs actual work, such as a machine tool, and is a component of a
- workstation, for example, a turning station, which is a component of a
- manufacturing cell, for example, a machining group, which is a component of an
- area, for example, a building of machining groups, which is a component of a
- plant, for example, a large manufacturing facility of several buildings, which is a component of an
- enterprise, for example, a worldwide manufacturing concern.

It should be noted that the above model contains a good many "levels" beyond four, and in fact the distinction of levels begins to get quite blurred as the functional paradigm is applied. In fact, the functional paradigm may be implemented in a flat network space, where all hardware platforms are connected to the same physical network. In this case, the hierarchy is completely implemented by administration of the application across a limited number of platforms, each of which supports one or more functions.

It is worth making the assertion that in the integrated state, the multitiered physical model we traditionally have dealt with has outlived its usefulness, and should be put to rest.
— is attained with frequently substantial and sometimes painful organizational and cultural changes.

It would not seem that the last statement should be at all controversial.

Capabilities Common to More Than One Application

In order to achieve the integrated state, some "enabling" capabilities emerge as prerequisites. An essential understanding required here is the realization that not all applications will have the need for all the enabling capabilities. Conversely, where any capability is required at more than one application, the implementation of the capability on all applications must be such that the "visible" attributes of the capability as implemented, from the perspective of interaction with other applications, are identical across all applications. In effect, this represents a formal requirement for the existence of integration standards. However, for the purposes of integration, identicality is required at the interface points between applications and an integrating infrastructure. For example, not all portable electrical appliances are alike, but they all use the same power source, and the plugs provided on all portable electrical appliances fit the sockets provided in all households. (This is at least a true statement within national borders.)

Adhering to this approach will ensure that future application interaction and, for that matter portability, when required, is not physically restricted. In an environment where change is assumed to be constant, flexibility takes on an increased importance. (When one moves to a larger, "upscale" home, one typically takes the portable electrical appliances along. Fortunately, they will fit the outlets in the new home. Shouldn't we be able to do this with existing applications moving to larger, faster "home" platforms at all "levels" in the hierarchy?)

Some of the required enabling capabilities include:

- The application development and production environments must be independent of the hardware platform. We see this realized today within the VAX environment, where a program developed under VAX/VMS on any VAX will operate successfully on any other VAX that supports VAX/VMS. The same flexibility must be extended in the future to include traditional "mainframe" platforms as well as the increasingly more powerful "micro" platforms. This will allow further extension of the capabilities of the application developers and maintainers, while preserving the benefits realized through the use of a few programming and operating system paradigms. It is worth making the assertion that the same requirement extends to the control and monitoring equipment in use on the shop floor, while recognizing that in order to do so requires a significant paradigm shift in how we think of control and monitoring equipment. The paradigm shift is required not because the technology (at a high level) is different, but because we've always managed control and monitoring equipment in a different way before. For example, the specialized nature of control and monitoring equipment has historically relegated the design of communication with such equipment to communication specialists, or in some cases constrained communication to a paradigm defined by and unique to the vendor of the equipment. However, in an ideal state there should be no requirement to recognize the type of equipment in use; only a knowledge of the function should be required. The benefits already realized in manufacturing through extensive use of VAX computers seem logically to extend to all development and production environments.

- There is a clear requirement to define the conceptual "domains" in which applications will function. The requirements of a database application are different from the requirements of an application indexing a shift register while monitoring and recording imperfection data in a moving web. Yet it is not an unreasonable assertion that most applications doing database access for read/alter/update will adhere to a common paradigm, which in turn fits within a conceptual "database interaction" domain. Similarly, domains may be defined for file transfer and access, monitoring and control messaging, electronic mail, electronic document interchange, and so on. Within each domain, the various capabilities should be standardized, and the way in which interaction occurs between applications must be standardized, so that our "plugs" will fit our "sockets," regardless of where we are. The ability to function within a particular (and well-defined) domain represents an essential enabling capability. Further, the application interface to a particular capability should, ideally, be standardized so that application flexibility and transportability are facilitated.

- A robust network infrastructure is essential to support application-to-application and application-to-database communication. The network becomes essential as infrastructure as soon as the business requirements of the corporation can no longer be met by a single physical computer. The network must provide "any-to-any" connectivity. Physically, the network structure will be necessarily hierarchical, and is expected, at least in the short term, to be constructed of an amalgamation of different protocols and vendor-proprietary networking products, but it is imperative that with the proper authorization and authentication any application may "associate" with any other application and exchange information, regardless of the geographic location of the corresponding applications. Similarly, the databases of the corporation represent "data assets" of the corporation. Applications with the proper authorization and authentication must be able to access any data asset of the corporation for the purposes of inquiry, update, or both, as authorized.

- Network and hardware reliability must be maximized. Some of the reasons for distribution of data in our current environment are based on the necessity to isolate the effects of hardware failure. It is worth making the assertion that the costs associated with maintaining duplicate data should be weighed against the costs required to install the equivalent of "nonstop" hardware and software. (And, for that matter, vice versa.)

Network Basics

For all intents and purposes, a network is nothing more than a common piece (or pieces) of wire connecting at least two computers. However, the way in which the right to transmit on the network is gained, how to identify the end destination on the network, and how to encode (represent) the information that is to be transmitted in a way that will be understood by the receiver are nontrivial problems that have been the subject of much study and experimentation.

For our purposes, we can simplify our view of a network by envisioning the cable plant or wires that physically connect the various computer hardware platforms as a logical "bus" structure, where all the platforms are connected equally. Technically, the bus structure represents a physical topology, and there are additionally "ring" and "star" topologies that are of great interest to network technical-types, and of mild interest to those attempting to link applications together for the purpose of supporting a commercial enterprise.

Within each hardware platform we must also envision a layered protocol "stack," so called because the specific protocols that are required to implement the network functionality are stacked one on top of the other. Each protocol layer within a stack implements a specific function — gaining access to the cable plant for the purpose of transmitting a message received from higher layer protocols, ensuring that the correct end-destination and routing instructions are provided, guaranteeing reliable end-to-end delivery, ensuring that the specified application receives the intended message (as opposed to a message intended for a different application which resides at the same platform), and so on.

At the topmost layer of the stack reside the so-called "application protocols," which provide the application-to-application semantics, or message meanings, and resort to common syntax, or message representation, in order to achieve intercommunication between applications. A proper view of networking must include both the application protocol(s) in use, and the specific stacks on which the application protocols are implemented. In rough terms, the stack provides the "bit delivery" services, while the application protocol provides a way to interpret the bits.

Standards in Support of Networking Capabilities

If there is a common vision to the work in progress in the standards community, it is the notion of full connectivity and interoperability within specific domains of file transfer, remote database access, etc. The connectivity issues are addressed by a variety of specific protocol stacks, including versions implementing the International Standards Organization seven-layer model for Open Systems Interconnection, or the "ISO seven-layer model," or even more simply, "OSI." There are also de facto standards and associated stacks in use, such as SNA, DECnet, and TCP/IP, which is an acronym for Transmission Control Protocol/Internet Protocol. TCP/IP has been a U.S. government standard, but has recently been replaced by a federal requirement for OSI. New applications utilizing networking and contracted for by the U.S. government will be required to provide OSI in lieu of TCP/IP. In the future, implementations of TCP/IP in government use could potentially migrate to OSI through sequential changes to the TCP/IP stack or could remain unchanged but also not interoperable.

For each conceptual application domain identified within the integrating standards community, a corresponding application protocol is either under development or exists as an international standard. Some application protocols are expected to appear over multiple varieties of stacks. There are also some identified application protocol/stack combinations targeted at specific application domains, where optimization for specific functions is viewed as an economic necessity.

The architectural vision for a networked approach to integrating multiple applications is based on OSI. Using a logically "flat" network space, where all hardware platforms are communicating peers on a shared resource, application protocols are used for the exchange of information between applications or for transparent access to remote databases. Because a single physical network is not capable of carrying all the potential traffic between the known and planned applications within large facilities, the network cable plant is expected to be divided into physical "segments," where each segment is itself a local area network. "Routers" and "bridges" are used to interconnect physical network segments. The use of multiple physical segments allows optimization of a specific segment for the type and volume of traffic anticipated. Such optimization is typically approached through the choice of network access algorithm (there are several), number of stations, physical segment length, "wire" selection (copper coax, twisted pair, or fiber), etc. However, because all physical segments are interoperable with OSI, and because the same application protocols are in use, application-to-application interoperability is preserved.

Two compatible "profiles" of OSI require brief comment. Manufacturing Automation Protocol, or MAP, and Technical and Office Protocol, or TOP, have been jointly developed by users and vendors as specific OSI profiles. General Motors was the principal sponsor of MAP, while Boeing was the principal sponsor of TOP. Both MAP and TOP represent specifications as opposed to standards. They call out specific standards that are used to populate the OSI stack, and specific options within those standards where options exist. Both MAP and TOP specify significant application protocols. The essential difference is found at the "physical" layer of the stack, where two different network media access algorithms are specified. Where it becomes necessary to join MAP to TOP, a bridge or a router will suffice.

The architectural vision for a networked approach to application integration includes several significant application protocols. Each is identified by an acronym (one quickly learns that technical people interested in communications and integration have all completed a course in creative abbreviations).

FTAM stands for File Transfer, Access, and Management. FTAM is intended to provide remote file access for read/write at a level as low as a field within a specific record. FTAM will also provide file transfer services, where the file is communicated from one application to another. FTAM resolves differences in data representation, for example ASCII/EBCDIC, byte swapping, and floating point representation during access or transfer. This capability allows two applications residing in totally incompatible hardware platforms to exchange file data, while preserving the native data representation as well as the file structure at each application. Because representation issues quickly become complex as additional incompatible platforms are introduced, FTAM relies on defined document types. Thus, a type A file may be efficiently transferred from one application to another with the mechanics of field translation facilitated by a knowledge of the desired representations at each end.

MHS stands for Message Handling Services. MHS has also been referred to as X.400, a designation it took on when introduced into the standards community via the European CCITT, a committee addressing mail, telegraphy, and telephony. (All CCITT documents acquire an X.NNN designation when progressed as CCITT standards.) MHS provides functionality similar to PROFS and DECmail, but does it in a vendor-independent way. As with FTAM, MHS resolves representation differences between hardware platforms. MHS also provides for office document exchange, and is expected in that capacity to provide the vehicle for EDI, Electronic Data Interchange.

MMS stands for Manufacturing Message Specification. MMS is intended expressly for communication with shop floor devices. MMS offers a total of 80 services, each of which approximates in functionality a remote procedure call. MMS services include the ability to read or write remote memory, upload/download all or part of another application program, upload/download data tables, manage the program remotely, take action and send a notification based on the occurrence of an event, coordinate the actions of multiple applications through the use of semaphores, and write/read entries to/from a process journal. MMS is different from other application protocols in that there is a core MMS document, which is in turn expected to be accompanied by a number of companion standards. The companion standards are used as a means of specifying the MMS semantics at specific classes of applications. Mapping of device specifics such as control and status variables to MMS variables is specified by companion standards. In some cases, the MMS syntax is extended by the companion standards in order to convey additional information. For example, the status of a robot arm may be conveyed as additional information in the response to a status service request, which in the core document is specified to contain only the basic status of the communicating device and communications system. Companion standards are under development for robotics applications, numerically controlled machine tools, programmable controllers, and process control applications.

RDA stands for Remote Database Access. RDA provides a way to open, close, and access databases using an OSI stack and additionally supports limited commit functionality where distributed update is required. RDA consists of a generic document, which specifies rules associated with databases in general, and also contains an SQL specialization, in which the use of Structured Query Language (SQL) in conjunction with remote, relational databases is specified. In theory, additional specializations could address other, nonrelational databases such as Network and Codasyl, but no work items have been identified or progressed.

Transaction Processing (TP) specifies the procedures for establishing and managing transactions across a network, including the all-important two-phase commitment procedure required to support distributed data in databases. TP defines Dialogue Trees, within which Transaction Trees are created and managed as atomic actions (essentially treated as a single unit that succeeds or fails as a whole). TP is somewhat different from other application protocols in that it provides the transaction management functionality, but requires the concurrent use of another application protocol to specify the effect of the transaction. For example, to write a field in a remote database using TP, RDA must also be utilized to specify the actions with respect to the database and (logical) database management system. TP, in conjunction with RDA and a standardized Information Resource Dictionary System (IRDS), is expected to provide distributed database capability in the future, although the timing is difficult to predict due to the fact that the thinking around standardized distributed database elements is still very much in the early stages.

An additional effort in progress in the standards community, known as the Fieldbus, introduces a capability adapted from OSI but not directly interoperable with OSI networks, optimized for communication with sensors and actuators as found in both the discrete parts manufacturing and process industries. The Fieldbus introduces an additional protocol stack that has been designed for multipeer communications as well as peer-to-peer communications, and is expected to be integratable to OSI networks on a peer-to-peer basis through the use of gateways. Physical Layer speeds are expected to be slower than those found in OSI networks, principally due to the requirements for minimal power consumption (some of the devices expected to be connected to this network will be powered from the communications cable itself). The application protocol will provide some semantics based on MMS, and will be coupled with a simplified syntax for less overhead in communication. The Fieldbus will also add semantics for communication in the multipeer environment, both with and without connections. It will employ a short stack, where some of the layers of the OSI model have null functions, in the interest of optimizing for low protocol overhead and low manufacturing/purchase cost. The Fieldbus standard is under development both nationally and internationally.

An Architectural Vision Based on Standards

The architectural vision offered for consideration here is designed to facilitate the attainment of the integrated state. It includes the Fieldbus where communication with process sensors and actuators is required. It uses the Fieldbus because the Fieldbus is expected to provide standardized communications with these devices, based on some of the MMS paradigms, so that integration with higher level functions and applications is facilitated. Standardization of communication with these devices is expected to reduce application configuration effort, thus speeding control development and reducing installation costs. Allowing (but not insisting) the Fieldbus to be integratable to higher levels facilitates the process of making changes to the controls as the business or product changes, with less effort to meet the requirements of change.

The architectural vision also includes a series of networks based on OSI. Applications reside on a variety of hardware platforms. Those platforms installed after a future date are equipped with a common, non-proprietary operating system. The operating system is pervasive, extending over a full range of hardware platforms from multiple vendors. The installed base of proprietary operating system equipped platforms are networked through OSI and appropriate application protocols to the newer installations, so that application interaction becomes possible regardless of the physical constraints of any application's location or platform.

In the common operating environment, applications developed on one platform operate successfully on platforms from other vendors. Application software packages are used extensively, because they were developed for the common operating system. Regardless of operating environment, databases are positioned as data assets available via the networks to applications with the proper authorization and authentication. Data is distributed to where it is needed most, and accessed from other locations, sometimes in conjunction with simultaneous access to still other locations. The details of communication are reduced to a few paradigms, defined primarily by the application protocols in use. Where database access is potentially both local and/or remote, the communication details are completely masked by user interfaces that are able to distinguish between local and remote data and apply local access techniques or employ the services of the networks. Concerns over the compatibility of applications, hardware platforms, and databases has become a nonissue.

Getting There from Here (Migration to a Future State)

The architectural vision discussed above clearly represents a future state. The vision includes the installed base of equipment currently in use, but it is clear that in order to reach the vision there will be necessary changes. Some of the changes required are merely philosophical, and while potentially traumatic to our minds, require no action beyond discussion and agreement on new philosophies through the consensus process. Other changes require overt action.

Two tactical steps seem essential if the vision is to be attained. First and foremost, an organization must agree on the vision or modify the vision so that agreement is reached. When agreement has been attained by the consensus process the vision must be shared with the organization's vendors. Users need their expertise in order to come to consensus as to technology selections with which to realize the vision. Involvement of multiple vendors will minimize any biases towards a particular vendor's viewpoint. Thereafter, it is necessary to ensure that the development efforts of the vendors are in alignment with the vision, since even visions will mature and change over time as the business and technology change. The first necessary step, then, is to fix the vision and determine the technical directions needed to help achieve it.

Second, having agreed upon the technologies that seem key to realizing the vision, each new IS project undertaking development should be encouraged (required?) to complete a technology assessment phase before proceeding. This phase is necessary in order to determine the current state of products available to help realize the vision and the state of readiness of such products for inclusion in production operations. In some cases, it may be possible to take actions that position applications for future inclusion of products when they become available, but minimize the changes necessary to upgrade an application into a different communications environment, for example, when real products become available. The second step, then, is for each project to define the gap between the vision and reality, and take as many actions as possible to close the gap.

The change process may be necessarily painful. Attempting to close gaps will induce more cost into the development cycle than will the "do nothing" approach. On the other hand, doing nothing to aggressively determine and attain a vision will assuredly prevent a vision from becoming a reality.

About the Author

Chris Williams is a systems engineer employed by Eastman Kodak Company in Rochester, New York. He is a graduate of the University of Iowa, where he received the BA, MFA and MSEE degrees. Born in 1944, his professional interests include systems architectures for communication and integration, communications protocols and enterprise integration.

Outside of Kodak, he is currently active in standards committees working on protocols for manufacturing communication. He chairs the Instrument Society of America committee developing the companion standard to MMS for process control, participates in both the U.S. and International Fieldbus efforts, is the International Rapporteur for the time critical communications effort in ISD TC184/SC5/WG2, and is the acting secretary for IEC SC65C/WG1, among other roles.

He is married, with one daughter, and has a passion for vintage sports cars.

Chapter

6

Concepts and Protocols of the OSI Network Layer

by Ashar Aziz

Overview of OSI Network Layer Functions

The primary purpose of the OSI Network Layer is to provide a subnetwork, independent, end-to-end data transfer service to a higher protocol layer, such as the transport layer.

In OSI terminology, a *subnetwork* is a collection of physical equipment commonly referred to as a "network" in normal English usage. Examples of a subnetwork include most local area network (LAN) technologies, such as 802.3 (similar to Ethernet), token bus (802.4), token ring (802.5), FDDI, X.25 Packet Switched Data Network (PSDN), Integrated Services Digital Network (ISDN), etc. Conceptually, it helps to think of a subnetwork as a single "wire" connecting various systems. In practice, a subnetwork may indeed be a single physical wire, or it may be something more complicated, such as an X.25 PSDN. The subnetwork concept is a useful abstraction for grouping these various technologies and treating them as similar.

The fact that the Network Layer provides for end-to-end transmission of data means that higher layers need not be concerned with the physical topology of the network. These networks could be formed by concatenating various subnetworks, both LAN types and subnetworks such as X.25 PSDN's that can be wide area networks (WAN's). The network layer is the layer most concerned with the physical topology of the network and provides for the routing and relaying of the data through such a (possibly interconnected) network.

Network Addresses

The primary means by which the Network Layer provides this independence from concerns of the network topology is by providing a logical network address mechanism to higher layers. This logical address is called the Network Service Access Point (NSAP) address. These network addresses are independent of the subnetwork addresses that are used on the individual subnetworks for the physical systems connected to them. A particular system can be assigned a new subnetwork address (such as a different Ethernet or FDDI address) and still be able to use the same NSAP address.

An NSAP address identifies a user of the network service on a remote system, as opposed to the remote system Network Layer itself. A component of the network address may identify the remote network layer itself.

Data Transfer Services

There are two basic types of data transfer services provided by the OSI Network Layer. One is a Connectionless (CL) type of service, and the other is a Connection-Oriented (CO) type of service. These are provided by two essentially independent Network Layer protocols.

In describing the operation of the Network Layer protocols and services, it is useful to describe some of the terms and concepts common to both types of network data transfer services. These terms and concepts can be described in the context of communication from one Network Service User (NS-user), call it A, to another (remote) NS-user, say B, as shown in Figure 6-1. NS-user A supplies data intended for remote NS-user B to the network service provider. The remote NS-user B is conceptually attached to a point, called the Network Service Access Point (NSAP). The NSAP address identifies this conceptual point. Thus, NSAP Address B identifies NSAP B.

The data as supplied by NS-user A to the NS provider is called a Network Service Data Unit (NSDU). This NSDU is processed according to the procedures that are defined by the particular network protocol in use. The activation of these procedures can be abstractly modeled as representing an entity following the rules of the protocol in use. The idea here is that communication can be modeled as the interaction of two active elements, termed entities, rather than the passive following of protocol procedures. The entity corresponding to the activation of procedures in the OSI Network Layer, is termed a *Network Entity*. This network entity is identified by a globally unique Network Entity Title (NET).

It should be emphasized that terms such as Network Service Access Points and entities are entirely conceptual models of the interaction between two NS-users. They have nothing to do with how these protocols are implemented inside a real system. There may be nothing in a real system that represents, for example, an NSAP. However, the identifiers of some of these things, such as NSAP addresses, are carried across the network as network protocol information.

Having followed the procedures of the protocol, network entity A tacks on Network Protocol Control Information (N-PCI), and passes the concatenation of the N-PCI and the NSDU down to the subnetwork service provider. This data unit formed by the concatenation of the NSDU and N-PCI is called a Network Protocol Data Unit (NPDU), as illustrated in Figure 6-2a. Note that, in general, an NSDU may map to several NPDU's, each of them with associated N-PCI, as shown in Figure 6-2b. This fragmentation of an NSDU into multiple NPDU's (officially termed segmentation in OSI) may be necessitated by the maximum size data unit that a subnetwork service provider is willing to accept.

These, possibly multiple, NPDU's are received by remote network entity B, reassembled into a single NSDU if necessary, and passed up as an NSDU to remote NS-user B.

Figure 6-1 is a simplified depiction of what could happen in practice in a real network. In particular, for the sake of simplicity, no intervening Network Layer entities are shown. An intervening Network Layer entity would be necessary if NS-user A and NS-user B were on systems on different subnetworks. The system containing a Network Layer entity that would relay NPDU's from one subnetwork to another is termed an Intermediate System (IS). A system that acts solely as the originator or recipient of NPDU's is termed an *end system* (ES). The figure here shows the data going in one direction only. In general, data could be going in both directions at the same time.

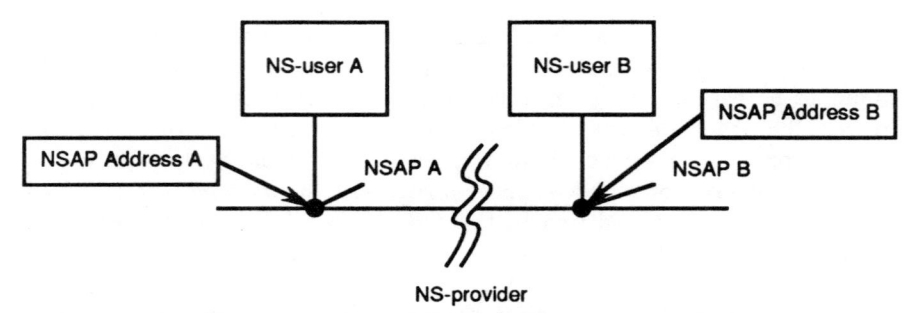

Figure 6-1 Communication from one network service user to another.

The interaction between the NS-user and NS-provider is modeled in terms of *service primitives*. There are four basic types of service primitives. A *request* service primitive type is one originated by the NS-user, as viewed by the originating NS-user. This request service primitive, when it reaches its intended destination NS-user, is called an *indication* of the same service primitive. There are two basic types of service primitives, which are abbreviated *req* and *ind*, respectively.

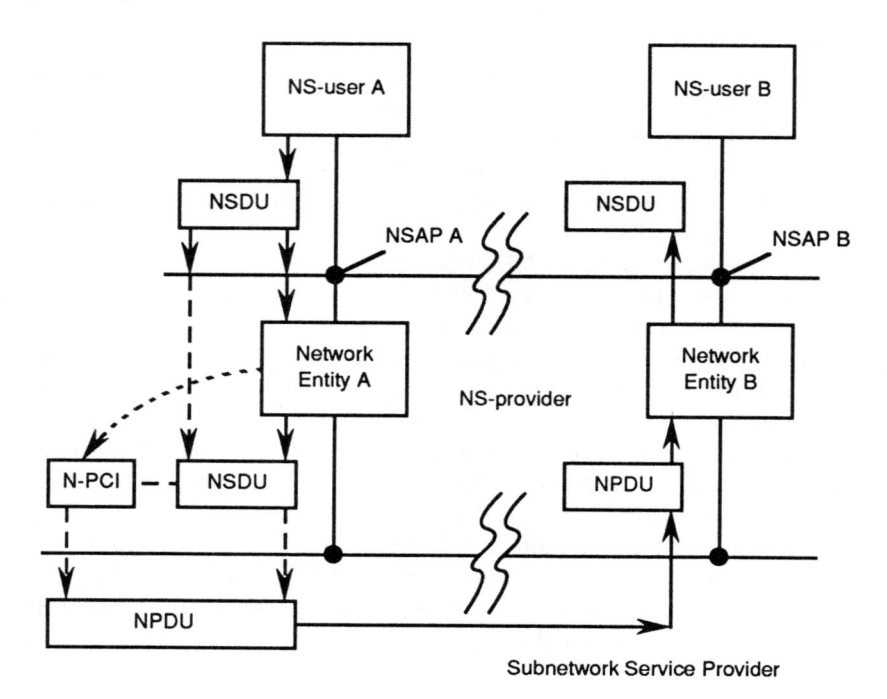

Figure 6-2a Network Protocol Data Unit.

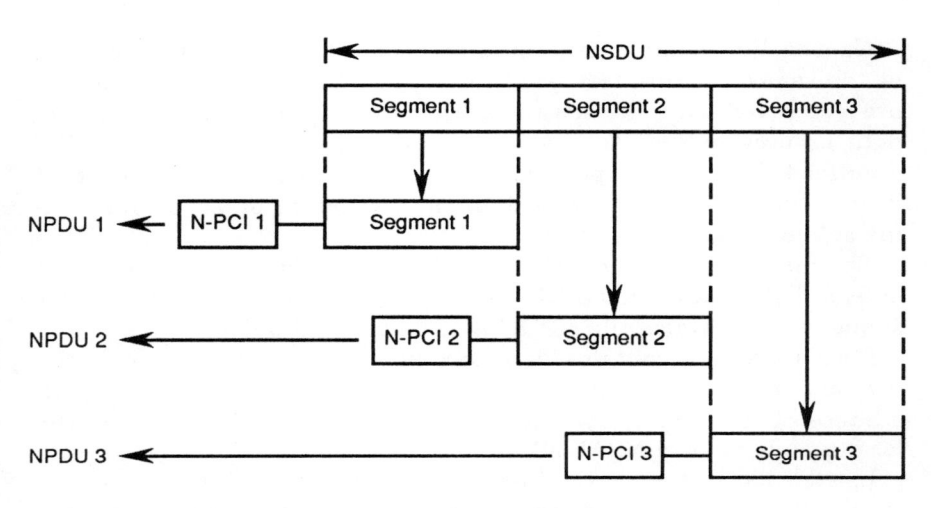

Concepts and Protocols of the OSI Network Layer   111

Figure 6-2b An NSDU may map to several NPDU's.

For connection-oriented services, there are two other types of service primitives. These are the response and confirm types. If the service primitive is a confirmed type of service, then the remote NS-user sends back a *response* service primitive after processing the corresponding request service primitive. This response service primitive is delivered to the requesting NS-user as a *confirm* service primitive. These two primitive types are abbreviated *rsp* and *cnf*, respectively.

Connectionless Network Service (CLNS)

A unit of transmission that is self-contained, and for which the network service provider needs no prior state in order to send or receive this unit, is called a datagram. The Connectionless Network Service (CLNS) provides the ability to send a datagram unit over to the destination system. The connectionless network service definition is provided in ISO 8348, Addendum 1.

Each datagram is an independent unit of transmission with no relationship to other datagram units that are sent over the same network service provider. In particular, the connectionless NS-provider may not preserve the order in which datagrams are delivered to the remote NS-user, and also does not guarantee delivery of data. If a datagram is lost en route to the remote user, there is no indication of this loss to the Network Service user (NS-user).

Upon delivery, the datagram is presented to the remote (NS-user) as the same unit that was transmitted, i.e., the datagram boundaries are preserved over the network. This means that a single unit of data as presented to the network service provider, e.g., the NSDU described above, will appear as the same unit in spite of the fact that it may have been fragmented into smaller pieces on some intervening subnetwork.

The maximum size of a single CLNS NSDU is 64512 octets (8-bit bytes). The maximum NPDU size is constrained by the particular subnetwork on which the NPDU is to be transmitted.

Each datagram contains in it sufficient information to reach the destination system. In particular, each datagram has in it the NSAP address of the remote system, as well as the NSAP address of the local system (source NSAP address).

In addition to the destination address, the user of the CLNS can specify the Quality of Service (QOS) parameter. The QOS parameter is actually a composite parameter, including in it provisions for five distinct subparameters. The first subparameter is the Transit Delay parameter. It specifies the minimum or maximum values for the elapsed time between an NSDU being given to the NS provider for transmission, called an N-UNITDATA request, and the time of its receipt by the remote NS-user, called an N-UNITDATA indication. Its specification is based on an average NSDU size. This parameter is made known to the NS-user by the NS-provider prior to transmission of data in a manner that is a local system matter.

The second subparameter is the Protection from Unauthorized Access parameter, which is used to specify one of four types of protection features in the NS. These features are used by the NS-user to request of the NS-provider a level of security for the particular NSDU being transmitted. The various levels of security are:

1. No protection features;
2. Protection from passive monitoring;
3. Protection against modification, replay, addition, or deletion;
4. Both 2 and 3 above.

The third subparameter is used by the NS-user to specify to the NS-provider the acceptable cost of the transmission of data. This can be specified in one of two ways. The first is by indicating that the NS-provider should use the least expensive mode of transmission, and the second is by specifying a ceiling to the cost of transmission, i.e., a maximum acceptable cost.

Concepts and Protocols of the OSI Network Layer

The fourth subparameter is used to specify what is termed the *residual error probability*. The residual error probability specifies the errors that will still be present after the NS-provider has taken all the steps that it can take, as defined by the protocol, in order to ensure proper delivery of data.

The fifth and final subparameter is used by the NS-user to specify a relative priority for the NSDU, in relation to other NSDU's that may be acted upon by that NS-provider. There are 15 relative priority levels. These priority levels are used to determine resource allocation by NS-providers, as well as the order of transmission or discarding of NSDU's or their fragments.

To summarize, the CLNS provides the following service primitive:

NS Primitive	Parameters
N-UNITDATA (req, ind)	Source NSAP address, destination NSAP address, QOS, user data

Connection-Oriented Network Service (CONS)

The CONS allows for the establishment of a virtual circuit with the remote NS-user. The service definition for the CO network is provided in ISO 8348.

The transfer of data using the CO network service follows three distinct phases. The first is connection establishment, the second is the data transfer phase, and the third is connection release. Each one of these implies a protocol action to the remote NS-provider/user.

First, a connection is established to the remote NS-user, by issuing an N-CONNECT-request service primitive. This remote NS-user is identified by an NSAP address in the N-CONNECT-request service primitive. The NSAP address is only specified during connection establishment time. Once a connection is successfully established, data units can be transmitted without the need to specify the remote NSAP address. If the connect attempt is succesful, the NS-user is given back an N-CONNECT-confirm indication. When a connection is established, the NS-user can send data on the connection using N-DATA request primitives.

If the remote NS-user (or provider) chooses not to accept the connection, it can send back an N-DISCONNECT-request. This traverses the network and appears as an N-DISCONNECT-indication on the side of the originating NS-user. In this case, the network connection attempt is considered to have failed.

All of the N-CONNECT-request, N-CONNECT-confirm, and N-DISCONNECT-indication primitives can carry up to 128 octets of user information (NS-user data). This user information can be used to pass, for example, passwords on an N-CONNECT-request.

The CONS preserves the order in which NSDU's are delivered to the remote NS-user. The CONS also preserves the NSDU boundaries across the network. Thus, a sequence of N-DATA-request service primitives appears as N-DATA-indication primitives to the remote NS-user in the same order with the same message boundaries.

By default, the N-DATA-request is not a confirmed service type. However, this does not mean that it is not a reliable service. The network protocol guarantees, within certain limits, reliable delivery of the data. This is done by the acknowledgment of data at the protocol level. However, this acknowledgment is only between the two network entities, and is not delivered to the NS-user. Thus, a distinction needs to be made between acknowledgment of data at the protocol level between the two network entities, and confirmation of the corresponding service primitive, which is between the two NS-users.

The CONS provides mechanisms for the reliable delivery of data, which may be acknowledged optionally to the NS-user sending the data by the receiving network entity. The data is acknowledged to the NS-user by means of an N-DATA-ACKNOWLEDGE primitive. If the NS-user sending the data wants a corresponding N-DATA-ACKNOWLEDGE, this is requested in the service primitive by setting a confirmation request parameter.

The data on such a network connection may also be subject to flow control if the recipient of the data is unable to keep up with the data flow. To bypass this regular stream of NSDU's on a network connection, the CONS provides for an expedited data service, which is not subject to the flow control restrictions of the regular data stream. The amount of data that may be sent in an expedited manner is limited to 32 octets. The expedited data is guaranteed to be delivered no later than regular data or expedited data sent later on the same network connection. The service primitives corresponding to this feature is the N-EXPEDITED-DATA request and indication primitives. Both expedited data and acknowledgment of data receipt to the NS-user are NS-provider options.

The Quality of Service (QOS) parameter for the CONS is similar to that of the CLNS. It has a few parameters, however, in addition to the ones described for CLNS. These are parameters associated with Network Connection (NC) establishment and release and throughput. There are two parameters for NC establishment, namely NC establishment delay, and NC establishment failure probability. The first one is an indication of the maximum acceptable delay between an N-CONNECT-request and an N-CONNECT-confirm. The second one is the acceptable probability of NC failure, either by refusal or misconnection. Similarly, there are two parameters associated with NC release. These are the NC release delay parameter and the NC release failure probabilty.

The difference between the QOS parameters for the CONS and for CLNS is that negotiation of these is possible between the two NS-users or the two network entities. This is done on the connect request/response sequence, with the N-CONNECT-request specifying the desired values for the QOS parameters, and the N-CONNECT-confirm containing the QOS values that are finally selected. These QOS values in the N-CONNECT-confirm are considered the outcome of the negotiation. The NS-provider can also be party to the negotiations.

There is also an N-RESET service primitive, available to the user. It is used to resynchronize the use of the network connection. When this primitive is used, it unblocks all normal and expedited data, and causes any pending normal and expedited data to be discarded. This service primitive may also be invoked by the NS-provider in cases of congestion. In this case, the corresponding N-RESET indication specifies that the originator was the NS-provider, in a parameter called the *originator* of the N-RESET.

To summarize, the CONS has the following service primitives and associated parameters.

NS Primitive	Parameters
N-CONNECT (req, ind)	Called NSAP address, calling NSAP address, receipt confirmation, expedited data selection, QOS, user data
N-CONNECT (rsp, cnf)	Responding NSAP address, calling NSAP address, receipt confirmation, expedited data selection, QOS, user data
N-DATA (req, ind)	User data, confirmation request
N-DATA-ACKNOWLEDGE (req, ind)	
N-EXPEDITED-DATA (req, ind)	User data

NS Primitive	Parameters
N-RESET (req)	Reason
N-RESET (ind)	Reason, originator
N-RESET (rsp, cnf)	
N-DISCONNECT (req)	Reason, NS-user data, responding NSAP address
N-DISCONNECT (ind)	Originator, reason, NS-user data, responding NSAP address

Routing and Relaying

From an abstract point of view, the routing function of the Network Layer takes a destination NSAP address and figures out a path through the network, composed of all the network entities and concatenated subnetworks, that can be used to reach the destination NSAP address.

In practice, in OSI the routing function is distributed among multiple systems so that each system, whether it is the originator of the data or an intervening system responsible for relaying the data, may know of only a fragment of the full path that must be traversed by the data to reach the destination system.

The relaying component of the Network Layer performs the actual act of taking data from one subnetwork interface and passing it to another subnetwork interface.

Network Layer Addressing

There are three types of addresses of interest at the Network Layer. One is the NSAP address, which identifies a user of the network service. The second is a Network Entity Title (NET), although strictly speaking this is a title and not an address, which identifies a network entity. The network entity, as noted above, is the element that embodies the rules and procedures of the Network Layer protocol. The third is the subnetwork address, also known as a Sub-Network Point of Attachment (SNPA) address. This is the address that identifies a real open system on a particular subnetwork, and is in the format of whatever addressing mechanism is used on that subnetwork. The network entity sends the NPDU inside a sub-

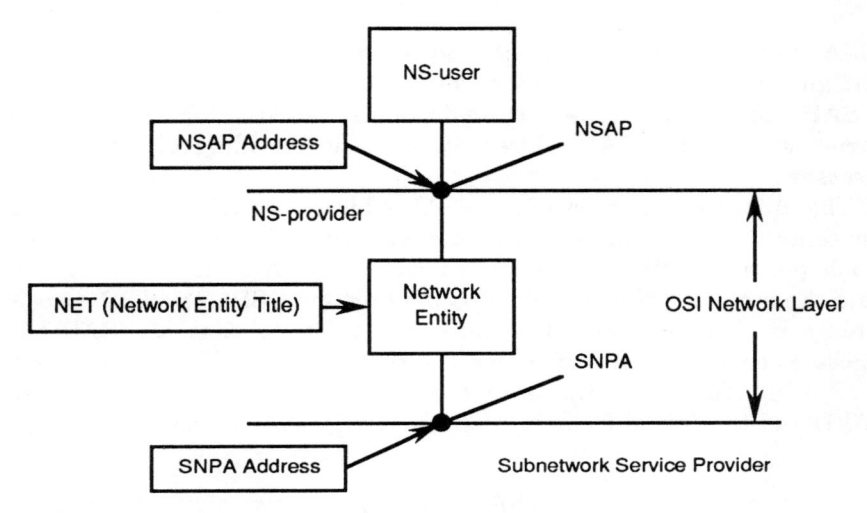

Concepts and Protocols of the OSI Network Layer   117

Figure 6-2c NSAP, NET, and SNPA.

network data request, using an SNPA address as the destination address for that subnetwork. These three concepts are illustrated in Figure 6-2c.

In a sense, an NSAP address can be viewed as a "logical" address to which an NPDU is to be sent. An SNPA address is then one of the series of "physical" addresses through which the NPDU traverses, wrapped inside subnetwork data PDU's. The term "physical address" should not be taken too literally. The SNPA address is only physical in the sense that it is the address type being used on a subnetwork. If the subnetwork is a single physical wire, such as FDDI, then the subnetwork addresses really are physical layer addresses. But if the subnetwork is an abstraction, representing something other than a physical wire, then the SNPA addresses would not, in normal discourse, be considered physical addresses.

An example of how these SNPA addresses can be something other than physical addresses is when the subnetwork is an IP (Internet Protocol, Internet RFC 791) network. In this case the IP addresses are the subnetwork addresses, which are really logical addresses from the point of view of IP.

NSAP Addresses

ISO 8348 (Addendum 2) describes NSAP addresses and NET's. The principal idea behind NSAP addresses is that these are assumed to be relatively stable (nontransient), globally unique identifiers of

NSAP's. The NSAP addresses, indirectly, identify open systems in the global network. There are three basic concepts used in describing NSAP addresses: the abstract semantics of NSAP addresses, the abstract syntax of NSAP addresses, and the encoding of NSAP addresses.

The abstract semantics of an NSAP address are the meaning of its contents. NSAP addresses have a structure that is composed of two basic parts. The first part is called the Initial Domain Part (or IDP), and the second is the Domain Specific Part (or DSP). The IDP associates a particular registration authority for that class of NSAP addresses, as well as a format for the rest of the NSAP address. The IDP itself consists of two parts, the Authority and Format Identifier (AFI) and the Initial Domain Identifier (IDI). This is shown below.

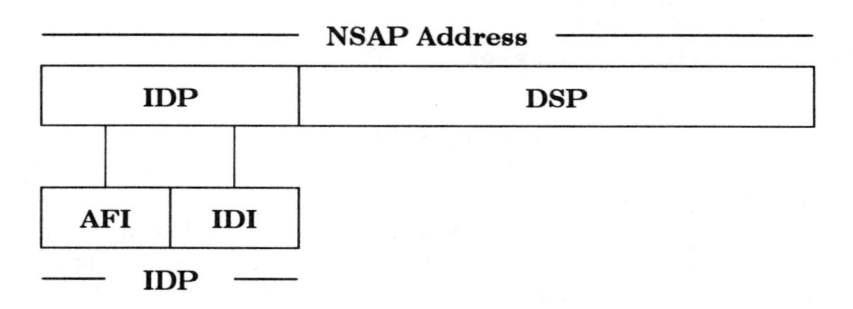

```
                         NSAP Address
    ┌──────────────────┬──────────────────────────────────┐
    │       IDP        │              DSP                 │
    └──────────────────┴──────────────────────────────────┘
    ┌────────┬─────────┐
    │  AFI   │   IDI   │
    └────────┴─────────┘
    ──── IDP ────
```

The AFI specifies the format of the IDI, the authority responsible for assigning values of NSAP addresses to different open systems, whether leading zeros are significant in the IDI, and the abstract syntax of the DSP. The rest of the structure of the DSP, i.e., whether certain fields in the NSAP address represent areas, organizations, subnetworks, SNPA addresses, or host ID's, etc., is implied by the IDP.

The abstract syntax is used to express the contents of NSAP addresses, without regard to how the network protocols will carry the addresses as Network Protocol Address Information (NPAI). What the network protocols carry across the wire are the encodings of these addresses. Each network layer protocol specifies what encoding rules will be used for the transmission of these addresses.

There are four general types of abstract syntaxes used to specify the contents of NSAP addresses: binary, decimal, character, and national character. These abstract syntaxes are descriptive devices that aid in the written description of NSAP addresses, without specifying

Concepts and Protocols of the OSI Network Layer 119

how these addresses are to be carried across the wire. Using the decimal digits 0–9 to write down addresses is a common way of representing addresses, as is using binary octets (by specifying all bits in each octet). The binary syntax can be written by specifying each bit individually as a 0 or 1, or by specifying each semi-octet using the hexadecimal digits 0–9 and A–F. To distinguish a hexadecimal notation for an NSAP address from a decimal one, the hexadecimal digits are preceded by the symbol /.

Thus, an IDP can be specified in decimal abstract syntax as,

/470005

Whereas, a DSP in binary syntax can be written as,

/0A78DD897600

If the DSP abstract syntax implied is the decimal syntax, then sometimes the DSP may be absent. It is required to be present for all other DSP abstract syntaxes being implied. The character and national character allow other means of specifying addresses, e.g., in some international character set. The encodings corresponding to these abstract syntaxes is the character encodings defined in the relevant character set document.

The IDP is always in decimal abstract syntax. The AFI is always two decimal digits with a value between 0 and 99. The IDI is a variable number of decimal digits. The following are the ranges of AFI values that are allocated.

AFI	How the AFI range is assigned
00–09	Reserved — will not be allocated
10–35	Reserved for future allocation by joint agreement of ISO and CCITT
36–59	Allocated to the IDI formats defined in clause 8.2.1.2 of 8348 AD 2
60–69	Allocated for assignment to new IDI formats by ISO
70–79	Allocated for assignment to new IDI formats by CCITT
80–99	Reserved for future allocation by joint agreement of ISO and CCITT

The fact that the first digit of the AFI is never 0 (0–9 is reserved) can be used by protocols as an escape sequence to inform the NSAP address decoding procedure that something other than a regular NSAP address follows the zero decimal digit. This can be used, for example, to convey that a partial NSAP address follows, and the rest of the NSAP address can be deduced from other aspects of the N-PCI. Alternatively, it may be used to escape to a completely different addressing scheme from the one specified by ISO.

The AFI range 36–59 allocated above is further specified in clause 8.2.1.2 of 8348 AD 2 as:

AFI (Decimal)	IDI Format	DSP Abstract Syntax	IDP Length (# digits)
36,52	X.121	Decimal	Up to 16 digits
37,53	X.121	Binary	Up to 16 digits
38	ISO DCC	Decimal	5 digits
39	ISO DCC	Binary	5 digits
40,54	F.69	Decimal	Up to 10 digits
41,55	F.69	Binary	Up to 10 digits
42,56	E.163	Decimal	Up to 14 digits
43,57	E.163	Binary	Up to 14 digits
44,58	E.164	Decimal	Up to 17 digits
45,59	E.164	Binary	Up to 17 digits
46	ISO 6523-ICD	Decimal	6 digits
47	ISO 6523-ICD	Binary	6 digits
48	Local	Decimal	2 digits
49	Local	Binary	2 digits
50	Local	Character (ISO 646)	2 digits
51	Local	National character	2 digits

Concepts and Protocols of the OSI Network Layer

For the pairs of AFI values that specify the same IDI format and DSP abstract syntax, the lower AFI value is used when the first significant digit of the IDI is nonzero, and the higher IDI value is used when the first significant IDI digit is zero. The IDI format refers to what the format of the IDI is like, and is typically a reference to another document, such as X.121 or E.163, which specifies address formats.

ISO 6523-ICD refers to the fact that the IDI consists of a four-digit International Code Designator (ICD) allocated according to ISO 6523. This code identifies an organizational authority responsible for allocating and assigning values of the DSP.

For the "local" AFI designation the IDI is null, and the format of the DSP is assigned by some local authority. Only the local types of NSAP addresses can have abstract syntaxes specified using the ISO 646 character set or some national character set.

The DSP may be in any one of the four abstract syntaxes. However, it is always in only one of the abstract syntaxes, not in a combination of these. For the decimal and binary abstract syntaxes, there are two encodings defined in ISO 8348 Addendum 2. The network layer protocol standards can refer to these encoding rules when they need to specify the encodings of the network addresses to be carried by the protocols as NPAI. These two encodings, called *preferred* encodings of network addresses, are the preferred binary encoding and the preferred decimal encoding.

Keeping the distinction between a value and its encoding is primarily why there is a distinction between how the value is represented using an abstract syntax and how it is encoded using a set of encoding rules. The same value may result in different encodings if different encoding rules are used.

The preferred binary encoding works as follows. The two decimal digits of the AFI are encoded as semi-octets, yielding for each digit in the range 0–9 a semi-octet (or "nybble") in the range 0000–1001. For example, an AFI of 49 would be encoded as 01001001. It is important to observe that the digits are encoded separately, and the decimal number 49 is not converted as a single decimal number to its binary encoding. The value of the AFI is specified in decimal, but after encoding it results in a binary number that would have resulted from treating the decimal number as a hexadecimal number. These rules are also known as Binary Coded Decimal (BCD) encoding rules.

The IDI is then padded with leading digits, if necessary, to obtain the maximum IDI length as specified above. Each decimal digit of the IDI is then encoded as a semi-octet in the range 0000–1001. If the DSP is not in decimal syntax, a filler semi-octet of 1111 is used after the last digit of the IDI, if necessary, to make the IDP an integral number of octets. The DSP, if in decimal syntax, is encoded similarly to the IDI, and each decimal digit is individually encoded as a semi-octet in the range 0000–1001. If this does not result in an integral number of octets, a final semi-octet of 1111 is used as a filler to yield an integral number of octets for the full NSAP address. The filler will always be recognized as such, as it does not map to a decimal digit. If the DSP is in binary abstract syntax, then each binary semi-octet is encoded directly into a semi-octet in the range 0000–1111.

These are the most commonly used abstract syntaxes and their encodings. The rest of the abstract syntaxes, namely the character and national character syntaxes, and their corresponding encodings are described in ISO 8348, Addendum 2, Clause 8.3.

The maximum size of an NSAP address, for all of the different NSAP address formats, never exceeds 40 digits (or 20 encoded octets).

NSAP Address Examples

Some examples of different classes of NSAP addresses follow. These classes are distinguished from each other by the IDP.

OSINET NSAP Address Format OSINET is an experimental network set up under the auspices of the National Institute for Standards and Technology (NIST), formerly known as the National Bureau of Standards (NBS). It is intended to be a test network for OSI. OSINET is based on an X.25 WAN, which is used as the subnetwork service provider for the CLNS.

The OSINET address format is under the AFI of 47. The IDI for this AFI, as described above, is used according to ISO 6523-ICD, and is assigned by ISO a four decimal digit ICD of 0004. The implied DSP abstract syntax is the binary abstract syntax. The full NSAP address is as follows:

```
<--AFI IDI --><---------------- DSP -------------------->
+----+------+----------+----------+-----------------+-----+
| 47 | 0004 | ORGID    | SUBNET ID|  SNPA Address   |NSEL|
+----+------+----------+----------+-----------------+-----+
   1     2       2          2             6            1
                                                  (# octets)
```

The two octets for ORGID represent an organization. These two octet organization codes are administered by the NIST. Each organization assigns subnet ID's and SNPA addresses for open systems that fall within its administrative domain. The SNPA address is typically a Medium Access Layer (MAC) address, such as an Ethernet address, FDDI address, etc. The last octet is the NSEL (Network SELector), which is used to identify different users of the network service on a particular open system.

The total length of an OSINET NSAP address is 14 octets. The NSEL is a common feature of an NSAP address, and NSAP addresses that are equal except for the NSEL are all meant for the same network entity, but (possibly) for different NS-users.

U.S. GOSIP NSAP Addresses The U.S. government, like many other governments, has stated that they will build government networks based on OSI protocols. In order to facilitate the procurement of systems providing OSI protocols, they have defined a Government OSI Profile (GOSIP). This specifies features such as which optional features of the protocols will be present, as well as which kinds of addressing schemes will be used. The documents specifying the GOSIP are revised periodically.

U.S. GOSIP version 1 and U.S. GOSIP version 2 specify two slightly different forms of NSAP addresses. The version 1 has an AFI of 47 and an IDI of 0005 (the ICD allocated to the U.S. Federal government and administered by NIST). The full NSAP address format is shown below.

```
 <-AFI IDI -->< - - - - - - - - - - -     DSP      - - - - - - - - - - - - - - - - - - - - ->
 +----+------+----------+-----------+-------------------+------+
 | 47 | 0005 |  ORGID   | SUBNET ID |   END SYSTEM ID   | NSEL|
 +----+------+----------+-----------+-------------------+------+
   1      2        2          2              4-8            1
                                                       (# octets)
```

This is fairly similar to the OSINET address format, apart from the variable length feature of the second-to-last field, called the End System ID. Each organization, identified by the ORGID code, is free to assign this field as well as to choose its length, which can be between four and eight octets. This could be a logical station ID, or it can be chosen from the ISO 8802 MAC address space, e.g., Ethernet or FDDI addresses. The ORGID codes are to be assigned by NIST.

The draft of version 2 of the U.S. GOSIP specifies a similar IDP, but has a different DSP structure. This NSAP address format is shown below.

```
AFI IDI <------------    DSP     ----------------------------------->
+---+----+--------+--------------+-----+---------------+----+------------+-------+
|47|0005|Version|Admin. Auth.|Rsvd.|Routing Domain|Area| End System | NSEL  |
+---+----+--------+--------------+-----+---------------+----+------------+-------+
 1   2     1          3            2          2          2       6         1
                                                                     (# octets)
```

The version 2 format supersedes the version 1 format by specifying this last DSP format as mandatory for addresses allocated under the ICD of 0005.

The various fields of the NSAP address are explained as follows. The first octet of the DSP is a version field, so that in the future different structures of the DSP may be permitted; these are distinguished from each other by using the version octet. The second field in the DSP is the Administrative Authority field, which identifies the entity responsible for the assignment of the Intermediate Systems and End Systems into various routing domains and areas. Routing domains and areas are concepts employed by routing protocols and will be explained later in the section on routing.

The third field in the DSP is the Reserved field of two octets. This can be used later to encode further levels of routing information. It also fills out the full NSAP address to be 20 octets.

The next field specifies a Routing Domain, using two octets. Following this is a two-octet field to specify an area for the purposes of routing. The End System ID is a six-octet field that uniquely identifies an ES within an area. This is usually done by assigning to this field a physical layer address, such as an Ethernet address, although this is not a requirement. Doing so would guarantee that this field is globally unique, and hence unique within an area as well.

The NSEL, as for all NSAP addresses, identifies a user of the network service, which is usually a transport entity. However, it can be used to identify direct users of the network service as well.

In addition to ICD 0005, NIST also has authority for ICD 0006, which it has delegated to the U.S. Department of Defense (DoD).

NSAP Addresses Used with CONS CONS networks are frequently implemented over an X.25 PSDN. The NSAP addresses used in these cases frequently relate to the DTE addresses assigned by the PSDN authority. The format of these DTE addresses is commonly the X.121 address format.

Concepts and Protocols of the OSI Network Layer

The NSAP address is either carried explicitly as NPAI, or it is implied by the DTE addresses being used. These DTE addresses are used in the framework of NSAP addresses in that the DTE X.121 address is used as the IDI of the NSAP address. The AFI used in these cases is either 36 or 37. If the AFI is 36, implying a decimal DSP abstract syntax, then the DSP can be null (i.e., absent). Given a DTE X.121 address of, say, 31344155551212, the NSAP address can be

```
AFI    IDI               DSP
36     31344155551212    (null)
```

Since most of the NSAP address is an X.121 DTE address, it can be deduced easily from the DTE address. This is in fact done when CONS is run over versions of X.25 subnetworks that do not support explicit carriage of NPAI, as is the case for X.25 subnetworks based on the 1980 CCITT recommendations. Of course, other NSAP addresses are possible and can be used when running CONS over subnetworks capable of carrying arbitrary NPAI, such as 1984 X.25 subnetworks.

Network Entity Titles (NET's)

According to ISO 8348 AD 2, NET's are syntactically the same as NSAP addresses. Conceptually, however, as noted above, they identify different objects. An NET is used to identify a network entity, which is conceptually a level lower in the OSI reference stack than an NS-user, which is what an NSAP address identifies. An NET can be allocated out of the same address space as an NSAP address; the only difference between the two is the way they are used.

A caveat here is that an upcoming IS-IS standard, currently DP 10589 (which describes protocols for routing), derives an NET from an NSAP address by excluding the NSEL field.

SubNetwork Point of Attachment (SNPA) Addresses

A subnetwork address, or an SNPA address, is an address which, when provided to the subnetwork service provider, is sufficient to send the subnetwork data PDU to the appropriate destination. Conceptually, an SNPA address is a level lower than an NSAP address. It identifies the point of attachment of a real system on a subnetwork (the SNPA), as shown in Figure 6-2c.

Indirectly, the SNPA address identifies the Network Entity and in this way is similar to the NET. However, the same Network Entity can, at different points in time, be attached to different SNPA's. The NET would not change in these cases, but it would have different SNPA addresses. Also, a network entity can be attached simultaneously to many different subnetworks and have a different SNPA address on each of these subnetworks. However, a network entity has only one NET at all times. Furthermore, the NET has significance only to protocols at the OSI Network Layer level, whereas the SNPA address is used for routing the subnetwork data within the subnetwork.

An example of an SNPA address is the DTE address on an X.25 PSDN. Another example is the Physical Layer addresses of IEEE 802 style LAN's, such as 802.3, 802.4, FDDI, etc. In these cases the SNPA address is the six-octet Ethernet address, FDDI address, etc. These addresses alone allow a system to reach a destination system on a LAN subnetwork, using the physical layer protocols.

Internal Network Layer Architecture

Before examining the protocols used for the transfer of data or routing of information, it is helpful to review the OSI model of the internal structure of the Network Layer. This architecture is described in ISO 8648. Briefly, the network layer is thought of as three sublayers, as shown in Figure 6-3. Each sublayer can have associated with it a sublayer protocol. For a given network protocol and subnetwork combination, not all sublayers need be present as discrete protocols. A single protocol may in fact suffice for doing the job of all three sublayers.

The first sublayer has associated with it what is called the SubNetwork Independent Convergence Protocol (SNICP). The protocol that implements this role of the network sublayer is constructed according to considerations that do not depend on the characteristics of a specific subnetwork type.

The second sublayer has associated with it a protocol termed the SubNetwork Dependent Convergence Protocol (SNDCP). This protocol is used to augment the role provided by the SNICP in order to realize the OSI network service on a particular subnetwork type. In the context of this discussion, a protocol does not necessarily imply exchange of PCI over a subnetwork. A protocol such as an SNDCP can consist of only a set of rules for manipulating the subnetwork service. These rules may not imply exchange of N-PCI over a sub-

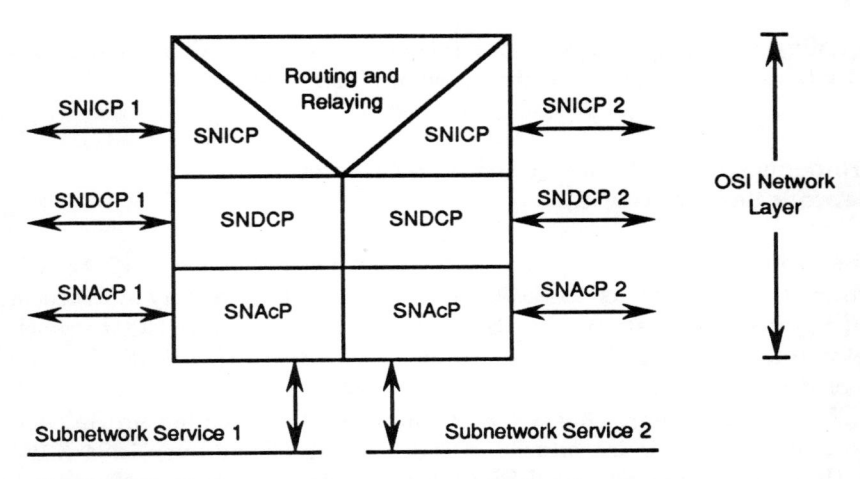

Concepts and Protocols of the OSI Network Layer 127

Figure 6-3 The network layer composed of three sublayers.

network. Often, in instances where the N-PCI associated with the SNDCP is null, the set of rules for manipulating the subnetwork service is also referred to as a Subnetwork Dependent Convergence Function (SNDCF).

The lowest sublayer has associated with it a protocol termed the SubNetwork Access Protocol (SNAcP). This protocol is concerned with routing and relaying within the subnetwork.

With reference to Figure 6-3, none of the respective protocols on both sides of the relay entity need be identical. It becomes the job of the relay entity to perform the appropriate functions and procedures for each one of the protocols on the subnetworks between which it is relaying.

Network Layer Data Transfer Protocols

There are two basic types of Network Layer protocols: one for providing the connection-oriented network service, and another for providing the Connectionless Network Service. It should be understood that, from the point of view of the Network Layer data transfer protocols, an NSAP address is treated simply as an opaque string of octets. Whatever underlying structure an NSAP address may have is ignored. For example, in order to determine the suitability of an NSAP address for a particular purpose, such as determining if the NSAP address is a local one, the NSAP address is simply tested for equality. Routing protocols and mechanisms (to be discussed later) may take advantage of the structure of NSAP addresses.

Protocols to Provide the Connection-Oriented Network Service (CONS)

The protocol for providing the CO network service maps to ISO 8208, which is the same as the 1984 CCITT X.25 Packet Layer Protocol (PLP) recommendation. The SNDCP for mapping the CO network service to 1984 X.25 PLP is specified in ISO 8878. ISO 8878 also has a provision to map the CONS to subnetworks supporting the 1980 X.25 recomendation. This SNDCP should really be called an SNDCF as no new N-PCI is introduced in order to run CONS over 1984 X.25. In this case an N-PCI based SNDCP is provided because of the insufficiencies of 1980 X.25 to provide the CONS.

Although the X.25 recommendation describes the PLP as running on top of LAPB, other ISO/CCITT documents describe how to run CONS over the LLC-2 protocol and ISDN. LLC-2 is a data-link protocol, similar to LAPB (which in turn is a subset of HDLC), meant to run in an IEEE 802.2 (ISO 8802) LAN environment, such as 802.3, FDDI, etc. Thus X.25 PLP can run between two systems connected by an IEEE 802 LAN.

All these various mappings are possible because of the similarity between the type of service offered by LAPB and LLC-2, and ISDN. The rest of the description of X.25 assumes LAPB as the data-link layer.

Since ISO 8208 (1984 X.25 PLP) requires no SNDCP to provide the CONS, a single protocol provides the role of the SNICP, SNDCP, and SNAcP.

Before examining the mapping from CONS to 1984 X.25 PLP, it would be instructive to briefly review the X.25 PLP recommendations and the major differences between the 1980, 1984, and 1988 versions.

Overview of X.25 PLP

X.25 PLP uses the data link protocol LAPB to provide a virtual circuit facility. All X.25 PLP frames are transmitted on LAPB information frames. LAPB is defined as part of the X.25 recommendations and corresponds to the OSI data link layer, whereas PLP corresponds to the OSI Network Layer.

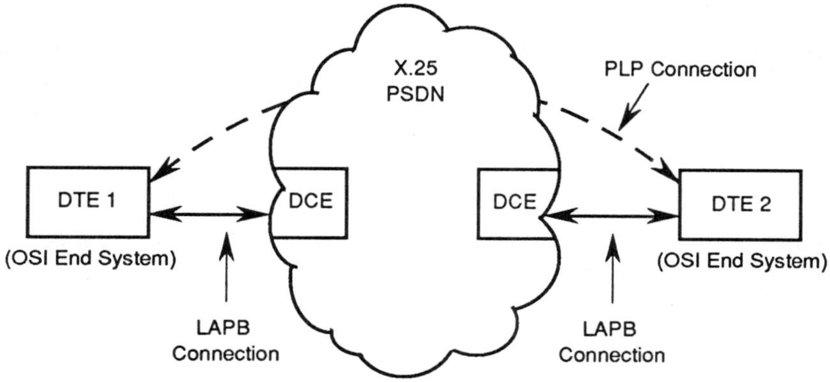

Concepts and Protocols of the OSI Network Layer 129

Figure 6-4 LAPB versus PLP.

LAPB is itself a connection-oriented data-link protocol that provides for error-free transmission over a line between a Data Terminal Equipment (DTE) and a Data Circuit Termination Equipment (DCE). The DTE is the end user of the network services, whereas the DCE side of the network provides for the actual routing and relaying of data in a reliable, sequenced packet stream.

In a way, the DTE can be thought of as analogous to a telephone. The DCE side would be the equivalent of the telephone service carrier. This analogy is actually not too far-fetched, considering that the X.25 model and protocols evolved from the work of the PTT's (national postal, telephone, and telegraph companies) of Europe.

Once a LAPB connection is established, X.25 PLP establishes a packet layer (Network Layer) connection on top of the LAPB connection, using LAPB data frames as an underlying service. LAPB has provision for flow control and error detection on the DTE-DCE link, but this is mostly transparent to PLP, which implements its own error detection and flow control. The primary difference between the two protocols is that LAPB exercises error detection and flow control on the DTE-DCE link, whereas the PLP multiplexes different virtual circuits over LAPB and performs flow control on a per virtual circuit basis. This is illustrated in Figure 6-4.

In the description that follows, rather than give a detailed account of the X.25 protocol, only the important packet formats, their parameters, and intended usage are covered. Protocol aspects related to flow control, packet sequencing, etc., not being directly relevant to CONS, are omitted.

The PLP connection is initiated by a Call Request packet. The X.25 Call Request packet format is given below.

Note: For all the X.25 packets described, the first name is used as the name of the packet when it is coming from the DTE and the second name is the name used when the packet is coming from the DCE side of the DTE-DCE interface.

```
        8      7      6      5      4      3      2      1   Octet #
    +----------------------------------+--------------------------+
    |           GFI                    |        LCGN #            |   1
    +----------------------------------+--------------------------+
    |           Logical   Channel   Number   (LCN)                |   2
    +-------------------------------------------------------------+
    |                  Packet Type Identifier                     |
    |     0      0      0      0      1      0      1      1     |   3
    +----------------------------------+--------------------------+
    | Calling DTE addr len             |    Called DTE addr len   |   4
    +----------------------------------+--------------------------+
    .                                                             .
    |                                                             |
    .                     DTE Addresses                           .
    |                                                             |
    .                                                             .
    +-------------------------------------------------------------+
    |                    Facility Length                          |
    +-------------------------------------------------------------+
    |                                                             |
    .                       Facilities                            .
    |                                                             |
    .                                                             .
    +-------------------------------------------------------------+
    .                                                             .
    |                     Call User Data                          |
    .                                                             .
    +-------------------------------------------------------------+
```

Call Request/Incoming Call packet format

All X.25 PLP packets contain at least three octets: the Logical Channel Group Number (LGCN)/General Format Identifier (GFI) octet, the Logical Channel Number (LCN) octet, and the Packet Type Identifier octet. Depending on the packet type as determined by the Packet Type Identifier octet, there may be subsequent octets in the packet.

The first octet contains the Logical Channel Group Number (LCGN) nybble, which, when coupled with the Logical Channel Number (LCN) octet, uniquely identifies a connection. The first octet also contains the GFI, which identifies the format and also the general type of packet (i.e., control packet or data packet). Bit 8 of octet 1 is used as the Qualifier bit (or Q bit) of data packets and is set to 0 in all nondata packets. The significance of this is described below.

Bit 7 of octet 1 is the D-bit. In call setup packets (Call Request, Call Accepted), it is used to negotiate end-to-end confirmation of data delivery. In data packets (described below), setting the D-bit to 1 causes the acknowledgment for that data packet to have end-to-end significance. It is set to 0 in all other types of packets.

The fourth octet contains the length of the calling and called DTE addresses. This is in the form of number of digits (semi-octets) in the DTE addresses. The low four bits contain the number of digits in the Called DTE address, and the high four bits contain the number of digits in the Calling DTE address. Octets 5 on, up to the length of the DTE addresses, contain the values of the DTE addresses. These DTE addresses values are encoded using the BCD encoding rules described above.

If the sum of the number of digits in the calling and called DTE addresses is odd, then a trailing semi-octet of 0000 is added to pad to an integral number of octets. Since the DTE address lengths are in number of digits, this last pad semi-octet will be ignored.

Following the DTE addresses is the Facilities field. This is similar to the Options field of the CLNP packet used for additional parameters. Annex G of 1984 X.25 recommedation describes several of the facilities needed to provide the CONS. The most important of these for CONS is the Address Extension Facility (AEF). There is a Called AEF and a Calling AEF, which correspond to the Called NSAP address and the Calling NSAP address in the various CONS primitives.

Each AEF facility has a type code, followed by a length octet. This AEF can be used either independently or in conjunction with the DTE address, to yield the NSAP address. 1984 X.25 provisionally allows 32 digits in the AEF value field, whereas the 1988 X.25 recommendation allows up to 40 digits of the AEF value.

There are other facilities to provide the QOS parameters and to negotiate use of expedited data on the network connection. The 1980 X.25 recommendation does not contain Annex G, so the QOS parameters and AEF facilities are not available on implementations of 1980 X.25.

Another facility, support of which was made mandatory in the 1984 and later X.25 recommendations, is the Fast Select facility. By specifying use of Fast Select, a DTE can send up to 128 octets of user information in the Call Request packet. When use of Fast Select is not requested, only 16 octets of user information may be sent. The

Fast Select facility was not a requirement for implementations of 1980 X.25 subnetworks; hence the amount of user information that can be passed over 1980 X.25 in certain packet types is either limited or zero.

When the remote DTE receives the Incoming Call packet, which has the same format as the original Call Request, it can issue either a Call Accepted packet or a Clear Request packet. The Call Accepted accepts the connection, and the Clear Request rejects the connection. The Clear Request can be issued subsequent to a Call Accept packet in the data transfer phase to release the connection.

The Call Accepted packet format is given below. The Call Connected packet has the same format as the Call Accepted packet, and results from the transmission of a Call Accepted packet from the called DTE to the calling DTE.

```
       8      7      6      5      4      3      2      1    Octet #
      +---------------------------------+---------------------------+
      |             GFI                 |         LCGN #            |   1
      +---------------------------------+---------------------------+
      |          Logical Channel Number (LCN)                       |   2
      +-------------------------------------------------------------+
      |                  Packet Type Identifier                     |
      |    0      0      0      0      1      1      1      1      |   3
      +---------------------------------+---------------------------+
      |    Calling DTE addr len         |    Called DTE addr len    |   4
      +---------------------------------+---------------------------+
      .                                                           .
                                                                        5
      |                                                           |
      .                      DTE Addresses                        .
      
      |                                                           |
      .                                                           :
      
      |                                                           |
      +-------------------------------------------------------------+
      |                    Facility Length                          |
      +-------------------------------------------------------------+
      .                                                           .
      
      |                       Facilities                          |
      
      .                                                           .
      +-------------------------------------------------------------+
      .                                                           .
      
      |                   Called User Data                        |
      
      .                                                           .
      +-------------------------------------------------------------+
```

Call Accepted/Call Connected packet format

The Call Accepted packet can contain NS-user information in the Called User Data field. This field can only be present if use of Fast Select was requested in the Call Request. In this case, the Called User data can contain up to 128 octets.

The following is the Clear Request packet format.

```
      8       7       6       5       4       3       2       1   Octet #
    +-------------------------------+-------------------------------+
    |            GFI                |           LCGN #              |   1
    +-------------------------------+-------------------------------+
    |              Logical Channel Number (LCN)                     |   2
    +---------------------------------------------------------------+
    |                    Packet Type Identifier                     |
    |    0       0       0       1       0       0       1       1 |   3
    +---------------------------------------------------------------+
    |                       Clearing Cause                          |   4
    +---------------------------------------------------------------+
    |                       Diagnostic Code                         |   5
    +---------------------------------------------------------------+
    |    Calling DTE addr len       |    Called DTE addr len        |   6
    +---------------------------------------------------------------+
    |                                                               |   7
    .                       DTE Addresses                           .
    .                                                               .
    |                                                               |
    +---------------------------------------------------------------+
    |                       Facility Length                         |
    +---------------------------------------------------------------+
    .                                                               .
    |                         Facilities                            |
    .                                                               .
    +---------------------------------------------------------------+
    .                                                               .
    |                       Clear User Data                         |
    .                                                               .
    +---------------------------------------------------------------+
```

Clear Request/Clear Indication packet format

As with the Call Accepted packet, the Clear Request packet can contain NS-user information only if Fast Select was requested in the Call Request packet. In this case, 128 octets of NS-user information can be passed in the Clear User Data field.

Once a Clear Request is received (as a Clear Indication), the receiving DTE sends back a Clear Confirm packet. This is shown below.

```
          8     7     6     5     4     3     2     1   Octet #
       +-----------------------------+-----------------------+
       |           GFI               |       LCGN #          |   1
       +-----------------------------+-----------------------+
       |          Logical Channel Number (LCN)               |   2
       +-----------------------------------------------------+
       |               Packet Type Identifier                |
       |    0     0     0     1     0     1     1     1      |   3
       +-----------------------------+-----------------------+
       |   Calling DTE addr len      |  Called DTE addr len  |   4
       +-----------------------------+-----------------------+
       .                                                     .   5
       |                                                     |
       .                  DTE Addresses                      .
       |                                                     |
       .                                                     .
       +-----------------------------------------------------+
       |                 Facility Length                     |
       +-----------------------------------------------------+
       .                                                     .
       |                    Facilities                       |
       .                                                     .
       +-----------------------------------------------------+
```

DTE/DCE Clear Confirmation packet format

If the Call Accepted packet is received by the DTE in response to its Call Request, it can enter into data transfer mode. This means that each DTE can send and receive data packets. The data packet format is given below.

```
          8     7     6     5     4     3     2     1   Octet #
       +-----------------------------+-----------------------+
       |   Q     D     0     1       |       LCGN #          |   1
       +-----------------------------+-----------------------+
       |          Logical Channel Number (LCN)               |   2
       +-----------------+-----+-----------------+-----------+
       |      P(R)       |  M  |      P(S)       |    0      |   3
       +-----------------+-----+-----------------+-----------+
```

```
  .                                                    .    4
  |              User Data                             |
  .                                                    .
  +----------------------------------------------------+
```

                    DTE/DCE Data packet format

The data packet is the only packet with a 0 in bit 1 of octet 3. The
rest of the bits in octet 3 of data packets are used for control information (related to flow control not discussed here), not for specifying
the packet type.

The above is only one of the possible packet formats. A 10 in bits 6
and 5 of octet 1 can specify a different packet format. The other
formats are not shown here. The M-bit (also More Data bit, bit 5 of
octet 3) is used to indicate that more "logically connected" data is to
follow in subsequent data packets. This bit is used to preserve the
logical boundaries of an NSDU segmented over multiple NPDU's
(DTE/DCE data packets).

The D-bit (bit 7 of octet 1) is used to request the delivery confirmation feature. The Q-bit (bit 8 of octet 1) is used to "qualify" the data.
It can be used, for example, to differentiate between user data and
control data. The control data (Q-bit set) can be used, for example, to
send parameters that are part of an SNDCP.

Either side may also send an "interrupt" to the other by sending
an interrupt packet. An interrupt packet is not subject to the flow
control of normal data and is handled out of band with respect to the
normal data on a connection. The interrupt packet format is given
below.

```
    8      7      6      5      4      3      2      1    Octet #
  +---------------------------+---------------------------+
  |          GFI              |         LCGN #            |    1
  +---------------------------+---------------------------+
  |          Logical Channel Number (LCN)                 |    2
  +-------------------------------------------------------+
  |   0      0      1      0      0      0      1      1 |    3
  +-------------------------------------------------------+
  .                                                       .    4
  |                       User Data                       |
  .                                                       .
  +-------------------------------------------------------+
```

                    DTE/DCE Interrupt packet format

1984 X.25 allows up to 32 octets of user information in the User data field, whereas 1980 X.25 allowed only 1 octet of user information.

Major Differences between 1980 X.25, 1984 X.25, and 1988 X.25 for CONS

1980 X.25 did not have the Address Extension facilities described in Annex G of the 1984 X.25 document. Thus, the only address information that can be carried in the defined fields of 1980 X.25 is the called and calling DTE addresses. Also missing in 1980 X.25 are the QOS parameter facilities and mandatory support of the Fast Select facility. Consequently, many implementations of 1980 X.25 subnetworks do not support the Fast Select facility. The Fast Select facility allows up to 128 octets of user information in the Call Request, Call Accepted, and Clear Request packets. Without this facility, the Call Request user information is limited to 16 octets and no user information can be passed in the Call Accepted and Clear Request packets.

The 1984 X.25 recommedation allows for 32 digits of network address information to be carried in the AEF parameter. Since an NSAP address can be 40 digits (or 20 octets), this is not enough for all NSAP addresses. The 1988 X.25 recommendation allows 40 digits in the AEF field.

1980 X.25 PLP allowed only 1 octet of user data in the interrupt packet. 1984 X.25 PLP allows 32 octets of user data in the interrupt packet.

The 1988 X.25 also has a feature that allows a Call Request to be "deflected" to another DTE address. The DTE that receives an Incoming Call packet can choose to deflect it to another DTE. The third DTE will receive the same Incoming Call packet, with an indication that the original call was deflected. This third DTE can accept the call, and the originating DTE can know the third DTE's address by examining the Responding DTE Address field. There will also be an indication in the Call Connected packet that the call was deflected by the DTE it was originally sent to.

Mapping of CONS Primitives to X.25 PLP

The mapping of CONS to X.25 PLP is described in ISO 8878 and CCITT X.223. One difference between the two is that X.223 does not specify how a mapping of the CONS can be achieved over 1980 X.25 subnetworks. Annex A of ISO 8878 specifies an SNDCP for mapping CONS to 1980 X.25.

Concepts and Protocols of the OSI Network Layer 137

The primary function of the SNDCP is to specify how the various CONS parameters are to be carried over 1980 X.25 packets. The most important of these parameters are the NSAP addresses, which cannot be conveyed by standard fields of the 1980 X.25 PLP fields. The SNDCP specifies how to convey the QOS parameters, among other parameters.

In practice, however, most of the existing implementations of CONS over 1980 X.25 subnetworks do not use the SNDCP specified in Annex A of ISO 8878. Instead, the calling and called NSAP addresses are restricted to a specific type of address that can be inferred from the calling and called DTE addresses. This is the type of NSAP address described above.

The QOS parameters are not conveyed using this approach, and neither is CONS-expedited data available. This approach, although unspecified as a valid approach in ISO/CCITT standards, is given temporary acceptance by implementors' agreements such as the NIST OSI Implementor's Workshop (OIW) (Clause 3.10.1 of Dec 1988 NIST OIW Agreements).

The following table details the mapping of the CONS primitives to X.25 PLP packets and parameters. There are two separate columns for the 1980 and 1984 X.25 subnetworks. Rather than describe the mappings that would result if one were using the SNDCP described in Annex A of ISO 8878 for 1980 X.25, instead we show the mapping when the SNDCP is null. This is the case for most existing implementations of CONS over 1980 X.25, such as SunNet OSI.

The following is the mapping for the CONS primitives and parameters for NC establishment phase:

CONS primitive/ parameter	1980 X.25 PLP packet (null SNDCP)	1984 X.25 PLP
N-CONNECT request	Call Request	Call Request
N-CONNECT indication	Incoming Call	Incoming Call
N-CONNECT response	Call Accepted	Call Accepted
N-CONNECT confirm	Call Connected	Call Connected
Called Address	Called DTE address	Called DTE Address + Called AEF
Calling Address	Calling DTE Address	Calling DTE Address + Calling AEF

CONS primitive/ parameter	1980 X.25 PLP packet (null SNDCP)	1984 X.25 PLP
Responding Address	Called DTE Address	Called DTE Address + Called AEF
Receipt Confirmation Selection	GFI Nybble (D-bit)	GFI nybble (D-bit)
Expedited Data Selection	–	Expedited Data Negotiation Facility
QOS Parameter Set	–	QOS Parameters Negotiation Facility
NS-user-Data	–	Call and Called User Data Field with Fast Select

The following is the mapping for the CONS primitives and parameters for NC release phase:

CONS primitive/ parameter	1980 X.25 PLP Packet (Null SNDCP)	1984 X.25 PLP
N-DISCONNECT-Request	Clear Request	Clear Request
N-DISCONNECT-Indication	Clear Indication Restart Indication Clear Request	Clear Indication Restart Indication Clear Requests
Originator and Reason	Cause Code and Diagnostic code	Cause Code and Diagnostic code
NS-user-Data	–	Clear User Data (with Fast Select)
Responding Address	Called DTE Address	Called DTE Address + Called AEF

Since 1980 X.25 does not mandate support of the Fast Select facility, no NS-user data is possible in the Call Request, Call Accepted, or the Clear Request packets.

Finally, the following is the mapping for the Data Transfer Phase:

CONS primitive/ parameter	1980 X.25 PLP packet (null SNDCP)	1984 X.25 PLP
N-DATA- Request	DATA	DATA
N-DATA-Indication	DATA	DATA
NS-user-Data	User Data, M-bit	User Data, M-bit
N-DATA-ACKNOWLEDGE-request	DATA, RR, RNR, REJ	DATA, RR, RNR, REJ
N-DATA-ACKNOWLEDGE-ind	DATA, RR, RNR, REJ	DATA, RR, RNR, REJ
N-EXPEDITED-DATA-request	–	Interrupt
NS-user-Data	–	Interrupt User Data
N-RESET-request	Reset Request	Reset Request
N-RESET-indication	Reset Indication Reset Request	Reset Indication Reset Request
N-RESET-response	–	–
N-RESET-request	–	–
Originator and Reason	Cause Code and Diagnostic Code Fields	Cause Code and Diagnostic Code Fields

Protocol to Provide the CLNS

ISO 8473 describes the Connectionless Network Layer Protocol (CLNP) which provides the CLNS. CLNP corresponds to the SNICP of the internal Network Layer architecture. It assumes a connectionless data-link protocol. Depending on the subnetwork type, an SNDCP (or more appropriately, SNDCF) may be required to provide this connectionless data-link protocol. For example, ISO 8473 specifies an SNDCF for mapping CLNP to a connection-oriented subnetwork such as an X.25 PSDN. This SNDCF makes the connection-oriented X.25 subnetwork appear as a connectionless medium on which a datagram unit may be sent.

An important funtionality offered by CLNP is the segmentation and reassembly of NSDU's into multiple NPDU's, and the segmentation of NPDU's into multiple NPDU's. If an NSDU is too large to be accommodated in a subnetwork data unit, CLNP will segment the NSDU into multiple NPDU's, each of which will individually fit in a subnetwork data unit.

It is the task of the remote network entity to reassemble the various segments of CLNP into one single segment and then pass it up to the NS-user. Sometimes an intermediate network entity may also perform the reassembly function if the subnetwork on which the reassembled NPDU is to be forwarded can handle the size of the reassembled NPDU in a single subnetwork data unit.

There is a timer associated with the reassembly function, so to avoid tying up system resources indefinitely on the system performing the reassembly. This timer is started when an incomplete NPDU (a segment) arrives at that network entity. If all the segments that comprise that NSDU arrive before this timer expires, then reassembly takes place and the reassembled NPDU is either delivered up to the NS-user or forwarded as the case may be. But if this timer expires while waiting for all the segments that make up that NSDU to arrive, then all the other NPDU segments are discarded.

The way segmentation is accomplished is by segmenting the data portion of the NSDU into small pieces. The size of the pieces is chosen such that once the N-PCI is added to the data portion, the combined piece, called a derived NPDU, will be small enough to fit in a single subnetwork data unit.

Each derived NPDU formed in this way contains information about which NSDU it belongs to, via a unique data unit identifier common to all segments of an NSDU, and by containing information regarding which piece of the original NSDU this is. This is accomplished by relating the beginning of the data portion of the derived NPDU segment to the offset in the data portion of the original NSDU. Also, each segment contains information on the total length of the original NSDU so that after reassembly is completed, the remote system can verify that all the segments are received.

There are two basic types of NPDU's. One is the DT-NPDU (Data NPDU), and the other is the ER-NPDU (Error NPDU). The DT-NPDU is used to convey the data of the N-UNITDATA request. The ER-NPDU is used to communicate information between network entities on errors or failures occurring before the NPDU can be delivered to the remote NS-user as an NSDU. The ER-NPDU comes (optionally) in response to the failure to deliver an NPDU and is generated by the destination network entity or some intermediate network entity.

The ER-NPDU information is not intended for the sending NS-user as much as for general system administration and error logging purposes by the originating network entity itself. The ER-NPDU does not have a corresponding service primitive to relay information back to the NS-user. Also, the addresses used in ER-NPDU's are Network Entity Titles, not NSAP addresses, meaning that the originating network entity is being informed of the failures, not the NS-user responsible for initiating the N-UNITDATA request. The NIST OIW agreements stipulate that the destination NET can be the same as the source NSAP address of the DT NPDU that caused the failure.

The general structure of DT- and ER-NPDU's is similar and is shown below:

```
+-------------------------------------------------+
|                  Fixed Part                     |
+-------------------------------------------------+
|                 Address Part                    |
+-------------------------------------------------+
|              Segmentation Part                  |
+-------------------------------------------------+
|                Options  Part                    |
+-------------------------------------------------+
|                     Data                        |
+-------------------------------------------------+
```

The fixed part has the following structure:

```
Bit#     8    7    6    5    4    3    2    1 Octet #
     +-------------------------------------------+
     | Network Layer Protocol Identifier (00 or 81(H)) |   1
     +-------------------------------------------+
     |         Length Indicator   (0-254)        |   2
     +-------------------------------------------+
     |    Version/Protocol ID Extension (01 H)   |   3
     +-------------------------------------------+
     |                 Lifetime                  |   4
     +----+----+----+---------------------------+
     | SP | MS | E/R|           Type            |   5
     +----+----+----+---------------------------+
```

```
|                  Segment Length                   |   6,7
+---------------------------------------------------+
|                     Checksum                      |   8,9
+---------------------------------------------------+
```

The Network Layer Protocol Identifier (the first octet in the NPDU) identifies the N-protocol being employed. This can be either 0 × 81 (Hex), which specifies ISO 8473, or 0 × 00, which specifies the Inactive Subset of ISO 8473.

If the Network Layer Protocol Identifier specifies the inactive subset (i.e., is 0 × 00), then there are no further octets in the fixed part, address part, segmentation part, or offset part, and this 0 × 00 octet is followed immediately by the data part. The inactive subset is run only on a single subnetwork, where no segmentation of an NSDU to mutiple NPDU's is required, and the NSAP addresses can be inferred from the subnetwork addresses. This can be true of a class of NSAP addresses that contain in them the subnetwork addresses.

If the Network Layer Protocol Identifier is 0 × 81 (Hex), then the rest of the fixed part octets are present, as is the address part. The segmentation part is present conditional on a flag in the fixed part of the header. The options part may not always be present either. Its presence is determined by examining the remainder of the header, after the fixed, address, and segmentation parts are processed. If there is still header data left to be processed, as indicated by the header length field, then this is the options part.

The second octet, if not running inactive, specifies the header length, and has a maximum value of 254 (decimal). The header length is the combined length of the fixed part, address part, segmentation part, and options part. It does not include the length of the data part. The value of 255 decimal is reserved and cannot be used as a header length.

The third octet is the version number and is always 01. The fourth octet is the PDU lifetime, which is a binary number representing the remaining lifetime of the NPDU in units of 500 milliseconds. It is set by the originating network entity, and as the NPDU is relayed from one network entity to another through interconnected subnetworks, this value is decreased by each of the network entities. This is normally decreased by 1, unless the sum of the transit delay in the underlying subnetwork and the local processing delay is estimated to be greater than 500 ms. In this case it is decreased by 1 for each estimated 500-ms combined delay. In SunNet OSI, this field is set to 16 by default. This allows the NPDU to traverse 16 500-ms hops before being discarded.

When the lifetime parameter reaches zero before reaching the final destination, it is to be discarded by that network entity. This can be used to prevent NPDU's from being caught in routing loops, and thereby congesting the network indefinitely.

The fifth octet is used to carry three flag bits and the type of the NPDU. The low 5 bits of octet 5 specify the NPDU type. For a DT-NPDU these bits are 11100, and for an ER-NPDU they are 00001. These are the only two allowed values for the type field in the fifth octet of the fixed part. The DT-NPDU is the NPDU most commonly used, and it provides the functionality of the N-UNITDATA service primitive. The ER-NPDU is used to inform the originating network entity of forwarding or other problems.

The generation of ER-NPDU's is controlled by the originating network entity by setting the E/R (Error Report) flag, which is bit 6 in the fifth octet. If this flag is 0, error report PDU's (ER-NPDU's) are not generated. If it is set to 1, then error report PDU's are generated if the NPDU is dropped somewhere along the way because of congestion, inability to find a route, or for some other reason. It should be clear, however, that the presence of ER-NPDUs does not make the CLNP a reliable protocol. In particular, nonreceipt of an ER-NPDU does not imply correct delivery of an NPDU.

The other two flags in the fifth octet of the fixed part of the header contain information for segmenting the NPDU. If the SP (segmentation permitted) flag, which is bit 8 of the fifth octet, is set to 1, then this NPDU may be segmented if it is to traverse a subnetwork on which this is necessary. If this flag is 0, then this NPDU may not be segmented on any intervening subnetwork. This flag is set by the originating network entity and (like the rest of the fixed part of the NPDU header) may not be changed by intermediate network entities. If the SP flag is not set, and the NPDU is to traverse a subnetwork that has a subnetwork service data unit size too small for that NPDU, then an error report PDU will be generated by that network entity, indicating its inability to forward the NPDU because segmentation is not permitted, provided that the E/R flag was set in the same NPDU. Furthermore, if the SP flag is not set, then the segmentation part of the NPDU header is not present.

The MS (more segments) flag, which is bit 7 of the fifth octet, indicates whether this NPDU is the NPDU containing the last octet of the user data of the N-UNITDATA service primitive. If this flag is cleared to 0, then this is the last (or only) segment of the NSDU; if it is set to 1 then this is not the last NPDU segment corresponding to the NSDU (either the first or some intervening NPDU). This flag may only be 1 if the SP flag is set to 1.

Octets 6 and 7 contain the total length of the NPDU, including the entire header and data portion, in octets. Octets 8 and 9 contain the checksum of the entire PDU header. The checksum does not include the data portion of NPDU. Usually, another checksum is employed for the data portion of the NPDU by a higher layer protocol, such as the transport layer, as part of the PCI of the higher layer protocol. A zero-valued checksum is used to indicate that the checksum field should be ignored. The checksum algorithm ensures that a zero value will not be generated through normal processing.

The address part has the following structure:

```
                                                        Octet #
+-----------------------------------------------------+
|        Destination Address Length Indicator        |    10
+-----------------------------------------------------+
|                                                     |    11
|                 Destination Address                 |
|                                                     |
.                                                     .
|                                                     |   m-1
+-----------------------------------------------------+
|          Source Address Length Indicator            |    m
+-----------------------------------------------------+
|                                                     |   m+1
|                   Source Address                    |
.                                                     .
|                                                     |   n-1
+-----------------------------------------------------+
```

The addresses that are passed in this part are NSAP addresses. They are always encoded using the preferred binary encoding specified in ISO 8348 Add. 2, and described above in the section on NSAP addresses. These addresses are of variable length, the length of each of them specified in a length field octet. As described above, ISO 8348 Add. 2 limits the preferred binary encodings to a maximum of 20 octets. Thus, the maximum length of each NSAP address as carried by by CLNP is never more than 20 octets. First comes the length of the destination NSAP address, then the destination NSAP address itself, then the length of the source NSAP address, and then the source NSAP address itself, as shown in the figure above. These source and destination NSAP addresses correspond to the source and destination NSAP addresses of the N-UNITDATA-request service primitive. Both NSAP addresses are encoded using the preferred binary encoding rules described above.

Concepts and Protocols of the OSI Network Layer

The segmentation part consists of six octets as shown below. This part is present only if the SP flag in the fixed part of the header is set to 1.

```
                                                              Octet #
+----------------------------------------------------+
|               Data Unit Identifier                 |   n,n+1
+----------------------------------------------------+
|                  Segment Offset                    |   n+2,n+3
+----------------------------------------------------+
|                   Total Length                     |   n+4,n+5
+----------------------------------------------------+
```

The Data Unit Identifier (DUI) (two octets) is the same for all the derived segments of a PDU. This may be all the derived segments corresponding to a single NSDU. The DUI stays the same for an NPDU no matter how many times it gets segmented further on intervening subnetworks.

The segment offset (two octets) is the offset in number of octets from the beginning of user data as seen from the point of view of the original NSDU from which the NPDU's are derived. Thus, the first NPDU segment corresponding to an NSDU has a segment offset of 0. This offset must always be a multiple of 8. This implies that NPDU segments must be made on eight octet boundaries. The Total Length field of the segmentation part specifies the total length of the NPDU, including the data and header portion.

Following the segmentation part is the options part, which is not always present. It is present only if there is header data left to be processed, as indicated by the total header length (given by the Length Indicator field in the Fixed Part), after processing the segmentation part. The options part contains optional parameters, which can be in any order in the options part. Each parameter is identified by a parameter code, indicating the type of parameter, the parameter length in octets, and then the parameter value.

The format is as shown below:

```
(k = n+6)
                                                              Octet #
+----------------------------------------------------+
|                  Parameter Code                    |      k
+----------------------------------------------------+
|            Parameter Length (e.g., 1)              |      k+1
+----------------------------------------------------+
```

```
    |                                                      |    k+2
    +                                                      +
    .              Parameter Value                         .
    +                                                      +
    |                                                      |    k+1+l
    +------------------------------------------------------+
```

This general format is repeated until the end of the header.

There are various types of optional parameters listed in ISO 8473. Some have to do with security, priority, and routing. They are described below.

The padding parameter is used to lengthen the NPDU header length to a convenient value. This may be used, e.g., to ensure that the data always begins at a fixed offset in the NPDU, even though the NSAP address lengths may yield differing fixed part header sizes for different addresses. The code corresponding to this parameter is 0 × CC (Hex). The parameter length is variable, and the value can be anything, since it most likely will be ignored.

Another parameter is the Security Parameter, which is used to assign a security level to an NPDU. This has the parameter code 0 × C5 (Hex). Its length is variable. The first octet specifies the type of security option being employed. This is encoded in the two high order bits of the first octet. If the two high order bits are 01, then it indicates a Source Address-specific parameter in the remaining parameter value octets. This implies that the security level is to be understood in the context of the classification system employed by the authority responsible for assigning the source NSAP address.

If the two high order bits are 10, then the security level parameter is to be understood in the context of the security classification system employed by the authority assigning the destination NSAP address. If the two high order bits are 11, then the security parameter is to be understood in the context of a globally unique security classification system. ISO 8473 does not specify what this globally unique classification system is. The rest of the bits of the first octet are always zero. The remainder of the octets are then used in the appropriate context as defined by the two high order bits of the first octet.

Another parameter is the Source Routing parameter. It has a parameter code equal to 0 × C8 (Hex). This is used to specify a route to be followed by the NPDU in terms of a list of network entities that the NPDU should traverse. This can be specified either as a complete list, meaning that all network entities to be traversed are in the list, or it can be a partial list, meaning that some network entities are listed, but there may be holes in the list.

Whether a complete or partial source route is in effect is specified by the the first octet of the parameter value octets. If this has the value 0×00 then a partial source route is specified in the remaining octets. If it has a value of 0×01 (Hex) then a complete source route is specified. If a complete source route is specified, and any one of the network entities is unreachable, then the NPDU is to be discarded. If a partial source route is specified, and one of the entities listed cannot be reached in the order specified, even through other unlisted network entities, then the NPDU is also to be discarded.

The second octet in the Source Route parameter value gives the offset where the Network Entity Title list begins. This is an offset from the beginning of the parameter value field. Then each entry of the list follows in succession. An entry consists of the length of each network entity title in octets, followed by the Network Entity Title itself.

The Recording of Route parameter has the parameter code $0 \times 8B$ (Hex). This parameter is used to instruct each network entity the NPDU passes through to record its title in the parameter value portion of the field. The total length of this parameter is set by the originator of the NPDU and does not change as the NPDU traverses various network entities. As the NPDU passes through a network entity, the network entity records its title at the end of the list that is formed in the parameter value portion of this parameter. Each new addition is added to the end of the list. The second octet of the parameter value portion is used to record the offset of the first unused octet in the parameter value portion. This is where a new Network Entity Title entry may be recorded. When there is no more space left, a value of $0 \times FF$ (Hex) in the second octet is used to indicate that route recording has terminated because no space is available in the recording of route parameter. In this case, network entities are still to forward the NPDU, albeit without making any additions to the recording of route parameter. The first octet is used to indicate whether complete or partial recording of route is in effect. This octet is identical to the first octet of the Source Route parameter described above. Each Network Entity Title is also identical with the one used in the Source Route parameter, i.e., the length followed by the network entity title itself.

If complete recording of route is in effect and an NPDU is segmented prior to reaching an intermediate network entity, the NPDU is reassembled only if all the segments took the same route. If they did not all take the same route, the PDU is discarded, and an ER PDU (if requested by the initiator) is generated.

If partial route recording is in effect and an NPDU has segmented prior to reaching an intermediate network entity, it may be reassembled even if the various segments took different routes. In this case, the route used by any one of them may be appended to the recording of route parameter of the reassembled NPDU.

The Quality of Service Maintenance parameter has the code 0 × C3 (Hex). It is used to convey information about the quality of the service parameter specified in the N-UNITDATA service primitive requested by the NS-user. Intermediate network entities can optionally make use of this information when processing an NPDU for forwarding and choosing the appropriate route.

As with the security parameter, the standard allows for mutiple QOS schemes to be employed. These schemes are classified in the same manner as the security parameter, i.e., they can be defined by the authority for assigning the source NSAP address, the authority for assigning the destination NSAP address, or a globally unique QOS scheme. While the first two schemes are left for the authorities that allocate various NSAP's, and hence an arbitrary number of schemes can be employed in total, the standard does specify the globally unique QOS scheme.

The parameter length is variable. The first octet of the parameter specifies the type of scheme being employed. As with the security parameter, a value of 01 for the two high order bits of the first octet specify the scheme defined by the authority for assigning the source NSAP address of the NPDU; a value of 10 is used for the scheme assigned by the authority for assigning the destination NSAP address. A value of 11 for the two high order bits of the first octet specifies a globally unique QOS scheme. The globally uniqe QOS scheme is described below.

When the globally unique QOS scheme is being employed, the parameter length is 1, and the remaining six bits of the first octet specify the QOS parameters. The bits are used as follows.

Bit 6 is reserved, and should not be used. When set to 1, bit 5 is used to indicate that a routing decision should be used to favor sending all NPDU's to the same destination NSAP address using the same path, and not optimize the routing decisions based on the best path to minimize the transit delay (i.e., time to reach the destination). This is in order to maximize the chances of preserving the order of delivering the NPDU's as they were received by the intermediate network entity. If the value of this bit is 0, then the network entity processing this NPDU should prefer the low transit delay option in favor of preserving the NPDU order by choosing the same path, even if the low transit delay option means different paths for different NPDU's going to the same destination NSAP address.

Bit 4 is the congestion experienced bit. It is set to zero by the originating network entity. If an intermediate network entity experiences congestion (e.g., lack of resources such as memory buffers) while processing this NPDU, that intermediate system will set this bit to 1, which will remain 1 until the NPDU reaches the destination end system. This is to notify the destination system that the path the NPDU traversed was experiencing congestion and the end system can take whatever action is necessary to alleviate the congestion condition.

Bit 3 is the transit delay vs. low cost bit. If this bit is set to 1, it specifies that, if possible, the decision on the route should favor low transit delay over a lower cost route. This is in case multiple routes exist to the same destination with different estimated values of transit delay and cost.

Bit 2 is the residual error probability vs. transit delay bit. If set to 1, it specifies that the choice of the route should favor the one with the lower residual error probability over the one with the lower transit delay. If it is set to 0, the sense is reversed, and the routing decision should favor the route with the lower transit delay, as opposed to the one with the lower residual error probability.

Bit 1 is the residual error probability vs. cost bit. If it is set to 1, it indicates that the choice of route should favor the one with the lower residual probability over the one with the lower cost. The residual error probability is the estimate of total lost/corrupted NPDU's to the total number of NPDU's transmitted on that subnetwork. If this bit is set to 0, then the sense is reversed and a lower cost route is to be favored over one with a lower residual error probability.

The last parameter defined for the options portion of the header in ISO 8473 is the Priority parameter. It is used to specify the relative priority of the NPDU in comparison with other NPDU's. This relative priority is to be used by the various network entities in allocating resources for this NPDU, as well as in ordering this NPDU for transmission. A higher priority means giving preference to this NPDU in allocating memory buffers and picking an earlier outbound slot on the transmission queue for this NPDU. The parameter code is $0 \times CD$ (Hex); its length is always 1. The parameter value ranges from 0×00 (lowest priority) to $0 \times 0E$ (highest priority). Thus a total of 15 priority levels is possible. All other values for the parameter value are reserved. If an intermediate system does not support the priority option, it treats all NPDU's as if they had a priority level of 0.

Following the options part of the NPDU is the data portion.

To summarize, there are two kinds of NPDU's defined in 8473. One is the DT (data) NPDU, and the other is the ER-NPDU. The overall DT-NPDU format follows.

```
Bit#      8    7    6    5    4    3    2    1         Octet #
      +----------------------------------------------+
      |    Network Layer Protocol Identifier (81(H)) |      1
      +----------------------------------------------+
      |           Length Indicator (0-254)           |      2
      +----------------------------------------------+
      |       Version/Protocol ID Extension (01 H)   |      3
      +----------------------------------------------+
      |                   Lifetime                   |      4
      +----+----+----+------------------------------+
      | SP | MS | E/R|   1    1    1    0    0     |      5
      +----+----+----+------------------------------+
      |               Segment Length                 |     6,7
      +----------------------------------------------+
      |                  Checksum                    |     8,9
      +----------------------------------------------+
      |     Destination Address Length Indicator     |     10
      +----------------------------------------------+
      |                                              |     11
      |             Destination Address              |
      .                                              .
      |                                              |     m-1
      +----------------------------------------------+
      |       Source Address Length Indicator        |      m
      +----------------------------------------------+
      |                                              |     m+1
      |               Source Address                 |
      .                                              .
      |                                              |     n-1
      +----------------------------------------------+
      |             Data Unit Identifier             |    n,n+1
      +----------------------------------------------+
      |                Segment Offset                |   n+2,n+3
      +----------------------------------------------+
      |                 Total Length                 |   n+4,n+5
      +----------------------------------------------+
      |                                              |    n+6
      |                   Options                    |
      |                                              |
      |                                              |    p-1
      +----------------------------------------------+
      |                                              |     p
      |                    Data                      |
      |                                              |
      .                                              .
      |                                              |     z
      +----------------------------------------------+
```

Concepts and Protocols of the OSI Network Layer 151

Under the Inactive Network Layer protocol, the DT-NPDU looks like this:

```
                                                     Octet #
   +-------------------------------------------------+
   |     Network Layer Protocol Identifier (00)      |    1
   +-------------------------------------------------+
   |                                                 |    2
   |                                                 |
   |                     Data                        |
   .                                                 .
   |                                                 |    z
   +-------------------------------------------------+
```

The full structure of the ER-NPDU is as follows.

```
Bit #     8    7    6    5    4    3    2    1            Octet #
        +-------------------------------------------------+
        |     Network Layer Protocol Identifier (81(H))   |    1
        +-------------------------------------------------+
        |            Length Indicator (0-254)             |    2
        +-------------------------------------------------+
        |        Version/Protocol ID Extension (01 H)     |    3
        +-------------------------------------------------+
        |                    Lifetime                     |    4
        +----+----+------+-------------------------------+
        |SP=0|MS=0|resvd |   0    0    0    0    1      |    5
        +----+----+------+-------------------------------+
        |                 Segment Length                  |   6,7
        +-------------------------------------------------+
        |                    Checksum                     |   8,9
        +-------------------------------------------------+
        |      Destination Address Length Indicator       |   10
        +-------------------------------------------------+
        |                                                 |   11
        |              Destination Address                |
        .                                                 .
        |                                                 |   m-1
        +-------------------------------------------------+
        |        Source Address Length Indicator          |   m
        +-------------------------------------------------+
        |                                                 |   m+1
        |                 Source Address                  |
        .                                                 .
        |                                                 |   n-1
        +-------------------------------------------------+
        |                                                 |   n+6
        |                    Options                      |
        |                                                 |
        |                                                 |   p-1
        +-------------------------------------------------+
        |                                                 |   p
        |               Reason for Discard                |
        |                                                 |
        .                                                 .
        |                                                 |   z
```

```
+-------------------------------------------------+
|                                                 |   z+1
|                                                 |
|                     Data                        |
|                                                 |
|                                                 |   z
+-------------------------------------------------+
```

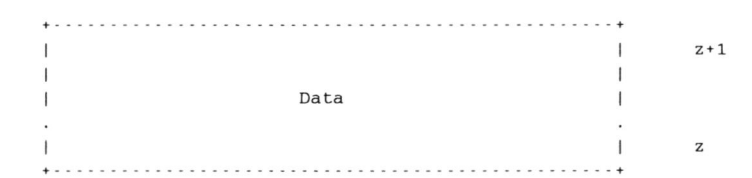

For the ER-NPDU, the destination NSAP address field specifies the Network Entity Title of the originator of the discarded PDU. The Source Address specifies the Network Entity Title of the intermediate system or end system generating the ER- NPDU. The ER-NPDU is never segmented and thus never has a segmentation portion.

In the options portion of the ER-NPDU, in addition to all the parameters possible for the DT-NPDU described above, there is an additional parameter called the Reason for Discard parameter. It has a parameter code of 0 × C1 (Hex) and always has a length of two octets. The first of the two octets contains an error code. If the error occurred while processing a specific field of the DT-NPDU, then the octet number of the beginning of that field is in the second octet. If the error cannot be localized in this fashion, or if it was a checksum error, then the second octet contains zero.

The error code contained in the first octet of the parameter value of the Reason for Discard parameter has the following values with the associated meanings.

Error code (hex)	Class of Error	Meaning of Error Code
00	General	Reason Not Specified
01	General	Protocol Procedure Error
02	General	Incorrect Checksum
03	General	PDU Discarded due to Congestion
04	General	Header Syntax Error (cannot be parsed)
05	General	Segmentation Needed but Not Permitted
06	General	Incomplete PDU Received
07	General	Duplicate Option
80	Address	Destination Address Unreachable
81	Address	Destination Address Unknown

Error code (hex)	Class of Error	Meaning of Error Code
90	Source Routing	Unspecified Source Routing Error
91	Source Routing	Syntax Error in Source Routing Field
92	Source Routing	Unknown Address in Source Routing Field
93	Source Routing	Path Not Acceptable
A0	Lifetime	Lifetime Expired while PDU in Transit
A1	Lifetime	Lifetime Expired in Reassembly
B0	PDU Discarded	Unsupported Option Not Specified
B1	PDU Discarded	Unsupported Protocol Version
B2	PDU Discarded	Unsupported Security Option
B3	PDU Discarded	Unsupported Source Routing Option
B4	PDU Discarded	Unsupported Recording of Route Option
C0	Reassembly	Reassembly Interference

Mapping CLNP to an X.25 Subnetwork

The mapping of CLNP, which assumes a connectionless data-link service, to an X.25 subnetwork, which is connection-oriented, requires the use of an SNDCF. The SNDCF is described in ISO 8473. It should be understood that the X.25 subnetwork is being used as a data-link service, not a Network Layer service as when it is used to provide the CONS. Because of this, whether the X.25 subnetwork is based on the 1980 recommendation or later is not as important, since all of the N-PCI is being carried by the CLNP protocol. The X.25 PLP protocol headers do not carry any N-PCI, and only provide an SN-UNITDATA (SubNetwork Unitdata) service to CLNP. The entire CLNP NPDU, both header and data, is passed in the data portion of the X.25 PLP data packets. In contrast with CONS, the N-PCI is carried as part of the header of the X.25 PLP packets. Only the user data portion of the CONS NSDU's is passed in the data portion of the X.25 packets.

The primary function of the CLNP to X.25 SNDCF is to create and tear down virtual circuits for passing the CLNP ER- and DT-NPDU's. When the CLNP network entity receives an N-UNITDATA request from the NS-user, it performs its protocol function and generates one or more NPDU's. These NPDU's are to be passed as the user-data of an SN-UNITDATA request. The SN-UNITDATA request contains as parameters the calling and called subnetwork addresses. These calling and called subnetwork addresses for an X.25 PSDN are the calling and called DTE addresses.

When the SNDCF receives this SN-UNITDATA request, it determines if there is already a virtual circuit established with the desired DTE. If so, it simply sends the CLNP PDU as user data of an X.25 PLP data packet. Otherwise, it keeps the CLNP PDU and tries to establish a virtual circuit with the desired DTE and goes through the Call Request and Call Confirm sequence. Once it has established a virtual circuit with the remote DTE, it sends the saved CLNP PDU. The remote side can then use the same virtual circuit for sending CLNP PDU's to the side that initiated the virtual circuit.

In establishing this virtual circuit, the SNDCF will pass as user data on the Call Request, a Protocol Identification of ISO 8473. This is the first octet of the Call Request user data field and is the same as the Network Layer Protocol Identifier octet of the CLNP PDU. This octet, which is the first octet of the CLNP PDU, is either 0×81 (Hex) or 0×00 (Hex), depending on whether full 8473 or the inactive subset is being employed.

The SNDCF may, as a local option, time out the virtual circuit after a certain amount of inactivity. In SunNet OSI, for example, the virtual circuit manager program (which is an implementation of the SNDCF) takes as a startup option the amount of time to keep the virtual circuit up. If no CLNP PDU's are sent or received during this time, the virtual circuit manager program will send a clear request to the remote DTE, thereby terminating the virtual circuit.

The SNDCF described in ISO 8473 specifies that, under normal circumstances, only one virtual circuit will be maintained between a pair of DTE's. If a new Call Request comes in to establish a virtual circuit with a DTE that already has a virtual circuit associated with it, the old virtual circuit is cleared and the new one is accepted.

In case the two DTE's initiate Call Requests simultaneously, which is termed a call collision, the SNDCF provides a way to pick only one of the Call Requests to result in a virtual circuit. This condition is detected if a Call Request is received from a DTE to which a Call Request was sent, but from which the Call Confirm has not yet been received. In this case, the DTE addresses of the two DTE's are compared. If the DTE addresses are of different lengths, the shorter one is padded with zeros on the left-hand side (most significant side) to be the same length as the longer one. Starting from the least significant digit, each digit of the two addresses is compared. The first digit found to be different between the two addresses is used to determine which DTE's call request is to succeed. The one with the higher digit is to have its call request confirmed. The other one is cleared by the SNDCF of the DTE with the higher digit.

If for reasons of reliability or throughput, multiple virtual circuits are desired between a pair of DTE's, then this is accomplished by passing in a Subnetwork Connection Reference (SNCR) in the Call User data field. This SNCR field follows the protocol discrimination octet, which is the first octet of the call user data. Octets 2 through 5 contain the SNCR. Octet 2 contains the length of this parameter, which is always 0 × 04 (Hex); octet 3 contains the SNCR version number, which is always 0 × 02 (Hex); and octets 4 and 5 contain the SNCR value. The value contained in these last two octets is chosen arbitrarily.

The call collision detection procedure described above is only followed if the SNCR value contained in the Call Request is the same. If no SNCR parameter is passed, then the SNCR value is assumed to be zero. Thus, an SNCR value is always communicated, either implicitly or explicitly, by sending four extra octets in the call user data. If the SNCR values are different, then both parties of a call collision are allowed to establish virtual circuits. This allows a large number of virtual circuits to be established between a pair of DTE's to improve, e.g., throughput, by using different SNCR values for new virtual circuits.

Mapping CLNP to 8802-2 Subnetworks

ISO 8802-2 described two classes of data-link protocols, termed Logical Link Control (LLC) protocols. These are run over various IEEE LAN's, such as 802.3 (CSMA/CD similar to Ethernet), 802.4 (Token Bus), 802.5 (Token Ring), and FDDI (100 Mbits/sec Fiber Optic LAN). The two classes are LLC-1 and LLC-2. LLC-1 provides for a connectionless unacknowledged data-link protocol. This is precisely the kind of data-link service assumed by CLNP. Thus, over various 8802-2 subnetworks, a CLNP PDU is carried as the data portion of the LLC-1 PDU's. The LLC-1 PDU's used to carry CLNP are the UI (Unnumbered Information) frames. No explicit SNDCP is carried or required to run CLNP over an 8802-2 subnetwork.

Network Layer Routing

The task of routing consists of finding a path, which is an ordered list of network entities, that an NPDU has to traverse in order to reach the destination ES.

On any given open system, the task of finding the path can be reduced to one of finding the next network entity to which the NPDU is to be forwarded. The next network entity has to be one that is adjacent to the network entity making the decision. An adjacent entity is one that is directly on one of the subnetworks to which the sending/forwarding network entity is connected.

The next network entity may be the destination ES itself, or the first of many IS network entities which, when concatenated, lead to the destination ES. From the point of view of the network entity, the task is further reduced to finding the SNPA address and the local subnetwork to which this next network entity is attached. Thus, a "route" for the purposes of this discussion means a tuple of the form

```
{Destination NSAP Address, Next SNPA Address, local subnetwork}
```

The routing table consists of an arbitrary number of entries of the general form above.

There are four basic ways of accomplishing the task of determining the next network entity to which an NPDU is to be forwarded. One way is static configuration of routing information. Another is algorithmic determination of routing information from the destination NSAP address. One can also employ a routing protocol operating at the Network Layer to disseminate this information. Lastly, one can use a network management protocol operating at the OSI application layer to affect routing decisions. This last approach will not be considered further here, apart from noting that once done, its effect is the same as if the information was statically configured.

Static Configuration of Routing Information

Full Destination NSAP Address Matching

The simplest way to configure a route statically is to manually enter the full route in a table somewhere. In SunNet OSI, such an entry is called a "host" entry, in that it identifies a specific ES (host) for which the entry is being made. Such a route entry takes a full destination NSAP address, an SNPA address, and the corresponding subnetwork identifier. An example of such an entry, which is entered in a routes file is:

```
host llc0 '[(user-defined) 490010203040506000]' '(802)
8:0:20:7:f9:96,fe'
```

In this case the entry is specified by

```
entry type, subnetwork, destination NSAP Address, SNPA Address
```

The subnetwork field identifies a particular interface "llc0," which is an LLC-1 interface on top of an 802.3 interface. The destination NSAP address is specified in hexadecimal syntax. The routing algorithm first searches for all complete matches of the destination NSAP address in the routing table to find an entry that contains it. If it finds such an entry, it uses the associated subnetwork and SNPA address to send the NPDU on.

Partial Matching of Destination NSAP Address

In an OSI network, it is expected that there will be a large number of end systems that will need to be reached. Keeping an explicit entry for each such system would require impractically large tables. One way to simplify this problem is to take advantage of the structure of NSAP addresses. When assigning NSAP addresses, certain prefixes are associated with certain subnetworks or certain "areas." This way a single routing entry can be used for an entire subnetwork or area.

After this is done, all systems having a certain class of NSAP addresses (such as sharing a certain address prefix) that are reachable through a particular IS can have one entry in the routing table for them. This entry would specify the class of NSAP addresses to which it is applicable (either by specifying an address prefix or, more generally, by specifying the common bit pattern these addresses would share) and the SNPA address and subnetwork on which the IS is reachable. This is what is meant by partial matching of NSAP addresses. The routing algorithm on SunNet OSI, for example, searches all the partial NSAP address entries if it doesn't find a full NSAP address match in the routing table. It is possible that there are prefixes that are subsets of other prefixes in different routing entries. In such cases the longest matching prefix entries are selected.

Default Routing Entry

If no match is found in either the fully specified NSAP addresses or the partially specified NSAP addresses, then a default IS may be selected. This default is specified in SunNet OSI by specifying a zero length prefix entry.

Algorithmic Determination of Routing Information

There are a number of ways to algorithmically determine the SNPA address from the NSAP address. One way is to take advantage of the fact that all the ES's on certain subnetworks have NSAP addresses that contain the SNPA address and subnetwork information, e.g., OSINET address formats. In the case in which an ES is directly connected to such a subnetwork, the SNPA address can be extracted directly from the NSAP address.

For CONS over X.25 subnetworks, when using NSAP addresses with an AFI of 36, the IDI contains the X.121 SNPA address (DTE address), so SNPA extraction can be performed on this class of NSAP addresses as well.

Routing Protocols at the Network Layer

The third alternative is to distribute the routing information through the network by means of Network Layer routing protocols. An advantage of this method is that these protocols can take into account changes in the network, in particular changes in the network topology caused by various IS's becoming inoperable or links going down. All traffic going through these IS's or links would have to be rerouted. The dynamic nature of network protocols can make this rerouting possible.

The OSI routing protocols use a distributed adaptive approach to routing. It is "distributed" in the sense that there is no central control of the global Routing Information Base (RIB). Rather, this global RIB is maintained by multiple cooperating network and application layer entities. It is "adaptive" in that systems sense changes in their local environment and compute new paths based on these changes.

In a large network, such as a global network, it is impractical for every ES to maintain a complete map of the network topology. In OSI, this problem of distributing and maintaining routing information through the network is solved by placing the network entities

Concepts and Protocols of the OSI Network Layer 159

into a multilevel hierarchy. At each level, network entities have access only to a subset of the routing information, but a sufficient subset to allow them to reach the next level in the hierarchy, until finally the NPDU is relayed to the destination ES. Naturally, the set formed by combining the subsets of information present at each level in the hierarchy should result in a complete global routing table. For reasons of practicality and scalability, this global RIB is distributed through various levels of the hierarchy. Each network entity is in one or more levels of the hierarchy. By decomposing the problem into this multilevel hierarchy, there is an immediate gain that a network entity deals with a reasonable size of the RIB, because it has to keep only a portion of it. A secondary gain is that different protocols can be employed at different levels of the hierarchy, simplifying the global routing problem into smaller, and hence simpler, problems.

The first level of the hierarchy is created by making a distinction between the two basic classes of network entities, ESs and ISs. You may recall that ES's only originate and receive NPDU's, but do not forward them. An IS has the task of forwarding NPDU's. Along this line, the routing protocols are divided into two basic types of protocols, ES-IS and IS-IS. The ES-IS protocols communicate information between ES's and IS's, whereas the IS-IS protocols communicate routing information between IS's.

The ES-IS protocols have a scope limited to a single subnetwork. They communicate information between all ES's and all IS's on a single subnetwork. These protocols do not consider intersubnetwork issues. This falls in the purview of the IS-IS protocols. An advantage of this approach is that implementation of the ES-IS protocol on an ES is very simple. This is important because in a typical OSI network there will be order of magnitude more end systems thatn in intermediate systems. Thus, keeping the protocol simple that has to execute on an ES translates to hiding the complexity of the routing problem to a limited number of network entities, the IS's.

ES-IS Routing Protocols

There are two basic ES-IS protocols, one for each type of network layer protocol. Thus, there is an ES-IS protocol, ISO 9542, for use in conjuction with CLNP and there is another ES-IS protocol (ISO 10030) for use in conjunction with ISO 8878/X.25 (protocols for CONS).

ES-IS for Use with CLNP (ISO 9542) The basic operation of this protocol is to transfer routing information between ES's and IS's by means of exchanging NPDU's. The essence of the protocol is very simple. Periodically, each ES transmits an end system hello (ESH), an NPDU containing all its local NSAP addresses, to a multicast address that is destined for all IS's on that subnetwork. The IS records information about all these NSAP addresses and the SNPA address from which this ESH came. Over time, it builds up a table of all the NSAP addresses and corresponding SNPA addresses for all the ES's on the subnetwork.

Similarly, the IS's periodically send out information about their NET's and corresponding SNPA addresses destined for all the ES's on the subnetwork. In time, if there is an IS on the subnetwork, the ES learns of its presence by receiving one of these NPDU's, called an intermediate system hello (ISH).

The way this communication is established is through well-known multicast SNPA addresses. This solves the chicken and egg problem of how to send information to a network entity if you do not have its SNPA address. There is a well-known address called the All-ES Multicast Address, through which all ES's can be reached. Similarly, there is a well-known multicast address, called the All-IS Multicast Address, which the ES's can use to send information to all IS's on the subnetwork to which they are attached. This assumes that the subnetwork supports the concept of multicasting, i.e., using a single SNPA address to reach a number of systems. This is true of all the IEEE 802 LAN's, such as 802.3, 802.4, FDDI, etc., but not X.25 PSDN's.

One stipulated way for the routing process to proceed is that, given no static routing information, an ES knows no route. As it needs to send an NPDU for which it doesn't have a route, it sends it to an IS on the subnetwork. The IS, which is assumed to have access to global routing information, has the task of forwarding the NPDU. This NPDU may be forwarded to an ES or IS on the same subnetwork as the originator of the NPDU, or it may be on another subnetwork. If the destination ES is on another subnetwork, the IS simply forwards the NPDU to the appropriate network entity, and that is the end of it. But, if the ES or IS is on the same subnetwork, then the IS can tell the originating ES that this is the case by sending a Redirect (RD) NPDU.

The RD-PDU contains information about the destination NSAP address and its corresponding SNPA address. If the NPDU was forwarded to another IS on the same subnetwork, not an ES, then the RD-PDU also contains the NET of this IS, informing the originating ES that this new IS is a better path for that NSAP address.

Concepts and Protocols of the OSI Network Layer 161

Optionally, the RD-PDU can contain information that applies not just to the destination NSAP address of the NPDU being forwarded, but to a class of NSAP addresses to which the given NSAP address belongs. This information can be in the form of the partial NSAP address matching described above for static routing. By means of specifying a bit pattern in the NSAP address, the redirect information can be made applicable to the class of NSAP addresses that match that bit pattern.

Another type of information that may be present in the RD-PDU concerns embedded SNPA addresses in the NSAP address. By specifying which bits, if any, in the NSAP address correspond to an SNPA address, along with the class of NSAP addresses to which this is applicable, the class being specified as described above, the originating ES receiving the RD-PDU can in the future perform SNPA extraction for that class of NSAP addresses. An ES can, at its option, use the redirect information for subsequent NPDU's.

For destination ES's on the local subnetwork, the step of sending the first NPDUs to a local IS works, but it can be slow. An optimization, which is allowed by the NIST OIW agreements, is to allow the ES's to listen for the ESH PDU's, normally destined for the ISs on the subnetwork. This way, NPDU's destined for an ES on the same subnetwork as the originating ES can be sent directly to that ES without going through the redirection step.

In the case in which there is more than one IS on a single subnetwork, the choice of which IS to use to send DT-NPDU's for which no route exists is a local matter. The originating ES is free to choose any IS, the idea being that if a nonoptimal IS is chosen, this IS will inform the originating ES of the optimal IS by means of a Redirect PDU.

Redirection is the only ES-IS (ISO 9542) functionality available on nonmulticast subnetworks, such as X.25 PSDN's. In such nonmulticast subnetworks, static configuration of the ES is typically employed to reach the IS in the first place.

For all the routing information passed in the ESH, ISH, and RD-PDU's, there is an associated time for which the information is to be kept. Each time the route entry is received in one of these PDU's, a timer is activated. If the information is not "renewed" by the arrival of another PDU containing the same information, before the timer expires, that route entry is deleted from the routing table. This way, changes in the network such as ES's, IS's, or subnetworks becoming operational or inoperational can be reflected in the routing table. A system that is inoperational will cease to send out ESH or ISH

PDU's, as the case may be, and the corresponding entries for that system will be timed out in the various routing tables. This is the major difference between the static approach to routing information and the network protocol approach. The network protocol approach can dynamically take into account topology changes caused by systems going down, whereas the static approach requires manual intervention to take into account such changes.

The above description of the protocol assumed that there was an IS on the subnetwork. There may be cases (on isolated subnetworks, for example) in which there is no network entity playing the role of an IS. In such cases, it is still possible for ES's to reach other ES's on the same subnetwork, by using an NPDU called a Query Configuration (QC) PDU. A QC-PDU is the same as a Data (DT) NPDU as described above for CLNP, except that the DT-NPDU is sent to the All-ES Multicast Address, as opposed to the actual SNPA address of the system that corresponds to the destination NSAP address. Since, in the absence of static configuration, the originating ES doesn't know the SNPA address corresponding to the destination NSAP address, it uses the well-known All-ES Multicast Address, since all ES's on the subnetwork can be reached through this address. All ES's receive this QC-NPDU, but only the one that has the same NSAP address as the destination NSAP address on the NPDU accepts the QC-NPDU. All others silently discard the QC-NPDU. Upon receipt of such a QC-NPDU, the destination ES will send back an ESH to the SNPA address of the originating ES. If the originating ES chooses to record this ESH, it will know for future NPDU's the real SNPA address corresponding to that NSAP address. An ES need only support this accept-and- response functionality to a QC-NPDU as a minimal subset of the ES-IS protocol. The periodic transmission of ESH PDU's is optional protocol functionality for an ES.

There is optional functionality of the ES-IS protocol associated with new ES's and IS's coming on-line. An ES or IS, when it comes on-line, will send out an ESH or ISH, respectively. An IS, upon receipt of an ESH corresponding to an NSAP address it did not have before, can send back an ISH directed to the SNPA address of that ES. This way, the ES can know of the NET and SNPA address of the IS without waiting for the periodic transmission of the ISH. Similarly, an ES, upon detecting a new IS coming on-line and receiving an ISH corresponding to an NET which it did not have before, can send an ESH directed to the SNPA address of that IS. This way the IS can know the route corresponding to that ES without waiting for the periodic transmission of the ESH.

Concepts and Protocols of the OSI Network Layer

The formats of the ES-IS PDU's are shown below. The three PDU's that are of interest are the ESH, ISH, and RD-PDU's.

The format of the ESH-PDU is as follows:

```
Bit#       8    7    6    5    4    3    2    1         Octet #
          +--------------------------------------------+
          |   Network Layer Protocol Identifier (82(H)) |    1
          +--------------------------------------------+
          |           Length Indicator (0-254)          |    2
          +--------------------------------------------+
          |       Version/Protocol ID Extension (01 H)  |    3
          +--------------------------------------------+
          |                 Reserved (00)               |    4
          +----+----+----+------------------------------+
          | 0  | 0  | 0  |   0    0    0    1    0     |    5
          +----+----+----+------------------------------+
          |                  Holding Time               |   6,7
          +--------------------------------------------+
          |                   Checksum                  |   8,9
          +--------------------------------------------+
          |          Number of Source Addresses         |   10
          +--------------------------------------------+
          |     Source Address Length Indicator (SAL)   |   11
          +--------------------------------------------+
          |                                             |
          .               Source Address                .
          |                                             |   m-1
          +--------------------------------------------+
          .                                             .
          +--------------------------------------------+
          |     Source Address Length Indicator (SAL)   |    k
          +--------------------------------------------+
          |                                             |   k+1
          |               Source Address                |
          |                                             |   q-1
          +--------------------------------------------+
          |                                             |    q
          |                  Options                    |
          |                                             |
          |                                             |    p
          +--------------------------------------------+
```

ESH-PDU Format

The structure of ES-IS PDU's is similar to that of the CLNP PDU's. The first octet that identifies the Network Layer Protocol is 0 × 82 (Hex) for ES-IS, as opposed to 0 × 81 (Hex) for CLNP. The second field indicates the length of the entire PDU. The third and fourth octet are always 0 × 01 (Hex) and 00, respectively.

The high three bits of octet 5 are always 0. The low five bits identify the type of the ES-IS PDU. An ESH-PDU is represented by the bits 00010, as shown. Octets 6 and 7 are the holding time for the information in this PDU. This field is encoded as an integral number of seconds.

Octets 8 and 9 are the checksum of the entire PDU header. A zero checksum value is reserved to indicate that the checksum should be ignored.

Octet 10 is used to indicate the number of source NSAP addresses that are to be identified by the SNPA address that is implicitly passed with this PDU. The subnetwork service, when it passes up a subnetwork data PDU, also passes the source and destination SNPA addresses corresponding to that PDU. Thus, the SNPA address is carried implicitly by the ESH-PDU.

Following the number of the NSAP addresses contained in the ESH-PDU are the NSAP addresses themselves. Each NSAP address is preceded by one octet of a length field, followed by the encoding of the NSAP addresses. The encoding used is the preferred binary encoding of NSAP addresses.

The options part is similar to the options part described for CLNP in that it contains optional parameters carried in the header. An ESH-PDU can contain the optional parameters of security and priority with identical syntax and semantics as in CLNP.

The format of an ISH is as follows:

```
Bit#        8    7    6    5    4    3    2    1         Octet #
        +-----------------------------------------------+
        |     Network Layer Protocol Identifier (82(H)) |    1
        +-----------------------------------------------+
        |              Length Indicator (0-254)         |    2
        +-----------------------------------------------+
        |         Version/Protocol ID Extension (01 H)  |    3
        +-----------------------------------------------+
        |                 Reserved (00)                 |    4
        +-----+----+----+-------------------------------+
        | 0   | 0  | 0  |  0    0    1    0    0        |    5
        +-----+----+----+-------------------------------+
        |                 Holding Time                  |   6,7
        +-----------------------------------------------+
        |                   Checksum                    |   8,9
        +-----------------------------------------------+
        |       Network Entity Title Length Indicator   |   10
        +-----------------------------------------------+
        |                                               |   11
        .          Network Entity Title (NET)           .
        .                                               .
        |                                               |  m-1
        +-----------------------------------------------+
```

```
|                                                    |   m
|                   Options                          |
|                                                    |
|                                                    |   p
+----------------------------------------------------+
```

ISH-PDU Format

This PDU is identical to the ESH-PDU until the type octet, which has 00100 as the low bits of octet 5 to specify an ISH-PDU. The holding time and checksum fields are identical to those in an ESH-PDU. Instead of source NSAP addresses, however, an ISH contains a single Network Entity Title. Since the NS-user is never involved in an IS, the only identifier of relevance is the NET. Implicitly, as for the ESH, there is an SNPA address for the IS.

The options part can carry the same parameters as an ESH, i.e., security and priority.

The format of an RD-PDU is as follows:

```
Bit#      8    7    6    5    4    3    2    1         Octet #
        +----------------------------------------------+
        |    Network Layer Protocol Identifier (82(H)) |    1
        +----------------------------------------------+
        |         Length Indicator   (0-254)           |    2
        +----------------------------------------------+
        |    Version/Protocol ID Extension (01 H)      |    3
        +----------------------------------------------+
        |              Reserved (00)                   |    4
        +----+----+----+-------------------------------+
        | 0  | 0  | 0  |   0    0    1    1    0       |    5
        +----+----+----+-------------------------------+
        |              Holding Time                    |    6,7
        +----------------------------------------------+
        |               Checksum                       |    8,9
        +----------------------------------------------+
        |    Destination Address Length Indicator      |    10
        +----------------------------------------------+
        |                                              |    11
        .         Destination NSAP Address             .
        .                                              .
        |                                              |    m-1
        +----------------------------------------------+
        |       SNPA Address Length Indicator          |    m
        +----------------------------------------------+
        |                                              |    m+1
        .              SNPA Address                    .
        .                                              .
        |                                              |    n-1
        +----------------------------------------------+
        |    NET Address Length Indicator  (NETL)      |    n
        +----------------------------------------------+
```

```
|                                            |    n+1
.                    NET                     .
.                                            .
|                                            |    p-1
+--------------------------------------------+
|                                            |    p
|                                            |
.                  Options                   .
|                                            |
|                                            |    q
+--------------------------------------------+
```

RD-PDU Format

The format of the first nine octets is similar to an ESH or ISH. The type bits (low five bits of octet 5) contain 00110 to specify an RD-PDU. Octet 10 contains the length of the destination NSAP address to which this RD-PDU is applicable. This is the same destination NSAP address that was used in the DT-NPDU that the IS forwarded to either an ES or IS on the same subnetwork as the originating ES.

Following the NSAP address parameter is the SNPA address to which future DT-NPDUs should be sent by the originating ES. Although at the time of this writing, ISO 9542 does not mention the encoding rules to be employed for the SNPA address, there are defect reports against the standard to remedy this situation. There is a need for such a specification, as different bit orders are used on different subnetworks, such as 802.3 and FDDI. In the absence of a specification of which encoding rules are being employed, an SNPA address as received in an RD-PDU may or may not be directly usable as the SNPA address for a given subnetwork.

If the DT-NPDU was forwarded to an ES, the NETL field contains 0 and is immediately followed by the options part. Otherwise, if the DT-NPDU was forwarded to an IS, then the corresponding RD-PDU contains a nonzero NETL field and is followed by the value of the NET of the IS to which the DT-NPDU was forwarded. The NET is encoded using the preferred binary encoding rules.

In addition to the options possible in an ESH or ISH-PDU, the RD-PDU can contain some further optional parameters. It can contain the QOS Maintenance parameter that was used in the DT-NPDU that caused the generation of the RD-PDU. It can also contain two additional parameters that can be present only in an RD-PDU.

One of these is the Address Mask parameter. This is used to convey the equivalence class of NSAP addresses for which the routing information in the RD-PDU is valid. The parameter code is $0 \times E1$

and the length is variable, up to 20 octets. The value field of the parameter contains a bit mask specifying a population of NSAP addresses. The way to determine that a trial NSAP address falls in the specified population is by first doing a bit-wise AND operation between the Address Mask parameter and the destination NSAP address field of the RD-PDU. Then a bit-wise AND operation is done between the trial NSAP address and the Address Mask parameter. For both bit-wise AND operations, the Address Mask is padded with trailing zeros to make its length the same as the length of the NSAP address to which it is being linked via the AND operation. If the results of both bit-wise AND operations are identical, i.e., the trial NSAP address is identical to the Destination NSAP address parameter everywhere the Address Mask contains a 1 bit, then the trial NSAP address falls in the equivalence class. The routing information specified in the RD-PDU is applicable to all NSAP addresses in the same equivalence class specified by the RD-PDU.

Another optional parameter is the SNPA Mask parameter, which is present only if the Address Mask parameter is present. If present, this parameter specifies that for the equivalence class specified by the Address Mask parameter, there is an embedded SNPA address. The parameter code is 0 × E2 (Hex) and the length is variable. The location of the SNPA address in the NSAP address is specified by the SNPA Mask parameter value. The place where there are 1 values in the SNPA mask corresponds to the field in the NSAP address where the SNPA address is contained. This is an area of the NSAP address "below" the Address Mask, i.e., a place where the Address Mask is logically 0.

ES-IS for Use with 8878/X.25 (ISO 10030)

ISO 10030 solves the problem of distributing and collecting routing information over a single subnetwork employing 8878/X.25. This may use X.25 over a LAN using LLC-2 or over a PSDN using LAPB.

This protocol runs only over subnetworks supporting 1984 or later versions of X.25. It requires that NSAP addresses be carried explicitly and not be determined by examining the DTE addresses. Thus, CONS running over 1980 X.25 subnetworks cannot use this routing protocol.

Each subnetwork has designated to it at least one supplier of routing information, called a Subnetwork Address Resolution Entity (SNARE). A SNARE may be implemented on a system functioning as either an ES or an IS. An ES wishing to know the SNPA address corresponding to a particular NSAP address can ask the SNARE on its subnetwork for this information. Normally, a local configuration is required to know the SNPA address of the SNARE in order to establish a connection with it.

A SNARE can also accept routing information from an ES that wishes to notify it of its NSAP addresses and corresponding SNPA addresses. It thus acts as the collector and distributor of routing information on a subnetwork.

There are two basic ways to interact with the SNARE on a subnetwork. One way is to query the SNARE for SNPA addresses corresponding to NSAP addresses, using a protocol to be described shortly. The ES can then try to establish the desired connection using the newly discovered SNPA address. Under this method, the ES is said to be using the Configuration Information subset of the protocol.

The other way is to try to establish the desired connection using the NSAP address of the destination ES but the SNPA address of the SNARE. The SNARE can then either deflect the call to the correct SNPA address using the X.25 call deflection facility, or it can clear the call and pass back the correct SNPA address in the Clear Request, or it can accept the call and act as an X.25 relay, provided it implements relaying functionality. When using the SNARE in this manner, the ES is said to be using the Redirection Information subset of the protocol.

It is a local matter for the ES which option it chooses to use, the Configuration Information subset or the Redirect Information subset. A SNARE has to be prepared to work with either subset. This protocol only describes interactions between an ES and a SNARE. SNARE-to-SNARE interactions are not discussed in ISO 10030.

Configuration Information Subset An ES using the Configuration Information subset has two basic procedures to implement, the Configuration Notification procedure and the Configuration Collection procedure.

Configuration Notification is similar in functionality to the ESH function described in ISO 9542. Its operation is controlled by a parameter called the Notification Required parameter. This parameter can have values indicating that Configuration Notification is required either periodically, or whenever the ES is attached to a different subnetwork. If periodic notification is required, then the time interval between notifications is also provided. This parameter is communicated to an ES from the SNARE whenever it has finished a communication session with it.

Concepts and Protocols of the OSI Network Layer 169

Configuration Notification and Collection, when needed and implemented, work as follows. The ES establishes an X.25 connection with the SNARE and passes in the Call User Data field of the X.25 Call Request, an End System Connect (ESC) PDU. The Fast Select facility with no restriction on response is specified in the Call Request. The structure of the ESC-PDU contained in the Call Request User Data field is as follows:

```
                                                      Octet #
+-----------------------------------------------------+
|      Network Layer Protocol Identifier (8A(H))      |    1
+-----------------------------------------------------+
|         Version/Protocol ID Extension (01 H)        |    2
+-----------------------------------------------------+
|                    PDU Type (03 H)                  |    3
+-----------------------------------------------------+
```

ESC-PDU Format

The first octet of this PDU identifies this ES-IS protocol (ISO 10030). The second octet is the version field and is always 01 (Hex). The last octet contains the PDU type and distinguishes this PDU from other PDU's employed in this protocol. The code of 03 (Hex) identifies an ESC-PDU.

When the SNARE receives the Call Request, with these three octets in the User Data field, then it knows that the Configuration Notification procedure is being performed. It then sends back an X.25 Call Accepted PDU, with a SNARE Notification Complete (SNC) PDU in the Call Accepted User Data field. The structure of this PDU is as follows:

```
                                                      Octet #
+-----------------------------------------------------+
|      Network Layer Protocol Identifier (8A(H))      |    1
+-----------------------------------------------------+
|         Version/Protocol ID Extension (01 H)        |    2
+-----------------------------------------------------+
|                    PDU Type (0B H)                  |    3
+-----------------------------------------------------+
|                     Request Time                    |    4
+-----------------------------------------------------+
```

SNC-PDU Format

This PDU is similar to the ESC-PDU, with a type field of 0B (Hex). If the Call Accepted User Data field does not contain a valid SNC-PDU, then the ES clears the call with an originator code of 0 and diagnostic code of 242 (Abnormal Condition). In this case, if the ES has knowledge of other SNARE's on the subnetwork that it hasn't tried yet it can attempt the same procedure with them. If, after trying all known SNARE's, it cannot get a valid SNC response in the Call Accepted, then the ES is to retry the procedure after a period of time called the Notification Retry Time.

Otherwise, if a valid SNC-PDU is in the Call Accepted User Data, the ES can enter into the X.25 data transfer mode. Each PDU transferred in this phase uses a single M-bit sequence without the Q-bit set, in accordance with the data transfer procedures of X.25.

The data transfer procedure consists of two parts, configuration notification and configuration collection. If it is the right time for the ES to perform the configuration notification procedure, as determined by the Notification Required parameter, then the ES performs this procedure. This essentially consists of sending an ESH for each NSAP address the ES is reachable at and terminating this sequence of ESH-PDU's with an End System Notification Complete (ENC) PDU. The ESH-PDU format for this protocol is different from the ESH-PDU format specified in ISO 9542. It is as follows:

```
                                                              Octet #
+-----------------------------------------------------+
|       Network Layer Protocol Identifier (8A(H))     |      1
+-----------------------------------------------------+
|         Version/Protocol ID Extension (01 H)        |      2
+-----------------------------------------------------+
|                    PDU Type (04 H)                  |      3
+-----------------------------------------------------+
|                 NSAP Address Length                 |      4
+-----------------------------------------------------+
|                                                     |      5
.                    NSAP Address                     .
|                                                     |     k-1
+-----------------------------------------------------+
|                                                     |      k
.                        QOS                          .
|                                                     |     k+m
+-----------------------------------------------------+
```

ESH-PDU Format

The QOS parameter specifies the associated QOS parameters with that NSAP address/SNPA address combination. The SNPA address is, as before, implicitly specified by virtue of the subnetwork service definition.

The ENC-PDU, which terminates the ESH-PDU sequence, is structured as follows:

```
                                                        Octet #
+----------------------------------------------------+
|     Network Layer Protocol Identifier (8A(H))      |    1
+----------------------------------------------------+
|        Version/Protocol ID Extension (01 H)        |    2
+----------------------------------------------------+
|                  PDU Type (02 H)                   |    3
+----------------------------------------------------+
```

ENC-PDU Format

After sending the ENC-PDU, which informs the SNARE that the ES is finished sending all the ESH-PDU's, the ES waits for a SNARE Received Notification (SRN) PDU. Receipt of this PDU tells the ES that the SNARE received all the ESH-PDU's successfully and that the configuration notification procedure has been successfully performed. The format of the SRN-PDU is as follows:

```
                                                        Octet #
+----------------------------------------------------+
|     Network Layer Protocol Identifier (8A(H))      |    1
+----------------------------------------------------+
|        Version/Protocol ID Extension (01 H)        |    2
+----------------------------------------------------+
|                  PDU Type (0C H)                   |    3
+----------------------------------------------------+
|              Notification Required                 |   4,5
+----------------------------------------------------+
```

SRN-PDU Format

The last two octets in this PDU contain the Notification Required parameter. If both octets contain 00 (Hex), then no periodic notification is required; otherwise the two octets represent the time period between notification as an integral number of seconds. The ES uses this value as its new Notification Required parameter every time it receives an SRN-PDU.

If the configuration notification is finished, or it was not needed in the first place, the ES moves on to the configuration collection phase. In this phase, the ES essentially inquires about the SNPA addresses corresponding to NSAP addresses it is interested in connecting to.

For each NSAP address the ES is interested in, the ES sends an End System Configuration Query (ECQ) PDU to the SNARE and waits for an SNARE Configuration Response (SCR) PDU. The ECQ-PDU contains the NSAP address the ES is interested in finding information about, and the SCR-PDU contains the corresponding SNPA address and associated QOS. The SNARE may send back multiple SCR-PDU's, corresponding to different SNPA addresses and associated QOS. The SNARE terminates the SCR-PDU's with a SNARE Configuration Complete (SCC) PDU.

The SCC-PDU contains a parameter called the Query Limit parameter. If this parameter is 0, then the ES is not allowed to inquire about more NSAP addresses; otherwise if it is 1, then the ES may make one more NSAP address query using the ECQ-PDU.

The structure of the ECQ-PDU is as follows:

```
                                                          Octet #
+--------------------------------------------------------+
|       Network Layer Protocol Identifier (8A(H))        |    1
+--------------------------------------------------------+
|          Version/Protocol ID Extension (01 H)          |    2
+--------------------------------------------------------+
|                    PDU Type (01 H)                     |    3
+--------------------------------------------------------+
|                  NSAP Address Length                   |    4
+--------------------------------------------------------+
|                                                        |    5
.                    NSAP Address                        .
|                                                        |   k-1
+--------------------------------------------------------+
```

ECQ-PDU Format

The last parameter contains the NSAP address about which the ES is interested in obtaining the corresponding SNPA address information.

The format of the SCR-PDU, sent in response to the ECQ-PDU is as follows:

Concepts and Protocols of the OSI Network Layer

```
                                                    Octet #
+-------------------------------------------------+
|    Network Layer Protocol Identifier (8A(H))    |    1
+-------------------------------------------------+
|        Version/Protocol ID Extension (01 H)     |    2
+-------------------------------------------------+
|                  PDU Type (0A H)                |    3
+-------------------------------------------------+
|               NSAP Address Length               |    4
+-------------------------------------------------+
|                                                 |    5
.                  NSAP Address                   .
|                                                 |   k-1
+-------+-----------------------------------------+
| Type  |       SNPA Address Length Indicator     |    k
+-------+-----------------------------------------+
|                                                 |   k+1
.           SNPA Address Parameter Value          .
|                                                 |   m-1
+-------------------------------------------------+
|                                                 |    m
.              Address Mask Parameter             .
|                                                 |   n-1
+-------------------------------------------------+
|                                                 |    n
.               SNPA  Mask Parameter              .
|                                                 |   p-1
+-------------------------------------------------+
|                                                 |    p
.                      QOS                        .
|                                                 |   p+q
+-------------------------------------------------+
```

SCR-PDU Format

The SCR-PDU contains the NSAP address about which it is supplying information. Following the NSAP address is an octet (k), the high two bits of which identify the encoding rules used for the SNPA address parameter value. If the high two bits of octet k are 00, then the encoding rules for the SNPA address are specified in ISO 10030. If the high two bits are 11, then some local encoding mechanism is specified. Other values for these two bits are reserved and not to be used.

The encoding rules specified in ISO 10030 when the high two bits of the SNPA length octet are 00 are as follows. The remaining low six bits of the length octet represent the length of the SNPA address. If the SNPA address is carried in the subnetwork access protocol as a string of octets, then that octet string will be used in the SNPA address parameter value field. This implies that, for example, ISO 8802 MAC addresses (Ethernet, FDDI addresses, etc.) are passed in the encoding mechanism used on the media. So on a LAN (e.g., FDDI) where the MSB is transmitted first, the same address, specified using a binary abstract syntax, would be encoded differently from a LAN where the LSB is transmitted first (e.g., 802.3).

If the subnetwork access protocol carries the SNPA address using BCD encoding, then a 1111 semi-octet will be padded at the end, in case the BCD encoding does not result in an integral number of octets.

Other ways of encoding an SNPA address include using a canonical octet encoding mechanism, such as LSB, first always, similar to the bit order on an 802.3 LAN. The advantage of using a canonical encoding mechanism is that in the presence of MAC layer bridges between LAN's using dissimilar bit ordering, the SNPA addresses are always in a known (i.e., the canonical) bit order and not a different one depending on which side of the MAC bridge the PDU came from. Conceivably, such an encoding rule could be employed using the "local" type encoding rules.

Following the SNPA address parameter value is the NSAP Address Mask and the SNPA Address Mask parameters. These two parameters have the same syntax (parameter codes 0 × E1 [Hex], 0 × E2, etc.) and semantics as these parameters described for ISO 9542. The last field is the QOS field, which specifies the QOS attainable using the provided SNPA address.

Redirection Information Subset An ES can optionally choose to use the Redirection Information Subset of ISO 10030. Using this subset, the originating ES makes the Connect Request using the NSAP address of the destination ES and the SNPA address of the SNARE.

The SNARE will either clear the call and in the Clear Request packet's user data field send a Redirect (RD) PDU, or it may deflect the call to the appropriate SNPA address. If it clears the call, it will use the NS-provider as the originator code in the Clear Request packet. If the originator code does not indicate NS-provider, the ES will not process any further. Otherwise, it will examine the user data field for an RD-PDU, which has the following format:

```
                                                              Octet #
+---------------------------------------------------+
|      Network Layer Protocol Identifier (8A(H))    |         1
+---------------------------------------------------+
|         Version/Protocol ID Extension (01 H)      |         2
+---------------------------------------------------+
|                    PDU Type (08 H)                |         3
+---------------------------------------------------+
|                    Holding Time                   |         4,5
+--------+------------------------------------------+
| Type   |      SNPA Address Length Indicator       |         6
+--------+------------------------------------------+
|                                                   |         7
.            SNPA Address Parameter Value           .
|                                                   |         m-1
+---------------------------------------------------+
|                                                   |         m
.            NSAP Address Mask Parameter            .
|                                                   |         n-1
+---------------------------------------------------+
|                                                   |         n
.            SNPA Address Mask Parameter            .
|                                                   |         p-1
+---------------------------------------------------+
```

RD-PDU Format

The RD-PDU contains in it a Holding Time parameter, SNPA Address, NSAP Address Mask, and SNPA Address Mask parameters similar to the RD-PDU described for ISO 9542 above. The SNPA address parameter is encoded as described for the SCR-PDU above.

If the SNARE decides to deflect the call, the ES should look at the SNPA address that comes back in the Call Accepted PDU. This SNPA address can be used in future attempts to connect to the destination NSAP address. This SNPA address should be used judiciously by the ES, however, as there is no holding time for it.

IS-IS Routing Protocols

As of 1990, work has progressed only on IS-IS protocols as they relate to CLNP. To examine the various types of IS-IS protocols, it is useful to understand a few relevant concepts. The routing universe is comprised of many *administrative domains,* which are sets of end systems and intermediate systems under the control of a single administrative authority. An example of an administrative domain would be all the network entities under the control of a corporation or a government agency. Each administrative domain can have in it multiple *routing domains.* A routing domain is a set of network entities operating according to the same set of protocols and procedures. An administrative authority may decide to administer multiple routing domains in order to run different routing protocols in the different routing domains.

Based on these concepts, there are two basic types of IS-IS routing protocols, the intradomain IS-IS routing protocol and the interdomain IS-IS routing protocol. An intradomain routing protocol disseminates and collects routing information inside a routing domain, while an interdomain routing protocol does the same between routing domains. Figure 6-5 summarizes these concepts.

One important distinction between the two IS-IS protocols is that when the interdomain routing protocol is routing between different administrative domains, issues such as security, access control, national regulations, etc., need to be considered. Inter-administrative-domain routing protocols assume a lesser degree of trust between systems that employ it. The intradomain (understood to be intra-routing-domain) protocol is concerned primarily with distributing routing information inside the routing domain.

DP 10589 is the ISO intradomain IS-IS routing protocol standard. This is not its final form as of 1990. It is at Draft Proposal (DP) stage, one of the earliest stages before becoming an International Standard (IS). It is premature, therefore, to give a detailed description of this protocol. Instead, the general concepts employed will be outlined. The interdomain routing protocols are not even at the DP level at this time. They will not be discussed further.

Intradomain IS-IS Routing (DP 10589) This protocol works in conjunction with ISO 8473 (CLNP) and ISO 9542 (ES-IS with CLNP) to provide a way for all IS network entities to obtain access to global routing information within the routing domain. This protocol operates over a variety of subnetwork types, including ISO 8802 LAN's (802.3, FDDI, etc.), point-to-point links, X.25 subnetworks, and multipoint links.

The general approach taken to routing in this protocol is called Link State Routing. The basic premise of this approach is that all IS network entities broadcast information about their local topological environment to all other IS entities. This is in contrast to another

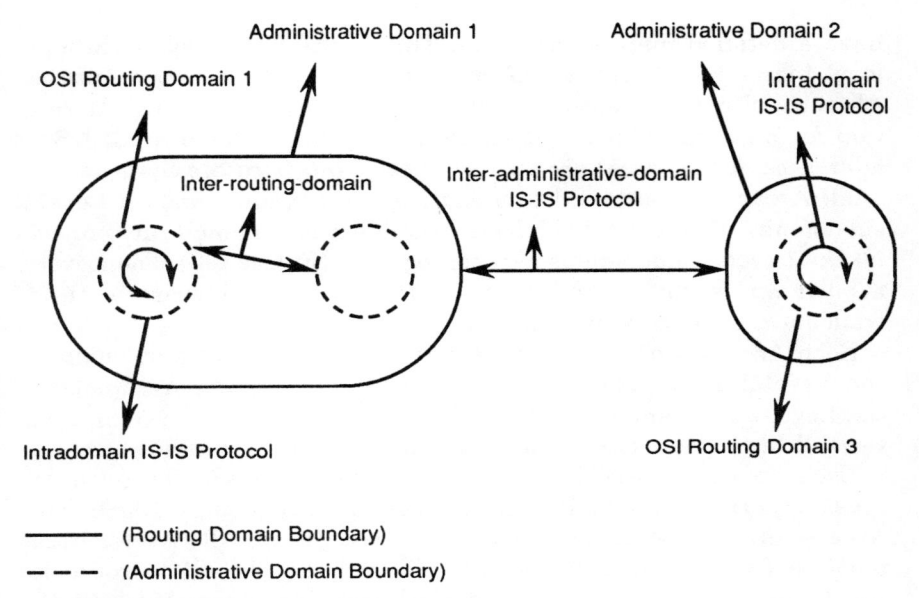

Concepts and Protocols of the OSI Network Layer   177

Figure 6-5 IS-IS routing protocols.

approach, called Distance Vector Routing. In the latter approach, network entities exchange global topology information with adjacent IS network entities.

Thus, with Link State local topology information is broadcast globally, whereas in Distance Vector global topology information is transmitted locally to the adjacent IS network entities. In Distance Vector Routing, the information being exchanged changes as it passes from one entity to another. Each entity recomputes its new map of the world, and passes this new map to all neighboring entities. In Link State Routing, the unit of information being exchanged remains the same as it passes from one entity to another. This unit of information contains only the local toplogy information of the network entity that originated it.

With Link State Routing, each IS network entity is able to compute the global map from all the individual pieces of local toplogy information. It then computes the path to a given NSAP address, using this global map. In DP 10589, the Link State concept is applied only within a routing subdomain, not for the entire routing domain. A routing subdomain is a set of ES and IS network entities that is wholly contained within a single routing domain.

A detailed global routing topology map is maintained only for routing subdomains termed *Areas*. All IS network entities within an area have a detailed map of that area. This is the first level of the two-level hierarchy of routing information kept by IS network entities. All such IS network entities that maintain detailed routing information for an area (which implies keeping optimal routes to all NSAP addresses in that area) are termed *Level-1 Intermediate Systems*.

All Areas are connected to a routing subdomain termed a Level-2 subdomain. The Level-2 subdomain is like a backplane that connects all the Level-1 subdomains (Areas) together (Figure 6-6). The Level-2 subdomain is the second level of the two-level hierarchy of intradomain IS routing information.

Each Area has one or more IS network entities that participate in the Level-2 subdomain. The IS network entity that participates in the Level-2 subdomain is called a Level-2 Intermediate System. Each Level-2 IS is also a Level-1 IS in the Area in which it resides.

Each area has associated with it an Area Address. The Area Address is part of the NSAP address structure assumed by 10589. This Area Address appears as an NSAP address prefix. All Level-2 Intermediate Systems have knowledge of which Level-2 IS to route towards, in order for the NPDU to reach the right Area. Much as the Level-1 IS's have a complete map of destination NSAP addresses in their area, the Level-2 IS's have a complete map of area addresses and their associated Level-2 paths.

Each End System is wholly contained within an Area. Thus, once the Level-2 Intermediate Systems has brought it to the Level-2 IS that is in the same area as the destination ES, Level-1 routing procedures take over to forward the NPDU to the destination ES. This is illustrated in Figure 6-7. Also shown in Figure 6-7 is another NPDU path that is entirely contained in an Area.

Much as the routing problem for an ES is simplified to that of simply finding an IS on the subnetwork, the routing problem for Level-1 Intermediate Systems is simplified to finding a Level-2 Intermediate system for NSAP addresses that are not resident in that Area. In the case of multiple Level-2 Intermediate Systems in an Area, the Level-2 IS chosen by a Level-1 IS may not be the most optimal one for a given destination NSAP address. This is the price that is paid by decomposing the full routing domain into smaller subdomains, each of which keeps detailed information relevant to its subdomain only.

By doing this sort of distribution of information, a given IS has to keep in its local RIB a smaller, and hence more manageable, amount of information. It is a goal of the protocol to be able to disseminate and maintain routing information for a very large number of End Systems.

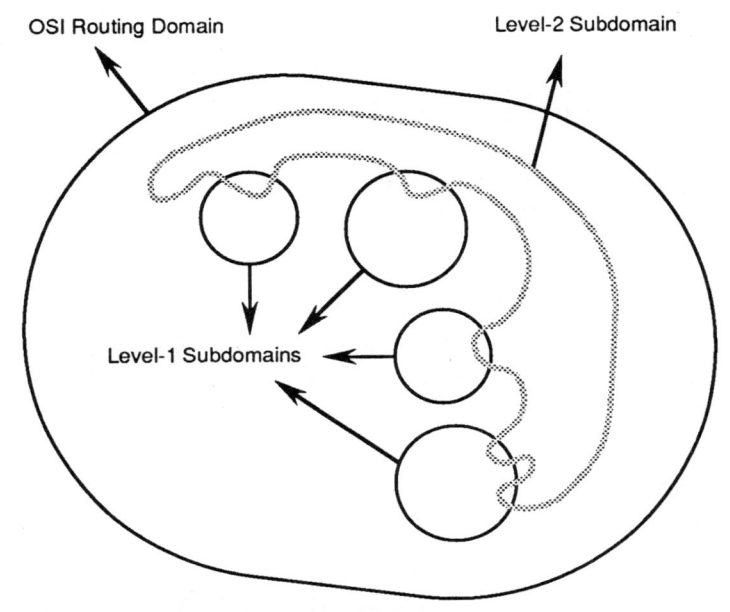

Figure 6-6 Level-1 and Level-2 subdomains.

An OSI routing domain is comprised of the Level-2 subdomain and all the ES's within this routing domain are reachable either via Level-1 or via Level-1 and Level-2 routing. Systems residing in other routing domains, either because they are under the control of a different administrative authority or because they are employing a different set of procedures and protocols, may be reached by doing static interdomain routing. This is the same kind of static routing as described above and usually takes the form of NSAP address prefix matching.

The way routing is done within and between areas is by assuming a given structure to the NSAP addresses. The general format assumed by DP 10589 is as follows:

```
| <-AFI IDI->| <----------------- DSP ------------------>|
+-------------+--------------------+-----------------+-----+
|    IDP      |      HO-DSP        |   Station ID    |NSEL |
+-------------+--------------------+-----------------+-----+
                                           6            1  (# octets)

|<--- Used by Level-2 routing --->|<- Level-1 routing -->|
|          (Area Address)         |
```

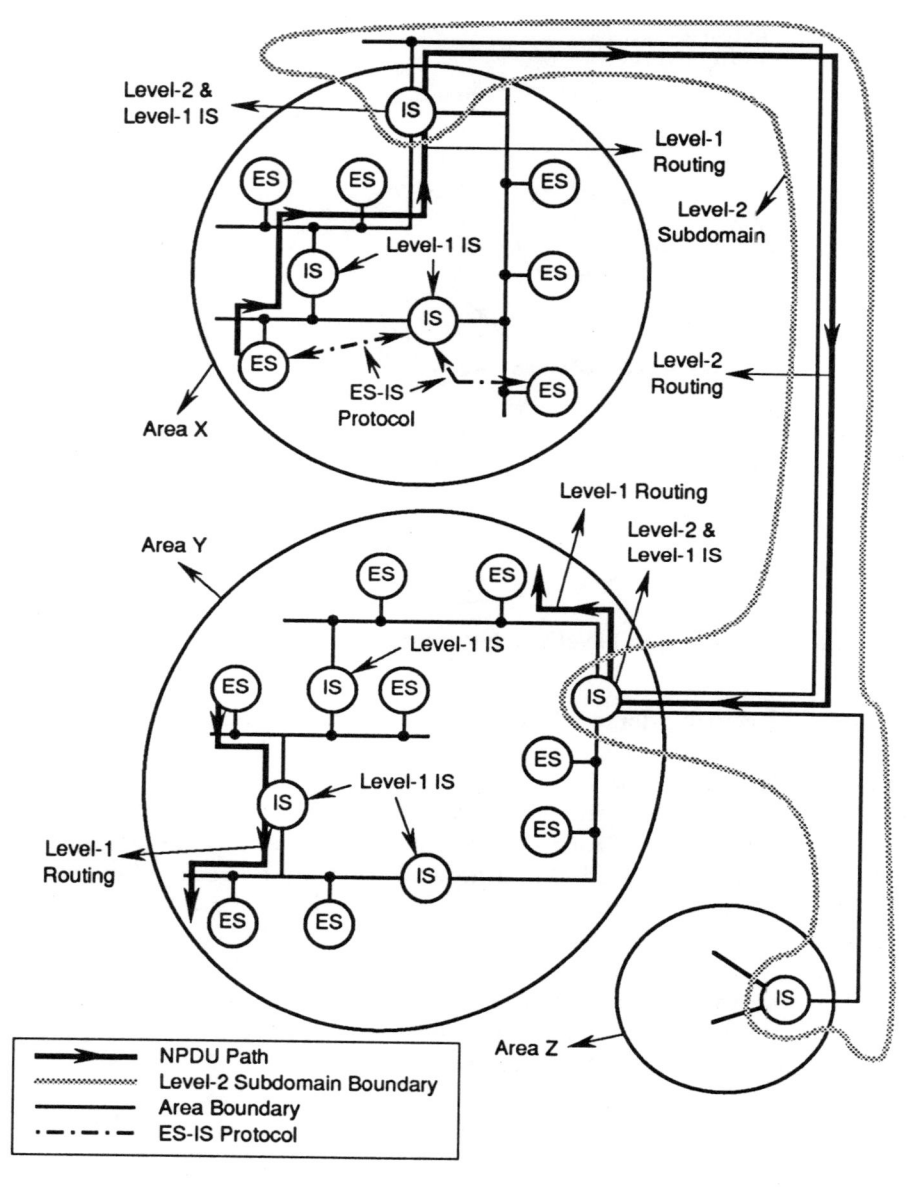

Figure 6-7 Intradomain routing.

In particular, the last seven octets of the NSAP address are assumed to contain six octets of a Station ID, followed by one octet of an NSEL. The exact form of the NSAP address above the low seven octets can be variable. The general idea is that the high part of the NSAP address (minus the low seven octets) is what is called the Area Address. All End Systems that reside in an area have the same Area Address but different Station ID's. The Station ID may be allocated out of the same address space as ISO 8802 addresses, which would make them globally unique, but the only requirement is for station ID's to be unique within an Area. End Systems in different Areas have different Area Addresses.

The HO-DSP is the High-Order Domain-Specific Part. The concatenation of the IDP and the HO-DSP forms the area address. Addresses that do not match the general requirement given above may still be reachable in the routing domain, but they require static configuration. The only requirement is that should an NSAP address's area address match that of a given area, it should reside in that area with a unique Station ID. An NET is similar to an NSAP address described above, except it does not include the NSEL field.

The U.S. GOSIP V.2 NSAP address format satisifies the general requirements described earlier. The area fields can be used to identify different Level-1 subdomains, the Routing Domain field can be used to identify different OSI Routing Domains, and the Administrative Authority can be used to identify different Administrative Domains. The fields are in that order, because areas are contained in a Routing Domain, which in turn is contained in an Administrative Domain. This simplifies static configuration of routing information for Inter-Routing-Domain and Inter-Administrative-Domain network traffic, by doing prefix based configuration.

If the area address of a given destination NSAP address is the same as the area address of the IS network entity fowarding the NPDU, then it computes the exact path based on its detailed routing knowledge of that area. Otherwise, the Level-1 IS passes it to the closest Level-2 IS, which may be itself. The Level-2 IS examines only the area address of the destination NSAP address. Based on this area address, the Level-2 IS passes the NPDU in the direction of the destination area. Once it has reached the destination area, the Level-1 IS of that area will examine the station ID and route based on that alone. The last octet of the NSAP address, the NSEL, is never used in making routing decisions.

The way in which routing information is disseminated within a subdomain is by means of a Link State PDU (LSP). The Link State PDU is broadcast to all IS network entities in the subdomain. The LSP contains the local environment of the network entity broadcasting it. Each LSP is broadcast to network entities within its subdomain, but not outside it. Thus, a Level-1 LSP is broadcast to all Level-1 IS network entities within an area, and a Level-2 LSP is broadcast to all Level-2 IS network entities in the Level-2 subdomain. An LSP is never propagated outside of the routing domain in which it is generated.

An LSP is sent either when a timer expires or the topology changes (such as when an ESH or ISH entry is timed out in a local RIB), or by some System Management action. An IS network entity builds up knowledge of its local environment by receipt of ESH's for ES adjacencies (through operation of the ES-IS protocol ISO 9542), or through various Intermediate System Hellos.

A Level-1 LSP contains information about all the IS and ES adjacencies of the Level-1 IS broadcasting it. This is in the form of the station ID's of the various IS and network entities that are directly attached to the originator of the LSP. The area address is assumed for all the network entities specified in the LSP, be they End Systems or Intermediate Systems. This LSP replaces information pertinent to the NSAP addresses and NET's that it describes and is entered into the local RIB of all the IS network entities that receive it. Since each Level-1 IS propagates its local environment information to every IS in the area, eventually all IS network entities in the area have a complete map of the topology of the domain. When a Level-1 IS receives a Level-1 LSP, it records the information and transmits the LSP to all other Level-1 IS entities it knows of. This is how broadcasting of the LSP takes place. An IS does not change the information in the LSP as it passes it on.

For the sake of robustness, an IS will only use IS adjacencies advertised in an LSP if the adjacent IS also reports the same adjacency in its LSP. If one IS reports another IS as adjacent, but the adjacent IS does not report the same adjacency, then that piece of information is ignored. ES adjacencies are not subject to this cross-check, since ES information is broadcast only on the subnetwork to which it is attached.

On a broadcast subnetwork to which multiple IS network entities are attached, it is useful to be able to reduce the amount of LSP traffic by considering that entire subnetwork as a "pseudonode." All the IS network entities are considered to be attached to that pseudonode, and only one of those IS network entities, called the Designated IS, generates LSP's on behalf of all the other IS's. The designated IS treats itself and all other IS's as directly connected to this pseudonode, and reports this information in its LSP. Since the LSP is marked to be as one originating from a pseudonode, the same topology can be derived from this one LSP, as from the LSP's from all the IS's on that subnetwork, each of which would have had to report a greater number of adjacencies in their LSP's. Furthermore, there would have been a greater number of LSP's generated, one for each IS on the network, had the subnetwork not been treated as a pseudonode. This is illustrated in Figure 6-8.

Having constructed this global map, each Level-1 IS then independently calculates the best route to all the NSAP addresses in the area. The "best" route is determined based on various metrics, which are the same ones that are specified in the QOS Maintenance field of the CLNP Data NPDU. These are the Default metric (by convention the throughput of the path), the Delay metric (based on transit delay of the associated path), the Expense metric (based on the monetary cost of using the path), and the Error metric (based on the residual error probability of the path). The best route is obtained with reference to optimize the metric. The Level-1 IS maintains separate forwarding information for each metric and applies the one specified in the Data NPDU being forwarded.

A Level-2 LSP contains information about the area addresses that each Level-2 IS is associated with. Each Level-2 IS builds up its knowledge of the local Level-2 IS adjacencies based on Level-2 Intermediate System Hellos. This local environment is broadcast to every Level-2 IS in the Level-2 subdomain. Thus, all Level-2 IS's eventually build up a complete map of which Level-2 IS to forward an NPDU to for a given area address prefix. The routes computed from this map are also based on the four metrics described above, one best route for each metric.

Each LSP has associated with it a "holding time." If the holding time passes before receipt of another similar LSP, then the information associated with that LSP is invalidated. This is how the protocol can dynamically keep track of changes in the network topology.

The algorithm used in computing these routes is a modified version of Dijkstra's Shortest Path First (SPF) algorithm. It is modified in that the algorithm does not compute a single best route for a given metric, but can compute multiple "equally good" routes. These alternative best routes are used when the local queue on a given route becomes too long and traffic can be distributed on the alternative routes. This is the only form of congestion control that is defined in 10589, i.e., one based on local congestion. No attempt is made to keep track of global network congestion or to compute paths based on it.

Within an area, if there are mutiple paths to a destination ES from an originating ES, and a link in one of these paths goes down,

184 Open Systems Interconnection Handbook

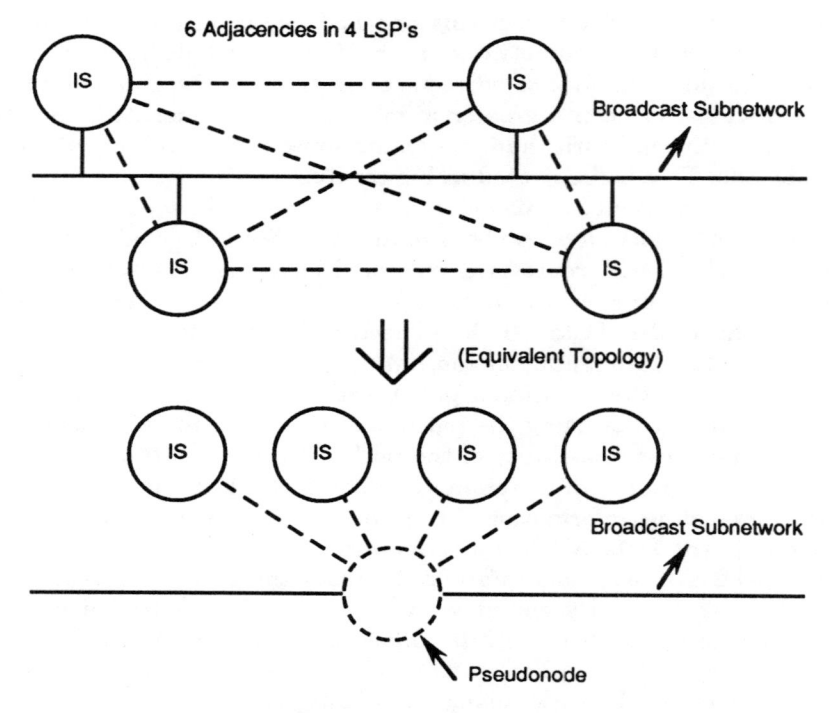

Figure 6-8 Topology derived from treating the subnetwork as a pseudonode.

the operation of the intradomain IS-IS protocol in conjunction with the ES-IS protocol will provide an alternative path to the destination ES.

If an area becomes completely partitioned in two, and there are Level-2 IS network entities attached to each partition of the area, it is possible to repair the area by use of a Level-1 repair path through the Level-2 subdomain. The reverse of this scenario, i.e., repair of the Level-2 subdomain through a Level-1 subdomain (an area) is not attempted by the protocol. To achieve logical connectivity through the entire routing domain, a connected Level-2 subdomain is assumed. If the Level-2 subdomain does get partitioned, areas on one side of the partition will not be able to communicate with areas on the other side, although connectivity will remain on either side of the Level-2 subdomain partition.

Acknowledgments

I would like to thank Raj Srinivasan, Jonathan Mills, Terry Gibson, Hemma Patel, Erik Nordmark, Mukesh Kacker, and Peter Vanderbilt for reviewing this chapter and providing useful comments.

About the Author

Ashar Aziz has been an engineer at Sun Microsystems, Inc., since 1987. His primary duties involve the implementation of OSI protocols and architectures. Ashar received a B.S. and an M.S. in Electrical Engineering and Computer Science from MIT and the University of California at Berkeley, respectively.

The leader in the workstation market, Sun Microsystems, Inc., has been pivotal in bringing about a new era of open systems — a significant departure from the industry's earlier days. The compatibility and connectivity that will result from the open systems movement will make workstations an essential component in automating the workplace.

The centerpiece of Sun's open systems strategy is SPARC, a high-performance RISC microprocessor architecture that is available to any company that wants to design and sell its own SPARC chips or systems. One of the most revolutionary aspects of SPARC is that all SPARC systems from every vendor — from laptops to supercomputers — can run the same binary-compatible software. Besides giving end users a new level of convenience and capability, this vastly simplifies the task of software developers, who can create a single product that will run on all SPARC hardware.

Sun develops and licenses other open standards, such as Open Network Computing (ONC) networking products, which include the Network File System (NFS), the standard for file sharing across heterogeneous systems. NFS is licensed by more than 300 companies and organizations worldwide.

Chapter 7

Using the OSI Model for Network Architecture Analysis

by Thomas G. DeVille

Introduction

The ISO/OSI model has proven to be a very powerful means for viewing communications among computing devices. The model divides the overall communication problem into seven smaller tasks to avoid being overwhelmed by the complexity of the technology. The model provides a frame of reference so that when viewing the details of one layer, one can still see how that piece fits into the overall scheme of communications.

Previous chapters have discussed the overall model, the details of each layer of the model, and the relationship of the ISO standards to other networking protocols, such as TCP/IP, DECnet, SNA, etc. The purpose of this chapter is to build on all three of the above — overview, details, and other protocols — to show an approach for using the OSI model to analyze and plan networks at a macro level.

Foundation

Purpose of Preparing a Network Architecture

The concept that will be developed in this chapter can be illustrated with a simple example as shown in Figure 7-1. In this example, there are three types of devices that need to communicate, labeled A, B, and C. The first question of concern is, "What are the required communication paths among A, B, and C?" In this case A needs to communicate with B and C, but B and C do not need to communicate with each other.

The next question is, "What type of application layer communication is required?" As shown in Figure 7-2, B is a data store that uses File Transfer, Access, and Management (FTAM), and C is a factory floor device that uses the Manufacturing Message Specification (MMS). Further, B is on a CSMA/CD (802.3) subnetwork, while C is on a token bus (802.4) subnetwork. For simplicity, the specifics of the application programs behind MMS and FTAM on A will be ignored for this example. The details of how the communication requirements are to be met for this example are shown in Figure 7-3. Note that A must have both MMS and FTAM in order to be able to communicate with B and C respectively. Further, a bridge is required because of the different physical layer protocols.

Why is this necessary? After all, the purpose of the ISO standards is to eliminate much of the concern over communications among computing devices. There are three reasons why this is important:

1. In many circumstances, other network protocols besides ISO are part of the problem of interest.
2. Even if all devices meet the ISO standards, there are several standards and/or choices for each of the OSI model layers.

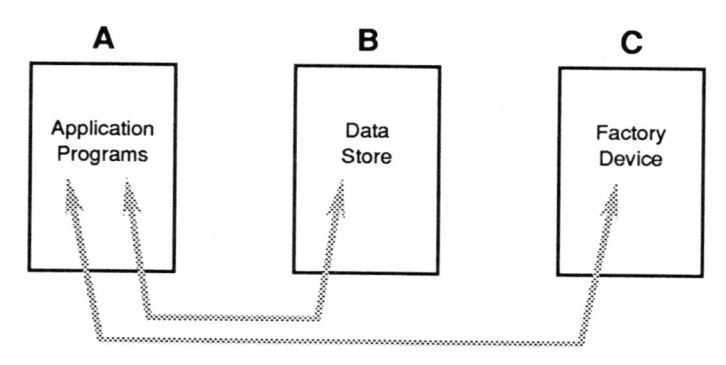

Figure 7-1 Example of three devices with two required communication paths.

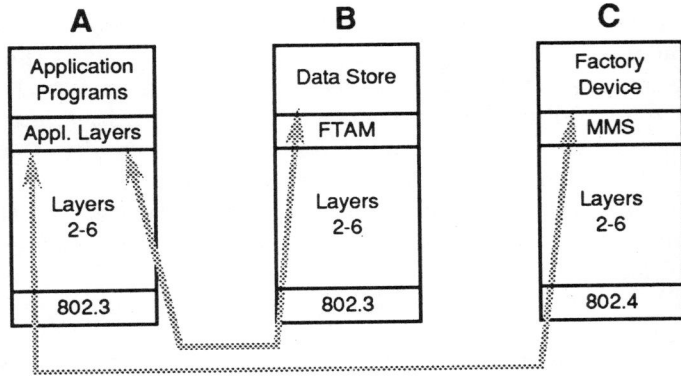

Using the OSI Model for Network Architecture Analysis   189

[Figure 7-2 diagram: Three stacks labeled A (Application Programs / Appl. Layers / Layers 2-6 / 802.3), B (Data Store / FTAM / Layers 2-6 / 802.3), and C (Factory Device / MMS / Layers 2-6 / 802.4)]

Figure 7-2 Example of three devices with two required communication paths showing components at the application and physical layers.

3. Communication among computing devices must account for all of the components involved in the communications. Besides the actual communication functions, there are operating systems, database management systems, programming languages, etc., to consider.

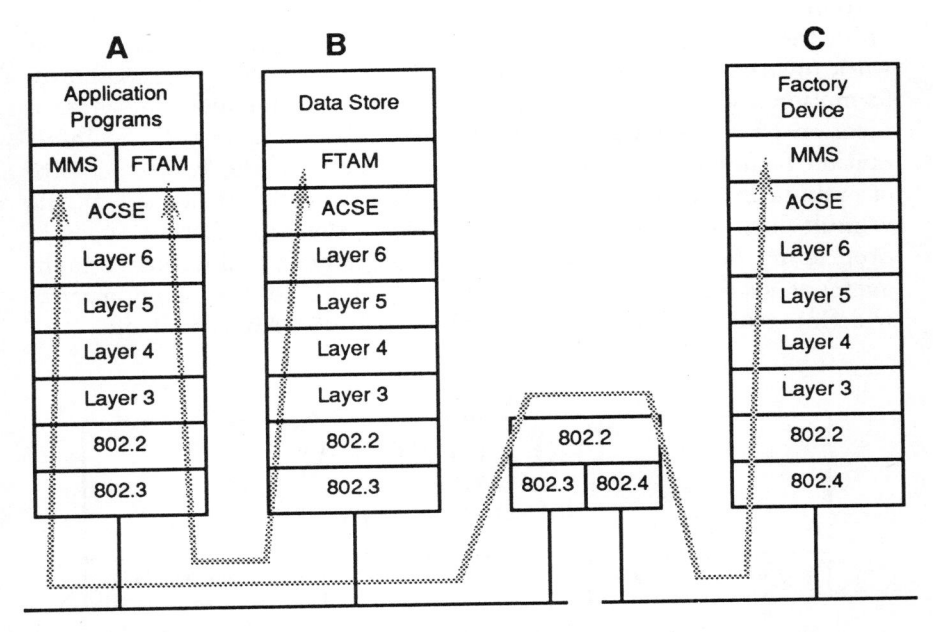

[Figure 7-3 diagram: Stack A (Application Programs / MMS | FTAM / ACSE / Layer 6 / Layer 5 / Layer 4 / Layer 3 / 802.2 / 802.3); Stack B (Data Store / FTAM / ACSE / Layer 6 / Layer 5 / Layer 4 / Layer 3 / 802.2 / 802.3); bridge (802.2 / 802.3 | 802.4); Stack C (Factory Device / MMS / ACSE / Layer 6 / Layer 5 / Layer 4 / Layer 3 / 802.2 / 802.4)]

Figure 7-3 Details of components in communication paths among three devices.

All of these components (network, operating system, data base management system, user interface, etc.) can be viewed as the "information technology infrastructure." Generally, the term *infrastructure* refers to roads, telephones, the mail, electricity, utilities, etc. These items are critical to any enterprise and are usually taken for granted. The purpose of the analysis approach described in this chapter is to methodically develop a network architecture that accounts for all of the components of the "information technology infrastructure" for an enterprise.

The Role of ISO Standards in the Information Technology Infrastructure

Figure 7-4 illustrates a basic objective of a typical enterprise of making information available when and where it is needed. Users (people) and machines (in the case of a manufacturing enterprise) create information that is needed by other users and/or machines. From a management perspective it is not important how the information gets from one point to another provided the information is timely and accurate. What information technology does is to allow the presentation, organization, and distribution of the information in ways that were impractical in the past.

In order to make use of the capabilities of information technology, all of the components at both ends of the communication path must work together. This is illustrated in Figure 7-5, which shows the information technology infrastructure components for just one communication path. As shown on Figure 7-6, the complexity of the information technology infrastructure can overwhelm the basic objective of making information available when and where it is needed. If this is multiplied several times over to reflect several different types of proprietary network protocols, operating systems, and database management systems, it becomes clear why the objective of enterprise-wide integration of information systems can be such a challenge.

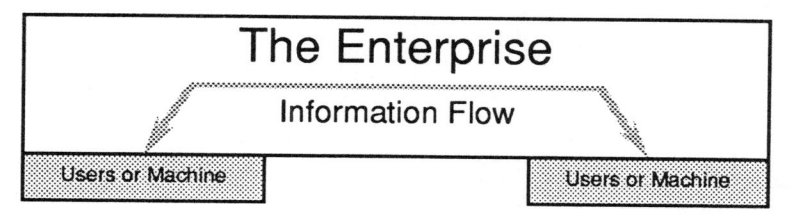

Figure 7-4 A "management" view of integration in which the objective is to make information available when and where it is needed.

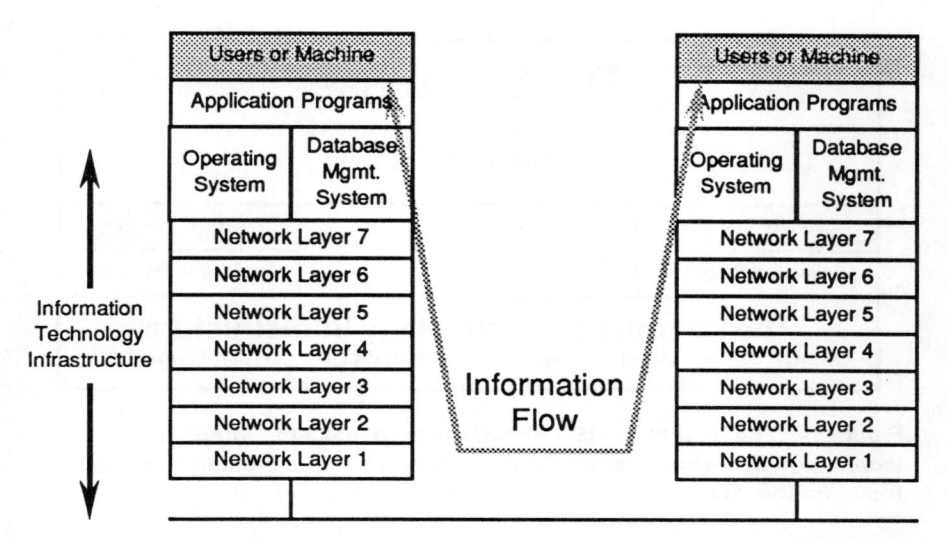

Using the OSI Model for Network Architecture Analysis 191

Figure 7-5 A "technical" view of integration that shows the components of the information technology infrastructure needed to communicate between the two users or machines.

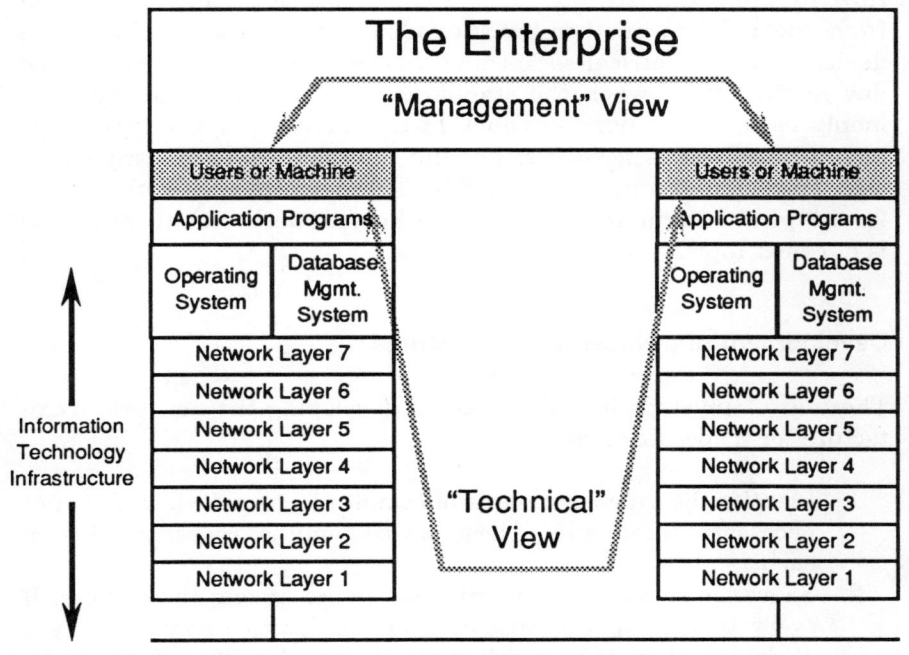

Figure 7-6 The combined view shows that the complexity of the information technology infrastructure can overwhelm the basic objective of making information available when and where it is needed.

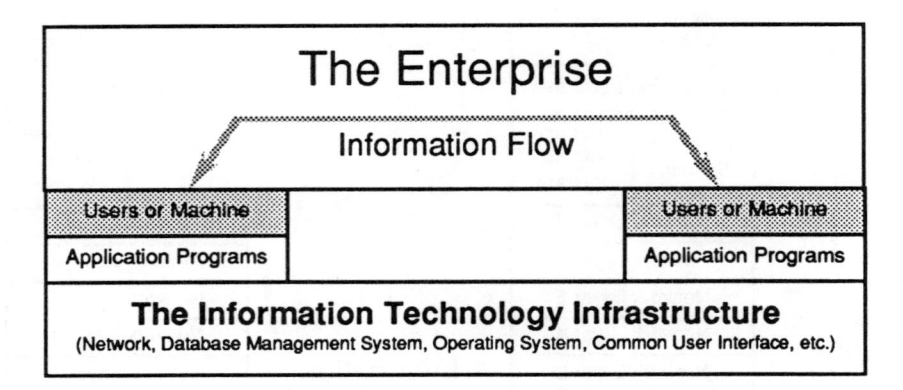

```
┌─────────────────────────────────────────────────────────┐
│                    The Enterprise                       │
│              ╱───── Information Flow ─────╲             │
│  ┌──────────────────┐         ┌──────────────────┐      │
│  │ Users or Machine │         │ Users or Machine │      │
│  ├──────────────────┤         ├──────────────────┤      │
│  │Application Programs│       │Application Programs│    │
│  ├──────────────────┴─────────┴──────────────────┤      │
│  │    The Information Technology Infrastructure  │      │
│  │ (Network, Database Management System, Operating│     │
│  │  System, Common User Interface, etc.)          │     │
└─────────────────────────────────────────────────────────┘
```

Figure 7-7 The goal of the ISO standards is to make the information technology infrastructure nearly transparent so that the enterprise can focus on the use of information rather than on the technology.

One of the purposes of the ISO standards is to provide commonality of the components used in the information technology infrastructure. Figure 7-7 illustrates the objective in which getting information from one point to another becomes almost as simple as plugging a device into an electrical socket and knowing that it will work. Some day in the future when the standards have matured and are commonly used, this may be possible. In the interim, for the typical enterprise analysis is needed to account for the variety of components that may or may not be compatible. The development of the model for a typical enterprise can be termed the "network architecture" and is our next topic.

Development of a Network Architecture

There are four steps in the process of developing the network architecture for a specific environment:

1. Identify the types or classes of communicating devices. It is not necessary to identify every device, only a representative of each.
2. Show the required communication paths among the devices. If every type of device must communicate with every other type of device, then the overall problem may be difficult to implement if there are a variety of types or classes of communicating

Using the OSI Model for Network Architecture Analysis 193

devices. Therefore, it is important to be clear as to why a particular type of device must communicate with another type.
3. Show the details of network protocols, the operating systems, the database management systems, etc., that are part of the information technology infrastructure in each communication path to determine how each of the components serves the communication requirements from device to device.
4. Finally, complete the network architecture to show all of the components and their relationships to the required communication paths.

This process is illustrated in Figure 7-8; each of the steps is discussed in the following sections, using an example of the devices involving data communication within a hypothetical enterprise.

Step 1: Identify the Types of Communicating Devices

Figure 7-9 shows an example with several types of devices for a hypothetical enterprise. The devices at the top represent computers that will be used for plant business management systems. There is also a database server connected to an office subnetwork. In the middle of the illustration are shown area controllers used to supervise factory devices. The factory devices themselves are controlled by process controllers and programmable logic controllers (PLC) shown at the bottom.

The first step in preparing the network architecture is to identify the types or classes of communicating devices. A communicating device could be a computer, a terminal, a programmable logic controller (PLC), a cell controller, a robot, a distributed control system (DCS) node, or in general any type or class of device that is an "end system" that creates or receives communication.

It is not necessary to identify every device. The idea is to be sure that each of the types of communication paths required are represented. For example, if communication between two similar computers is required, then two computers should be shown. If there is to be communication among computers that are on different subnetworks, then a representative on each subnetwork should be shown. If there are different network protocols involved, then a representative device for each of the protocols should be shown.

Figure 7-10 shows the results of completing the first step for the hypothetical enterprise. It is a simplified version of the previous illustration that shows one of each type of communicating devices.

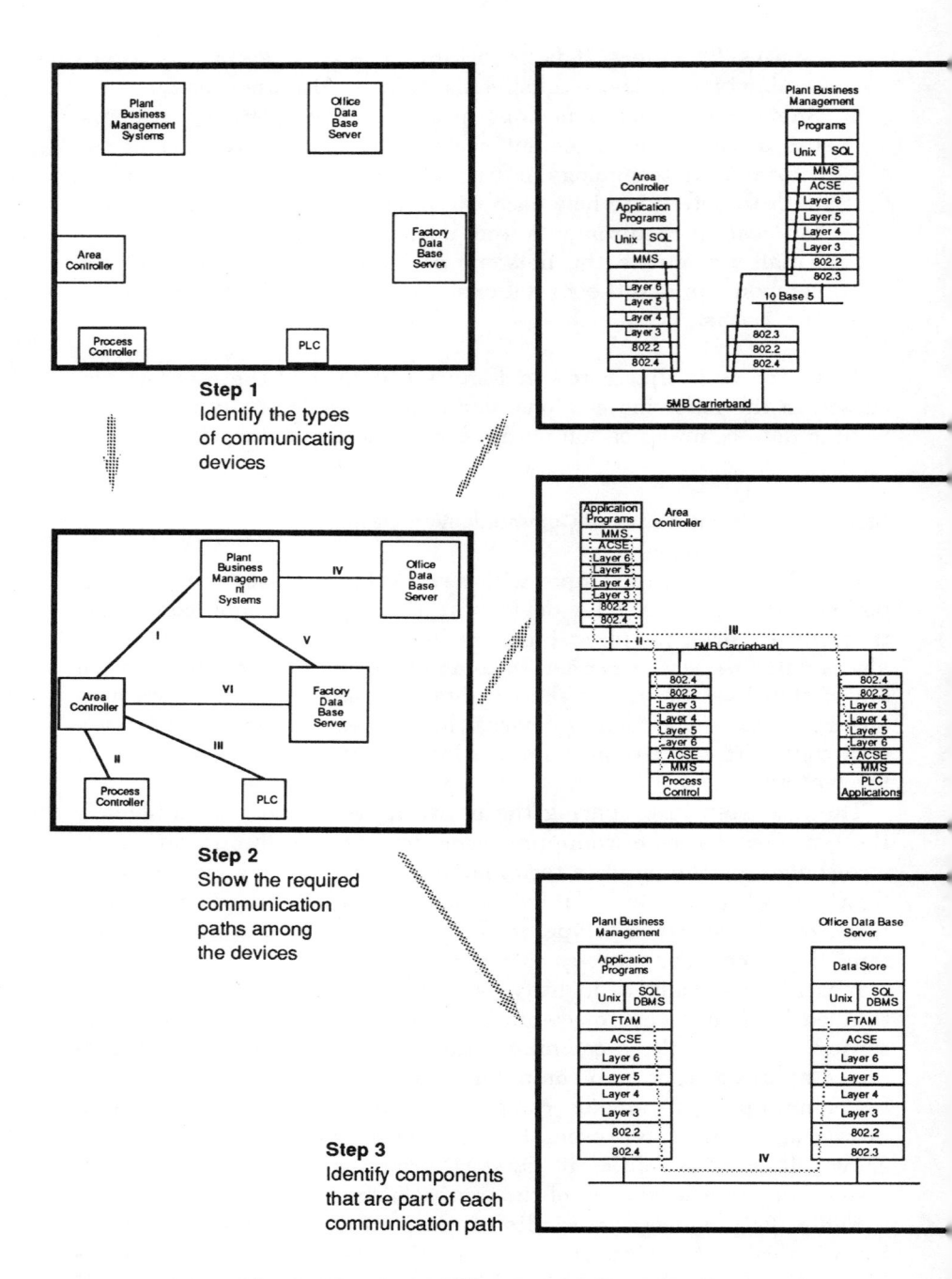

Figure 7-8 Steps in the development of a network architecture.

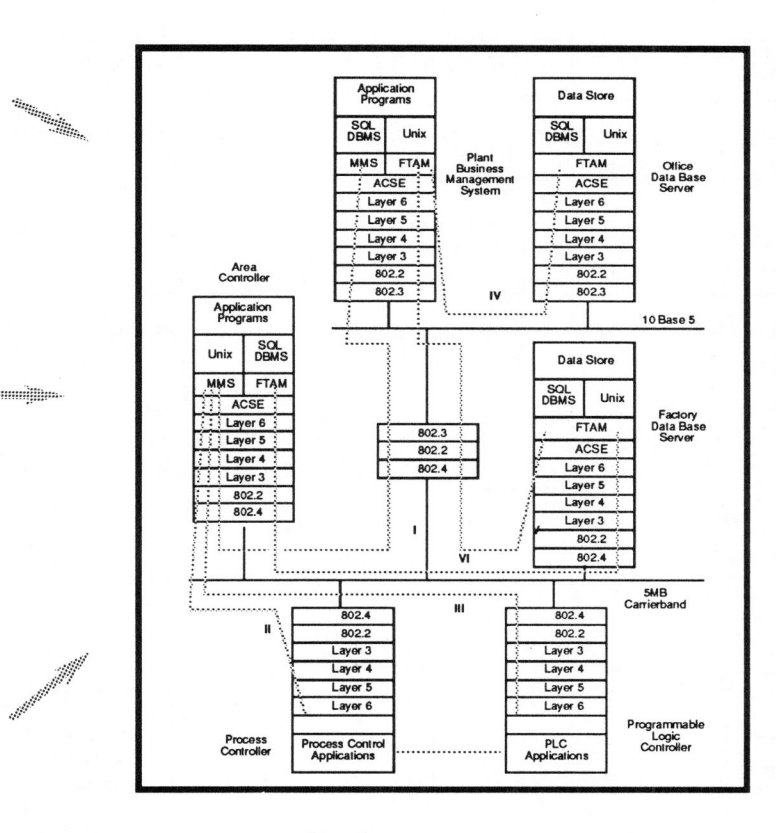

Using the OSI Model for Network Architecture Analysis 195

Step 4
Combine and prepare the overall network architecture

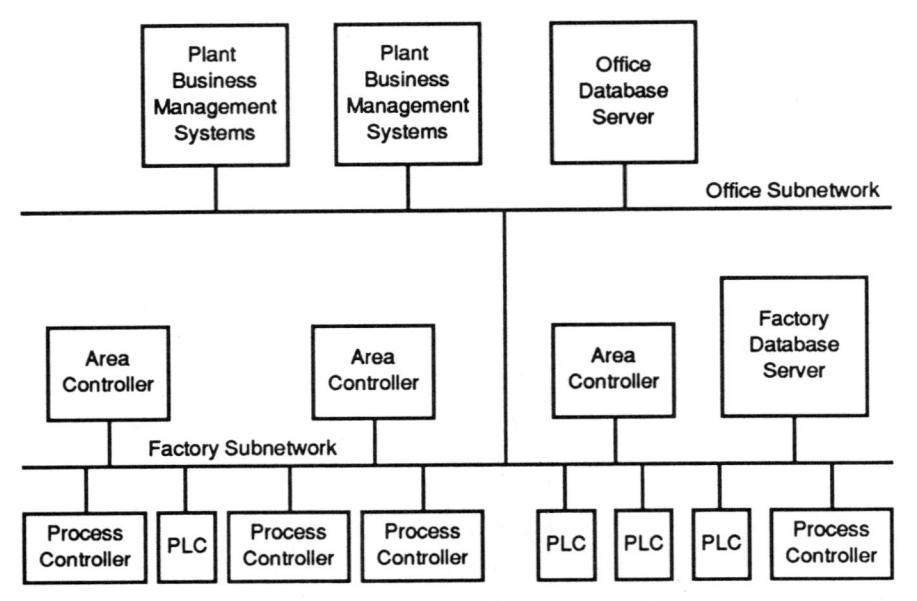

Figure 7-9 Overview of communication devices for the hypothetical enterprise.

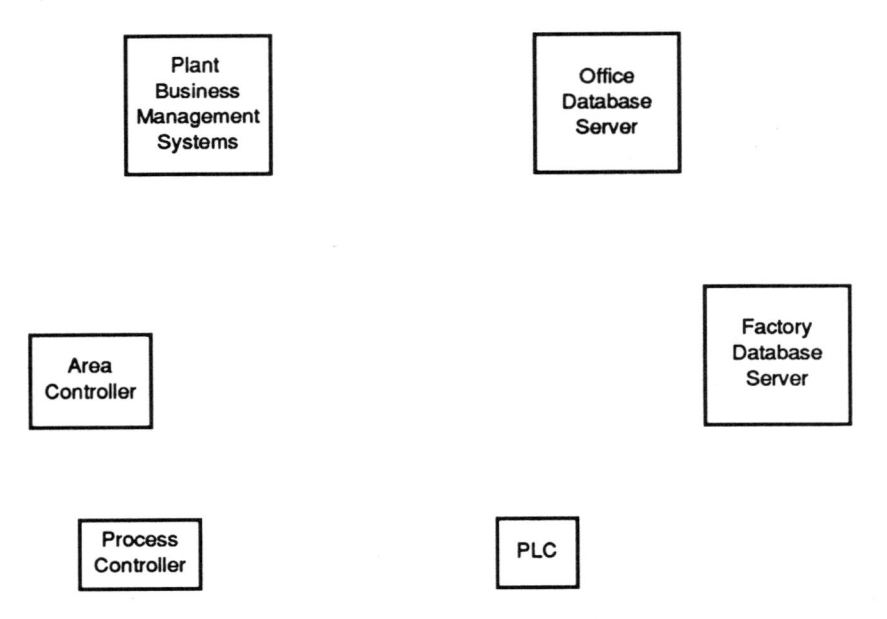

Figure 7-10 Overview of the different types of communicating devices for the hypothetical enterprise.

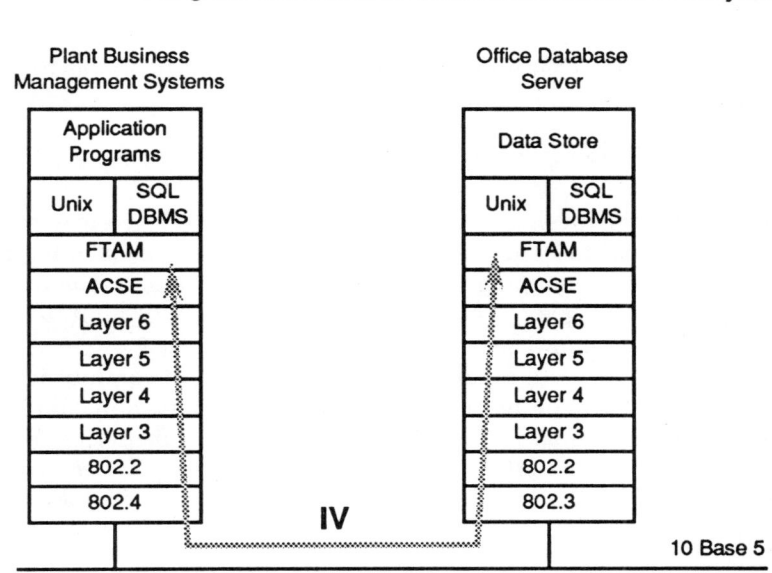

Using the OSI Model for Network Architecture Analysis   197

```
  Plant Business                    Office Database
Management Systems                      Server
```

Application Programs			Data Store	
Unix	SQL DBMS		Unix	SQL DBMS
FTAM			FTAM	
ACSE			ACSE	
Layer 6			Layer 6	
Layer 5			Layer 5	
Layer 4			Layer 4	
Layer 3			Layer 3	
802.2			802.2	
802.4			802.3	

IV

10 Base 5

Protocols Common on Each Device
Layer 6   ISO Presentation Kernel
Layer 5   ISO Session Kernel
Layer 4   ISO Transport Class IV
Layer 3   ISO CLNP

Figure 7-11 Overview of required communication paths for the hypothetical enterprise.

Step 2: Show the Required Communication Paths Among the Devices

The next step is to show the required communication paths among the devices. This is illustrated in Figure 7-11 in which are shown six types of required communication paths.

The plant business management systems will need to communicate with the area controllers. This is represented by communication path I. The area controllers will need to communicate with the process controllers and the PLC's, as represented by communication paths II and III respectively. Paths IV, V, and VI are for access to the database servers from the plant business management systems and the area controllers.

There are other paths that would likely be required, but for simplicity they are not included in the example. For example, plant business management systems would likely need to communicate with one another; the area controllers would also probably need to communicate with one another. There might be terminals on the factory subnetwork that might need to communicate with the area controllers. PLC's might need to pass messages from one to another. Each of these additional communication paths would need to be investigated for an actual enterprise network.

Step 3: Identify the Components of Each Communication Path

The third step is to show the components involved in each of the communication paths. These include the network protocol to be used at each layer, the operating system, the database management system, application programs, etc. In our example we will analyze each of the required communications paths separately.

Figure 7-12 shows the details of the components in communication path I between the plant business management systems and the area controllers. The two subnetworks use different protocols for the physical layer. For the office subnetwork, the physical layer protocol is CSMA/CD (802.3), and for the factory network it is token bus

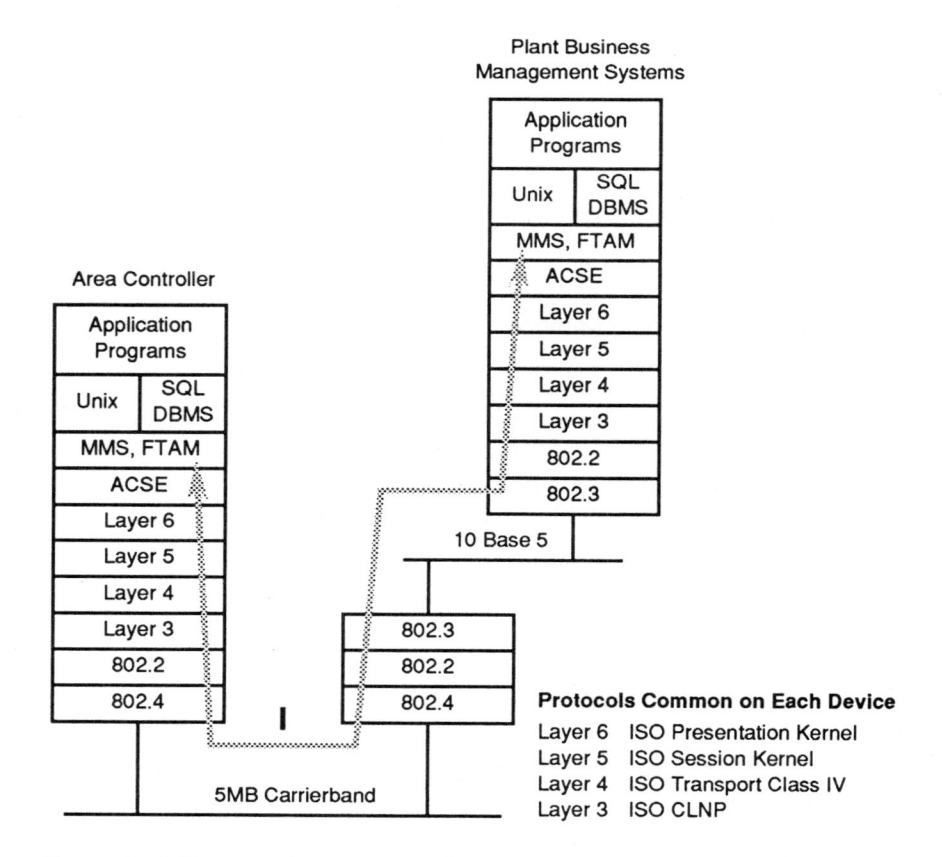

Figure 7-12 Details of components in communication path I between plant business management systems and area controllers.

(802.4). Therefore, a bridge is required to connect them. The bridge is relatively simple since the upper layer protocols are not affected by the physical media used. This is one of the big advantages of basing networks on the ISO standards. In fact, if it were decided to use 802.3 instead of 802.4 for the factory subnetwork, the applications and basic communication strategies would be unaffected. For the time being, the protocols for layers 3 through 6 will be assumed to be the same throughout the overall network. (Generally, the selection of the protocols to be used at layers 1 and 7 will be the ones of interest.)

For this hypothetical enterprise, it is intended that MMS and FTAM be used for communications between the plant business management systems and the area controllers. In addition, a Unix operating system and a database management system based on SQL will be used on each. The actual type of communication between the two may involve messaging between application programs (MMS), file transfer (FTAM), and perhaps a distributed database management system. The reason for showing the operating systems and the database management systems is to be sure the full impact of the communication at each end is considered. Both the operating system and the database management system are key components of the information technology infrastructure and are important in making communication work. If, for example, there were different proprietary operating systems and/or database management systems at each end, the communication could still be accomplished with MMS and FTAM, but the way the data and/or files would be handled at each end could be different. In this hypothetical case, it is intended that the systems at each end be symmetrical so that in the future applications can be moved from machine to machine.

The protocols to be used on layers 3 through 6 are to be the same throughout and therefore are not shown in the details for each device. If communication via telecommunication to other networks were required, then the protocols at these layers would have to be included. The same would be true if it were necessary to interconnect with proprietary network protocols.

Figure 7-13 shows communication paths II and III from the area controllers to the process controllers and the PLC's. MMS will be used for communication between the area controller applications and the process controller applications and between the area controller applications and the PLC's applications. Notice that on the area controller, the components of interest for these communication paths are fewer than in Figure 7-12. This is not because the operating system is not important. Rather, it is because in this case the messages are from application to application and other services of the area controller will not be used directly. If, however, the process controllers were

```
        Application       Area            Protocols Common on Each Device
         Programs      Controller         Layer 6  ISO Presentation Kernel
           MMS                            Layer 5  ISO Session Kernel
           ACSE                           Layer 4  ISO Transport Class IV
          Layer 6                         Layer 3  ISO CLNP
          Layer 5
          Layer 4
          Layer 3
           802.2
           802.4
                                 III
   II
                            5MB Carrierband
```

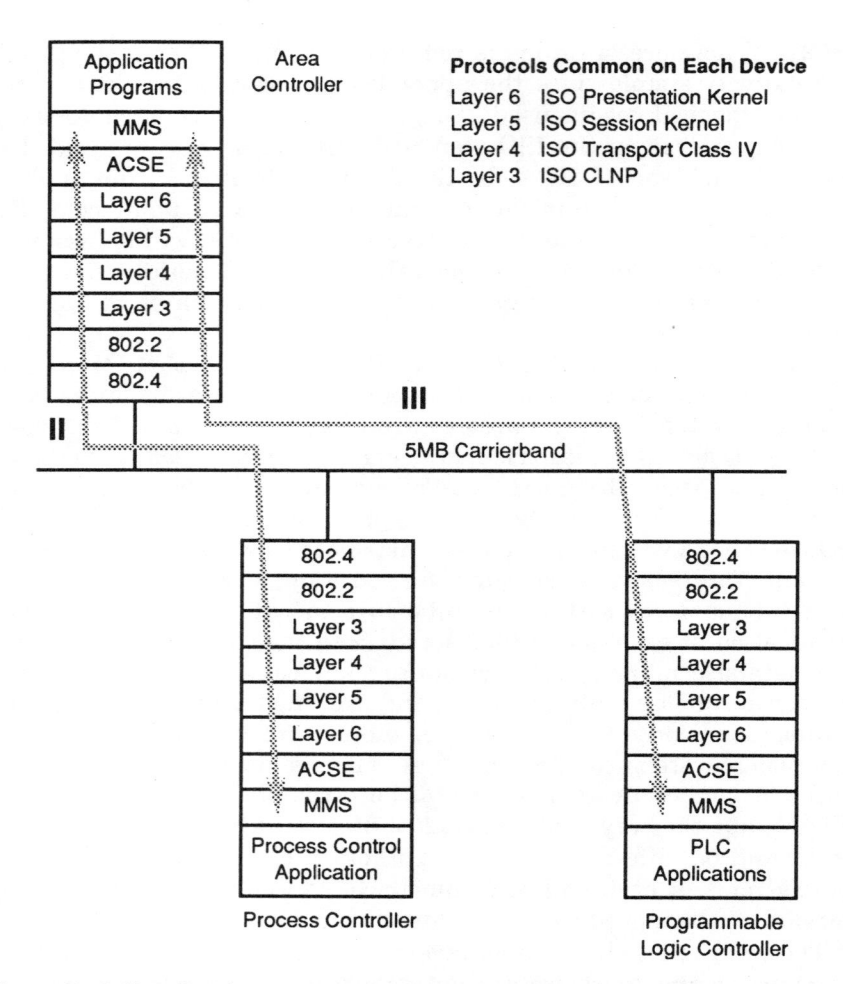

802.4		802.4
802.2		802.2
Layer 3		Layer 3
Layer 4		Layer 4
Layer 5		Layer 5
Layer 6		Layer 6
ACSE		ACSE
MMS		MMS
Process Control Application		PLC Applications

Process Controller   Programmable
                                  Logic Controller

Figure 7-13 Details of components in communication paths II and III from area controllers to process controllers and PLC's.

to have a separate database management system that the area controllers were to utilize, then this would have to be included and analyzed to determine how it entered into the communications.

Figure 7-14 shows communication path IV, which provides the access between the plant business management system and the office database server. The other two paths, V and VI, are similar. In this case FTAM, Unix, and SQL will be used on each end.

As mentioned above, for an actual facility, communication between process controllers, between PLC's, and from process controllers to PLC's might also be required. This would also need to be analyzed. It is not included in this simplified example, but it can be seen that the

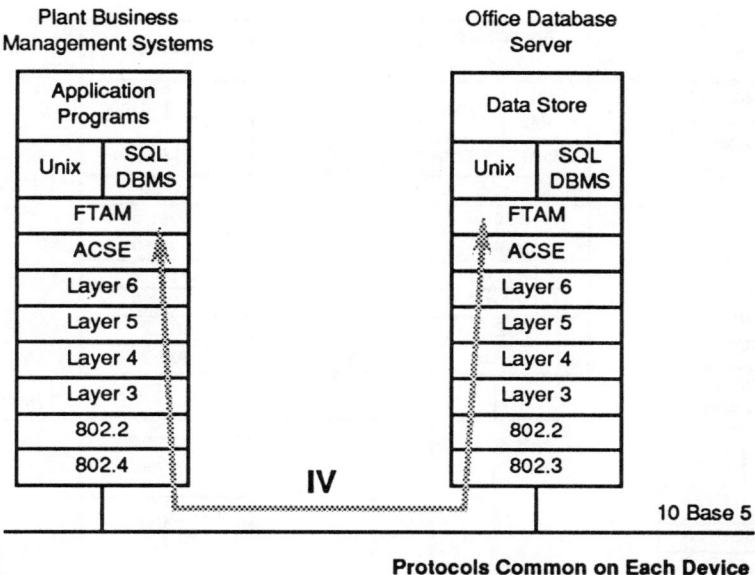

Using the OSI Model for Network Architecture Analysis 201

```
Plant Business                          Office Database
Management Systems                      Server

┌─────────────────┐                    ┌─────────────────┐
│  Application    │                    │   Data Store    │
│   Programs      │                    │                 │
├──────┬──────────┤                    ├──────┬──────────┤
│      │   SQL    │                    │      │   SQL    │
│ Unix │  DBMS    │                    │ Unix │  DBMS    │
├──────┴──────────┤                    ├──────┴──────────┤
│      FTAM       │                    │      FTAM       │
├─────────────────┤                    ├─────────────────┤
│      ACSE       │                    │      ACSE       │
├─────────────────┤                    ├─────────────────┤
│     Layer 6     │                    │     Layer 6     │
├─────────────────┤                    ├─────────────────┤
│     Layer 5     │                    │     Layer 5     │
├─────────────────┤                    ├─────────────────┤
│     Layer 4     │                    │     Layer 4     │
├─────────────────┤                    ├─────────────────┤
│     Layer 3     │                    │     Layer 3     │
├─────────────────┤                    ├─────────────────┤
│      802.2      │                    │      802.2      │
├─────────────────┤         IV         ├─────────────────┤
│      802.4      │····················│      802.3      │
└────────┬────────┘                    └────────┬────────┘
                                                    10 Base 5
```

Protocols Common on Each Device
Layer 6   ISO Presentation Kernel
Layer 5   ISO Session Kernel
Layer 4   ISO Transport Class IV
Layer 3   ISO CLNP

Figure 7-14 Details of components in communication path IV between plant business management systems and office database server.

network shown would also permit these communication paths since the same components would be used. However, in an actual facility, there might also be proprietary protocols used on the process controllers and/or PLC's. In this case, a detailed analysis would be needed of communication between PLC's and process controllers. It may turn out that direct communication is not feasible and that alternative means, such as indirect communication through the area controller, would be required. This makes it clear why nonproprietary ISO standards are important when more than two types of devices must communicate.

Step 4: Combine and Prepare the Overall Network Architecture

The final step in completing the network architecture is to show all of the components and their relationships to the required communication paths. Figure 7-15 shows this for the hypothetical enterprise. It is a composite showing the devices, the required communication paths, and the components involved in the communication.

202 Open Systems Interconnection Handbook

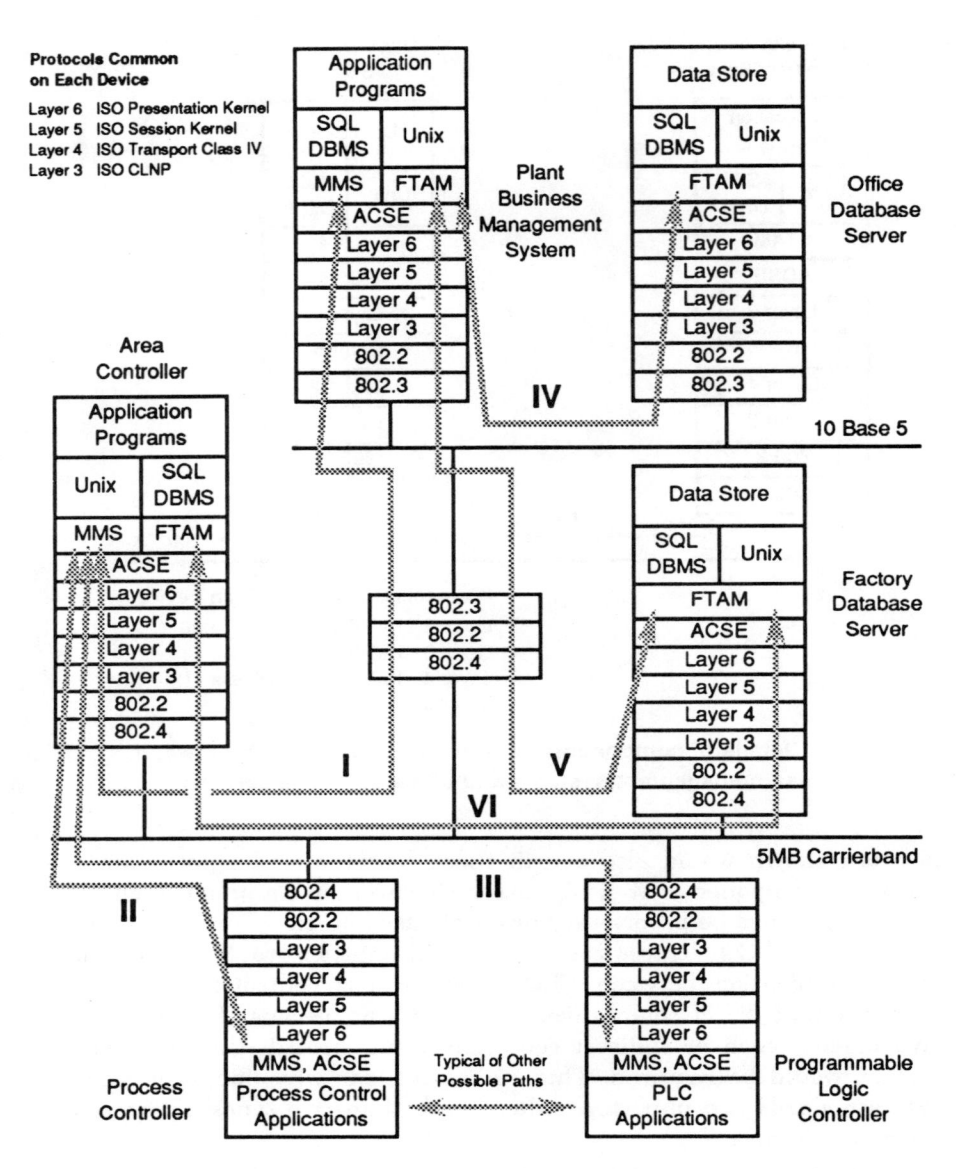

Figure 7-15 Network architecture showing the required communication paths.

With all of the basic components shown, "what if" analyses can be made. For example, should a Virtual Terminal (VT) protocol be included on area controllers so that terminals in the factory can access the plant business management systems? What about the terminals on the plant business management system accessing the area controllers? Whether this is required or even desirable would depend upon the operating practices and philosophy of the enterprise. This is an example of how the implementation of an open architecture could have an impact on the operation of the enterprise by making information available directly without filtering through an organizational hierarchy.

Another condition that could be investigated in this example is the communication between similar devices, such as between plant business management systems. Because they use the same components, the communication would be similar to that shown for path I. In the same way, communication from process controller to process controller or from PLC to PLC would in principle be possible. The question would be whether the applications on these devices would be able to initiate and use the communication path.

Finally, there are some important "housekeeping" protocols that are not included in the example above that need to be included. These include directory services and network management, which have been discussed in other chapters. Although they do not enter directly into the analysis procedure described above, they must be incorporated into the overall design.

Analyzing the Network Architecture When Non-ISO Protocols Are Included

The above example was of a hypothetical enterprise in which all of the communication protocols are based on the ISO standards. However, in most situations there are proprietary and non-ISO protocols that already exist within the enterprise. How are these to be handled? The procedure discussed above still applies, but the problem and its analysis are more complex.

A frequent solution is to use a gateway. The term *gateway* in the context of the ISO standards refers to a device that has all seven layers of one network protocol and all seven layers of a "foreign" network protocol. Typically, gateways are offered by vendors to allow their proprietary network to communicate with another popular proprietary network.

In general, incompatibility at the lower layers is much less of a problem than incompatibility at upper layers. For example, as shown in Figure 7-3, the means for interconnecting a CSMA/CD-based subnetwork with a token bus network is relatively simple and requires a bridge. This is because the translation is on the method of modulation, signaling, etc.

On the other hand, translation at the application layer can be very complex or even impractical. This is because the meaning and context of communication is at issue. For example, MMS, an application layer protocol, has many commands that are similar to commands used by proprietary PLC network protocols, such as starting, stopping, and downloading programs. Translation of simple commands such as these is feasible through gateways. However, MMS also has some rather sophisticated commands that depend on the context in which the commands are used. A gateway to handle these would be rather complex, which could make such a solution impractical. Therefore, a gateway might be a solution for a specific type of communication, but the specific requirements need to be analyzed.

Figure 7-16 illustrates how non-ISO devices would be included in the network architecture. In this case, the process controllers and the PLC's have their own proprietary network protocol. Special interface drivers and network interfaces are required for each of the proprietary networks. Intercommunication among the process controllers, as well as among the PLC's, is possible. However, intercommunication between the process controllers and PLC's would most likely not be feasible, nor would intercommunication between a process controller or PLC and any other device other than the single area controller.

Summary

This chapter has shown how to analyze and plan networks from a "macro" view. It has discussed the importance of the information technology infrastructure for the typical enterprise and how the goal of standards is to minimize the difficulty in making information available when and where it is needed. Because of the complexity and variety of network protocols in the current state of affairs today, it is not possible simply to plug any given computer into a network and have the information get to the destination desired in the form needed. Even if only ISO standards are used, there still are variations in the types of protocols that can be applied. Also, in the typical enterprise there are usually proprietary network protocols that must be accounted for in developing a network strategy.

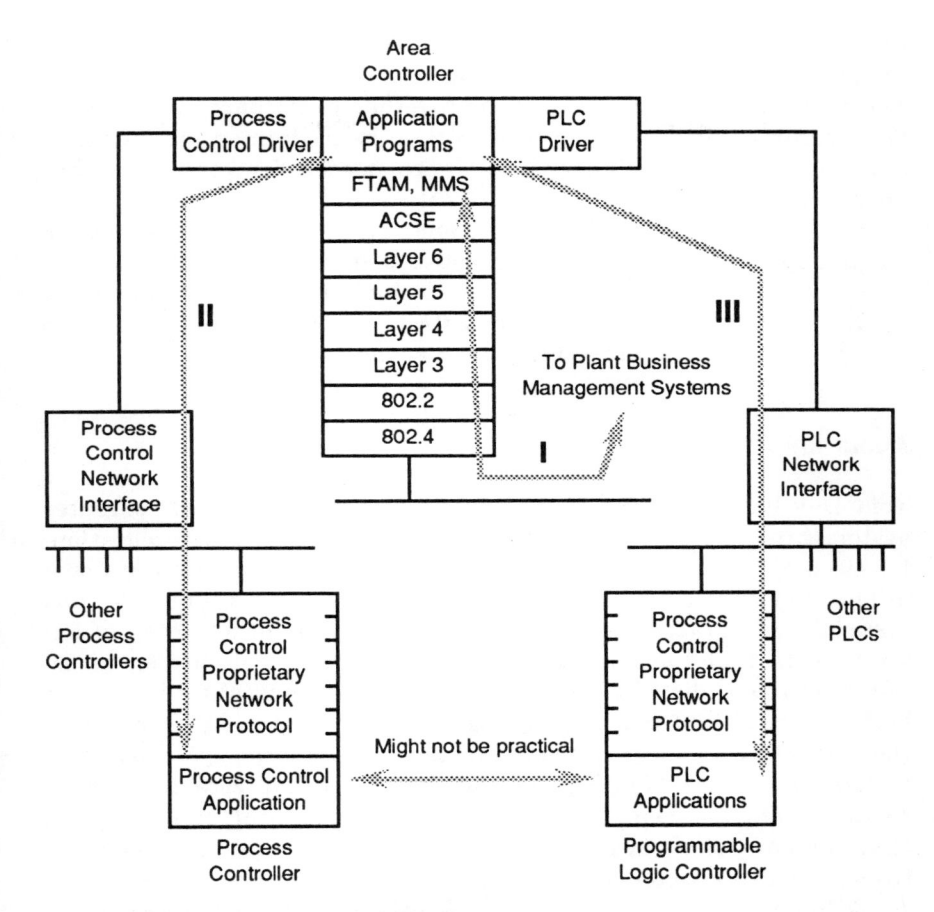

Using the OSI Model for Network Architecture Analysis 205

Figure 7-16 Use of non-ISO devices.

A means of methodically analyzing the components involved in the required data communication paths has been presented. The purpose of this was to develop for the enterprise an overall network architecture that accounts for how each of the types of communication paths will be realized. The approach presented divides the overall problem into four steps. The first step is to identify the types of end system devices that will be involved with communications with other end system devices. These devices might be computers, terminals, PLC's, robots, automated guided vehicles, etc. The second step is to show the types of required communication paths among the devices. The third step is to show all of the information technology infrastructure components that will be part of each of the communication paths. The final step is to put all of this together to prepare the network architecture. "What if" analyses can then be performed to determine if there are other components that are needed for conditions that may occur in the future.

The reason for performing this analysis is to prevent surprises when implementing networks. Because of the complexity of the issues involved, it is important to have looked at all of the components of the information technology infrastructure from a macro view to ensure that the desired results can be achieved.

About the Author

Tom DeVille has 22 years' experience in engineering and computer system integration. Currently he is Manager, Systems Integration, for Bechtel Corporation and is responsible for managing all systems integration projects in Bechtel's industrial business line. He has planned and managed implementation of systems in a variety of environments that have included mainframes, minicomputers, microcomputers, and distributed control systems. He has M.S. degrees in both electrical and mechanical engineering from the Massachusetts Institute of Technology, specializing in control of large systems. He is a member of the MAP/TOP Steering Committee that establishes user requirements for computer networking in industrial and technical environments. He is also a member of ISA, IEEE, and SME, and is a registered Professional Engineer in California. He may be contacted as follows: Thomas G. DeVille, Manager, Systems Integration, Bechtel Corporation, P.O. Box 3965, San Francisco, CA 94925, Tel: (415) 768-9924.

Bechtel Corporation is a broad-based technology company that provides technical and management services to design, engineer, build, and operate facilities throughout the world. It provides these services to clients in a variety of industries including food, microelectronics, pharmaceuticals, petroleum, chemicals, power generation, metal processing, pulp and paper, environmental, and aerospace. Bechtel has been a leader in the application of information technology in the design and engineering of facilities. In addition, Bechtel provides systems integration services to clients in the industries it serves. Besides activities in MAP/TOP, Bechtel is a charter member of the Corporation for Open Systems.

Section C

X.400 and X.500

Chapter

8

Successful OSI Migration Strategies

by Peter R. Westwood

Introduction

Because the OSI technologies are still evolving, some users are concerned that they cannot benefit from connectivity solutions based upon the standards in their current form. This chapter discusses connectivity alternatives, then presents case studies of successful uses of the OSI X.400 protocols; the basic migration and implementation strategies used to ensure success are also documented. The case studies have been selected from the banking, communication, and defense industries. In all cases the organizations have multivendor hardware and software environments.

We are in the information age, an age in which information is a major strategic asset. Communication of information and access to information systems are fundamental to the survival and success of organizations today. For instance, without advanced communication systems, brokerage companies cannot compete in the modern markets in which stocks and bonds are traded twenty-four hours a day on exchanges throughout the world. Similarly, the connection of automobile companies' manufacturing systems to their parts suppliers' systems using "just-in-time" inventory management is essential for the automobile manufacturers to increase their productivity and lower their manufacturing costs. As another example, airline reservation system companies have become more profitable than the airline companies themselves. A reservation system company's sole business is the communication of information.

Despite the many successful, well-known cases of demonstrated increased productivity and profitability, most organizations still have islands of information systems. Users of departmental systems cannot communicate directly with colleagues on other departmental systems, nor can they communicate with their clients and their systems.

The computer and communication industry has recognized these user "connectivity" needs. As a result, the standards conforming to the OSI model have been developed and are still being further developed. By using systems that conform to these standards, users can connect their heterogeneous systems.

Interconnect Alternatives

Before the advent of these industry standards, organizations had three choices if they wished to interconnect their disparate systems:

1. Develop a custom solution
2. Utilize a proprietary solution
3. Utilize a de facto standard

Each of these options has considerable drawbacks, as evidenced by the lack of implemented interconnections between dissimilar systems.

Although the custom solution should exactly meet an organization's specific needs and result in complete control over its business, the investment associated with developing and installing custom systems is immense. Development of communication software is a highly specialized discipline, fraught with risk. To develop software with a reasonable degree of functionality takes years and costs millions, and the costs do not stop after the initial investment. The software has to be supported, maintained, and enhanced as the requirements and business evolve and as applicable new technologies arise.

A company that elects to use a proprietary solution is totally dependent upon the business viability of the vendor supplying that proprietary solution. Not only has the vendor to develop the software, but he must also adapt and support it for all the different computer systems available today. There is a high risk that either the vendor's product will not remain current with the technological improvements that become available and that the proprietary software could benefit from, or the vendor of the proprietary solution will no longer support that solution, or even go out of business. Even the very largest system vendors are moving away from proprietary communication protocols because of the research and development costs and the incompatibilities with other vendors' systems.

Another significant disadvantage of both custom and proprietary solutions is that the investment resources of only one company are committed to the solution. The industry as a whole is not placing its research and development resources behind the solution, and a user organization cannot take advantage of all the millions of dollars being invested in standards-based interconnection products and applications.

Proprietary solutions gain viability when they become de facto standards, and other vendors implement such solutions. The major problem with such standards is that they are too closely dependent upon the system architecture and whims of the original vendor. Other vendors lag behind in implementing the de facto standards on their systems. Most large organizations today have evolved from being primarily single-vendor shops, to being multivendor shops, recognizing the specialized and unique capabilities of the different system vendors. To use a single vendor's proprietary communication protocol is, therefore, to many organizations a step backward.

The most beneficial solution for both vendors and users is based upon industry-approved standards. This removes the overdependence on particular vendors and provides more compatibility and connectivity among different information systems, increasing the value of the organization's information asset. What previously had been islands of information assets and systems, used by isolated groups, can be readily expanded into a network of interconnected information systems spanning the globe.

However, despite the apparent soundness of the above analysis, some organizations are reluctant to commit to and implement OSI-based solutions. Why?

- They question the vendors' commitment to implementing the standards.
- They wonder, with the new particular standards still being developed and the older ones being revised, whether or not the standards are viable for use today.

- They need to be able to protect their existing investments yet take advantage of the benefits that can be obtained by implementing standards-based solutions.

Although as recently as a year or two ago, certain vendors' commitments to OSI products were suspect, this should no longer concern anyone. All vendors have not only announced their commitments, but also have been spending significant amounts of money developing OSI products, many of which are already available, with more soon to become available. The two other concerns can be answered by examining successful implementations that have used OSI technologies to solve organizations' problems. This chapter discusses three such cases with which the author was personally involved. The chapter concludes with a review of the migration strategies that were used to ensure success and that would be applicable in many other situations.

Case 1

A major international public e-mail supplier was providing e-mail services to user organizations whereby users had to use dumb terminals or PC's, communicating over a network directly with their mailboxes on the public e-mail host system. Many of the user organizations were already using IBM's PROFS electronic mail product to communicate with many others in their own organization. Most users had access to only one type of terminal and one e-mail system. Those that had access to both types of terminal and e-mail had to key common messages into both systems, which was intolerable.

The solution to the users' problems was to connect their PROFS systems directly to the public e-mail system. Then, to a PROFS user a public e-mail user looked just like another PROFS user at another PROFS node. And to a public e-mail user, a PROFS user appeared to be another public e-mail user in a particular domain.

Figure 8-1 shows a configuration for achieving this system-to-system interconnection using OSI X.400. On one IBM mainframe PROFS node in the user organization is installed on OSIware Inc.'s PROFS/X.400 Gateway software. This consists of the PCF (PROFS Conversion Facility) and the X.400 compliant MTA, RTS, Session, Transport software integrated with IBM's NPSI X.25 software. In this way the IBM mainframe, with the X.400 software, can communicate over a packet-switched network with any other system running X.400 software. The public e-mail service communicates with

Successful OSI Migration Strategies 213

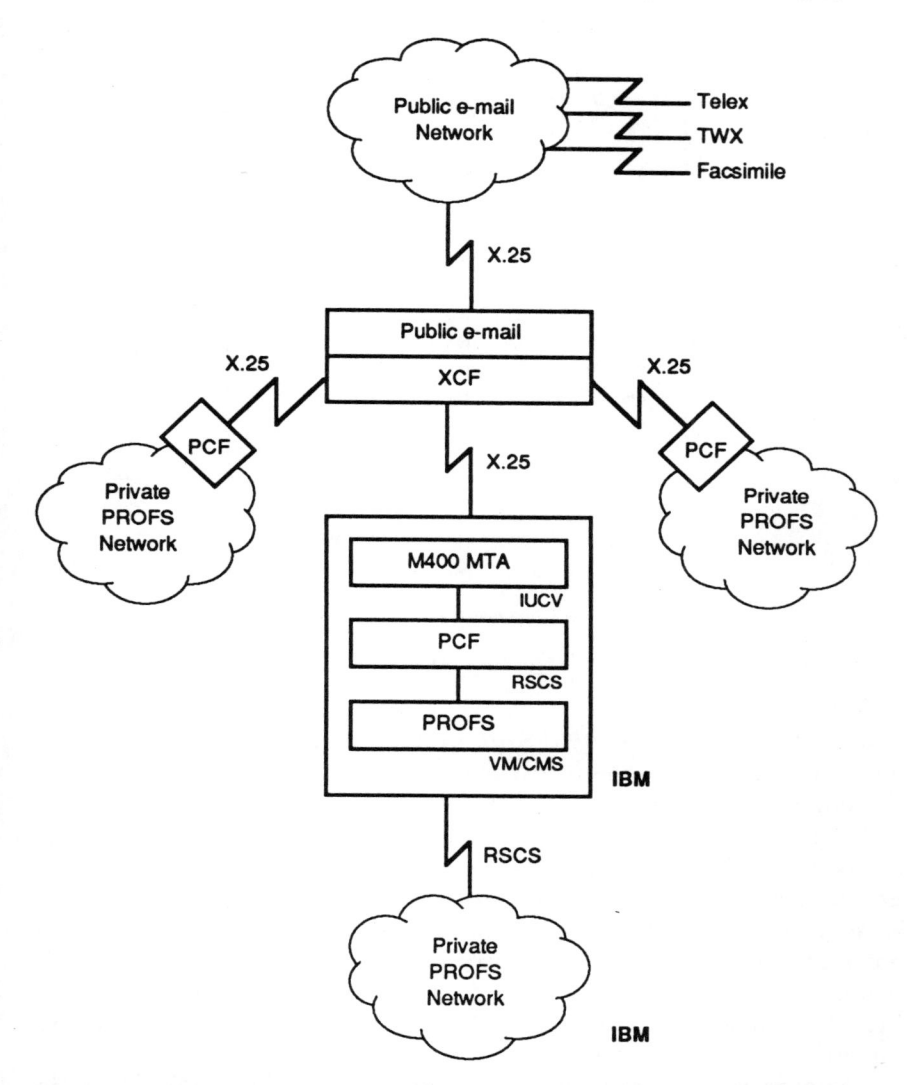

Figure 8-1 Configuration 1: PROFS and public e-mail interconnection.

the IBM mainframe X.400 system (and then with PROFS) via the public e-mail X.400 Gateway services.

Clearly X.400-compliant software has certain features that PROFS doesn't have and vice versa. Figure 8-2 lists all the message header fields that an X.400 system supports, along with those supported by PROFS.

214 Open Systems Interconnection Handbook

FIELD	PROFS	M400 (X.400)
to	Yes	Yes
from	Yes	Yes
subject	Yes	Yes
cc	Yes	Yes
bcc	No	Yes
auto-forward	No	Yes
expiry-date	No	Yes
importance	No	Yes
in-reply-to	No	Yes
message-ID	No	Yes
obsoletes	No	Yes
references	No	Yes
reply-by	No	Yes
reply-to	No	Yes
sender	No	Yes
sensitivity	No	Yes

Figure 8-2 PROFS/X.400 message header support.

In addition, because PROFS users can be addressed only with an eight-character ID, when a PROFS user wishes to send a message to a public e-mail user, the public e-mail user's ID must be preregistered in a specialized PROFS PCF directory by the system administrator. This directory translates the PROFS ID to an X.400 address. Because of the greater flexibility in X.400 addressing, messages coming from the public e-mail world to the PROFS world do not have to be addressed to preregistered recipients in the PCF directory. However they have to follow a convention in which the PROFS node and ID are contained in the public e-mail address using the standard attribute facilities within X.400 addressing.

For example, a message from PROFS to "VM(M400USR1)" is converted, using the PCF directory, to "S=M400USR1/ O=VM/ a ADMD/ C=CA/ P=PRMD." A message from the public e-mail system to "S=SMITH/OSIWARE/OSIVAN/ A=ADMD/ C=CA/ P=PRMD" is delivered to the PROFS PCF node, where the X.400 addressing is stripped off, and then presented to the PROFS node as "OSIVAN(SMITH)."

With this network-to-network connection, the need for two different terminals is eliminated, as is duplicate keying of messages. Easy access to a larger e-mail community is the major benefit. In addition, the PROFS users can take advantage of other services provided by the public e-mail service, such as sending messages to Faxes, Telex and TWX, and overnight hard copy. Multiple PROFS networks can be interconnected with the public e-mail network. PROFS users can even use the public e-mail service to send messages to other PROFS users, taking advantage of the reliability and efficiency (unlike PROFS, one copy of a message to multiple users is transmitted between nodes) of X.400 over X.25 networks when compared to using IBM's RSCS protocol over leased or dial-up lines.

Case 2

In this second scenario, a number of defense industry suppliers had individual PROFS networks, another proprietary e-mail network conforming to the DARPA Internet RFC822 standard, IBM-compatible PC's, and DEC machines running the VMS and Ultrix operating systems. None of these systems were interconnected until they were connected using OSI-conformant software, as shown in Figure 8-3.

On one node in each organization's PROFS network is installed PROFS/X.400 Gateway software running over IBM NPSI X.25; on the DEC VAX machines is installed OSIware Inc.'s native X.400 Messenger 400 e-mail product, integrated with DEC's PSI X.25 software. On the DEC systems running Ultrix, OSIware's RFC822/X.400 Gateway software is installed to connect to the Internet network. That network consists of a series of Altos systems running a proprietary distributed mail package called V6MAIL. In addition to the Internet mailers, UUCP, CSNET, and BITNET mailers (such as Sendmail, MMDF, and UUCPmail) conform to the RFC822 specification.

One of the features of this network is the inclusion of LAN's and stand-alone DOS PC's. Consumers Software Network Courier e-mail software through the Network Courier X.400 Gateway using an Eicon Technologies X.25 board interconnects to the X.400-connected network. Consumers Software ModemMail version of Network Courier connects the stand-alone PC's via the Network Courier Post Office on the LAN to the X.400-linked network.

The result of all this interconnection is that users on any of the mail systems can communicate with any of the other users whatever their e-mail base. PROFS to X.400 addressing is handled as in case 1. Internet addressing uses the X.400 domain-defined attribute facili-

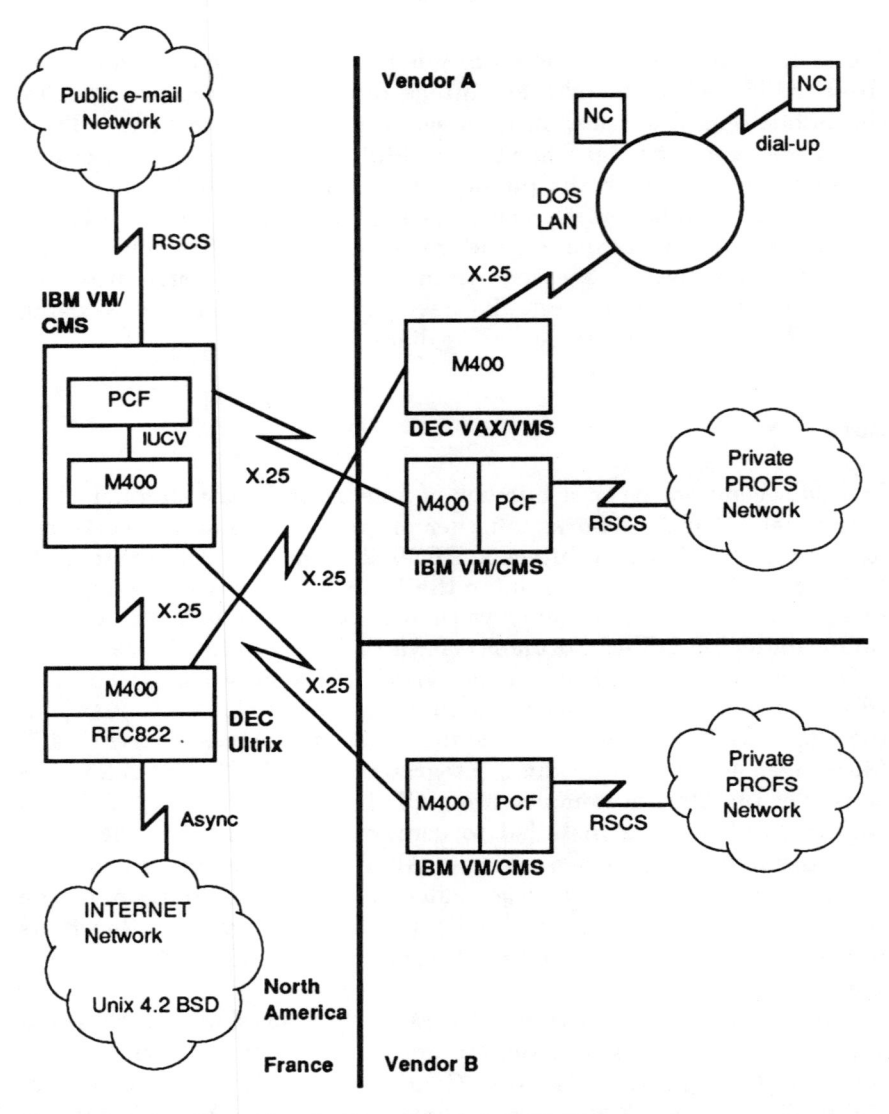

Figure 8-3 Configuration 2: Case 2 interconnection.

ties. Network Courier handles full X.400 addressing. The support of certain messaging features depends upon the commonality of features among the different mail systems. Message header fields between PROFS and X.400 are as in Figure 8-2; Figure 8-4 shows the level of support of message header fields between the Internet and X.400 domains.

Successful OSI Migration Strategies 217

FIELD	M400 (X.400)	RFC822
to	Yes	Yes
from	Yes	Yes
subject	Yes	Yes
cc	Yes	Yes
bcc	Yes	No
auto-forward	Yes	No
expiry-date	Yes	No
importance	Yes	Yes
in-reply-to	Yes	Yes
message-ID	Yes	No
obsoletes	Yes	No
references	Yes	Yes
reply-by	Yes	No
reply-to	Yes	Yes
sender	Yes	Yes
sensitivity	Yes	Yes

Figure 8-4 X.400/RFC822 message header support.

Case 3

The last case to be discussed is that of a large, multinational oil company. The company had a number of unconnected proprietary e-mail systems distributed throughout the world, including IBM's PROFS, DEC's All-in-1 and VMS Mail, DG's CEO, and British Telecom's Telecom Gold public e-mail service. These systems are now interconnected using an X.400 over X.25 backbone, as in Figure 8-5.

As in cases 1 and 2, OSIware's PROFS/X.400 Gateway integrated with IBM NPSI X.25 is installed on a PROFS node that serves as the gateway to the PROFS network. DEC's All-in-1 and VMS Mail products interconnect to the network via DEC's MRX X.400 Gateway. Similarly, DG's X.400 option for CEO is installed. Telecom Gold can now communicate with other X.400 systems. IBM-compatible PC's and LAN's are now connected using the Network Courier X.400 and ModemMail software described in case 2 above. In addition, Macintosh PC's on Appletalk LAN's using the Macintosh version of Consumers Software Network Courier are connected to the Consumers Software IBM-compatible PC LAN's, and via those to the X.400 network. The X.400 interconnections are channeled through a DEC

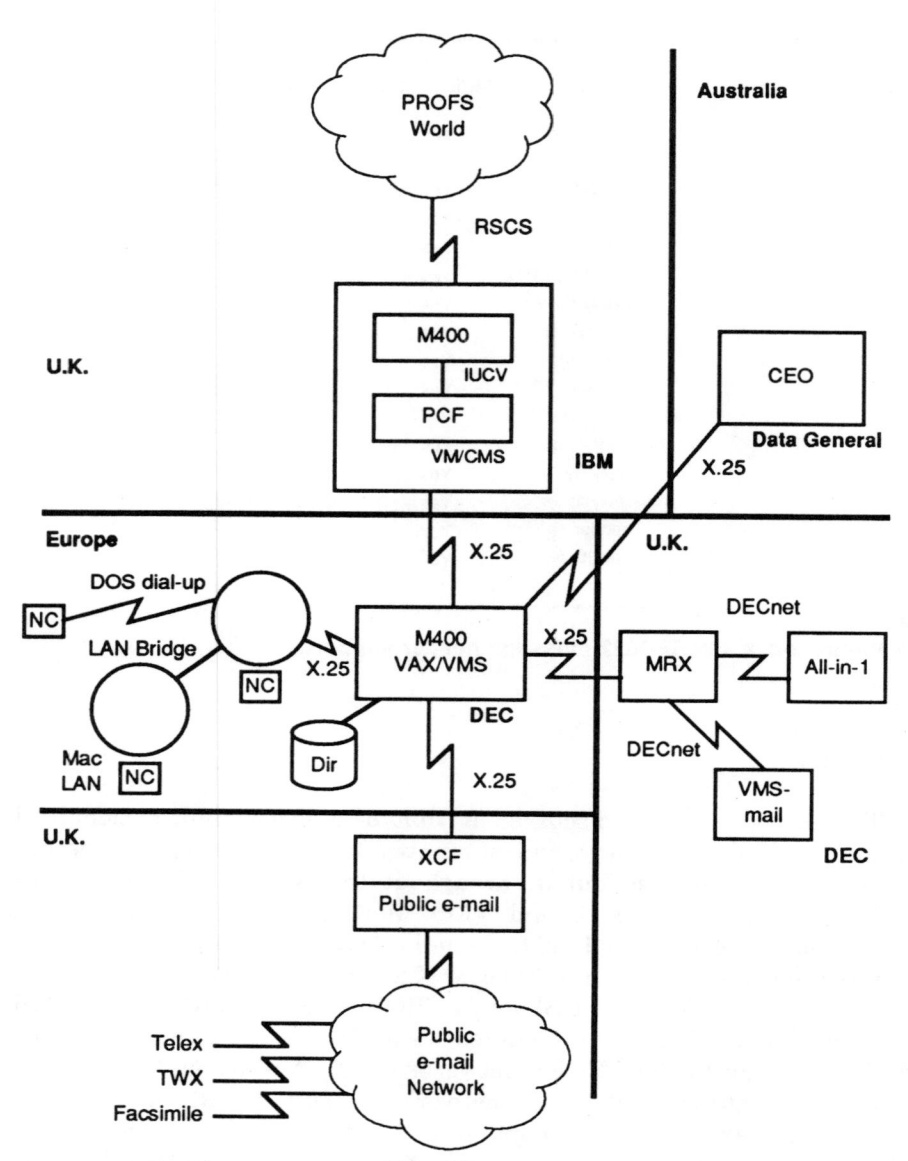

Figure 8-5 Configuration 3: Case 3 interconnection.

VMS system running OSIware's native Messenger 400 X.400 software. This DEC machine acts as the hub of the network; network management is performed from that central system.

As a result of the installation of this X.400-based network, different units throughout the world can now communicate with each other much more effectively. The oil company is using the public e-mail connection to allow direct communication with its clients.

Key Implementation Strategies

Certain underlying strategies were used in the above cases and have been found to work in other situations. These strategies are:

1. First make sure that the appropriate technology to solve the particular problem at hand is being used.
2. Usually use X.400 as the backbone of the interconnect network, definitely when more than two types of mail systems are being interconnected.
3. Don't require that users replace their existing applications.
4. Provide users with added features in addition to increased connectivity.
5. Provide integrated end-to-end solutions; don't let vendors provide pieces that don't all fit together.

Let's elaborate a little on each of these strategies:

Appropriate Technology

In the examples given above and in many other implementations that the author has been involved in, X.400 has been the most appropriate, cost-effective base technology. X.400 is used primarily to connect remote text-messaging systems, but it is a most effective transport mechanism for any type of messages, such as documents, graphics, fax, files, image, voice, and EDI. It is a store-and-forward, peer-to-peer protocol. End-to-end reliable message transfer is a key feature of the protocol. X.400 is ideally suited for connecting distributed applications that need rapid interconnection but not instant real-time connections. The store-and-forward protocol does not require that machines be on-line at all times — an impossible situation if systems are managed on a distributed basis and clients and departmental systems are in the network.

OSI and X.400 as the Backbone

X.400 (and the OSI stack) has considerable functionality, both from a user and reliability viewpoint. On a network-wide basis, application-to-application communication has to function at the lowest common denominator. Because of the extensive functionality of X.400, proprietary e-mail users have little if any loss of mail functionality. (The same is not true for native X.400 e-mail users when communicating with the proprietary systems.)

Users Do Not Replace Existing Applications

There is now usually an X.400 Gateway available for most proprietary e-mail packages, if not from the original developer of the package then from a third-party software vendor. This means that users who are happy with their e-mail do not have to give it up and learn a totally new system, just how to use the gateway if it's not a transparent operation.

Added Features to Users

The number one added feature is of course the increased connectivity and the ability to communicate more rapidly and easily with a larger community of users. Often the connection to other proprietary systems means that the users on a system can access the extra facilities offered by the system, such as fax communication, telex, and hard copy local delivery. Again, a good X.400 e-mail system will have an API permitting distributed applications to be connected on a reliable, store-and-forward basis.

End-to-End Solutions

Putting networks together and connecting hardware and software from a multitude of vendors is a challenging project. Vendors do cooperate with other vendors; most of them have checked their systems against each other. However, everything has to be planned, coordinated, and managed on an operational basis. One single individual/organization must have overall coordinating and decision-making responsibility. This coordinator has to determine what local addressing standards are to be followed, the common functions and procedures, the implementation schedule, problem resolution procedures, vendor liaison — the list is extensive.

Summary

If a systematic, methodical approach is followed, OSI X.400 can be successfully used today to connect heterogeneous systems and to provide significant, increased benefits and functionalities to the users of those systems. By using X.400 today, an organization not only achieves the immediate benefits associated with the latest technology, but it is also in a position to reap the benefits of future OSI and X.400 products as they become available. Since the bulk of vendor communication R&D is now devoted to OSI products, the majority of new products will be OSI-based.

About the Author

Peter Westwood is a management consultant. One of his areas of specialization is providing OSI application planning, marketing, and implementation services to business managers in both communication and information technology vendor companies and to user organizations. He has successfully directed numerous X.400 and X.500 projects. With over 24 years of experience in the communications and computer field and extensive involvement in OSI projects since 1984, Mr. Westwood has also given talks and papers on emerging communication and office automation applications and markets at numerous international conferences; he has also published many articles. Immediately prior to forming his own company, Westwood Technology Management, he was C.O.O. of the software company that was the major initial developer of X.400 and that also developed X.500 software. Eighteen of the top thirty of the world's largest computer and communication companies licensed that X.400 software, and it was installed in over 40 countries. Mr. Westwood has B.A. and B.Sc. degrees from the University of Durham, U.K., and an M.B.A. from Simon Fraser University, Canada. He can be contacted at Westwood Technology Management, 943 Inglewood Avenue, West Vancouver, B.C., Canada V7T 1X8 {Tel: (604) 922-8734, Fax: (604) 926-3297}.

Chapter

9

X.400 and Xerox Network Systems Mail

by John Stidd

Introduction

In this chapter we discuss a distributed electronic mail system that gateways to X.400. The Xerox Network Systems (XNS) Mail System grew out of the work on office computer systems and networks done by Xerox's Palo Alto Research Center in the 1970s and early 1980s. During the latter part of this period, the Consultative Committee for International Telephony and Telegraphy (CCITT), one of the main standards bodies for telecommunications, was developing the standard for electronic mail that was to become the X.400 Series of Recommendations in 1984. X.400 was influenced by the XNS Mail architecture; the converse was also true. The purpose of this chapter is to compare X.400 with the XNS Mail implementation at all seven of the OSI layers and to briefly recount the history of one vendor's involvement with this standard. At the end, an attempt is made to analyze some of the difficulties involved in moving from Xerox Network Systems standards to ISO standards.

The Grapevine System at PARC

In the early 1980s, the Grapevine system was developed at Xerox's Palo Alto Research Center. Grapevine linked multiple computer systems together through the Ethernet local area network technology, also developed at PARC. Grapevine used an early version of Ethernet with a 3-megabyte transfer rate and the PARC Universal Packet (Pup) protocols above Ethernet (Boggs, 1979). Grapevine was a distributed and replicated mail system in the sense that the service to the user was provided by multiple computers interconnected in a network, instead of by the user's host computer. The distinction is that in a host-based mail system, each user is the client of, and is addressed by, a specific host computer system. This host is used to exchange mail among its own users; networked hosts can support mail interchange among users on different hosts. A user's mail address is tied to the specific computer system of which he or she is a client.

In a distributed and replicated mail system, the service is provided by multiple computers called *servers*, each of which is interchangeable with the others from the user's point of view. The mail service is provided by the network, not by a single host computer. If one of the servers becomes unavailable, other servers can perform its tasks in a manner that is transparent to the user. The user's mailing address is now a name that is independent of the structure of the network or of the addresses of the computers attached to it.

In the Grapevine system, the name space was structured as a two-level hierarchy. Names were character strings of the form <user name>.<registry>, where <user name> was normally the actual name or perhaps nickname of a human user. The <user name> was a made-up name if the user was a process running in one of the computers on the network, or if the <user name> identified a group of users, called a *distribution list*. The <registry> component of the name could correspond to organizational, geographic, or any other subdivisions of user community that were convenient. There is no architectural significance to the fact that two levels of naming were used. The two-level scheme was convenient for the particular community that implemented and used Grapevine, but more levels would not have resulted in any significant changes to the overall architecture.

The citizens of the Grapevine were either intelligent workstation client implementations or servers of some type. Types of services provided to the user included messaging (ASCII text only), registration, authentication, and filing. Grapevine also supported a gateway func-

X.400 and Xerox Network Systems Mail 225

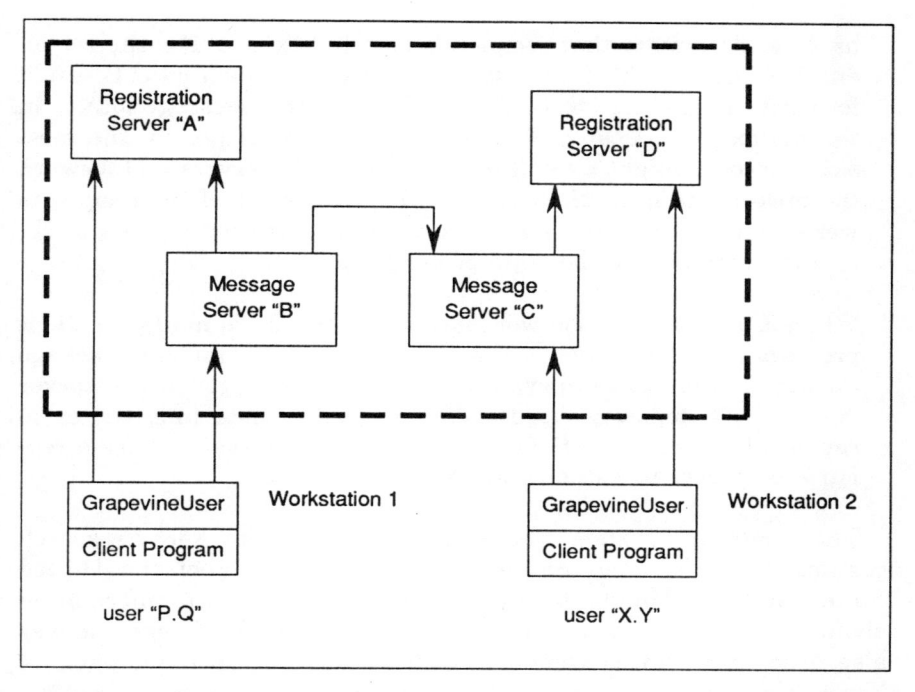

Figure 9-1 Example of how Grapevine works (adapted from a figure in Birell).

tion that linked the Ethernets through telephone lines. Each user had one or more in-boxes located on servers attached to the network. An example of how this worked appears in one of the papers on Grapevine written at PARC (Birrell, 1982). In the excerpt that follows, "GrapevineUser" is a package that provides support for the Grapevine protocols for communication between clients and servers and is bound with the user's application program:

With Figure 9-1 we consider an example of how Grapevine works. If a user named P.Q were using workstation 1 to send a message to X.Y, then events would proceed as follows. After the user had prepared the message using a suitable client program, the client program would call the delivery function of the GrapevineUser package on workstation 1. GrapevineUser would contact some registration server such as A and use the Grapevine resource location functions to locate any message server such as B; it would then submit the message to B. For each recipient, B would use the resource location facilities, and suitable registration servers (such as A) to determine that recipient's best in-box site. For the recipient X.Y, this might be message server C, in which case B would forward the message to C. C. would buffer this message locally in the in-box for X.Y. If the message had more recipients, the message server B might consult other registration servers and forward the message to multiple message servers. If some of the recipients were distribution lists, B would use the registration servers to obtain the members of the appropriate groups.

When X.Y wishes to use workstation 2 to read his mail, the client program calls the retrieval function of the GrapevineUser package in workstation 2. GrapevineUser uses some registration server (such as D) that contains the Y registry to locate in-box sites to retrieve his messages. Before allowing this retrieval, C uses a registration server to authenticate X.Y.

The Grapevine system was a success within the Xerox research community. It enabled researchers on both coasts of the United States and in Canada to electronically communicate information about research projects and technical discoveries. The Grapevine was also used in advanced customer installations and in other parts of Xerox.

The Development of Xerox 8000 Network Systems

The next step was to develop a commercial product line based on key developments at PARC: the Alto workstation, Ethernet, and the Grapevine.

The Alto was the predecessor of the commercial product that was developed, later known as the Star. Star was conceived as an office workstation that enabled the creation of documents with advanced typography and integrated text and graphics, embedded in an intuitive user interface that simulated artifacts and procedures used in the office. On the screen were "file drawers," "folders," and "documents" that, when not open, appeared to be little pieces of paper with the upper right corner turned down. The file drawers were really references to file servers located within the internetwork to which the workstation was always connected. To enable the user to manipulate these "icons," a mouse was provided in addition to the workstation keyboard.

Ethernet was experimentally developed at PARC beginning in 1972 (Metcalfe, 1976; Shoch, 1982). Ethernet is a high-speed local area network, so called because the distance spanned is limited to less than about 1.74 miles. The tradeoff is that rate of data transfer is much higher than that achievable over the networks that were then offering service over a wide area — 10 megabits per second on the Ethernet versus several hundred bits per second over, for example, the public telephone network (at that time). Since most business communication takes place within local working groups, the researchers at PARC reasoned that a high-speed local networking technology would fill a need. Later, a number of other organizations developed Ethernet-like local area networks. A standard Ethernet specification was developed jointly by Xerox, Digital Equipment, and Intel (Xerox, 1982) and became the basis for the IEEE 802.3 and ISO 8802/3 standards for local area networks.

Finally, higher-level protocols above the Ethernet were needed to support networks of office workstations and servers. Ethernet itself only implemented the physical and data link layers of the OSI Reference Model. There was no provision in the Ethernet for the interconnection of multiple networks or for application layer services such as mail. Both of these issues had been addressed in the Grapevine. Further work in these areas and in functions corresponding to the middle layers of OSI was done during the development of the Xerox 8000 Network System products and the Xerox Network Systems (XNS) communication protocols (White, 1982).

The 8000 NS offered a variety of application layer services to the advanced office workstation, in particular the ability to store and retrieve documents from file servers and the ability to send, along with documents, instructions on paper size, number of copies, and other options to the Xerox laser printers available on the network. Mail service was initially supported as an option of the file service. In the mid-1980s, the mail service became a distributed service in its own right, incorporating many of the architectural concepts of Grapevine. Figure 9-2 shows an 8000 Network System with many of its components, including in particular the file, print, and mail services, and the internetwork routing service that allowed the 8000 NS to expand beyond a single Ethernet.

The Incorporation of the X.400 Mail Gateway

Almost since its inception, the XNS Mail service had supported gateways to other networks, including the Grapevine Xerox Research Internet, the ARPA Net, and an External Mail Gateway that enabled the exchange of mail between distinct XNS networks through the

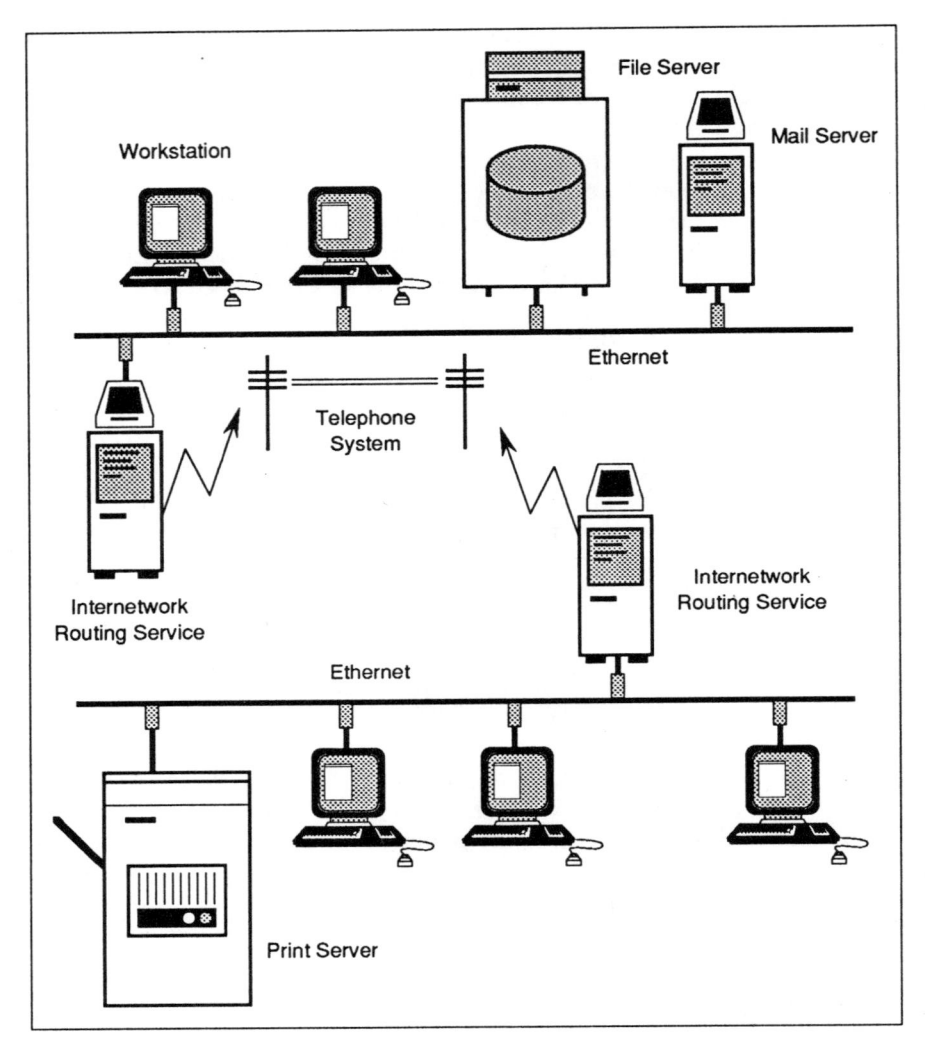

Figure 9-2 Xerox 8000 Network System.

telephone system. The purpose of the EMG was to let companies exchange business transactions and other information without allowing complete access to their private networks by outsiders. It had been intended right along that this gateway eventually would support the standard X.400 protocols, but when the mail service was first designed and implemented, the CCITT 1984 Study Period was not complete, and the X.400 standard was not available in final form. After the close of the 1984 Study Period, work began in earnest on X.400 support. The X.400 External Mail Gateway was first demonstrated by Xerox at CeBIT, Hanover Fair, in March 1987, along with X.400 implementations from eleven other computer companies and telephone service providers.

Xerox's Early Influence on X.400

Xerox had actively participated in the development of the CCITT X.400 Series of Recommendations. James White, manager of electronic mail at Xerox's Office Products Division was special rapporteur (chairman) of the CCITT Question 33/VII committee that developed the X.400 (1984) Recommendations and continued in this capacity during the subsequent 1988 Study Period, although not as a representative of Xerox. While some work on X.400 had been done earlier, the "Redbook" X.400 of 1984 (CCITT, 1984) was the basis of the first commercial implementations of the standard for electronic mail.

One of the lessons of the 1984 Study Period was that the level of standardization prescribed by the X.400 Recommendations did not guarantee interoperability of products developed in accordance with them. In both the United States and Europe, and later, Japan, groups composed of the engineering and marketing representatives of computer vendors and telecommunications carriers were established to make agreements about how the new Recommendations would be supported. The issues were threefold:

1. What should be the maximum lengths supported for variable-length fields such as personal names and for the number of occurrences of repeated fields such as Recipient O/RNames?
2. Which of the optional services need to be supported or not supported as a package in order to guarantee interworking?
3. What, if any, extensions to the standard were needed to provide viable commercial services and products? These were few and far between; the groups took the position that they were not there to do standards, but rather "profiles" that enable interworking.

Nonetheless, there were a small number of nonstandard extensions that appeared in some of the profiles, at least on a temporary basis. In particular, the European X.400 profile during the period 1986–1988 included support for the ISO 6937 character set, which enabled the transmission of accented Latin alphabetic characters used by many western European languages.

In the United States and Canada, the profiling work was done by the National Bureau of Standards (now NIST) OSI Implementor's Workshop, X.400 Special Interest Group. The OSI Workshop also established profiles for OSI layers 1 through 6 and for OSI File Transfer, Access, and Management (FTAM) at layer 7. The output of the OSI Workshop, the OSI Implementor's Agreements (National Bureau of Standards, 1987), is the technical foundation for the U.S. Government OSI Profile (National Bureau of Standards, 1988), now required for government network procurements. Xerox was represented at the X.400 SIG by JoAnn Read, the XNS Mail team leader during 1985–1988, and by this author, who chaired the X.400 SIG during the latter part of this period.

Comparison of XNS and OSI Stacks

Like OSI, XNS is a layered communication architecture. Figure 9-3 shows the correspondence between the individual layers of XNS and OSI. At the bottom of the stacks, XNS Ethernet is essentially equivalent to the ISO 8802/3 physical and data link layers. The Ethernet specification was agreed to jointly by Xerox, Intel, and Digital, and was published in its current version in November 1982 (Xerox, 1982). A few years later, a variant of Ethernet was standardized by the IEEE 802 committee and later by the International Standards Organization. (The only difference between Ethernet and IEEE 802.3 or ISO 8802/3 is that a field in the data link PDU that Ethernet thinks of as an encoded packet type is treated as a packet length field by the standard.) At layers 3 and 4, the XNS Internet Transport Protocols are collectively the equivalent of the ISO Network and Transport Protocols. These protocols are described briefly here and are specified in the Xerox Internet Transport Protocols (Xerox, Internet, 1981).

- *Internetwork Datagram Protocol (IDP).* IDP is the XNS network layer. Its function is to address, route, and deliver standard packets traversing the internet. Each packet is an independent entity with no relation to other packets. IDP is unreliable in the sense that it gives its best effort to deliver the packets, but cannot guarantee that they are delivered once and only once, nor that they are delivered in the same order as transmitted. It is analogous to the ISO 8473 Connectionless Network Protocol.

X.400 and Xerox Network Systems Mail 231

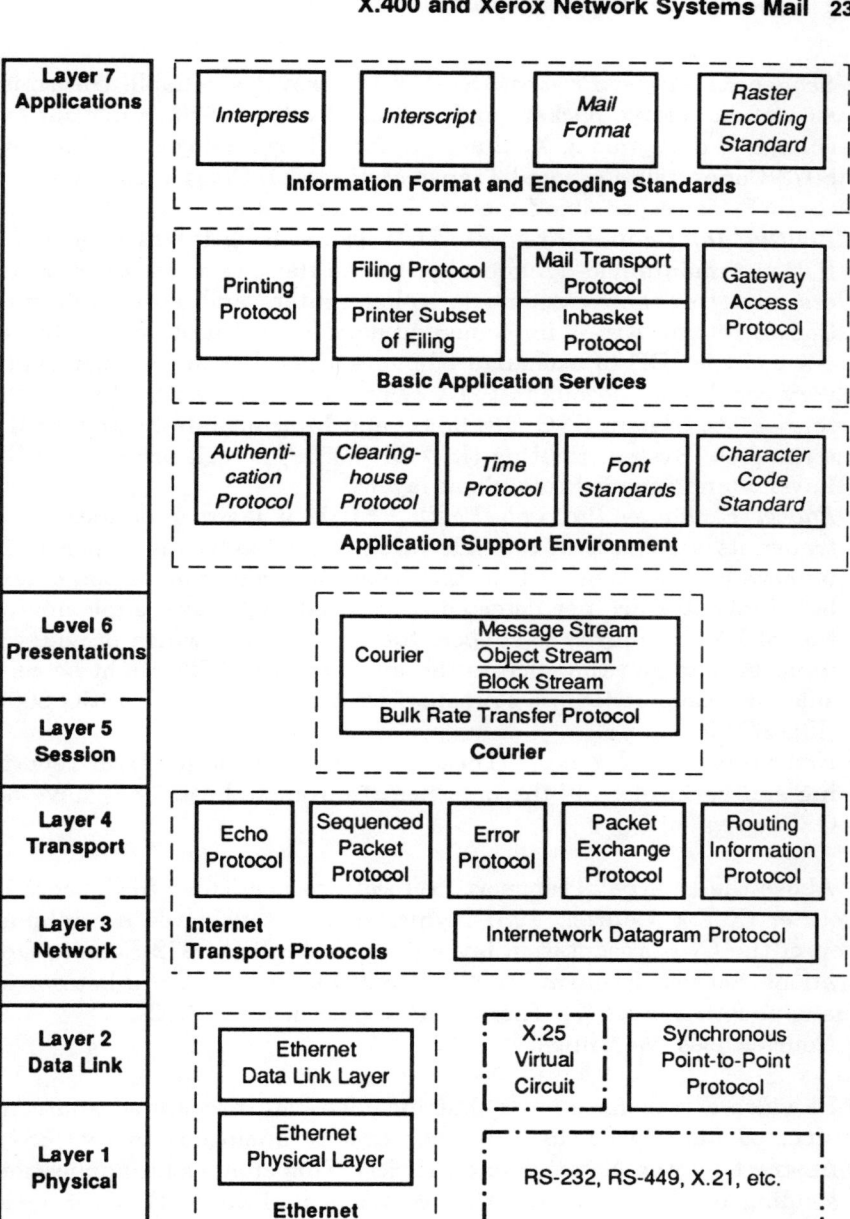

Figure 9-3 XNS and OSI (reprinted by permission of Xerox Corporation).

- *Sequenced Packet Protocol (SPP).* SPP provides reliable transmission of successive packets and is typically used for the normal exchange of data among XNS applications. It is analogous to the ISO 8073 Connection-Oriented Transport Protocol, Class 4, in the sense that SPP is responsible for error detection and recovery.
- *Routing Information Protocol (RIP).* The routing tables supporting IDP are maintained dynamically. RIP is the means by which routers advertise their existence to other routers and obtain information in return. RIP is implemented as a layer 4 protocol; i.e., routers use the IDP to exchange RIP messages. RIP is therefore only very roughly analogous to the ISO protocols for End System to Intermediate System (ISO DIS 9542) and Intermediate System to Intermediate System Routing (ISO DP 10589), which are technically Layer Management Protocols at layer 3.
- *Packet Exchange Protocol (PEP).* PEP is a layer 4 protocol that transmits a request in a single packet and receives a response. It is more reliable than IDP in the sense that retransmissions occur, but duplicates are not detected. It is used in Xerox's implementation of XNS primarily to support the time service, which provides a uniform date and time across the internetwork. PEP might be considered a Connectionless Transport Protocol analogous to ISO 8602 (ISO 8602).
- *Error and Echo Protocols.* These protocols provide for error reporting and verification of the presence of a remote host. They have no OSI equivalent.

Above the Internet Transport Protocols, in particular SPP, there is Courier (Xerox, Courier, 1981), which can be considered a combination of the OSI presentation layer (6) and the ISO 9072 Remote Operations Service Element (ROSE) (ISO/IEC 9072) at the bottom of the application layer (7). There is no session layer in XNS.

Courier does two things:

- Provides a transfer syntax that includes both predefined and constructed data types, in a manner exactly analogous to ISO 8824 Abstract Syntax Notation one (ASN.1). This enables an application sending a message to tell the receiving application that the next thing in the data stream is, for example, an integer as opposed to a string or some other data type. This is the presentation layer function.
- Provides a request/response remote procedure call protocol that enables an application to request service from another application located anywhere in the internetwork. This is also the function of the OSI ROSE.

XNS applications, including filing, clearinghouse (the directory service), printing, and mail service use Courier to communicate with clients and with each other. Only the mail service will be discussed here; information about the other applications is available in the references.

Architecture of XNS Mail

In what follows, the term *service* will be used in two different senses, depending on whether XNS or OSI is being discussed. In the context of XNS, a service is an application layer function that provides requested network functionality to a "client." For example, the mail service provides the ability to send mail to and receive mail from a workstation. In the context of OSI, a service is provided by a layer to the layer above it; e.g., a transport entity uses the network service to send Transport Protocol Data Units to a peer Transport entity. It is hoped that the meaning of service will be clear from the context. Changing this terminology for the sake of clarity is not a viable option, since all of the references depend on these two very different definitions.

The XNS Mail Service is a network service that supports multiple clients. From the viewpoint of a client, XNS Mail provides an internetworkwide store and retrieve service for messages to other clients. A "client" in this context is a process running on one of the computers attached to the network. The most common occurrence of this type of process is the software in a user's workstation that interchanges mail with other users by communicating with the Mail Service. There are also automatic processes that use the Mail Service. In particular, the clearinghouse application (the XNS distributed directory service) uses the Mail Service to update the distributed directory of the internetwork. Clearinghouse will not be covered in detail here. Interested readers may refer to Xerox, 1984.

Many of the elements of XNS Mail have direct X.400 counterparts. In particular, the addresses supported by XNS Mail, called distinguished names, are similar in concept to the X.400 originator/recipient name (form 1, variant 1). The distinguished name includes a personal name component, along with the person's (or other entity's) domain, which is the equivalent of the X.400 organizational unit, and organization. Information about the distinguished names is maintained in the clearinghouse. Aliases are supported by the clearinghouse, enabling user-friendly addressing in mail messages.

XNS Mail is implemented as a distributed system. This means that many, possibly even hundreds of mail services located around an internet, cooperate to form a unified service. Most of the services of XNS Mail can be performed by any instance of the mail service, although not necessarily with the same level of performance. The exception to this is that a user's mailbox is located on a specific server; if this becomes unavailable, the user is unable to read mail until it returns to service. However, the user can send mail from any instance of the mail service. An X.400 mail system is also distributed, assuming that it has more than one Message Transfer Agent (MTA).

Figure 9-4 shows an architectural model of the XNS Mail system, including the protocols used between mail clients and the service. There are two primary protocols used between a client and the mail service, the MailTransport and Inbasket Protocols. XNS Mail also supports a MailFormat, which is analogous to the X.400 Interpersonal Message Body Part (P2) (CCITT, 1984). In addition, there is a MailTransportEnvelopeFormat, which allows XNS Mail clients to implement most of the basic and essential optional service elements defined in X.401, with the exception of deferred delivery, deferred delivery cancellation, probe, and registered encoded information types.

MailTransport Protocol

The MailTransport Protocol is used for the submission and delivery of messages. As shown in Figure 9-4, this protocol is used by the client to send a message to the mail service. For message submission, the MailTransport Protocol provides approximately the same level of functionality as defined for SUBMIT used with the P3 Protocol in CCITT X.411 (1984). SUBMIT is the X.400 message submission service provided to a User Agent (UA) by a Message Transfer Agent (MTA). P3 is the X.400 protocol used between an MTA and a UA that are located in different computers. The information carried in the MailTransport Protocol during message submission includes the names of the recipients, requirement for delivery reports (a response from the mail system indicating whether or not a message has been delivered), the types of messages being submitted (body part types, in X.400 terminology), and various other items as defined in XNSS 148812 (Xerox, 1988).

Before a message is submitted, a mail server willing to accept it for transmission must be located. This is done by polling the servers

X.400 and Xerox Network Systems Mail 235

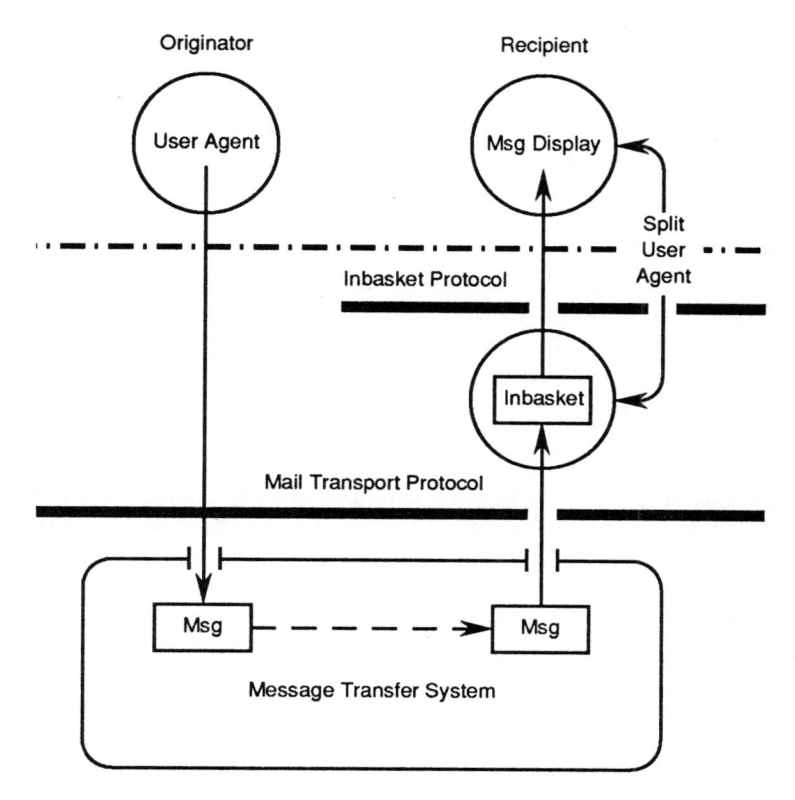

Figure 9-4 XNS Mail System architecture (reprinted by permission of Xerox Corporation).

to determine their level of willingness to accept new messages. Of the servers responding, the optimal choice is made based on proximity within the network, ability to handle the required message sizes, and availability. Once a mail server has been chosen, a session is established and the entire message, including all of its parts, is transmitted. (That is "session" with a small s — not the OSI Session Service. A session, in this context means the posting of a single message, with a separate remote procedure call for each body part.)

In order to improve the efficiency of polling, expedited procedure calls are supported for server polling. The procedure calls are expedited in the sense that the Packet Exchange Protocol is used, thereby eliminating the need to establish a Sequenced Packet Protocol connection. Normally the expedited calls are confined to servers located on the same local area network as the client.

The mail service uses a separate protocol, the MailTransportEnvelopeFormat, to provide a standard format for the message envelope. The other function of the MailTransportEnvelopeFormat is to describe the set of message body parts associated with delivery and nondelivery reports.

Inbasket Protocol

The P3 Protocol defined in X.411 (1984) is unsuitable for use in XNS because the typical client is a user's workstation that may be unavailable, i.e., turned off, when a message is ready to be delivered. X.411 assumes that the UA is always available and provides the P3 Protocol for the MTA to spontaneously deliver a message to a remote UA. If the UA is not available, the MTA has only the options of repeated attempts at delivery or the nondelivery of the message with optional notification and return to the sender. (The service supported by P3 has some similarity to Telex: the Telex machine is assumed always to be on and connected to the network. You come to work in the morning and read the messages that have been received and printed out overnight. A mail system supporting workstations as intelligent terminals could be designed this way, but the world is moving away from this. People turn off their computers, these days.) Instead of this, XNS Mail supports the idea of a user's mailbox, or Inbasket. As can be seen from Figure 9-4, messages are delivered not directly to the user, but to a mailbox located (usually) on the same server as the mail service. As the figure shows, the X.400 User Agent is conceptually split between the server and the client. The Inbasket Protocol allows the client to retrieve the mail in the Inbasket.

The Inbasket Protocol is functionally similar to the P7 Protocol of X.411 (1988). During the CCITT 1988 Study Period, the X.400 Special Rapporteur's Group confronted the same question about the interaction of a mail system with workstation/personal computer clients and arrived at a similar solution: provide a mailbox as part of the service. In the case of X.400, the mail store service defined by CCITT is not required to be located on the same computer as the Message Transfer Agent. The P3 Protocol can now be used to deliver a message either directly to a client, as in X.400 (1984), or to a mail store, for subsequent retrieval using the new P7 protocol. A block diagram of the latter option would look like Figure 9-4. (It is not clear that there is any user demand for a configuration that separates the mailboxes from the mail service, but CCITT allowed for the possibility in order to provide complete generality in the definitions of the services. The case in which the MTA and mail store have the same location is also supported and is likely to be more commonly implemented.)

In XNS, each client has a specific Inbasket located on a specific instance of the mail service. This is in contrast to message submission, in which any available mail server can be used to send a message. Later releases of XNS Mail provide optional support for multiple mailboxes (Inbaskets) in order to allow a user to receive mail when the primary mail server is unavailable. The expedited procedure calls described above also are available for checking the Inbasket to see if mail is available.

MailFormat Protocol

There is also an entity corresponding to the P2 format used in the interpersonal messaging service of X.400. The XNS MailFormat Protocol supports multiple body parts in a message, just as X.400 does. For compatibility with other X.400 systems, both the standard IA5 text (ASCII is the U.S. version of the International Alphabet 5 character code) and the ISO 6937 body part implemented by many European vendors are supported. (ISO 6937 is one of several character set standards that provide a way of representing the alphabetic characters with accent marks needed by many European languages. The fact that more than one standard exists for character sets continues to be a problem.) XNS Mail also allows for sending and receiving any other objects used by entities on the internetwork, including in particular documents and *folders* (subdirectories containing documents or other objects).

The XNS/X.400 Mail Gateway

The support of the X.400 (1984) mail protocols under XNS is through the X.400 External Mail Gateway. The X.400 Gateway supports the full OSI stack specified by the U.S. GOSIP (National Bureau of Standards, 1988) and other international profiles. Let us briefly review this stack:

Application:	X.400 Series, except X.430 (Teletex access)
Presentation:	Provided by X.409 Transfer Syntax and Notation
Session:	X.215, X.225 (known as "version 1" session)
Transport:	Both Class 0 and Class 4 are supported
Network:	Both X.25 and the connectionless network service
Data Link:	Both X.25 link level and ISO 8802 LLC Type 1
Physical:	Both ISO 8802/3 LAN and CCITT X.21 bis (RS 232)

Where possible, advantage is taken of common network facilities. In particular, the LAN packets of 8802/3 can share a common circuit with XNS's Ethernet packets.

The Gateway itself operates at the application layer. The components of XNS distinguished names are mapped into their counterparts in X.400 O/RNames in a manner described earlier. The presence of a country code and a domain name tells the XNS Mail service (and clients) that an originator or recipient name is not local to the XNS internetwork but is from the "outside" X.400 world. Some facilities are provided in the workstation mail tool to support the easy field-by-field entry of X.400 names, since these have multiple parts. When an X.400 message is received by the Gateway, the reverse mapping is done to derive the XNS distinguished names of the recipients. The X.400 P1/P2 Protocol information is extracted from incoming messages and reformatted into the corresponding XNS MailTransport, MailTransportEnvelopeFormat, and MailFormat Protocols. The reverse is done for outgoing messages. This is facilitated by the fact that virtually all of the X.400 P1/P2 Protocol elements have counterparts in XNS Mail. The Gateway also takes care of lower-level OSI connections with outside entities in a manner that is transparent to XNS users.

Conclusion and Lessons

As we have seen, Xerox mail developers were active in the X.400 standards process almost from its inception. How, then, did the XNS Mail system turn out different enough from X.400 to require a gateway?

The first and most obvious consideration is that X.400 or any OSI Application Protocol depends on all of the layers below. "Native" support for X.400 must mean either native support for all of OSI's seven layers or possibly the implementation of a mapping of the lower layer OSI services into their counterparts in XNS; i.e., a gateway below the application layer. In the former case, a wholesale replacement of XNS must be done. It is not practical to do this for an entire line of current products; such migrations must be done in stages, with the new communication architecture incorporated into new products and careful thought given to backward compatibility with the old products.

The second approach, mapping the lower layers, looks superficially more promising. Conceivably, an OSI gateway could be constructed at, say, the presentation layer that would allow any OSI application to be run over XNS. Unfortunately, details get in the way of this, as is often the case with grand schemes.

To begin with, the OSI presentation layer is not really present in X.400 (1984). The function of the presentation layer is provided by X.409, Presentation Transfer Syntax and Notation, but it is integrated into the application itself; no services are defined, only protocols. The chart on page 231 shows X.409 as the presentation layer, but this is technically incorrect — the correct answer is "null." (After the 1984 Study Period, X.409 became Abstract Syntax Notation one [ASN.1], the foundation of the Presentation Protocol, and the presentation service was itself standardized by both ISO and CCITT.) The same thing is true of XNS. Courier is the XNS equivalent of presentation. Courier doesn't exist as a separate "service"; it is a protocol and transfer syntax used between application entities to implement remote procedure calls. A general translation between X.409 transfer syntax and courier might be possible, but it would be pointless since OSI applications only connect to other OSI applications and not to XNS applications. There is no session layer in XNS, so the gateway, if it existed, would have to operate at OSI Transport, which corresponds to the Sequenced Packet Protocol in XNS. (Exactly this type of thing is done in the public domain ISO Development Environment package [ISODE] developed by Marshall Rose. ISODE implements the OSI session, presentation, and application layers over the Transport Control Protocol of TCP/IP.)

A more difficult problem is the architectural correspondence, or lack of it in specific areas, of X.400 and XNS Mail. There is a definite family resemblance between the XNS Mail server and the X.400 MTA. However, the User Agent is a problem. The X.400 (1984) UA is imagined by the standard to be either colocated (in the same computer system) or remote. If remote, the UA is imagined to be like a Telex in that it is always capable of receiving messages. The latter is unacceptable for UA's implemented as workstations on a distributed network. (Earlier, the XNS Mail UA was presented as split between a workstation and mailbox on a server, with a P7-like protocol used to retrieve mail. Another way to look at it is that the XNS Mail UA is "colocated" with the MTA in a manner that happens to include non-OSI communications.) The 1988 version of X.400 solves this nicely with the mail store and P7 Protocol. Unfortunately, these facilities are not available in the 1984 version, on which the X.400 External Mail Gateway and most other current X.400 products are based, although draft versions of the text that was incorporated into X.411 (1988) were certainly available during the period 1985–1988, when the Gateway was developed. (The implementation of products based on draft standards is called an "intercept strategy" in the trade and is a dangerous game. The standard usually comes out different from the product.)

Finally, there is the issue of backward compatibility with existing XNS Mail clients. There was a need to implement X.400 in a manner that caused minimum disruption to existing customer installations. This could best be accomplished by modifying the existing mail protocols to support the additional features of X.400 instead of imposing new protocols. An issue here is that XNS at the courier layer is a client-server communication architecture, as opposed to the peer-to-peer OSI architecture. Another is that the XNS Mail server-server protocols, not discussed here, already provided all of the functionality of X.400 and more within the XNS internet itself. Since clients never directly use these protocols, there was no strong motivation to replace them with the X.400 P1 Protocol. There was, of course, a substantial disincentive to do anything with them resulting from increased development expense and a genuine loss of functionality in the mail service. For example, XNS Mail has always supported the concept of distribution lists, i.e., a single name identifying a group of recipients. This concept is not supported at all in X.400 (1984), but it is present in the 1988 version.

As of this writing, most of the X.400 products on the market are really gateways to networks implementing proprietary architectures. With the completion of the OSI Network Layer Management Protocols (ISO DIS 9542, ISO DP 10589), dynamic routing will be supported, making large-scale distributed internetworks based on OSI practical.

References

Birell, A. D.; Levin, R.; Needham, R. M.; and Schroeder, M. D. *Grapevine: An Exercise in Distributed Computing*. Xerox Corporation: Office Systems Technology, A Look into the World of the Xerox 8000 Series Products, 1982. See also *Communications of the ACM* 25(4) (April 1982).

Boggs, David R.; Shoch, John F.; Taft, Edward A.; and Metcalfe, Robert M. *Pup: An Internetwork Architecture*. Xerox Palo Alto Research Center: CSL-79-10, July 1979.

CCITT. *Blue Book,* Volume VIII — Fascicle VIII.7 (Data Communication Networks, Message Handling Systems, Recommendations X.400–X.420). Melbourne: IXth Plenary Assembly, November 14–25, 1988.

CCITT. *Red Book,* Volume VIII — Fascicle VIII.5 (Data Communications Networks, Systems Description Techniques, Recommendations X.200–X.250). Malaga-Torremolinos: VIIIth Plenary Assembly, October 8–19, 1984.

CCITT. *Red Book,* Volume VIII — Fascicle VIII.7 (Data Communications Networks, Message Handling Systems, Recommendations X.400–X.430). Malaga-Torremolinos: VIIIth Plenary Assembly, October 8–19, 1984.

CCITT. *Yellow Book,* Volume VIII — Fascicle VIII.2 (Data Communications Networks, Services and Facilities, Terminal Equipment and Interfaces, Recommendations X.1–X.29) Geneva: VIIth Plenary Assembly, November 10–21, 1980.

ISO 8602. Information Processing Systems — Open Systems Interconnection — Protocol for providing the connectionless-mode transport service.

ISO 8802/3, ANSI/IEEE Std 802.3. Information Processing Systems — Local Area Networks — Part 2: logical link control; Part 3: carrier sense multiple access with collision detection (CSMA/CD) access method and physical layer specifications.

ISO 8824. Information Processing Systems — Open Systems Interconnection — Specification of Abstract Syntax Notation One (ASN.1).

ISO DIS 9542. Information Processing Systems — Open Systems Interconnection — End System to Intermediate System Routing Exchange Protocol for use in conjunction with the protocol for provision of the connectionless network service.

ISO DP 10589. Information Processing Systems — Open Systems Interconnection — Intermediate System to Intermediate System Routing Exchange Protocol for use in conjunction with the protocol for provision of the connectionless network service.

ISO/IEC 9072. Information Processing Systems — Text Communication — Remote Operations.

Metcalfe, Robert M.; Boggs, David R. *Ethernet: Distributed Packet Switching for Local Computer Networks.* CACM Vol. 19, No. 7,

July 1976. Reprinted in CSL-80-2, February 1980, Xerox Palo Alto Research Center.

National Bureau of Standards. Federal Information Processing Standards Publication 146. *Government Open Systems Interconnection Profile,* August 24, 1988.

National Bureau of Standards. *Stable Implementation Agreements for Open Systems Interconnection Protocols,* Version 1, Edition 1. NBS Special Publication 500-150, December 1987.

Redell, D., and Hall, A. *Mail Service Functional Specification (Services 8.0).* Xerox Corporation: July 3, 1984 (unpublished).

Shoch, J. F.; Dalal, Y. K.; Crane, R. C.; and Redell, D. D. *Evolution of the Ethernet Local Computer Network.* Xerox Corporation: Office Systems Technology, A Look into the World of the Xerox 8000 Series Products, 1982. See also *IEEE Computer Magazine* 15(8) (August 1982): 10–27.

White, J. E.; Dalal, Y. K. *Higher-Level Protocols Enhance Ethernet.* Xerox Corporation: Office Systems Technology, A Look into the World of the Xerox 8000 Series Products, 1982. See also *Electronic Design* 30(8) (April 15, 1982): 33–41.

Xerox Corporation. *Clearinghouse Protocol,* XNSS 078404. Xerox: April 1984.

Xerox Corporation. *Courier: The Remote Procedure Call Protocol,* XNSS 038112. Xerox: December 1981.

Xerox Corporation. *The Ethernet, A Local Area Network, Data Link Layer and Physical Layer Specifications,* Version 2.0. Xerox: November, 1982.

Xerox Corporation. *Internet Transport Protocols,* XNSS 028112. Xerox: December 1981.

Xerox Corporation. *Mailing Protocols,* XNSS 148812. Xerox: December 1988.

Xerox Corporation. *Xerox Network Systems Architecture General Information Manual,* XNSG 068504. Xerox: April 1985.

About the Author

John Stidd is the Manager of Standards Development and Planning for Xerox Corporation and was the Product Manager for Xerox's X.400 Mail Gateway described in this chapter. He chaired the X.400 Special Interest Group of the NIST OSI Implementor's Workshop during the period when the U.S. Implementor's Agreements on X.400 were developed (1984).

Xerox Corporation, headquartered in Stamford, Connecticut, is a major manufacturer of electronic equipment, including copiers, electronic printers, and computer workstations and servers.

Chapter

10

An X.500 Overview

by Peter R. Westwood

Introduction

This chapter is a brief introduction to a set of new data communication standards called the X.500 Directory Recommendations. It is intended for the use of both nontechnical and technical personnel. It is a general overview; no particular implementation or application is assumed.

Before discussing the specifics of the X.500 Directory Recommendations, let's briefly review the need for an electronic directory and how the X.500 Directory Recommendations address this need.

Communication has become an increasingly important aspect of a business's competitiveness in today's global economies. As the different types of communication systems proliferate — facsimile, voice, electronic mail, telex, overnight mail, etc. — there is an increasing need for a global electronic directory of communication systems and users. Users at their own PCs and computer terminals need to be able to quickly obtain information from a directory without the assistance of a telephone operator.

Existing Directories

The existing communication directories are primarily manual. They are fragmented, containing inconsistent, incomplete, and often obsolete information. As a consequence, locating communication information on someone can be extremely awkward, expensive, and often impossible. For example, at present there is a variety of manual methods that can be used to obtain telephone numbers — white and yellow pages, Directory Assistance, internal directories, and operator information. The information supplied (telephone numbers, names, and addresses) is extremely limited and often out-of-date, and the search process is very slow (often multiple directory sources must be accessed). Some electronic directories do exist, specifically for electronic mail networks. However, these directories provide access to only a limited number of individuals and information, and no inter-directory searching is possible. Often in large organizations, an individual may be entered in a number of directories with different e-mail addresses reflecting membership in a variety of proprietary electronic messaging networks.

X.500 Objectives

The purpose of the X.500 Directory Recommendations is to provide a global electronic directory that contains information such as name, organization, address, telephone number, e-mail address, and facsimile number on all kinds of communication users and systems. The X.500 Directory is accessible to both users and computer programs via modern database and communication technologies. Conceptually there is one global electronic directory information base; in reality the information is distributed among different computer systems. The X.500 Recommendations dictate how these systems interrelate, describing how and what information can be stored within the directory, along with the basic user access capabilities.

Benefits of X.500

With access to the X.500 Directory a user can communicate much more easily and rapidly with others. Knowing a person's name and organization, a user can easily find that person's communication information such as phone number, e-mail address(es), and facsimile number. If the user is not sure of the correct spelling of the person's name or organization, the user can electronically search the Directory and select from the list of entries returned. No longer do users have to remember each different communication address or name for a person or organization. The Directory can also be used to find supplemental information such as title, correct spelling of a name, and ZIP/postal code.

In addition to these extended "white pages" directory capabilities, the X.500 Directory provides the user with "yellow pages" directory capabilities, including the ability to search the Directory for organizations or individuals that perform a certain function or service. For instance, the X.500 Directory can be used to determine which companies provide a public electronic directory service within a particular location, or who is the purchasing officer for a particular company.

Security

For any global directory to be successful, the security of the information contained within a particular subset of the directory must be locally controllable. This must include who is permitted to access and maintain which information within a subset of the directory. The X.500 Recommendations define certain global security features and how they might be implemented within organizations.

CCITT/ISO

Before discussing the X.500 Directory in more detail, let us review some background information on the Recommendations. The CCITT Blue Book on "Data Communications Networks: Directory, Recommendations X.500–X.521," which we have been referring to as the "X.500 Directory Recommendations," are a series of standards developed by the CCITT (a group composed of the world's telecom companies) in collaboration with the International Standards Organization (ISO). (The corresponding ISO standards are the series ISO 9594-1 to 9594-7.) The X.500 standards are part of the Open System Interconnection (OSI) series of standards, belonging in the Application Layer of the OSI model. (Perhaps the best known of the other Application Layer standards is the X.400 Message Handling System series of Recommendations.)

The CCITT Blue Book that specifies the X.500 Recommendations states, "The Directory provides the directory capabilities required by OSI applications, OSI management processes, other OSI layer entities, and telecommunication services. Among the capabilities . . . are those of user-friendly naming . . . and name-to-address mapping. . . ."

X.500 Time Frames

The X.500 Recommendations were first approved in November 1988, and initial research and pilot implementations started to appear in 1989. If the adoption of the X.500 standard roughly follows the adoption model for the X.400 Message Handling Systems Recommendations (first approved in 1984) then widespread interconnection of different vendors' X.500 Directories will occur in 1993/94, with early users being companies that use communication systems extensively as part of their competitive business strategy. These firms will already be using a variety of communication networks and e-mail systems that need to be better integrated and more readily usable. Using X.500 will allow such organizations to meet their immediate communication needs as well as to reap further benefits as the more widespread implementation of X.500 systems occurs.

The remainder of this chapter provides more specific information on the Recommendations: what information the Directory can contain; how users can retrieve and manage the information within the Directory; how the different distributed components of the Directory work together; what is not presently covered within the standards. The main body of the chapter concludes with a discussion of a variety of applications of the Directory and likely future directions. In the appendices are a definition of some of the key terminology used within the Recommendations and a summary of each of the individual Recommendations X.500 through X.521.

Directory Information

What information is contained in the X.500 Directory, and how is it structured?

Objects

Each entry in the Directory represents an "object" from the real world. The Recommendations define certain classes of objects, including: Country, Locality, Organization, Organizational Unit, Person, Application Process, and Device. The set of all Directory entries is called the Directory Information Base.

Attributes

Each entry for an object in the Directory Information Base (DIB) is composed of a series of *attribute types* and associated values. The attribute types that are contained within an entry depend upon the class that the object entry belongs to. Again the Recommendations define certain types of attributes, including: Country Name, Organization Name, Organizational Unit Name, Postal Address, Title, Common Name, Business Category, Description (of object entry), Telephone Number, Facsimile Number, International ISDN Number, and Telex Number. A certain attribute type can be associated with more than one object class.

One of the strengths of the Recommendations is that implementors can define additional object classes and attribute types as they require them. For example, the X.500 Directory can include e-mail objects and attributes such as those defined in the X.400 MHS series of Recommendations.

DIT

The entries in the Directory Information Base are organized in a hierarchical, inverted tree structure called the Directory Information Tree. Figure 10-1 shows a simplified example of a Directory Information Tree (DIT), with the entries at the nodes of the tree. Each entry in the DIT is a child of a parent entry, with the exception of the initial (root) entry. Names are the means by which entries in the DIB are accessed; that is, names are the keys to the database. Each entry is uniquely named among its siblings; the name is termed the *Relative Distinguished Name* and is a combination of some of the attributes of the entry. Each entry then has a globally unique name (called the *Distinguished Name*), which is the ordered sequence combination of the Relative Distinguished Names encountered on the path from the root of the DIT to the entry. A typical sequence of object classes in descending order from the root is: Country, Organization, Location, Organizational Unit, Person; another typical example is Country, Location, Person.

DIT Structure and Schema

The structure of the DIT is defined by the Directory Schema. The Schema defines which attribute types make up an entry's Relative Distinguished Name and the relationship between different object classes. For example, certain object classes cannot be subordinate to

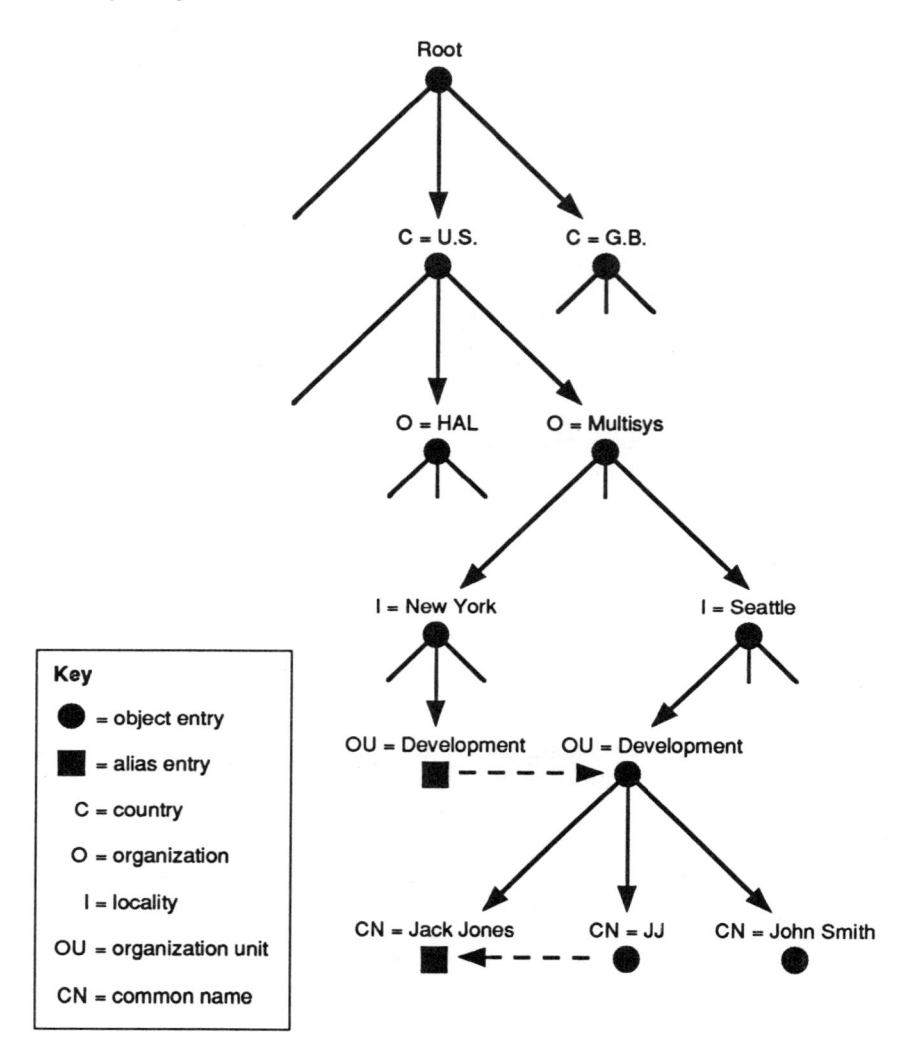

Figure 10-1 Example of a directory information tree.

certain other object classes (e.g., Organizations cannot be subordinate to People). The Schema also defines the relationships between object classes and attributes and the characteristics of attributes. For example, it may be mandatory that the Person object class contain the attributes common name and telephone number, and that the telephone number must have certain numeric structures.

The Schema is used by the Directory software to ensure the integrity of the information contained within the Directory. The Directory Schema can be distributed like the Directory Information Base. Though the Recommendations provide a suggested DIT structure and common naming practices, the form of the DIT, its growth, the Directory Schema, and the selection of distinguished names for entries are all the responsibility of the various Directory management authorities. The relationship between each authority is defined by the shape of the inverted tree. Figure 10-1 shows a typical DIT structure.

This hierarchical, inverted tree structure not only closely represents the intuitive approach for searching a directory (based upon existing manual directory uses) but also greatly facilitates the distributed management of the Directory. For example, distributed name management is achieved by assigning the responsibility for choosing an entry's Relative Distinguished Name to its parent, making the parent the naming authority for that entry. Similarly the set of entries subordinate to a particular entry can be more easily physically distributed and managed.

Aliases

Though each entry has a unique distinguished name, alternative names can exist through the use of "alias" entries. An alias entry contains only attributes that form the Relative Distinguished Name for that entry. Alias entries are "leaf" entries in the inverted tree; that is, they have no subordinate entries. They simply point to object entries providing an alternative name for the each such entry. Figure 10-1 includes an example of an alias entry.

Use of DBMS

One final comment on the DIB. The Recommendations do not make any statement about the underlying DBMS. As long as the DBMS provides the necessary functions, it can be a relational DBMS, a hierarchical type, or conceivably some other type.

This concludes the overview on the information that can be maintained in the Directory. The next section discusses the operations that are available to users to access the X.500 Directory.

User Access to the Directory Information

The X.500 Recommendations define certain operations that users can perform in order to access the Directory Information Base. There is a group of Directory interrogation operations and a group of Directory modification operations.

Interrogation

The Directory interrogation operations are:

- *Read* — used to obtain the requested attribute information on a selected entry in the DIB.
- *Compare* — typically used to handle security needs, such as password checking, when the value of an attribute must be kept confidential; used to determine whether the value of a selected attribute within a selected entry matches the input value.
- *List* — used to obtain a list of entries immediately subordinate to a selected entry in the DIB.
- *Search* — used to obtain information only from those entries that satisfy input selection criteria (filters); for example, finding which organizations within a certain locality have a business category value of "Communications Software Developer."
- *Abandon* — used to instruct the Directory to abandon processing a user input interrogation request, discarding any preliminary results obtained.

Modification

The Directory modification user operations are:

- *Add entry* — the added entry can only be a leaf entry (object or alias).
- *Remove entry* — the entry that is being deleted can only be a leaf entry (object or alias).
- *Modify entry* — used to modify the values of the specified attributes within an entry; the entry does not have to be a leaf entry.
- *Modify Relative Distinguished Name* — used to change the values of the attributes that make up the RDN of a leaf entry (object or alias).

Access Control

The user can control how these operations (which are all included within the Directory Abstract Services elements of the Recommendations) are performed by specifying such things as the method and extent (scope) of access to the different distributed portions of the DIB, use of copies (as opposed to original master entries) to satisfy requests, priority for processing a request, and the maximum entries that may be returned that satisfy a list or search operation request.

Security

In a large distributed, networked database system like the X.500 Directory, security is extremely important. The Recommendations refer to two aspects of security: *authentication* (the verification of users and the distributed, communicating Directory components) and *authorization* (what information a user can access).

The Directory itself was designed so that it could be used to authenticate users and applications (not only Directory applications). Two levels of authentication are currently defined within the Recommendations: *simple* and *strong*. Simple authentication uses passwords, strong authentication uses public key encryption techniques that assume the existence of an independent certifying authority. The use of encrypted, digitized signatures as certificates is covered in the Recommendations.

As mentioned in the Introduction of this chapter, the Recommendations do not define a global security policy; rather they define certain authentication mechanisms. The implementation of security policies is a local matter. Though the Recommendations refer to authorization, no such elements are in the current version of the Recommendations. However, in order for the X.500 Directory to be operationally viable and used by multiple organizations, some level of authorization process is essential. The Recommendations expect such to be defined locally and to be mutually agreed upon by cooperating distributed Directory managers. The Recommendations suggest this authorization process could use access control lists. These lists would define which users (individuals or groups) could access what information (such as subtrees, object classes, attribute types). With such an authorization process, portions of private directories could become publicly accessible, linked to public directories, all forming the global X.500 Directory.

This completes the description of user access to the information in the Directory. The next section is an overview of the internal workings of the Directory.

Internal Operations of the Directory

As previously mentioned, the X.500 Directory is a distributed directory that is logically viewed as one global directory. The information component of the Directory, the DIB, is a hierarchical, inverted tree-structured database containing communication-related information on objects. Typical objects are people, organizations, communicating devices, and applications. The DIB can be physically at one physical location, or more likely physically distributed.

DUA

Users of the Directory, which can be computer programs or people, access the Directory through an application process called a Directory User Agent (DUA). There is one and only one DUA for each user. The user, via the DUA, accesses the Directory via the Directory interrogation and modification operations discussed in the previous section. Local DUA functions (not defined in the Recommendations) can be used with the Directory operations to provide the user with the facilities required.

DSA

The Directory itself consists of one or more application processes called Directory Service Agents (DSA's) and the DIB. The DUA access point to the Directory is via a DSA. A DSA can service multiple DUA's and can access different DSA's. The DSA's provide access to and manage the DIB. The Directory is distributed when there is more than one DSA. If the DIB itself is distributed, then each distributed component of the DIB is accessed via its own DSA, which in turn services requests from other DSA's. If a DUA request for access cannot be satisfied within the portion of the DIB managed by the DSA servicing the DUA, then the DSA routes the request for service to other appropriate DSA's. Figure 10-2 shows a representation of users and the major components of the Directory.

Note that in the case in which a DSA is used just for routing purposes, the DSA manages only that portion of the DIB needed to route service requests to other DSA's (this distributed routing information

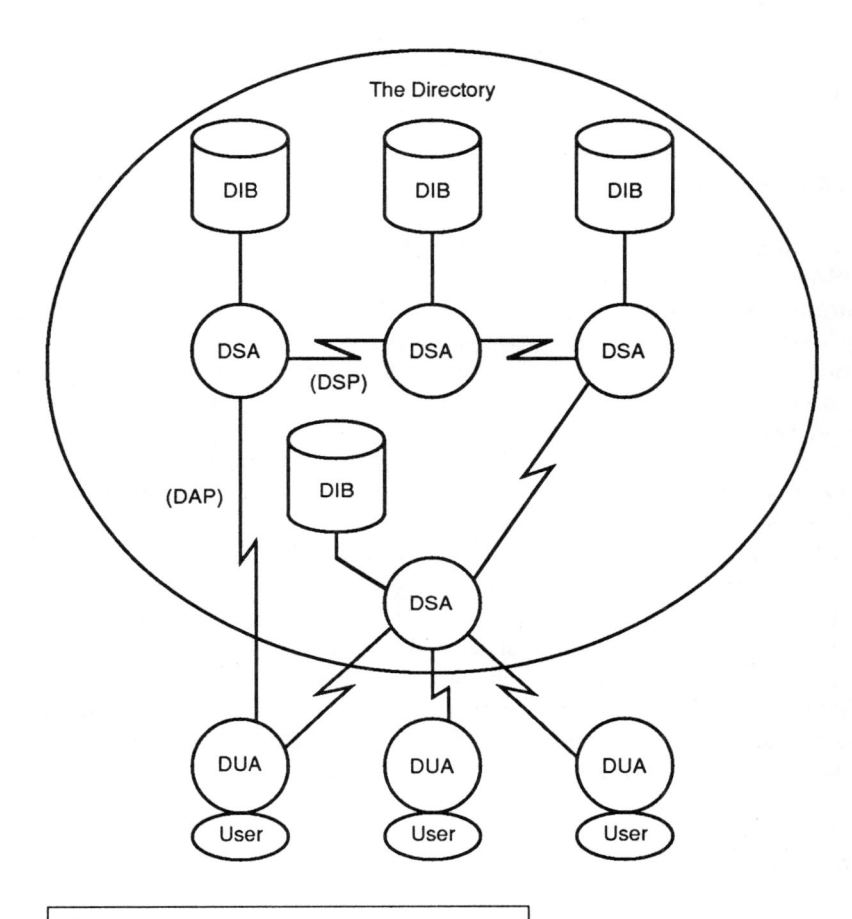

Figure 10-2 Major components of the X.500 Directory.

Key
DUA = Directory User Agent
DAP = Directory Access Protocol (DUA-DSA)
DSA = Directory System Agent
DSP = Directory System Protocol (DSA-DSA)
DIB = Directory Information Base

is called "knowledge," explained further below). In the case of one centrally located, nondistributed DIB (other than distributed routing information), one DSA would directly access and manage the DIB. Other DSA's could be distributed if required to route DUA requests to the central DSA, which would then access the DIB as required to service the requests, or the DUA's could all access directly the one central DSA.

DSA Interaction

The Recommendations define three modes of interaction between DSA's: chaining, multicasting, and referral. In chaining, if a DSA cannot satisfy some part of a DUA's request for service, then, subject to user control over the extent (scope) of the DSA's to be accessed and subject to security, the unsatisfied portion of the request is passed on to another DSA. If that DSA cannot satisfy the request, then the DSA can pass the request on to another DSA that it believes can satisfy the request, and so on (still subject to the controls). The responses to the requests are passed back through the DSA chain in reverse sequence.

Multicasting DSA interaction occurs when a DSA passes the identical request to multiple DSA's (either in parallel or sequentially).

Referral interaction occurs when a DSA in response to a request for service refers the requesting DSA to another DSA. The requesting DSA then directly interacts with the referenced DSA. In addition to DSA's interacting on a referral basis, a DUA can also interact with DSA's on a referral basis. In this case the DUA would directly interact with each referenced DSA.

Knowledge

In order for the different DSA's to interact as described, the DSA's must maintain certain information, called "knowledge," in the DIB that enables a DSA to know which DSA's to interact with in order to service access requests. This knowledge enables DSA's to navigate the requests to cooperating DSA's. The Recommendations define what knowledge information is maintained in the DIB, but the implementation and management of the distributed knowledge is left up to the Directory implementors and cooperating administrators.

Protocols

The Recommendations term the protocol that defines the DUA to DSA interactions the Directory Access Protocol (DAP) and the protocol that defines the DSA to DSA interactions the Directory System

Protocol (DSP). These protocols use underlying OSI services. The other Application layer services used are ROSE (Remote Operations Service Elements) and ACSE (Application Control Service Elements). The Application layer services in turn use the OSI Presentation layer services. X.500 requires a Session layer below that provides both Kernel and Duplex functional units and a Transport layer that supports at a minimum class 0. An underlying network supporting OSI Network Services (X.25-based) is assumed.

Though outside of the Recommendations, cooperating DSA's and DUA's can substitute for lower elements of the OSI stack with networks that provide the equivalent functionality.

Replication

The X.500 Directory functions in real time (unlike the X.400 MHS, which functions in a store-and-forward basis). Obviously, in a distributed environment performance could be an issue. The topology of the Directory has to be carefully planned in order to meet user expectations. One of the features of the Directory is the ability to service requests from replications (copies) of portions of the DIB. This of course could significantly improve the time to respond to user requests. A user can designate whether or not requests can be serviced from replications of the required objects and attributes in the DIB or only from the original (master) version. The information returned in response to a request includes whether or not the information was obtained from a replicated copy.

Though the Recommendations define how requests for service handle replicated information, the management of the replicated information is outside the current scope of the Recommendations.

This completes our overview of the Directory. The next section discusses applications of the X.500 Directory and possible future directions for the Directory.

Directory Applications and Future Directions

The application potential of the X.500 Directory is considerable, particularly because of the global aspects of the distributed directory and the extensibility of the information that can be supported in the Directory Information Base.

E-Mail

Initial uses of X.500 are likely to be in association with electronic mail networks. It's been estimated that there are currently as many as 8 million e-mail users worldwide. One obstacle to global e-mail communications has been the lack of interconnection among the different systems. The increased implementation of X.400 capabilities in these systems is addressing that obstacle. Other major obstacles include: users, particularly when sending occasional messages to recipients, just don't know or can't find out the recipient's e-mail address; the address is difficult to use and remember; or the address has changed.

The X.500 Directory will overcome these obstacles. Users will be able to browse through the Directory to find the required addresses, using the "yellow pages" capability when the name of the individual or organization is unknown. The Directory could be used to expand or to verify an input e-mail address and to provide alternate e-mail network addresses. It could be used by various components of the e-mail software. For example, an X.400 MTA (Message Transfer Agent) could use the Directory to verify e-mail addresses, to expand distribution lists, verify passwords, and verify UA (User Agent) capabilities. An X.400 RTS (Reliable Transfer Service) could use the Directory to obtain the OSI addresses required to make a connection to a remote MTA. Such an application would combine the use of the two specific applications of the X.500 Recommendations that have been standardized: OSI intersystem communication and X.400.

Users are already using PCs and terminals to send and receive e-mail. X.500 will make e-mail more user-friendly and provide users with more access to, and information on, more people and communication devices. As such, X.500 should be readily adopted by e-mail users.

Telephone Directories

An even greater potential exists for X.500-based telephone directory systems, covering white and yellow pages, internal organization directories, and directory and operator information. In addition to regular voice phone numbers, such a directory could include facsimile numbers, e-mail addresses, and more extensive organization and personal information.

One factor that will impact the use of the X.500 Directory for these communication methods is the penetration of communicating PCs into the workplace, and the ease of using the Directory from a PC when combined with using the targeted communication network, i.e., the phone or facsimile. PC penetration of the North American workplace is already high. Over 50 percent of the 70 million plus knowledge workers in North America have PCs on their desks. Over 30 percent of these PCs have a communication capability, which is expected to grow to 50 percent by 1991. As these knowledge workers use their PCs more and more in their everyday work, they will require that the PC integrate with their other communicating devices. Already some users have replaced their Rolodexes with electronic personal directories that will initiate voice phone connections.

Similarly, users will want integrated, easier access to the 5 million facsimile machines that are presently installed in North America alone. The number of vendors that provide hardware or software that allows communication between PCs and facsimile machines is rapidly growing, as is the number of users. As business users combine the operation of a PC with voice phone messaging and with facsimile messaging, PC-based X.500 Directory access will provide many benefits and should be well accepted if the user interface is well designed and integrated with the different communication devices.

The major question, in the United States at least, is how can the telephone companies, which are the best sources of much of the directory information and supply most of the directory manuals and services, supply electronic directory databases? At present the U.S. telephone companies are prevented by federal regulations from supplying electronic databases when they own the contents; recently, however, the F.C.C. has permitted Southwestern Bell (on the basis that Southwestern Bell is only providing access and not supplemental customer information) to offer its customers direct electronic access to its directory assistance database. Other telcos have applied for similar rights. This service is targeted at large users of the directory assistance services, such as credit and collection agencies and insurance companies.

Much of today's telephone directory usage is consumer-based. In North America over 20 percent of homes have PCs in them, and this percentage is growing. Significantly, close to 60 percent of the new PCs purchased for home use in 1989 were IBM compatibles. The French Minitel system (with 5 million users) has demonstrated that under the right conditions consumers will use an electronic phone directory. As PCs penetrate the homes in North America and are used for more than games (already more than 40 percent of the home computers are used for business-related activities), an X.500 capability will become of significant value to many consumers.

Without question the X.500 Directory is going to dramatically change the phone directory business, particularly in the highly profitable "yellow pages" industry. How long this change will take is hard to say.

Initial X.500 phone number directories are very likely to be extensions of the initial X.500 e-mail directories. Organizations will integrate their phone directories with their e-mail directories using X.500. Associations of companies that are linked by e-mail systems will implement a distributed X.500 Directory listing the phone numbers, e-mail addresses, facsimile numbers, etc., of the employees in the associated companies and their business partners.

Direct Mail and Telemarketing

Another application in which the X.500 Directory could have significant impact is in direct mail and telemarketing. At present, companies that supply such services spend a considerable effort maintaining their own computerized databases, which are often out-of-date and inaccurate. Tying these databases into the X.500 Directory would diminish this problem and increase their potential use.

General Directories

The Recommendations define communication directory-related object classes and attribute types, but as has been discussed, implementors can define their own object classes and attributes. The X.500 Directory could then be used to support any type of directory information; for instance, object classes such as computer files, products, and services, as well as communication users, systems and devices. One example of this is the recent selection by the Open Software Foundation of X.500 as the directory component of their to-be-developed standardized distributed computing environment (DCE) technology.

X.500 in the Future

One closing comment on the X.500 Directory Recommendations. As was mentioned above, they were first published at the end of 1988. As they presently stand, the Recommendations provide an excellent basis for a solution to any distributed directory requirement. As with all CCITT standards, they will be updated and enhanced every four years. Already work is underway on a number of extensions, specifically in the areas of replication (copying), knowledge propagation, and access control management. There will be other refinements as technologies advance and more operational experience is gained. As an analogy, X.25 first became a standard in 1976 and is still being used extensively in 1990. It is not unreasonable to expect at least a twenty-year life cycle for X.500 with a form very similar to its current form.

Appendix A. Glossary of Selected X.500 Terminology

The CCITT *Blue Book,* Data Communications: Directory, Recommendations X.500–X.521 defines all of the X.500 terminology. This appendix defines only a selected subset. The reference accompanying each definition is to the main section(s) in the *Blue Book* that describes the term.

Abstract Services — Services (operations) provided by the Directory to the Directory user via the DUA. (X.511, p. 85)

Access Control — Definition and management of who can access what information within the DIB. (X.501, p. 38; Appendix F, p. 46)

Alias — An entry that is used solely for the purpose of providing an alternate name to another entry. (X.501, p. 30)

Attribute — A particular type of information about an object that appears in an entry in the DIB describing that object. (X.501, pp. 26, 191)

Authentication, simple — A password-based method used by the Directory to authenticate users and by DSA's to authenticate other DSA's. (X.509, p. 50)

Authentication, strong — Encryption-based method used by the Directory to authenticate users and by DSA's to authenticate other DSA's. (X.509, p. 50)

Chaining — Method by which requests for, and responses to, Directory services are passed from one DSA to another in the form of a chain. (X.518, p. 116)

DAP (Directory Access Protocol) — Protocol that defines the requests and outcomes between a DUA and a DSA. (X.519, p. 177)

DIB (Directory Information Base) — Complete database of information that describes the objects that are represented within the Directory. (X.501, p. 24)

DIT (Directory Information Tree) — Hierarchical, inverted tree-like structure of the DIB. (X.501, p. 24)

DSA (Directory Service Agent) — Directory process that provides DUA's and other DSA's with access to the DIB. (X.501, p. 22)

DSP (Directory System Protocol) — Protocol that defines the requests and outcomes between a pair of DSA's. (X.519, p. 177)

DUA (Directory User Agent) — Process that accesses the Directory and obtains services from it on behalf of the user. (X.501, p. 22)

Knowledge — Information that a DSA maintains in its own local portion of the DIB that enables the DSA to operate with other fragments of the DIB held by other DSA's. (X.518, p. 127)

Multicasting — Method by which a DSA directly submits the same request for Directory services, in parallel or sequentially, to other DSA's, with the responses being directly returned to the originating DSA. (X.518, p. 116)

Object Class — An identified family of objects that share certain common characteristics. (X.501, p. 25; X.521, p. 214)

Recommendations — CCITT term for standards.

Referral — Situation in which a DSA cannot satisfy a request for service from either another DSA or a DUA and refers the originator of the request to other DSA(s) it believes can service the request. (X.518, p. 116)

Replication — Distribution of copies (which are marked as copies) of selected DIB entries; implemented to improve user response times. (X.518, p. 125)

Schema — The set of DIB rules that describes the DIT structure, object class definitions, attribute types, and syntaxes. (X.501, p. 31)

Shadowing — See *Replication*.

Appendix B. Summary of X.500 Recommendations

X.500 (ISO 9594-1) The Directory — Overview of Concepts, Models, and Services. Provides an overview of the Directory, its applications, the major components, the information within the Directory, and the services provided to Directory users. (p. 3)

X.501 (ISO 9594-2) The Directory — Models. Describes the overall functional model together with the organizational, informational, and security models of the Directory. (p. 19)

X.509 (ISO 9594-8) The Directory — Authentication Framework. Defines how the Directory authenticates users and how DSA's authenticate other DSA's. (p. 83)

X.511 (ISO 9594-3) The Directory — Abstract Service Definition. Defines in an abstract way the user services (access operations) provided by the Directory. (p. 83)

X.518 (ISO 9548-4) The Directory — Procedures for Distributed Operation. Describes how the DSA's interact together in forming the distributed Directory. (p. 118)

X.519 (ISO 9548-5) The Directory — Protocol Specifications. Specifies the protocols that provide the user services described in X.511 (the DAP protocol) and those that provide the distributed Directory services in X.518 (the DSP protocol). (p. 175)

X.520 (ISO 9548-6) The Directory — Selected Attribute Types. Defines standard attribute types. (p. 189)

X.521 (ISO 9548-7) The Directory — Selected Object Classes. Defines standard object classes and the associated groups of attributes (attribute sets). (p. 212)

About the Author

Peter Westwood is a management consultant. One of his areas of specialization is providing OSI application planning, marketing, and implementation services to business managers in both communication and information technology vendor companies and to user organizations. He has successfully directed numerous X.400 and

X.500 projects. With over 24 years of experience in the communications and computer field and extensive involvement in OSI projects since 1984, Mr. Westwood has also given talks and papers on emerging communication and office automation applications and markets at numerous international conferences; he has also published many articles. Immediately prior to forming his own company, Westwood Technology Management, he was C.O.O. of the software company that was the major initial developer of X.400 and that also developed X.500 software. Eighteen of the top thirty of the world's largest computer and communication companies licensed that X.400 software, and it was installed in over 40 countries. Mr. Westwood has B.A. and B.Sc. degrees from the University of Durham, U.K., and an M.B.A. from Simon Fraser University, Canada. He can be contacted at Westwood Technology Management, 943 Inglewood Avenue, West Vancouver, B.C., Canada V7T 1X8 Tel: (604) 922-8734, Fax: (604) 926-3297.

Chapter

11

The Distributed Computing Environment

by Sumner Blount

Section 1. The Role of a Distributed Computing Environment

Recent changes in the computer industry have had a dramatic impact on the way information is processed. In particular, the growth of personal computers, graphic workstations, and networks (both LAN's and WAN's) have caused many businesses to alter dramatically their normal techniques for meeting their computing needs. These changes have, in turn, created a need for computing services to allow users and application developers to utilize more easily the increased capabilities of these new systems. How well these businesses integrate new technologies may very well have a major impact on their overall success.

This chapter focuses on the core services required for a comprehensive distributed computing environment (DCE). It discusses briefly each distributed service in turn and explains the salient characteristics of each. Some attention is also given to the DCE as specified by the Open Software Foundation (OSF). These technologies are worthy of attention for two reasons. First, each component in the OSF DCE has been combined with the others to form a unified distributed environment. Second, the OSF DCE is expected to have a major impact in the computing industry over the next few years.

This first section contains an overview of distributed computing, including its evolution from earlier computing models, and a comparison with centralized and networked systems. Then comes a discussion of the relationship of the OSI model and its relevant standards to distributed computing, followed by the essential attributes of a distributed computing environment that allow it to provide enhanced capabilities over earlier systems. Finally, this section introduces the most important distributed services and illustrates how they can be integrated to form a unified DCE.

Section 2 is devoted to a discussion of one of the key components of any distributed environment, the name service. It will discuss the major tradeoffs that must be made in the architecture and design of an effective distributed name service. In addition, the naming architecture contained in the OSF DCE is used to illustrate some of the important characteristics of this core technology.

The Evolution of Distributed Computing

Distributed processing is not a new concept. In fact, there has been a gradual but unmistakable movement toward distributed processing over the last twenty years, which could be characterized as having three distinct phases:

1. *Centralized (timesharing) systems (1970s)* These systems are based on a model of "many users, one computer." During this period, the cost of hardware was high enough that to make computers cost-effective, many users had to share each computer. This was very effective for many different types of environments, especially those that were typically interactive in nature.
2. *Networked systems (1980s)* The advent of the workstation in the early 1980s gave rise to the "one user, one computer" model of computing. This was made possible by dramatic hardware price decreases, increased disk capacity, integrated graphics processors, and sophisticated networking software.

    Workstations allow a form of distributed computing, in the sense that both computing power and data are moved closer to the user. This is certainly an improvement over the earlier timesharing or batch machines that required users to compete for all computing resources, thereby often indirectly penalizing some users because of the usage requirements of others. Still,

it can be difficult for a workstation user to share resources on another user's machine, especially processor resources. Also, this model generally is implemented in the form of multiple systems connected together via a network, instead of as a single operating system distributed across the network.
3. *Distributed computing (1990s)* The next decade is expected to make distributed processing truly a reality. This could be viewed as the "one user, many computers" phase of computing. In particular, users will view all the resources within a computing environment as comprising a single, comprehensive distributed system. These resources will include not only processors and data, but also users, devices, and services.

Full distributed processing will allow application developers and users to gain the maximum benefit from the numerous heterogeneous systems that typically comprise today's networks. Users will be able to execute their applications on the most appropriate processor within the network, in a way that is transparent to them. For example, if a single processor is underutilized, applications can be migrated dynamically to execute on that processor, thereby increasing total system throughput.

In addition, the specific data formats of each machine architecture can be hidden from both users and application developers. For example, even though some machines store data differently from others (known as the "big or little endian" problem), these machine differences can be masked by distributed software that converts data from one format to the other, transparent to the applications.

What Is a Distributed System?

A distributed system is a group of computers doing something together. To be more specific, distributed systems are typified by the following set of characteristics:

1. The system consists of a set of hardware, software, and data components, which are generally heterogeneous in nature.
2. All components are connected by a network, which may be quite large and may span huge geographical areas.
3. The system provides a comprehensive set of services, which are available from any location within the distributed system (subject to security constraints).
4. The services provided have certain global properties that are uniform throughout the system.

These characteristics are required for a truly distributed system. A group of machines, even heterogeneous, that are simply connected together by a network does not possess all these properties and therefore does not qualify as a distributed system. In particular, a uniform set of services and global properties gives a distributed system its sense of coherence and distinguishes it from simply a large collection of networked machines.

Why do we need distributed systems? Why is so much attention being devoted to them in recent years? The answer is very simple. Distributed systems can provide computing capability that more closely typifies the way many businesses operate and can yield significant reliability and availability advantages over either centralized or networked systems.

Let's consider the specific advantages of a distributed environment:

1. *Closer correspondence to business practices* Distributed systems mimic most modern businesses. The major components of many businesses are often distributed: people, information, and computing resources. Centralized systems don't adequately support this type of organization because they force a computing model upon companies that seldom reflects their normal business practices. This leads to inefficiencies, bottlenecks, and often frustration.

2. *More widespread resource sharing* The problem of sharing of information and computing resources is one of the most significant problems facing today's businesses. A company's information is often its lifeblood. It generally must be shared among the corporate groups for the company to effectively respond to changing business conditions.

   Similarly, distributed systems allow more efficient use of computing resources. This includes not only the sharing of basic resources such as printers, but also more effective use of the actual processors within the system. Underutilized processors, especially expensive specialized ones like supercomputers can be a problem in many nondistributed systems. The ability to dynamically migrate processes to the most appropriate processor can be a major advantage of distributed systems.

3. *More modularity and expandability* Centralized systems are often difficult to expand. Other than simply acquiring more memory or disk capacity, there is relatively little that one can do to significantly expand the capacity of many centralized systems. Distributed systems can be easily expanded simply by

adding more components and by expanding the scope of the set of distributed services to include the new components.

The increased modularity of distributed systems requires that the interfaces to all distributed services be very carefully designed. Interfaces must be precise, well thought-out, and relatively stable, in order for the distributed system to function effectively. This is one impetus behind the increased trend toward standardized interfaces as specified by such groups as ISO, X/OPEN, and POSIX. These interfaces enable services to be built that can more easily accommodate a wider range of hardware and software platforms, and thereby offer increased portability to the applications that are built on top of these services.

4. *Better availability and reliability* The availability of a computer system can be viewed as being the probability that it will be available to perform the work you want it to do. Distributed systems generally offer significantly better availability than centralized systems. This is due to their innate capacity to replicate services and resources within the distributed environment and to dynamically manage these services so that if one service is unavailable, another instance of the service can be located and used to perform the same function. The key concept here is that a distributed system is much less likely to have a single point of failure for any critical function or resource than is a comparable centralized system.

It is easy to replicate services that have no state (preinvocation data that must be stored between calls). Simply by initiating many instances of the service, one can easily increase availability. Unfortunately, any nontrivial service will almost certainly require some sort of state information (e.g., knowledge that a file is already in use). Also, whenever the service replicates the state (which includes such things as namespaces and even the contents of files), then the goal of availability meets head on the problem of maintaining consistency of this data. It's trivial to guarantee consistency by locking all replicas until each one has been updated. However, this would lower overall availability to unacceptable levels. We will examine more of this availability vs. consistency tradeoff in a later discussion of name services.

One distributed system expert has observed, somewhat facetiously, that a distributed system is one in which you can't get your work done because some computer you never even heard of has failed. Although this may certainly be true for some systems that purport to be distributed, it doesn't describe our model of how a distributed system should function. An analogous way of expressing how a distributed system *should* operate is to say that a distributed system is one in which a computer you never even heard of will help you get your job done.

Reliability is a broader concept than availability. A reliable system is one that both is available when you need it and performs correctly even in the face of sporadic component failures. Distributed systems offer the potential for better reliability because they have more modular and well-defined interfaces, with fewer cross-component side-effects that could cause system failures.

5. *Better scalability* Scalability of an algorithm or service occurs when the complexity of the algorithm or service grows no more than linearly as the size of the distributed system grows. Algorithms that perform well on small networks, but perform poorly on very large networks, are not scalable.

Distributed systems generally are more scalable than centralized ones. One major reason for this is simply that distributed systems typically have no centralized components. They therefore can grow much more easily than nondistributed systems. Another reason is that distributed systems are not simply centralized systems that have been "tweaked" a little. Distributed systems are designed from the ground up, or are composed of a set of independent distributed services, each of which was usually designed with a large, distributed system in mind. In short, most distributed systems are scalable because their originators designed them to be that way. Most centralized systems are not for the converse reason.

Distributed Systems vs. Centralized and Networked Systems

As discussed above, distributed systems are a natural evolution of the earlier centralized systems and the more recent (and current) networked systems. Let's summarize the salient characteristics of each computing model.

Centralized systems had many advantages for the period in which they were predominant. As an example, they typically provided a wealth of functions and capabilities, often sufficient to meet the needs of most application developers. This richness of capability was necessary because there was often a wide diversity of users and applications utilizing these systems simultaneously. In effect, centralized systems often had to be "all things to all people."

In addition, these systems possess a high degree of functional coherence. Similar functions tend to operate in similar ways, resources can be managed in consistent ways, etc. This makes some centralized systems relatively easy to manage and administer, as well as enabling them to provide a coherent base for application development.

Networked systems provide significant benefits over centralized systems. They allow easier sharing of resources, primarily devices and data. This greatly increases the cost-effectiveness of networked systems. Sharing in networked systems, though, can be somewhat cumbersome. Sharing is often at a high granularity (whole files instead of records, for example), and simultaneous sharing with synchronization mechanisms is often not supported.

Another major advantage of networked systems over centralized ones is their capacity to expand as computing requirements grow. Nodes can generally be added easily to a network, with no decrease in function to the existing nodes. This is not as common in centralized systems, where the addition of a few more users or applications can often have a dramatic (and negative) impact on existing users.

The emergence of distributed systems has shown that they can provide the richness of function and the coherence of centralized systems, while also allowing easy expandability and resource sharing as networked systems do. Further, distributed systems provide significantly better reliability and availability than either of these earlier types of systems. This, then, is the key to the promise of distributed systems, and why it is expected that their importance will grow significantly during this decade.

Figure 11-1 summarizes the advantages of each type of system.

OSI and Distributed Systems

In one sense, the suite of emerging OSI (Open System Interconnection) standards are orthogonal to much of what constitutes a distributed system. The bulk of a distributed environment (as we will view it in this chapter) exists only at OSI layer 7, the application layer. These distributed services could theoretically run on top of any suite of network protocols, whether it be OSI or the Internet protocol suite (e.g., TCP/IP).

One issue that distributed system designers must face is the amount of protocol and interface standardization that one is willing to use in a distributed system, since many standardized protocols are by intent very general and provide a wide range of functions. This is often contradictory to the design goals of the distributed system, in

```
┌─────────────────────────────────────────────────────────────────┐
│   Centralized systems:      Distributed systems:    Networked systems:   │
│                                                                 │
│   Richness of function  ──▶  Richness of function               │
│                                                                 │
│   Coherence             ──▶  Coherence                          │
│                                                                 │
│                              Resource sharing  ◀──  Resource sharing     │
│                                                                 │
│                              Easy growth       ◀──  Easy growth         │
│                                                                 │
│                              Cost-effective    ◀──  Cost-effective      │
│                                                                 │
│                              Availability                       │
│                                                                 │
│                              Reliability                        │
└─────────────────────────────────────────────────────────────────┘
```

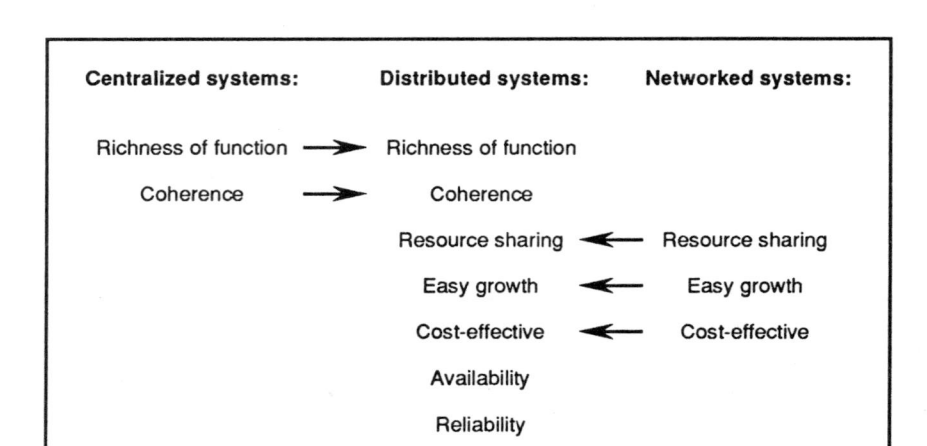

Figure 11-1 Advantages of each type of system: centralized, networked, and distributed.

which there is usually a lightweight mechanism for communication and information transfer among components.

Yet, there are some OSI standards that play a key role in the architecture of a distributed system. The X.500 Directory Service is the most obvious example of this. We will consider the role of this standard in more detail when we discuss name services.

Pervasive Properties of a Distributed System

In an earlier section, we saw that one of the key distinguishing characteristics of a distributed system is that it possesses a set of global properties that are uniform throughout the environment. This is the primary attribute that separates distributed systems from earlier networked systems, which were often simply large numbers of computers whose interactions were limited to asynchronous message-passing applications. Only a truly distributed system provides services common to all machines in the system, so that it essentially presents the illusion of a single system to the user or application. In a comprehensive distributed system, the boundaries between machines are transparent, in terms of data files, resources, users, their names, and even physical distances. It is the set of global properties of a distributed system that makes this possible.

The following are essential properties of a distributed system:

1. *Global Names* In this context, "global" means everywhere in the system. The concept of global names implies that each object has a unique name throughout the system. Objects such as users, files, resources, and services all have complete names that are constant regardless of where in the system those objects are referenced. The full name (as opposed to any sort of nickname or abbreviation) of a resource on my machine is always exactly the same, whether I reference it or you reference it from your machine.

   The fact that an object has the same name when referenced from anywhere in the system does not imply that each object has only one name (that is, one way to locate it within the object space). It is common for a single object, especially files, to have aliases (sometimes called softlinks) such that two distinct full names reference the same object.

2. *Global Access* Each service in the distributed system should be usable from anywhere in the system. This implies that I can access the system from any workstation and have available to me all the services that I have on my own workstation in my office (subject only to security restrictions). There may be some (hopefully) minor performance degradation, especially if the workstation I'm using is physically distant from the services and resources that I'm accessing. But, other than a minor performance impact, my location within the distributed system should be transparent to me.

   One of the most difficult problems in achieving global access is that of insuring *data coherence*. This means that as the distances between components of the system become larger (and presumably more prone to errors of different kinds), and as multiple heterogeneous operating systems exist within the distributed system, it becomes increasingly more difficult to assure consistency of data across many users and applications. For example, if I (in Boston) open a file on another workstation (in Los Angeles) while its owner is editing it, I ought to be able to actually see those changes to the file as they appear. That is, subject to transmission delays, I should always see the latest data within the file. The fact that I can do this is the basis of global access, and yet it is quite complex to achieve in its full generality.

3. *Global Security* All the security mechanisms in the distributed system should operate consistently throughout the system. There are several aspects to this concept. First, user authentication works the same across the entire system. This implies

that I can authenticate to any process in the system, and my access rights are exactly as if I were using my own workstation. Second, all the objects in the system (printers, services, files, etc.) use the same access control mechanism. Thus, users are granted (or denied) access to each resource in a consistent way, and each object uses this global mechanism to control access to it.

4. *Global Management* It should be possible to manage all of the resources and objects in a distributed system from a single location in the system. This means that I (with appropriate privilege) should be able to control the entire system from my office. Although it's very unlikely that a single person could or would want to manage the entire system, there should be no constraints imposed by the system on how the objects within it should be managed.

An associated characteristic of this principle is the ability to manage the entire system from *anywhere* in the system. Not only should I be able to manage the entire system from my workstation, but I should also be able to do it from *any* workstation in the system. The limiting of all management functions to a single location is unnecessarily restricting to the flexibility of the system. Still, if centralization of system management is required due to security requirements, then this capability should also be possible.

To achieve global management, each object to be managed must export a well-defined and consistent set of interfaces. These interfaces should be accessible either by programs or by users (via management tools). There should be management functions required only in cases where human judgment is required to manage certain objects. In general, the less management is required, the more effective the distributed system will be.

5. *Global Availability* Improved availability is a key advantage of a distributed system. Global availability means that all services are available to clients, even after some failures in the system. This level of availability is achieved through replication of services and objects. As long as the failure rate is less than the level of replication provided by the system, the critical services and objects will always be available to applications.

The degree of replication should be controlled by the system administrator. Some objects, such as a heavily used subtree of the namespace, might be highly replicated while other resources, such as a specialized printer, might not be replicated at all. The level of redundancy is determined by the access patterns of that resource and by the impact caused by its unavailability. If a set of replicated services is designed to fail independently, then any level of availability is possible simply by increasing the level of redundancy of the service.

One important way to achieve availability is to provide transparent fail-over when a service fails during processing of a client request. One of the ways this is done is by having a module in the client computer that is responsible for creating and managing communication links between the client application and the desired service. This module, called a *clerk* or *server agent* can detect when a server has failed and redirect service requests to another, similar server. This operation should always be transparent to the client program, which will never know that its original server has stopped processing requests.

Core Services for a DCE

In order to have a comprehensive DCE, a set of core services should be available to all applications. Each of these core services should possess the global properties listed in the previous section. This will allow the set of services to form a uniform, consistent environment for the development of distributed applications.

The following are the core services for a comprehensive DCE. Note that there are variations or extended capabilities for each service (for example, a record manager within the file service), but these are the most important basic services:

1. *Global Naming Service* A global naming service is a distributed system facility that allows network objects (resources, users, services, etc.) to be conveniently located. It is the glue that holds the distributed system together. A name service simply maps an object name into a set of attributes of that object. Typically, these attributes are system-controlled things such as the object's location, time of creation, and access control list.

    A global naming service provides information about objects within the distributed system and provides a convenient mechanism for sharing this information across the distributed system. It also provides location transparency for network objects, so they can be moved from one machine to another without changing their full global name and, by extension, the applica-

tions that reference them. A global name service stores system-related information that is generally stored in the file system on timesharing computers.
2. *Support for Distribution of Applications* For many years, programmers have found that organizing programs as a set of separate procedures aids the debugging and maintenance of the program. This procedure-call paradigm presents a request/response protocol that is easily adapted to the client/server environment.

    Remote procedure calls (RPC's) extend the model for higher-level language procedure calls by supporting direct calls to procedures on remote systems. This makes distributed applications almost as easy to develop as regular nondistributed (single system) applications.

    Use of an RPC facility allows distributed applications to be written without concern for the location or architecture of the machines on which they will be run. Since RPC's usually require no special purpose language constructs, the resulting source code is generally portable to machines of other types. Some RPC's allow client and server to be written in different programming languages. In fact, it is a goal of RPC that the client not need know the programming language of the server.
3. *Distributed File System* A distributed file system (DFS) provides transparent access to files in the network, regardless of the physical location of either the application or the data. Users of a DFS generally see a single, large file namespace, instead of a series of disjoint file systems for the different nodes in the network.

    Distributed file systems are much more complex to implement than traditional file systems. In the distributed environment, issues such as synchronization of file access (locking), and error detection and recovery become extremely complex. In addition, distributed file systems often need to support replication of the file system data in order to increase overall availability. Finally, the problems that might be encountered in a distributed file system are much more difficult to isolate and reproduce than in a centralized system.
4. *Authentication Service* A key component of any distributed computing environment is a comprehensive security architecture. In order to provide sufficient security, this architecture must be fully integrated into the global naming service, the RPC mechanism, the file system, and management capabilities.

    A major portion of any security architecture is the authentication service. This service authenticates principals (users) to

services, in order to guarantee the identity of the user of the service. It can also authenticate the service to the user, in order to guard against a false program, such as a virus, masquerading as a system service.
5. *Synchronization of System Time* In a large network environment, it is important that each machine in the network have a consistent view of the current time. A distributed time service provides a mechanism to synchronize time clocks among all the machines in the system. Synchronization of time permits the coordination of various functions, such as event and error logging, error recovery, name service operations, and access to distributed databases. These functions require a consistent time value to be able to accurately determine the order of events. Synchronized time values also enable systems to accurately determine the interval between two time values that were taken in different parts of the network.

It is essential that time synchronization occur continuously (or at relatively small intervals), so that the time values stored by different machines don't start to drift apart. When this happens, the differences in these time values can cause many distributed algorithms to function incorrectly. This can, in some cases, cause major failures such as database inconsistency, inability to recover from other failures, etc.

Summary

We have discussed briefly each of the critical services required for a DCE. However, the mere presence of each of these services is not sufficient to provide a comprehensive system. There are two important criteria that must be met for the system to be an effective environment for distributed applications. First, each service must be based on the same conceptual model. For example, it is of no benefit to combine a name service based on hierarchical names with another service that expects a flat namespace. Each service must therefore subscribe to the same basic model of how resources and services are named, how they are located, how applications interface to the services, etc.

Second, it is very important that these core services be well-integrated with each other. This implies that each service should use, where appropriate, the capabilities offered by the others, so that each one doesn't have to reinvent the features it needs. As an example, the RPC facility should be integrated with the authentication mechanisms that are present. This allows all applications and services that use RPC's to automatically get the benefits of authentication without having to call the authentication service directly. Similarly, if the file system, authentication service, and naming service are closely integrated, there can be a single namespace that can be used by each service. For example, the file service could use the name service to traverse parts of the namespace tree, down to the point where the file system naming structure began.

Figure 11-2 illustrates the basic services of a DCE and an approximation of their logical layering. Note the well-integrated nature of these services, as indicated by the many lines of communication across the service interfaces. The key areas of integration are the RPC and authentication services (since this allows all applications to have an authenticated RPC facility) and the use of RPC as the communication mechanism by all services (since this makes these services independent of the actual transport facility).

The Open Software Foundation DCE

The Open Software Foundation (OSF) is a nonprofit company whose charter is to analyze, select, and license the best technology within the industry. As of 1990, the OSF had selected technologies in two general areas: a graphical user interface (MOTIF) and a distributed computing environment (DCE).

The OSF DCE is composed of six core components, each one of which represents an innovative technology. These technologies have

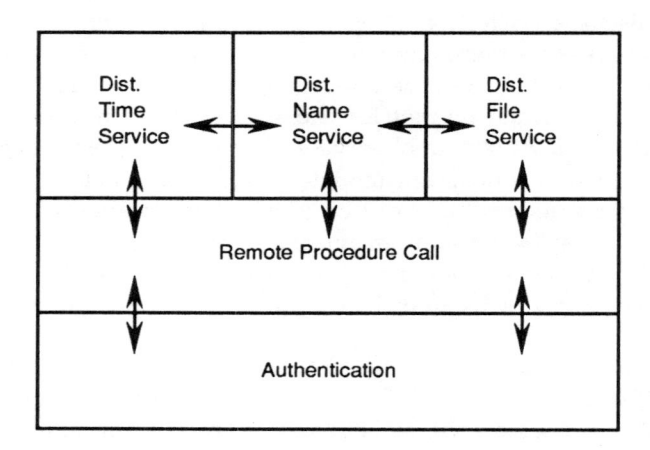

Figure 11-2 Core services for a distributed computing environment.

Table 11-1 Contents of OSF DCE

Service	Technology	Sponsor
RPC	NCS RPC	HP/Apollo, Digital Equipment
Name Service	DECdns, DIR-X X.500	Siemens AG
Dist. File System	AFS	Transarc
Security	Kerberos, Password, etc.	HP/Apollo
Time Service	DECdts	Digital Equipment
Multithreading	Concert Multithread Arch.	Digital Equipment

been closely integrated with each other, and this integration is what gives the OSF DCE its uniqueness in the industry.

Table 11-1 lists the core technologies in the OSF DCE and the originating company.

The name service architecture of the DCE is the glue that provides much of the coherence of the system. The next section focuses on name services in general, and the specific attributes of the OSF DCE name service in particular.

Section 2. Distributed Name Services

One of the main impediments to the effective use of computer networks is the growing difficulty of identifying, locating, and accessing network resources. Much of the power of existing and future computer networks may go unused simply because the users are either unaware of the facilities available to them or are simply overwhelmed. The difficulty can be expected to increase over time for the following reasons:

1. *Networks are getting very large.*

    Thousand-node networks are now common, with million-node networks on the horizon for the world's larger public and private organizations.

2. *Networks are heterogeneous.*
   There are more kinds of computers participating in networks all the time — workstations, servers, personal computers, minicomputers, supercomputers, and mainframes. Even more important is the loose, heterogeneous composition of a large network, which makes central control and management of the entire conglomeration infeasible.
3. *There are whole new classes of distributed applications.*
   Once the communication capabilities of the network itself become ubiquitous and reliable, new applications spring up to exploit the power of a large computer network. Applications such as network file systems and network-based electronic mail systems are already common. New applications, such as fully distributed databases, are being deployed today. To a great extent, the difficulty in accessing network resources arises from the lack of a consistent, globally accessible directory of network resources.

What Is a Global Name Service?

A global name service provides a mapping between the names of network objects (users, node names, distributed services, resources, etc.) and the set of attributes defined for each object. The most common application of this is the presenting of a network name to the name service, which returns all (or some) of the attributes for that object. Some recent name services (especially those based on the X.500 model) also provide attribute-to-name mapping. As we will see later, this is useful for searching for network objects that meet a specified set of criteria.

Though very general in their use and application, name services are different from distributed databases. The major ways in which a name server differs from a distributed database are:

1. The objects stored in the namespace tend to change their names and their attributes quite slowly, while database entries often have high rates of change.
2. Name services typically have much weaker consistency requirements than do database systems. In a network namespace, it is acceptable for the entries to be inconsistent for relatively short periods of time. This is acceptable because of the high availability requirements that name services have. It would be very

bad if the entire network namespace (or even parts of it) were to be unavailable each time that a change had to be propagated around the world to all the replicas in the name service. Therefore, temporary inconsistency is acceptable for a name service, whereas this would likely cause major problems for many database applications.
3. Name services have a high query-to-update ratio. Database entries typically change much more often.
4. The frequency of updates to a name service depends on the characteristics of the people and organizational groups, not on the networking environment.

Name services also differ from distributed file services in their requirements. File systems need very fast lookup access for files in their directories, whereas name services don't require that level of performance for object name lookup. File system directories also tend to be smaller than the namespace supported by most name services. Some name services can support networks with hundreds of thousands of nodes and more than one million objects in the namespace.

How Are Network Objects Named?

There are several different ways of naming objects in a network (see Figure 11-3).

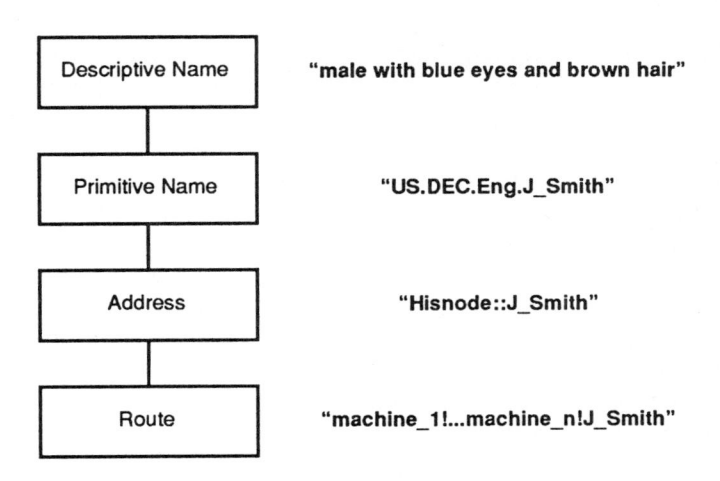

Descriptive Name	"male with blue eyes and brown hair"
Primitive Name	"US.DEC.Eng.J_Smith"
Address	"Hisnode::J_Smith"
Route	"machine_1!...machine_n!J_Smith"

Figure 11-3 Types of network names.

A *descriptive name* names a resource or object by enumerating enough of its attributes to distinguish it from other objects. A descriptive name is of the form "a male with blue eyes and brown hair."

Descriptive names are most useful to human users who are browsing the network to discover a resource that meets certain user-specified criteria. Descriptive naming systems are potentially the most powerful kind of naming systems, but they are also the most demanding of computing resources and are difficult to distribute effectively. The CCITT and ISO are developing a standard, known as X.500, for a descriptive naming system primarily oriented toward international electronic mail systems.

A *primitive name* is a string of symbols that identifies a single object or resource in the network. A primitive name is like the name of a person or business. If you know the name of the resource you seek, the primitive name gives you an extremely convenient identifier to use to locate the resource or to discover more about it. A principal feature of primitive names is that they are unambiguous; no two objects or resources in a network can have the same primitive name at the same time. Because they are simple and straightforward, naming systems based on primitive names are technically easier to design for speed, scalability, and robustness.

An *address* is a form of name that identifies a resource based on its location in the network. Addresses are the kind of name usually used in computer networks lacking a global naming service. For example, in the Internet, all resources are identified by the node on which they reside. There are a number of difficulties with using addresses as names. As a network grows, the relationship between the nodes and the resources that live on them becomes increasingly complex and arbitrary. It is unnatural to use addresses to name resources that are either replicated or not inherently tied to one location in the network for a long period of time. Also, reconfiguring resources as new nodes are added or old nodes removed causes some pain to the users, since when this happens the names they were using become invalid.

A *route* names a resource by enumerating the path from the accessing user to the location of the resource. Routes suffer from all of the disadvantages of addresses, and some more as well. Route names are dependent on who is accessing the resource as well as where the resource is. Different users must use different names to access the same resource. Worse, if any portion of the network is reconfigured and the path to a resource is affected, its name changes.

Network Naming Structures

Network names in a primitive naming system could have one of a number of possible structures. The simplest of these would be a flat namespace, in which the names are simply strings of symbols with no internal structure. Flat names are easy for users to understand but suffer from a number of serious deficiencies, especially when allocation of new names is considered. In a flat namespace, a single authority is needed to arbitrate the assignment of names to ensure that all names are unambiguous. This is difficult even on single computers and is infeasible in large computer networks.

A second possible structure for network names is a *tree*, a type of graph in which each node has exactly one parent but may have any number of children. Computer file systems such as those supported by Unix use a tree-structured namespace for naming files. In these systems, the tree is rooted, meaning that there is a single node that is the ancestor of all others. Trees have the advantage of allowing a decentralized method of assigning names and giving users a natural hierarchical scheme for organizing their network namespace. Trees suffer from a number of deficiencies, however. The most serious is that a node in the graph can have only one name (because each node has a single parent). This makes names in a tree unique as well as unambiguous, preventing users from using more than one path through the graph to name the same network resource.

In order to avoid the uniqueness limitations of trees, a third possible structure for network names is that of a directed graph, in which names consist of paths from some initial node to the desired terminal node (i.e., a node with no arcs emanating from it). Some computer file systems, such as Unix, augment their basic tree with a capability called Symbolic Links, which allows users to view the file system as a directed graph rather than a tree.

Naming structures based on directed graphs have two major subtypes, which have quite different semantics as seen by their users. The graph can be either rooted or unrooted. In a rooted graph, like a rooted tree, there is a distinguished node which is the ancestor of all others and is globally known to all users. In an unrooted graph, there is no such node, and each user must choose a starting node in the graph from which to specify names.

Rooted graphs produce a structure with absolute names. Absolute names are desirable because they are accessible to the entire community of network users; the node in the graph that is the starting point for all paths is globally known. This allows the names to be stored, communicated in network protocols, or written on business cards without fear that the starting point for the path cannot be found by some user.

Unrooted graphs produce a structure with relative names. Although relative names suffer seriously from a lack of global usability, they have certain advantages. The major flexibility derived from relative names is avoiding the need to designate a single node in the graph as a root. In some environments picking the global root is very difficult due to a nonhierarchical relationship among the participants in the network or an unwillingness to delegate responsibility for a highest-level naming authority to any one organization.

As noted above, there are several major advantages to a name service based on a hierarchical tree model. First, hierarchical names are generally intuitive and easy to use. Second, tree structures are inherently more scalable than other models, particularly flat namespaces. As new names are added to the tree, the complexity of namespace operations goes up only logarithmically. Given the size of today's network namespaces, this can easily become the dominant reason for using a hierarchical model. Finally, the X.500 Directory Services standard is based on a hierarchical naming model. For these reasons, we will use a hierarchical naming model in our examples.

A namespace is stored in a partitioned database. This implies that parts of the database are stored in different locations within the network. The database is generally also partially replicated. This means that certain subtrees can be stored in multiple places, in order to increase the availability of the database and to improve performance by storing portions of the namespace closer to the applications that use it.

Design Criteria for Name Services

Now that we have considered the general characteristics of a name service, let's look at some of the more important design criteria that must be considered when designing, or choosing, a distributed name service. This is not a complete view of all the design issues relating to name services, but simply an introduction to the more important technical issues.

1. *Replication and Consistency* In a large network, it is infeasible to store all names in one central location. Apart from the problems attendant with such single points of failure, a centralized

service suffers from poor performance since the cost of accessing the service from distant parts of the network is high and the service provider can quickly become both a processing and communication bottleneck to the entire network. Thus, any practical global naming system must provide some form of partitioning of the namespace to allow some names to be stored in a different location from other names. Different naming structures give rise to different partitioning techniques. In a tree-based naming structure, a natural approach to partitioning is to store each node, or an entire subtree, in its own database.

It is important not to allow single points of failure in the name service. The most appropriate technique for achieving this reliability is to replicate the data in multiple locations. Adding data replication to a system leads to two important decisions. The first is to determine what the unit of replication should be. One could decide to replicate each name individually, to replicate the entire database, or to replicate individual nodes. The second issue is the effect of replication on data consistency. One must decide if all copies of the data should be kept tightly synchronized. If the data is not synchronized, then a decision must be made as to what consistency facilities and semantics will be offered.

A common tenet underlying the architecture of most name services is that the data in the namespace need not be guaranteed to be totally consistent at any instant of time. This characteristic is different from the requirements for most distributed database systems. The reason is that availability of the namespace is considered to be much more important than absolute consistency. In applications we are more willing to tolerate the slight possibility of getting old data than the possibility of not being able to get *any* data at all due to a namespace being locked for update.

In general, the greater the degree of redundancy (replication) supported by the system, the greater the complexity of the update problem. If each directory in the namespace is replicated, then updating all of these replicas can be time-consuming and more likely to encounter errors during processing. This namespace convergence operation can be done when the update is made, continuously over short-term periods (every five minutes, for example), or over a longer interval (say, every twelve hours). This interval should be controllable by the system manager, since he or she is in the best position to judge the data consistency requirements of the applications.

2. *Scalability* So that a network's growth is not constrained by the ability of the naming system to continue growing, the naming system must be highly scalable. In practice this means avoiding data storage techniques in which the amount of overhead grows too rapidly with the size of the namespace. It is essential to avoid algorithms or data structures that grow faster than linearly, and desirable if all processing and storage overheads grow no faster than logarithmically.

    Scalability is a much more critical requirement in distributed systems than in earlier centralized systems. With a centralized system, it was generally possible to estimate the maximum size (in terms of users, number of applications, memory, etc.) that the system would reach over time. This limit was typically reached much earlier than was expected, but it was usually obvious when the system was becoming saturated. Distributed systems don't share this trait. They tend to grow indefinitely without limit, and therefore they must be designed with scalability in mind.

    Hierarchical namespaces provide good scalability. The complexity (processing required for each operation) of namespace access grows only logarithmically as the namespace grows. The complexity of an operation on a flat namespace generally grows linearly as the number of entries increases, and therefore this model is not suitable for a large distributed system.

3. *Caching* Namespace access often exhibits a high degree of locality. That is, names that are referenced by applications are often referenced again over a short period of time. This trait, coupled with the fact that network delays can often cause communication with a name server to be slow, make client caching a virtual necessity for adequate performance. When a reference to a particular object is made, the data returned from the server is stored in the client machine for subsequent use. When the same name is used soon thereafter by the application, a server request does not have to be made. Virtually any information that is retrieved from the name server can be cached. This includes not only specific object names and attributes, but also whole subtrees of the namespace and network addresses of other name servers.

    It is also possible to cache the nonexistence of a particular name. The client machine will store the name with an indicator that the name was not found in the namespace. This facility, called negative caching, does not provide the same performance improvement as normal caching, but it is relatively easy to implement.

It is impractical for the name server to keep track of what data is cached for each client. This implies that when the namespace is modified, some of the cached information on some client machines might not be valid. This condition is acceptable because any client must be capable of dealing with slight inconsistencies in the data returned by the name server. When the client discovers that the cache contains stale information, then that part of the cache can be flushed and the correct information obtained from the name server.

Functional Name Service Model

There is a set of functional components that a name service must have. Although the terminology for these components may vary across name services, their basic purpose is similar in most implementations. Figure 11-4 gives the functional name service components and their X.500 nomenclature (in parentheses).

The *clerk* (also called the "client agent" in some systems and the Directory User Agent [DUA] in X.500 systems) is generally coresident on the application host machine. It coordinates access to multiple name servers, caches and processes results from each operation, and in some cases does treewalk processing of the namespace tree. The clerk passes service requests to any one of the instantiations of the name servers. The protocol used for this is called the Directory Access Protocol (DAP) in X.500.

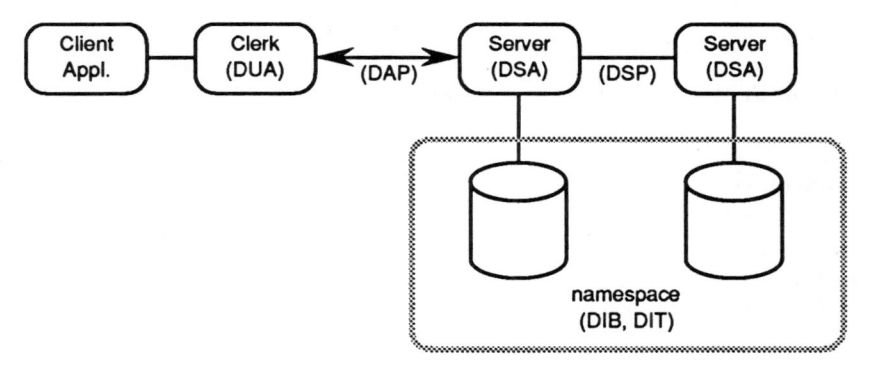

Figure 11-4 Functional name service components.

The entire set of information about the objects managed by the name servers is called the namespace. In X.500 terms, this consists of a Directory Information Base (DIB), which is the actual object data, and the Directory Information Tree (DIT), which comprises the control information that defines the logical structure of the namespace. The namespace is generally partitioned (and replicated) across a set of machines.

The name servers (called Directory Service Agents [DSA] in X.500) process service requests and return results to the clerks. The DSA's each typically control a portion of the total set of data contained within the namespace. When a server must communicate with another server in order to process the request, a specific server protocol is used. In X.500 implementations, this protocol is called the Directory Service Protocol (DSP).

There are several ways that communication between name servers can satisfy each service request. The first, called *referral*, occurs when a particular server cannot satisfy a request and returns to the clerk the name of another server that may be able to perform the request. It is then the clerk's responsibility to establish communication with that other server and issue the service request to it. *Chaining* occurs when the original server passes the request directly onto another server for processing. This process is analogous to nested subroutine calls and can continue to other servers until the request is satisfied. This technique removes the burden of processing referrals from the clerk. *Multicast* is a special case of chaining and involves the simultaneous forwarding of the request to multiple servers for concurrent processing. This is often used for decomposition of a compound request into simpler operations, in which case the partial results from each server are collated by the original server, and a single, complete response is then returned to the naming clerk.

Section 3. The OSF DCE Name Service

Introduction

The heart of any DCE is its name service. The OSF DCE is built around an innovative yet proven naming architecture, which is implemented by three complementary technologies (a local name service, the Domain Naming System, and an X.500 directory service). These technologies are intended to be seamless in their integration and provide a consistent application interface.

The naming architecture builds on the concept of a "cell," which is a (potentially large) collection of machines that share an administrative and security domain. The OSF DCE naming architecture has three components: a name service that provides local (i.e., relative to the cell) naming, and two that provide global (i.e., outside the cell) naming. The local name service is DECdns from Digital Equipment Corp., and the global name services are the DIR-X X.500 product from Siemens AG, and the Domain Naming System.

How Is the Namespace Organized?

There are several terms that are important in the understanding of the OSF DCE name service. An *object* is some entity in real life that is identified or described by an entry in the name service. The object represents reality, and its entry represents a snapshot of its attributes at a given instant of time (usually very recently). The entry cannot be guaranteed to completely reflect the true state of the object.

Directories are collections of entries. Each directory is identified by a pointer contained within the superior directory in the naming tree. Directories thus essentially represent nonleaf nodes in the naming graph. The set of all directories organized into a tree is called the *namespace*.

To increase availability, directories can be replicated to suit the specific needs of the environment. There are three types of replicas supported:

1. Master: can support all operations on the namespace.
2. Secondary: can support all operations except creation of new directories in the tree.
3. Read-only: can support only entry read operations.

What Is a Cell?

A cell is a key concept in the OSF DCE. It represents a (potentially) large group of machines that are commonly administered and often correspond to some organizational entity. A cell may have as few as two systems in it, or as many as several thousand. Many organizations need to organize into only one cell, while others need many cells. Machines within the cell typically share several characteristics. The following are the most important traits:

1. *High connectivity* Nodes within a cell typically are physically near one another. This follows from the assumption that the nodes in a cell share some sort of organizational or functional affinity for each other.
2. *Trusted administration* Machines in a single cell are often administered by the same person or group. The implication of this is that all machines in a cell would use a common authentication service. Machines outside the cell would not necessarily be controlled by an administrative entity that was trusted by the users inside this cell.
3. *Optimized protocols* Communication among machines within the cell should be optimized as much as possible. Because of the relative physical proximity and organizational affinity, there is no need for full generality of standardized protocols.

This naming model has a single global directory and supports a single application programming interface (API). This interface (the X/Open Directory Services API) is designed to allow access to the full X.500 features and semantics, yet still provide optimized operation within a local cell.

The concept of cells has several important advantages:

1. It is modeled after the way most businesses are structured organizationally.
2. It generally reflects the security trust relationships that exist in most environments. That is, users in the same organization (usually an entire company) tend to trust the administration of those users, yet often do not trust the administration of a distant set of users (often in another company).
3. It supports a single API for applications.
4. It allows for optimized interfaces to be used by the DCE components themselves.
5. It supports international standards (e.g., X.500). Yet, it also supports optimized protocols for intercell communication among clients and servers in different cells, once that communication is established using standard protocols.

To illustrate the cell concept, consider Figure 11-5. The tree represents a portion of the global namespace, specifically those objects located at DEC. The machines whose root is /dec/eng constitute a cell.

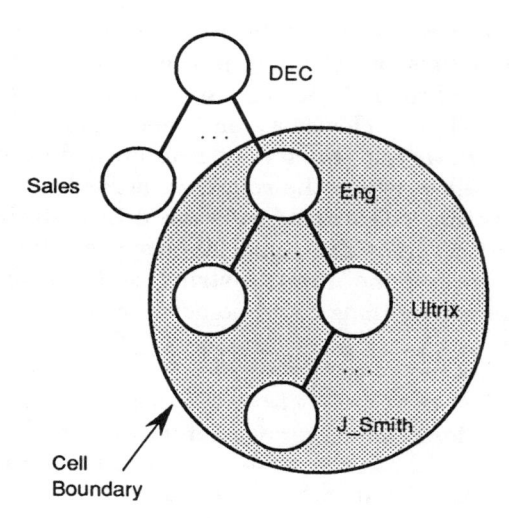

Figure 11-5 Example of cell structure.

What Is a Name?

A name in the OSF DCE is simply a printable string that defines a path from some root (either the global root or the local cell root) to the directory entry containing information for the target object. The name consists of a series of components, each one of which is an arc of the global naming graph. The global root is denoted by the string "/..." preceding the object pathname. A similar string, "/cns," denotes that the namespace search should be only in the "cell namespace," and hence should start at the local cell root. These strings were chosen because they are easy to use and remember and do not conflict with other Unix file-naming syntax.

Consider the following example. Assume that my application is running in a cell called "/.../com/dec/eng." Then the string "/cns/ULTRIX/J_Smith" would reference an object with the name "J_Smith" that exists in the ULTRIX directory within the local cell. This is termed an intracell reference because the search begins only at the local cell root.

One could have also used the string "/.../com/dec/eng/ULTRIX/J_Smith." This would have caused the search to start at the global root and would have followed the tree path down to the com/dec/eng cell, at which point the local name service would have resolved the reference down to the object entry. The above strings cause the pathname resolution to start at different roots (local or global), but the target object entry is the same. Note that an object name that starts with "/..." can be used in any cell and will always denote a single object. However, an object name that starts with "/cns" is cell-relative and thus may reference different objects depending on the cell in which the reference is made.

Objects in another cell can be referenced in a similar way, except that the search traverses the global namespace. There are two ways in which this can be done. First, a string conforming to the Domain Naming System conventions could be used, such as:

```
/.../com/HP/Apollo/S_Jones
```

In this case, the local name service sends this string to the Domain Naming System to locate the object. Second, the name string might contain typed values (as in X.500), such as:

```
/.../C=US/O=GOV/OU=EXEC/George_Bush
```

In this case, the string would be passed from the local name service to the X.500 global service for further resolution.

How Does the Application View the DCE Name Service?

The OSF DCE name service represents the integration of three different technologies (DECdns, DIR-X X.500, and the Domain Naming System), all of which have slightly different approaches to solving the problem of naming network resources. Yet the view that an application has of the DCE naming facilities is that of a single, consistent interface that supports all three technologies. This means that applications can be written to be independent of the cell environment in which they will operate, and they don't have to be changed as their access patterns go from objects within the cell to those outside the cell.

The API for naming services is the X/Open Directory Services interface (XDS). This interface was chosen because it is the only internationally recognized directory services application interface and is expected to become the industry standard.

Applications use XDS to access both local and global objects and operations. However, there are some operations that are supported only by the global name service. For example, the ability to search the namespace based on a set of attribute criteria is supported by the X.500 service, but not by the local service. An attempt to perform this type of function within the cell will cause DECdns to return an error condition.

There are three cases to consider when an application references an object name. The target object might be:

1. within the local cell (intracell)
2. in another cell (intercell)
3. in the X.500 global namespace, but not in any specific cell (extra-cell)

The XDS library determines whether the target object is within either the local cell or another cell. If so, it passes the request directly to the DECdns clerk. If the name does not reside within a cell, then a service request is made to the X.500 service for name resolution.

The DECdns clerk determines whether the object is inside or outside the local cell. If the reference is cell-relative, then the request is sent to the DECdns servers that manage the cell namespace. If the object is within another cell, DECdns must transmit the request to the local name servers within that cell. To do this, it first must find the location of the name servers in that cell and then establish communication with one or more of them.

When the cell name service detects that this is an intercell reference, it essentially transfers the operation to a gateway component, called the Global Directory Agent (GDA). There are two types of GDA's within the OSF DCE: an X.500 GDA and a Domain GDA. The purpose of the X.500 GDA is to map the local protocols into the regular X.500 standard protocols and to find the addresses of the local name servers that are stored in the X.500 namespace. It interfaces directly to the X.500 name service to resolve references to other cells into a list of DECdns server locations within that cell. The Domain GDA performs a similar function, except that the cell name and its server locations are stored in the Domain global namespace.

The X.500 GDA incrementally strips off each component of the X.500 object name. It attempts to resolve the name down to the component that delineates a cell boundary. Once it has determined the cell name of the object, it makes a service request to the appropriate server to determine the locations of the local name servers that support that cell. When the X.500 server returns the list of local server locations, the GDA returns them to the DECdns clerk as a server referral.

Once the list of server locations has been returned to DECdns, it can make a decision as to which one it should initiate contact with.

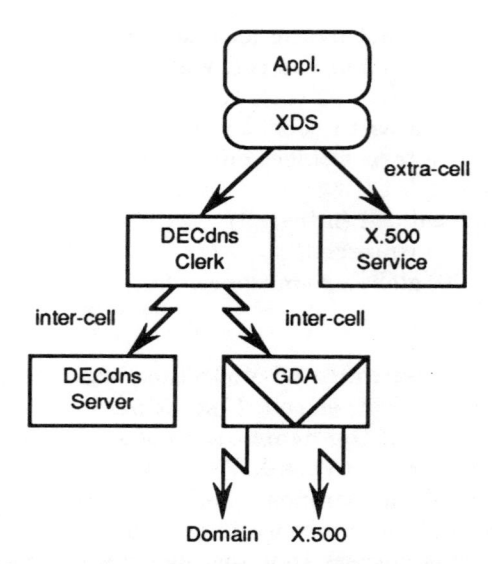

Figure 11-6 Interaction between local and global name service.

It then issues RPC calls directly to the target name server using optimized protocols, not the more general-purpose X.500 protocols. This maximizes efficiency because it allows local name servers to communicate with each other almost as if the communication was completely intracell. Figure 11-6 illustrates how the application views the DCE name service and the interaction among the components.

The integration of these GDA's with both the local and global name services allows the boundary between these services to be transparent to applications. This architecture also allows applications to pay for (in terms of performance) only that level of naming generality that they need.

Summary

Distributed computing will likely become the dominant computing paradigm in the next decade. A comprehensive, well-integrated set of distributed services is the foundation of an effective DCE.

The heart of any DCE is its name service. This chapter has considered the essential characteristics of a flexible name service. The OSF name service represents a melding of proven technologies, which form an innovative naming architecture for the development of distributed applications.

Sources

Lampson, Butler. Internal Digital Equipment Corporation Communication.

Oran, David. "The Digital Distributed Name Service," *Digital Technical Journal* (June 1989): pp. 9–15.

About the Author

Sumner Blount is currently a Senior Manager in the Distributed Processing Engineering group at Digital Equipment Corporation. He has spent a total of 11 years at Digital, in both development and management positions. He was the development manager for the TOPS-10 and TOPS-20 development groups.

He also has worked at Prime Computer, where he was the Operating System Development Manager, and at Pathway Designs, where he was Director of Software. He holds a B.S. degree from the University of North Carolina and an M.S. from the University of Connecticut.

Digital Equipment Corporation, headquartered in Maynard, Massachusetts, is the leading worldwide supplier of networked computer systems and services. Digital offers a full range of computing solutions and systems integration for the entire enterprise — from the desktop to the data center. Digital is also a leader in the area of OSI networking.

Section D

Implementation Considerations

Chapter

12

How to Justify an OSI-Based Network

by Bill Andrews

Introduction

As companies begin to rely on computers to aid in their daily operations, the need to share "electronic" information increases. Information systems are integrated into the computer environment to allow users to share data. Because information systems often share data from computers from different manufacturers running different applications, the need for standards for data communication and data exchange grows. This is one of the justifications for the development of the ISO/OSI model and related standards.

However, now that communication specifications (e.g., MAP, TOP, GOSIP) incorporating the OSI standards are defined and products available, end users have a difficult time convincing management that OSI is right for them. It is often difficult to quantify the intangible benefits OSI provides over proprietary networks or to describe to management how the inherent benefits of OSI can meet short-term needs and follow long-term corporate strategic directions. The lack of a network selection guideline procedure has prevented many corporations from justifying OSI as their communication direction.

This chapter will provide insight on how to quantify the intangible benefits of OSI; it will also include cost justification issues, a network selection guideline procedure, and a case study that was performed at a major petrochemical facility.

LAN Selection Overview

The basic theme of the selection process is the comparison of *prerequisite information* (what you want) to *network selection parameters* (what is available). A rating procedure is performed using the prerequisite information and the selection parameters to obtain a *closeness of fit*. The results of this analysis are correlated to the *network selection goals*. The tradeoffs are examined, and a sensitivity analysis is performed, from which a recommendation is generated (see Figure 12-1).

Prerequisite Information

Prerequisite information consists of a project mission statement and the information on the computer environment that the network will be integrated into. Prerequisite information is used to establish a foundation for network selection.

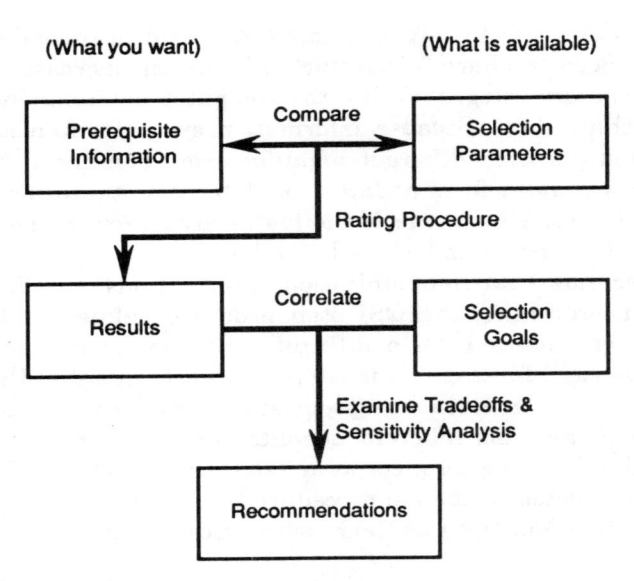

Figure 12-1 Selecting a Local Area Network.

The project mission statement should answer the following:

Why? This defines the purpose of the project, needs/requirements, and problems to be solved.

Where? This defines the functional and physical area(s) that the project encompasses.

What? This defines what has to be done to meet the project needs/requirements and includes any proposed solutions to the problems outlined.

Information on hardware, software, modification/replacement schedules, facility blueprints, communication transactions/volumes, and performance requirements is needed to answer these questions and entails:

1. List of planned automation and computer hardware required to meet the functionality of the project mission. This includes:
   - Computers
     — Plant host
     — Area managers
     — Cell controllers
     — Workstations
   - Terminals
     — Basic I/O
     — Forms
     — Graphics
   - Factory floor devices
     — Robot, PLC, CNC, CMM, tool presetter
     — PCS, DCS, loop controller, historian
     — Any computer/controller-based intelligent devices
2. List of the planned software required to meet the functionality of the project mission. This includes:
   - Databases
   - Operating systems
   - Application software
     — Off-the-shelf
     — Modified off-the-shelf
     — Custom
   - System support tools
     — Editors
     — Diagnostic tools
     — Backup

3. The schedule for modification and replacement of existing systems. In most cases, existing equipment will be integrated into the new system or modified to work with the new system (e.g., retrofitting a robot controller with a communication board and modem). This requires changes in:
   - Hardware
     — Communications
     — CPU
     — Memory
     — Storage
   - Software
     — Application
     — Operating system/control software
     — Support functions
   - System requirements
   - Future network operating procedures
4. Facility blueprints to determine the physical placement and distance of computers, terminals, and factory floor devices. This includes:
   - Current wiring diagrams
     — Existing communication systems
     — Power
   - Distance between equipment and required areas
   - Location of the planned hardware
   - Building, electrical, and fire code requirements
5. Communication transactions/volumes. Before selecting a network, one has to know what kind of traffic will be on the network. The communications required for the project must be established. This prerequisite is important for performing a cost analysis and network comparison, yet it is frequently done prior to the selection of a network.

   When documenting communication transactions, the transactions have to be broken down to an *atomic* level. An atomic transaction occurs between two devices with no intermediate devices. For example, robot status reporting to an area manager is a *compound* transaction:

   robot → cell controller → area manager

   This compound transaction consists of two atomic transactions: robot to cell controller and cell controller to area manager. These transaction distinctions are important in performing detailed cost analysis and network project planning. Required information on communication volume includes:

- List of transactions
  — Type
  — Source
  — Destination
  — Length
  — Frequency
  — Priority
  — Appropriate responses for sender and receiver
- System peak volume in characters per second
- Average message volume in characters per second
6. Performance requirements:
   - Response time
   - Response type
     — Deterministic (e.g., token passing)
     — Probabilistic (e.g., CSMA/CD)

Network Selection Parameters

Selection parameters are the functional attributes of a LAN used for cost analysis and comparison of networks. They correspond to the physical and logical characteristics of the communication solutions that are being analyzed.

Physical selection parameters deal with hardware and operational functional attributes of a LAN and include:

Architecture. The availability of LAN support for the hardware selected during the planning phase can be considered a fundamental issue. If there is no support, gateways (e.g., computer LAN to PLC network), front-end workstations (e.g., PC with MAP connected to a machine tool controller via RS-232), or tophats (e.g., PLC LAN connected to a robot via discrete I/O) are required. These components add cost and are directly related to the network selection goals, such as performance, manageability, flexibility, risk level and integration.

Media. The issues of media support for LAN's are important physical selection parameters. Some physical selection parameters involving media are:

- Access technique (CSMA/CD, TOKEN PASSING, TOKEN RING) impacts performance.
- Topology (BUS, RING, TREE, MESH, STAR) impacts cost, flexibility, performance, and reliability.

- Geographic integration and distance impacts cost, expandability, reliability, manageability, performance. (For example, broadband can span a greater distance at less cost than baseband.)
- Number of stations that can be supported.
- EFI/RFI immunity impacts reliability, cost.
- Throughput impacts performance.
- Ease of installation impacts cost.
- Communications supported impacts integration, expandability, flexibility, cost (for example, broadband supports voice, data, and video while baseband supports only data).
- Media integration. Media of different types can be connected transparently and cost effectively through the use of routers and/or bridges. This has an effect on cost, reliability, flexibility, expandability, and manageability.

Maintenance. Maintenance is one of the physical selection parameters whose cost and requirements can "come back to haunt you." Selection parameters related to maintenance include:

- Diagnostic procedures and tools available.
- Spare parts inventory required.
- Preventive maintenance required. (For example, a broadband system should be checked out every year, while this is unnecessary with baseband. Although this adds to the maintenance cost, broadband provides more capacity and performance than baseband.)
- Troubleshooting. More complex hybrid networks (e.g., a computer LAN connected to a factory device network) can be harder to troubleshoot than a homogeneous solution.

Maintenance issues have a direct relationship to performance and reliability (for example, a "kink" in a broadband system can cause reflections that can impact performance).

Change. The ability to change aspects of the LAN impacts many of the network selection goals. Changes can occur in:

- New drop cables.
- Application movement from one device to another or physical movement of a device (for example, do the network address, application titles, interface board DIP switches, board jumpers, and modem tuning, change?).
- Expansion of the trunk cable system.
- Addition of new legs to the cable system trunk.
- Addition of new ports to cable system legs.

These changes have an impact on the cost, flexibility, expandability, and manageability of network selection goals.

Logical selection parameters involve the functional attributes of a LAN that support and impact applications; they include:

Application Services. The application services support for communication transactions is one of the fundamental logical selection parameters. In performing a comparison, the transaction types must be supported by the application services. For example, if a variable read transaction is required and the network does not support that variable read, the variable could be embedded in a file and the entire file transferred, or variable read services will have to be created. This would directly impact cost, reliability, performance, and manageability.

In general, if the LAN does not support the required transaction types it will have a negative impact on the majority of the network selection goals.

Performance. The definition and determination of performance metrics for the application services of a LAN may be an important logical selection parameter. For example, the prerequisite for file transfer performance could be 50 Kbs.

Network Management. The management of the network through LAN-supported procedures and products is an important consideration for large network installations. Support for configuration, fault, performance, accounting, and security management can impact all of the network selection goals to some extent.

Protocol Service Support. Protocol services provides support for network connection and network communication. Some networks adopt a layered protocol (for example, MAP has seven layers, MAP EPA has three layers, TCP/IP has four layers). It is important to verify that protocol services for network connection can support the physical selection parameters and the logical selection parameters.

Network Selection Goals

A network selection goal is any factor used as a selection criterion. A set of network selection goals is established and prioritized for use as a baseline in which to make decisions regarding the selection.

Typical network selection goals include:

Cost. Cost must be considered for the entire life of the project, from implementation to long-term maintenance. All cost components must be accounted for; for example, physical connection of a device to a cable is not the only cost component of communication.

Flexibility. Ability to add devices from different vendors, physical movement of devices, moving software applications from one node to another, changing the communication board/modem, and changes in the network address are all important considerations.

Expandability. A network should have sufficient capability and capacity for the future or be easily expanded to accommodate growth.

Uptime/Reliability. If uptime/reliability is a key issue, then redundancy, system backup procedures, status monitoring, and fault recovery procedures become major issues.

Manageability. As a network grows and becomes complex, the ability to handle and control the action and use of the network becomes increasingly important. Configuration, fault detection/correction, performance, accounting, and security management make up the core of network management functions.

Integration. How well the network fits into the overall business plan and meets current and future requirements is an important consideration.

Risk Level. Availability of vendors' products with respect to the timing of the project and the use of products with short product histories are elements of risk.

Performance/System Throughput. If response time, response type, and network loading are important for the proposed project, performance should be a high network selection goal.

Security. Security encompasses protected access to applications, workstations, databases, and subordinate intelligent devices (e.g., robots, discrete I/O). Access can be granted for a portion or all of the available resources.

Network Guideline Procedure

In order for a selection procedure to provide meaningful results, it should quantify how closely a network meets user requirements rather than comparing networks to each other. For example, consider the case in which network A supports video and data transmissions, and network B supports only data transmissions. One could not say that network A is "better" than network B without considering the user requirements. If the user requires video, then network A would be the better choice; but if the user does not require video, then network B might be the better choice due to cost savings.

Another important consideration for using a network selection procedure is viewpoint. The selection procedure will best serve the corporation if the corporate viewpoint rather than that of an individual engineer is considered.

The network guideline procedure documented in this chapter compares a network to user requirements and encompasses the corporate viewpoint. The procedure consists of four phases:

Phase I: Guideline Prerequisites
Phase II: Interview Process
Phase III: Comparison and Analysis
Phase IV: Management Report

Phase I: Guideline Prerequisites

Phase I consists of documenting the project mission and collecting information on the environment the computer will be integrated into. This information is used to establish a foundation for the guideline procedure. Refer to LAN Selection Overview for information that has to be documented in Phase 1.

Phase II: Interview Process

The purpose of conducting interviews in Phase II is to gather information to be used in conjunction with the project mission statement to define a baseline for network comparison. The information is collected in such a manner that:

The company viewpoint, rather than the viewpoint of a single engineer, is used in the selection of a network.

Networks are not compared to each other. They are judged on how well they meet the requirements of the process and the company's strategic direction.

Individuals to be interviewed should be selected from a large spectrum of job classifications in order to get a complete view of the networking requirements as related to the project needs. Interviews should be arranged with the:

Operator/user
Operator supervisor
Maintenance engineer/manager
Computer systems engineer/manager
Network systems engineer/manager
Process engineer/manager
Upper management

Interviews should be given to pairs of individuals in similar job functions. Two people from the same job classification can embellish each other's answers. Individual interviews do not gather robust information, while interview groups of more than two individuals are difficult to document and control.

The interviews should encompass business, project, and technology issues. Though the network should satisfy the project and technology needs, it is also important to include business issues so that the network does not form "islands of business."

Business Planning Questions

The purpose of the business planning questions is to gather information regarding corporate commitment to the project, as well as assuring that the project follows defined corporate strategic directions.

Before any project planning activity has begun, the project should have been accepted by upper management and tied into the corporate business plan. Additionally, the communication and information systems should support the corporate business plan. If these issues have not been addressed, selecting a local area network or beginning a project plan is inappropriate.

Some business planning questions are:

Describe the business plan in relation to the use of automation, computers, communication, and the integration of information systems to meet the objectives (e.g., become the leading supplier of product *xyz*) and end goals (e.g., sell 1 million units of product *xyz*) of the business plan.

What are the future market requirements? What is the impact on the need for additional communication and information systems? Requirements may include decreased product design times to meet changing market demands, shorter product delivery times, increased product quality to penetrate into more demanding markets, etc.

How will future products impact the need for additional communication and information systems? How will this relate to current operations?

How will future organizational growth impact the need for additional communication and information systems?

What is the level of commitment in the business plan to communication and information systems? Provide financial and strategic examples of corporate commitment to the integration of information systems through the use of communication systems.

What is the corporate short-term strategy (one to three years) for communication and information systems? What is your perception of the short-term needs, and how does it differ from the corporate view?

What is the corporate long-term strategy (three to ten years) for communication and information systems? What is your perception of the long-term needs, and how does it differ from the corporate view?

Project Planning Questions

The purpose of the project planning questions is to gather information on individual perspectives on the project. Answers to these questions may uncover additional computer, automation, and communication requirements.

Some project planning questions are:

What is your function in relation to the project? Are you an active part of the project, a manager, or support personnel?

Based upon your knowledge of the project and personal impressions of what is needed to make the project better, what information that a communication network can provide is required to improve the project?

How can information provided by a communication network improve your job function in relation to the project?

Technology Planning Questions

The purpose of the technology planning questions is to gather information on the current communication systems, if any, and on the scope of a future communication system. Answers to these questions may uncover additional computer, automation, and communication requirements.

In addition to the questions there are two worksheets, "Technology Planning Worksheet — Current Communications" (see Figure 12-2) and "Technology Planning Worksheet — Future Communications" (see Figure 12-3). The "Technology Planning Worksheet — Current Communications" documents the current communication architecture

Location: Page #:

Data	From	To	Function	Media	Protocol

Figure 12-2 Technology Planning Worksheet — Current Communications.

Location: _____   Page #: _____

Data	From	To	Function	Benefit

Figure 12-3 Technology Planning Worksheet — Future Communications.

and flow of information as it appears to the individual being interviewed, while the "Technology Planning Worksheet — Future Communications" is used when documenting the answers to the third question below.

Some technology planning questions are:

What are the benefits of the current communication systems? What aspects of the current communication systems would you not change?

What are the problems with the current flow of information through the communication systems? What would you modify in the current communication systems to alleviate problems in the current flow of information?

If you could "start from scratch," what would the future communication systems and flow of information look like? What would you like to see in a future communication system? What benefits and advantages should a future communication system have over the current communication systems?

What communication system planning has occurred to date to improve the flow of information through the design/manufacturing process? Is there facility and/or corporate backing (e.g., strategic, financial, research, technical committees, technical departments) for this communication technology? Include both local and corporate efforts.

What is the required implementation time of additional automation, computer, and communication systems technology to improve the flow of information through the design/manufacturing process?

Network Selection Goal Scoring

This portion of the interview is used to gather information that will be used to quantify the desired end goals of an appropriate network based on your specific requirements. Weight, rank, and priority goal scores should be collected for each of the network selection goals. Any additional requirements or constraints for each selection goal should be recorded at this time. Three "Network Selection Goal Summary Worksheets" (see Figure 12-4) should be filled out, one for each goal score.

Measurement: Location:						
Cost						
Flexibility						
Expandability						
Uptime/Reliability						
Manageability						
Integration						
Risk Level						
System Throughput						
Security						
Accountability						

Figure 12-4 Network Selection Goal Summary Worksheet.

Measurements used in the scoring procedure include:

Weight. This measure is used to show the individual importance of a network selection goal independent of other network selection goals. Each selection goal is weighted from 1 to 10, with 10 the highest in importance and 1 the lowest. Each number can be used more than once during the weighting procedure (for example, cost and security could both have weights of 7).

Rank. This measure is used to show the importance of a network selection goal in relation to other goals. Each selection goal is ranked from 1 to 10, with 1 the most important goal, 2 the second most important goal, etc. Note that the weighting of a goal occurs independent of the other goals, while ranking shows the importance of the goals in relation to each other. While in the weighting of goals the numbers 1 through 10 can be reused, in the ranking of goals each number 1 through 10 can be used only once; there is only one goal of rank 1, one goal of rank 2 . . . and one goal of rank 10.

Priority. This measure is used to group rankings into levels of priority. For example, goals ranked 1, 2, 3, 4 could be priority 1, goals ranked 5, 6, 7, 8, 9 could be priority 2, and the goal ranked 10 could be priority 3. You *cannot* assign priority levels that conflict with the ranking (for example, goals 1, 2, 4, 5 being priority 1 and goal 3 being priority 2 is not allowable). The priority procedures define levels of ranked goals.

A priority of 1 is assigned to the network selection goals that cannot be traded off; a 2 is assigned to goals that must be met after priority 1 goals are met; a 3 is assigned to goals that must be met after priority 2 goals are met; and so on.

Phase III: Comparison and Analysis

The purpose of Phase III is to:

Define potential communication system profiles (CSP's) and preliminary network architectures.

Determine initial and life cycle cost estimates.

Compare each CSP against the process, business, technology, and selection goal requirements and obtain CSP weight scores for use in network selection.

314 Open Systems Interconnection Handbook

Summarize the network selection goal worksheet information.

Provide the scoring of intangible benefits by network selection goal priority level for each communication system profile.

CSP (Communication System Profile) Definition

For each network architecture under consideration, a communication system profile (CSP) is documented. The CSP consists of information relating to the protocol and media for the main network and subnetwork alternatives, if applicable. Each CSP architecture is constructed from the prerequisite information.

CSP Cost Estimates

The initial cost estimates are based on the communication transactions from the prerequisite information section. It is important to note that many factors come into play when doing a cost comparison for networks. The standard sales pitch for LAN vendors is their cost of connection to a cable system. However, the physical attachment of a device to a cable is not the only cost component of communication. For example, factory floor networks must include the appropriate equipment to pass information from the factory floor to a manufacturing computer-based application. This requires that devices have the ability to communicate with each other. All the cost components must be accounted for. As you can see in Figure 12-5, "Communication vs. Connection Cost," the total cost of communication is more than the cost of connection.

Figure 12-6, "Connection Components," illustrates the components that may be required. On each device, you may have to include costs for the:

Application interface
Application communication services
Communication protocol
Communication board
Media controller
Physical connection/modem
Network connector/interface cable

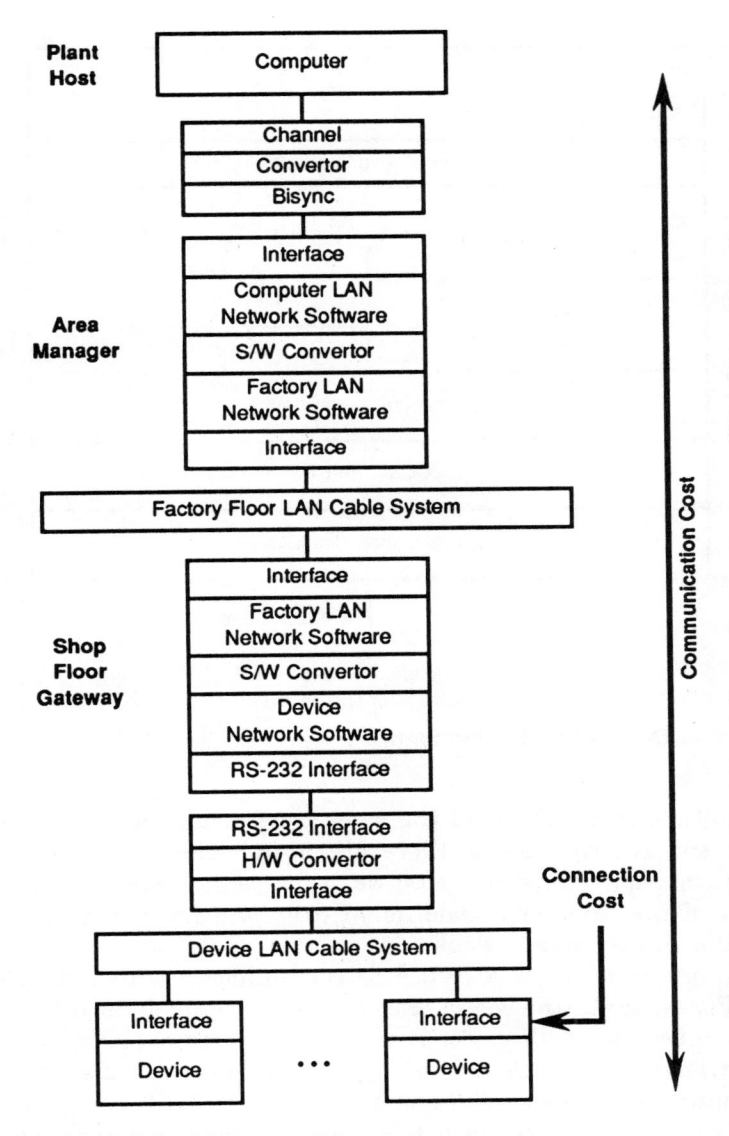

Figure 12-5 Communication vs. Connection Cost.

Some communication products may have many of these components combined into one product. For example, the communication board and communication board driver usually are bundled into one product.

```
┌─────────────────────────────────────────────────────────┐
│                  Application Program                    │
├─────────────────────────────────────────────────────────┤
│                  Application Interface                  │
├──────────────────────────┬──────────────────────────────┤
│       Application        │                              │
│     Comm. Services       │       Operating              │
│                          │        System                │
├──────────────────────────┤                              │
│     Communication        │                              │
│       Protocol           ├──────────────────────────────┤
│                          │       Board Driver           │
├──────────────────────────┴──────────────────────────────┤
│                  Communication Board                    │
├─────────────────────────────────────────────────────────┤
│                    Media Controller                     │
├─────────────────────────────────────────────────────────┤
│               Physical Connection/Modem                 │
└─────────────────────────────────────────────────────────┘
```
(bordered left and right by: Management & Configuration)

Network Connector

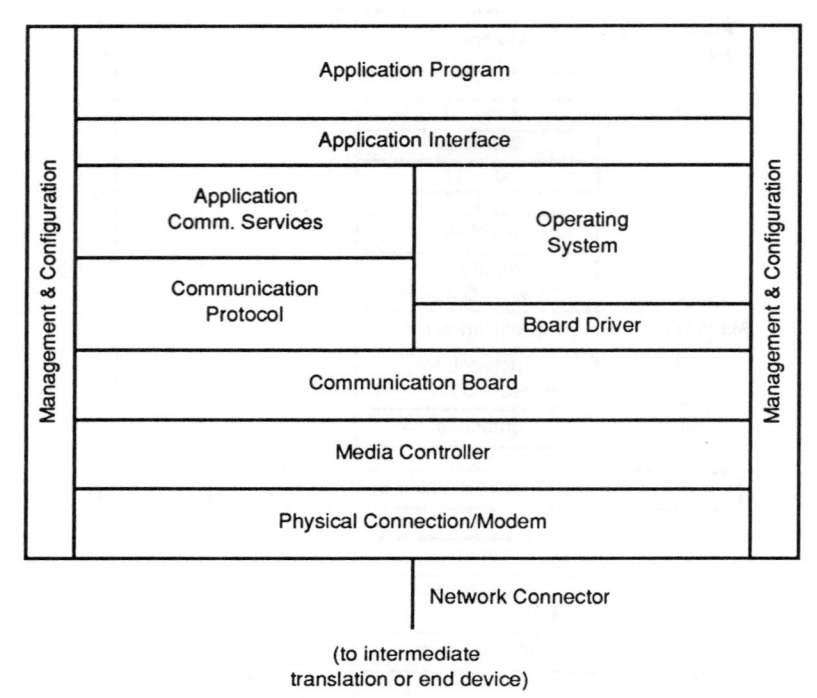

(to intermediate
translation or end device)

Figure 12-6 Connection Components.

If multiple transactions of the same type occur between the same sender and receiver nodes, there are no additional communication costs. If multiple transactions between the same sender and receiver are not of the same type, additional costs will have to be added to make that transaction possible.

Many products allow a device to communicate with multiple devices. For example, the communication components defined for device A for transactions with device B may be the same required for device A for transactions with device C. Transactions may use the same communication component as another transaction, if component capacity and performance do not become an issue (for example, how many devices can make use of a gateway before capacity and/or performance become an issue?). These costs can be averaged over many devices and transactions as long as capacity and performance do not become an issue.

The initial installation costs and issues are a part of the overall life cycle of the project. Additional costs and other issues are addressed throughout the planning, design, implementation, installation, debugging, operations, and change of a network over time. Life cycle issues include costs for:

Implementation: Software development, test development (database, design, network conformance, performance), testing and debugging of software, and test software modules.

Debugging: Symptom categorization, problem identification, design modification, testing, and fix verification times.

Installation: Hardware installation, hardware acceptance, software integration, system acceptance, and training.

Operations: Spare parts inventory, preventive maintenance, unscheduled maintenance, diagnostic tools and procedures, and network management/administration.

Change: Moving a device, adding a device, expansion of the physical cable system, adding new channels to the cable system, physical movement of an application from one hardware platform to another, change of validation procedures, and debugging.

For the implementation, debugging, installation, operations, and change phases, functional attributes for each of the LAN alternatives have a cost component. These costs will vary based upon the characteristics of the LAN alternatives used for comparison. For example, a spare parts inventory for an OSI LAN will be smaller than a spare parts inventory for a hybrid solution composed of multiple device and computer LAN's. As another example, the manpower time and costs vary depending on the complexity and "newness" of the factory LAN; to install RS-232 cable is less costly than to install a fiber optics cable system.

For all phases in the network life cycle, costs should be accumulated for hardware, software, cable system, manpower (all types of labor, project manager to cable installer), diagnostic procedures and tools, and training. These cost components can "come in many flavors." For example, training is required for products, programming, operations, users, system administrators, testers, and so on.

Before beginning the justification procedure, you should decide to what degree the cost analysis should be conducted. While a cost analysis based upon a complete network functional model can provide a good estimate for the initial cost of the candidate factory network solutions, additional analysis should include estimates for the magnitude of cost for the other network life cycle phases.

For example, if a network was chosen because of the initial ease and cost of installation, additional costs and considerations regarding expansion, change, and maintenance may not have been accounted for. Once the pilot network needs to expand to meet the needs of a production environment, the expansion, change, and maintenance issues could indicate that the factory network chosen was not the most technically or financially sound selection.

Prerequisite Information/CSP Selection Parameter Comparison

This comparison corresponds to the first step in Figure 12-1, comparing the prerequisite information (what you want) to CSP selection parameters (what is available). By comparing each CSP against the process, business, technology, and selection goal requirements, a score can be obtained on how well the CSP satisfies the project requirements; this is more useful than just comparing the technological benefits of network alternatives against each other in a sterile academic environment. This comparison score will be correlated with the network selection goal scores collected during the interview phase in order to select the best network based on user requirements.

The output of this portion of Phase III is the "Communication System Profile Weight Summary Worksheet" (see Figure 12-7). To obtain the CSP weights for each selection goal you must:

1. Review the CSP network selection parameters.
2. Review the process information, business information, technology planning, and network selection goal requirements and constraints from the worksheets you completed during the interviews. Answers on these worksheets may provide additional insights into life cycle issues as they pertain to your project.
3. Review the CSP functional and cost architectures that you constructed in the preceding section.
4. Review the definition of each network selection goal.
5. Fill out a "CSP Weight Worksheet" for each CSP. The CSP weight is a measure of how close the selection parameters of a CSP match the prerequisite information across the life of the project, with respect to each network selection goal. Each CSP weight is from 1 to 10, with a 10 indicating a "perfect match" of the CSP to the needs of the project throughout the entire project life cycle. A 1 is the lowest score and indicates that the CSP does not meet any of the selection goal requirements. A 5

CSP: Location:	Weight
Cost	
Flexibility	
Expandability	
Uptime/Reliability	
Manageability	
Integration	
Risk Level	
System Throughput	
Security	
Accountability	

Figure 12-7 Communication System Profile Weight Summary Worksheet.

would indicate that the CSP meets approximately half the requirements throughout the project life cycle.

For example, consider a new networking technology "Z" that is still in the specification development process with no product releases. Suppose that you discovered during the interview process that networking could make significant improvements in the project (project information), the project is backed by the corporation at a strategic and financial level (business plan information), with an immediate technology implementation time frame (technology planning information). When determining the CSP weight for "Risk Level," you would assign a 1 to that category. The reason for such a low weight is the implementation technology "Z" would jeopardize the success of the project due to its specification instability and product immaturity.

You can get information on CSP selection parameters from:

Vendors
Third party vendors
Vendors of competing technologies
Users
User groups
Magazine articles
Published case studies

When gathering information on CSP selection parameters and life cycle issues, be sure to consider the source. Your information source may have a "hidden agenda" when supplying you with information.

Summary of Network Selection Goals

During the interview phase the weight, rank, and priority scores were collected for each selection goal from each individual. The purpose of this section is to average all the individual scores into a corporate score.

For each network selection goal, compute the average and standard deviation for the weight, rank, and priority from the individual scores. While the average gives a mathematically correct score, one has to take into account the source of the information. For example, the process engineer's input may reflect a better view of the "total picture" than that of a user of a specific aspect of the entire process. Using information gathered through the interview process and the computed average and standard deviation, determine overall weight, rank, and priority scores for each network selection goal.

Prior to determining the overall weights, rankings, and priorities, inspect the individual scores for each network selection goal. If the data appears to be scattered (e.g., 4, 7, 6, 1) or heavily lopsided (e.g., 7, 2, 2, 2), you may want to perform some follow-up investigations to determine if there is any undue bias. Begin the investigation into suspicious data groupings by reviewing the interview data sheets, and then follow up with phone calls to the individuals who furnished the questionable data.

Remember that rankings for the network selection goals have to be ordered from 1 to 10, and no number can be used more than once.

Once the overall priority is computed, compare it to the overall ranking. Make sure that the overall priority levels do not conflict with the overall ranking (e.g., goals 1, 2, 4, 5 of priority 1 and goal 3 of priority 2 is not allowable). Remember that priority defines levels of ranked goals. If conflicts occur, refer back to the individual priority, overall ranking, and overall weight scores in order to resolve the conflicts.

When overall scores have been determined, fill in the "Network Selection Goal Overall Summary Worksheet" (see Figure 12-8).

Quantify the Intangible Benefits of Each CSP

At this point each CSP has weights for each network selection goal, and the corporate network selection goals have been determined.

How to Justify an OSI-Based Network 321

Location:	Weight	Ranking	Priority
Cost			
Flexibility			
Expandability			
Uptime/Reliability			
Manageability			
Integration			
Risk Level			
System Throughput			
Security			
Accountability			

Figure 12-8 Network Selection Goal Overall Summary Worksheet.

From this information a magnitude vector of how closely the CSP meets the user's requirements can be computed.

Priority and weight information from the "Network Selection Goal Overall Summary Worksheet" (see Figure 12-8) is entered into the "Network Goal Comparison Worksheet" (see Figure 12-9); one worksheet is completed for each CSP. The corresponding CSP weight information (see Figure 12-7) is also entered into this worksheet. An overall goal score is then computed. The overall goal weights are accumulated at each priority level in order to compute a priority score. The raw score is computed by accumulating all the priority scores.

The step-by-step procedure is:

1. Make copies of the "Network Goal Comparison Worksheet," one for each CSP.
2. Document the network selection goals, priorities, rankings, and weights on the worksheet using the information from the "Network Selection Goal Overall Summary Worksheet." The network selection goals should be documented in ascending priority level, and within any given priority level, the network selection goal should be documented in ascending ranking. For example, document the network selection goal with priority 1, ranking 1 first, priority 1 ranking 2 second, etc. Fill out one worksheet for each CSP.

322 Open Systems Interconnection Handbook

Network Selection Goal	Priority	Ranking	CSP Weight	Goal Weight	Goal Score	Priority Level	Priority Score
		1					
		2					
		3					
		4					
		5					
		6					
		7					
		8					
		9					
		10					

Location:
Communication Systems Profile:

Raw Score

Figure 12-9 Network Goal Comparison Worksheet.

3. Steps 3 through 7 are done on a "Network Goal Comparison Worksheet" for each CSP.
4. Fill in the CSP weights in the corresponding CSP Weight column, per the CSP Weight Worksheets.
5. Compute the overall goal score by subtracting the Goal Weight from the CSP Weight. Do this for all the network selection goals. A negative number indicates that the CSP did not meet your predetermined goal requirement.
6. For each priority level, compute the priority score by accumulating all goal scores for a priority level. For example, if you have

PRIORITY	GOAL SCORE	PRIORITY SCORE
1	3	
1	−1	2
2	1	
2	0	1

the priority score for priority 1 is 2 and for priority 2 is 1. Note that the priority score is entered into the worksheet on the line of the last goal within a priority level.

7. Compute the overall raw score by totaling the priority scores.

Phase IV: Management Report

Prior to preparing the management report, you need to determine which network best meets your needs based on the CSP scores and cost information.

CSP comparison should be done by priority level scores rather than the overall raw score, which may be deceiving. For example, CSP "A" may have negative scores for priority levels 1 and 2 with very high scores for priority levels 3 and 4, making a high overall raw score. CSP "B" may have a high score for priority level 1, an average score for priority 2, and large negative scores for levels 3 and 4, with an overall low raw score. In this case, even though CSP "A" has a higher overall raw score, it would not be a better selection than CSP "B," which would have met the primary criteria per the priority 1 and 2 network selection goals, while CSP "A" would not have. Remember, priority levels are based on what you feel is important for the selection of a network.

The purpose of a management report is to justify and document the selection process, using information gathered, processed, and analyzed during Phase I (Guideline Prerequisites), Phase II (Interview Process), and Phase III (Comparison and Analysis). The following is an example of how to structure the information in report form.

I. Executive Summary

1. Interview Introduction and Guideline Overview.

II. Project Mission

III. Business Plan Overview

1. Business plan in relation to the use of automation, computers, communications, and the integration of information systems.

2. Business justifications for communication and information systems.
    a. Future market requirements
    b. Future products
    c. Future organizational growth

3. Level of commitment to communication and information systems.

a. Financial
   b. Strategic

4. Communication and information systems strategy.
   a. Immediate timing
   b. Short term
   c. Long term

IV. Communication System Overview

1. "As Is."
   a. Provide a two-paragraph overview of any current communication system you are using).
   b. Technology Planning Worksheet — Current Communications
   c. Benefits of the current system
   d. Problems with the current system

2. "To Be."
   a. What has to be modified in the current system to alleviate current problems
   b. Overview of what the future system should consist of
      (1) Architecture overview
      (2) Benefits and advantages over current system
      (3) Technology Planning Worksheet — Future Communications

V. Network Selection Goal Overview

1. Definition of a network selection goal.

2. Definition of weight, ranking, and priority.

3. List and definition of network selection goals (Network Selection Goal Summary Worksheet).

4. Description of interview process and the use of individuals from users to corporate management to get network selection goals.
   a. Corporate feedback rather than a single engineer making corporate decisions

5. Network Selection Goal — Overall Summary Worksheet.

6. Network selection goals — requirements and constraints "scratchsheet" (an unstructured list of site-specific requirements such as total user up-time and standard payback).

VI. Communication System Profiles

1. Definition of a CSP.

2. List of CSP's used in the selection process.

VII. Life Cycle Comparison

1. Discuss the initial CSP totals.

2. Discuss the need to consider life cycle issues.

3. Describe the life cycle comparison components.
   a. Life cycle issues
   b. Network selection parameters

4. Describe comparison procedure.

5. For each CSP complete CSP Weight Summary Worksheet.

VIII. Recommendations

1. Justify selection by referring to:
   a. Network selection goals
      (1) Describe network selection goal comparison procedure (Network Goal Comparison Worksheet)
      (2) Priority level scores
      (3) Raw scores

2. Cost.
   a. CSP initial costs
   b. Life cycle cost issues

Case Study — Tank Car Project

This network guideline procedure was used to justify an HMD Tank Car project at a major petrochemical facility. This was one of the first production MAP 3.0 networks, an OSI-based communication specification for the manufacturing environment.

The HMD Tank Car (HMD is a chemical abbreviation) project involved an Allen Bradley PLC 5/15 that monitors and controls the filling of an HMD railroad tank car. The operator monitors information from the PLC and sets various parameters. The filling information is stored and sent to the Vax Cluster for reports.

The following sections will illustrate some of the techniques of the network guideline procedure, using real data from the HMD Tank Car justification study.

Case Study — Prerequisites

The project mission was to integrate the PLC, operator workstation, and Vax Cluster into the existing computer and communication architecture. The current environment consisted of:

Computers
VAX Technical Cluster and associated equipment
Multiple PDP 11/70–84
IBM mainframe and associated equipment

Factory Floor Devices
Lab-adept robot
Allen Bradley PLC's
Moore Products, Foxboro, Bailey, Honeywell, and Fisher
  Distributed Control Systems
EMC
CPI

Terminals
VT 100
VT 240
VT 241
VT 320
VT 340

Databases
RS1
DB2

Operating Systems
VMS
RSX11M+
MVS

Application Software
Proprietary lab information management and process monitoring systems
All-in-One
Mass 11
20/20, Lotus, MiniTab
Intergraph CAD/CAM

Communication Systems
Sytek Terminal Network
Intra-Plant DECnet and LAT (Broadband and Ethernet)
Inter-Plant DECnet and LAT (X.25 and Ethernet)
XNS CAD Network
Sneaker Net
Corporate Worldwide SNA Network

Performance Requirements
People ↔ Machine < 1 second
Machine ↔ Machine < 3 seconds
Machine ↔ Front end < 1 second

The communication nerve system for the facility is a broadband cable system in a star topology. The head end for the broadband cable system is located in the Powerhouse building. Video, CSMA/CD, point-to-point, and Sytek Terminal Network services reside on the broadband.

Figure 12-10 shows the existing computer and communication architecture. Figure 12-11 illustrates typical communication transactions at the facility.

Case Study — Interview Process

Plant trips for interviews with key employees were scheduled. Employees were interviewed on various aspects of current and future networking requirements and related daily operation scenarios. A wide spectrum of job classifications were required in order to get a complete view of the networking activities and related operations. This included employees from:

Polymer Products Department

- —Senior Engineer

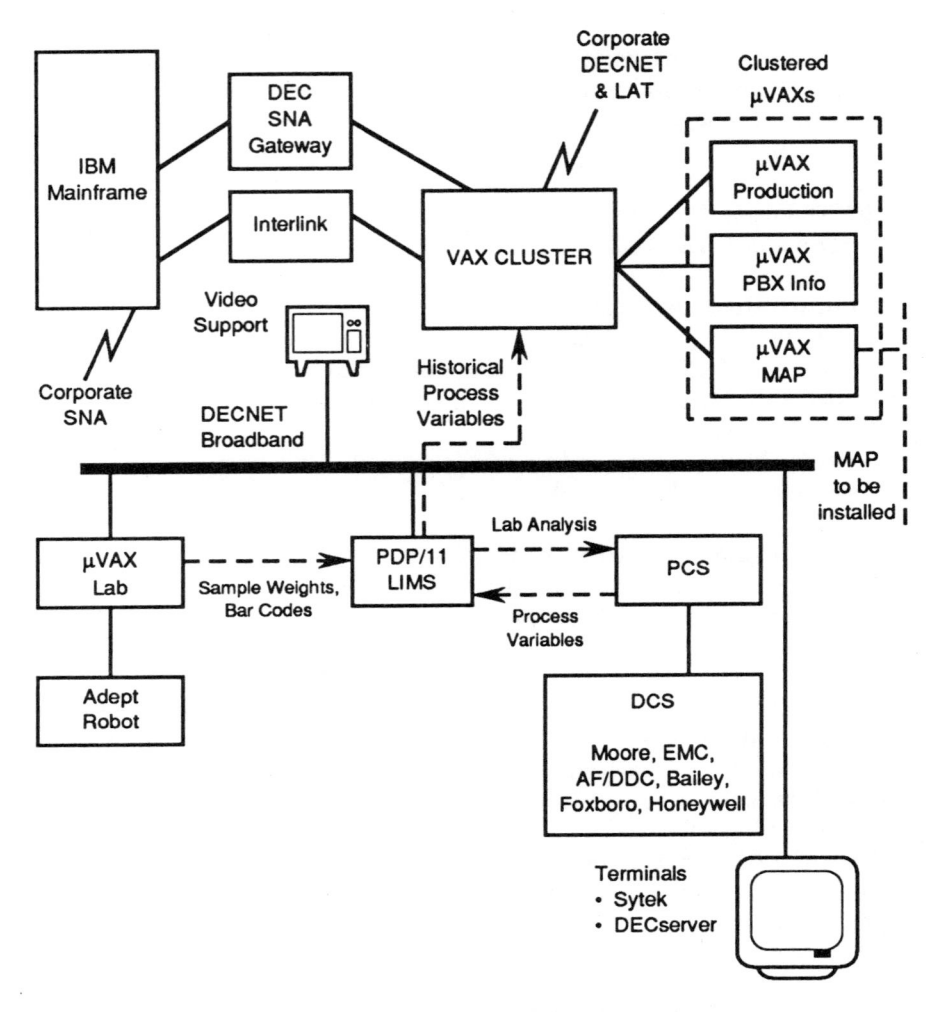

Figure 12-10 Computer and Communication Architecture.

Technical and Engineering Services — Computer and Telecommunications Systems

- —Computer Specialist
- —Network Technician

MIS Application and Communication Systems

- —Systems Analyst
- —Systems Implementor

How to Justify an OSI-Based Network 329

Date	Computer/Applications	Function	Network
Lab Analysis	PDP 11/LIMS –> PDP 11/PCS	Quality Feedback, Product Release	DECNET/File Transfer
Lab Labels	PDP 11/LIMS –> Field Printers	Schedule Samples	Broadband Pt. to Pt.
Sample Weights, Bar Codes	PDP 11/LIMS <–> mVAX (Adept Robot)	Sample Preparation	DECNET/File Transfer & Task-Task
Production Data	Field –> PCS	Data Collection, Process Control	Digital I/O Analog Pneumatic Proprietary
Production Data	PCS <–> PCS	Data Collection, Accounting, Coordination, Optimization	DECNET/ Task-Task
Production Data	PCS <–> VAX Cluster	Process Data, Process Modeling, Expert Systems	DECNET/File Transfer & Task-Task
NC Data	Intergraph –> Paper Tape/Bubble Memory	Machine Source	Broadband Pt. to Pt.
CAD	Intergraph <–> Workstation	Drafting Prints	XNS
AutoCAD	PC –> Intergraph	Drafting Prints	Sneaker Net

Figure 12-11 Typical Communication Transactions.

These individuals provided feedback on process requirements, process computer and communication systems, and MIS computers and communication systems.

Case Study — Business Planning Information

The following information is paraphrased from actual interview data. The focus of each question is in bold, with the answers as bullet points. Each question was phrased in the context of communication and information systems.

Business Plan Overview

- Very aggressive. Corporate management realizes that without communication and information systems they cannot compete.
- The business plan is to provide communication and information system services for all job classifications.

Future Market Requirements

- The use of EDI and external communication to suppliers and contractors.
- More emphasis on links to other data centers.
- Anticipate increased communication traffic due to more graphics and image data.

Future Organizational Growth

- The facility is in the process of becoming the regional waste disposal center and central location to store cranes. Communications are required to do the scheduling for the region through the use of a proprietary management information system.
- Reorganization underway to streamline management through the reduction of midmanagement. The remaining management is being given responsibility over a broader base. Communication and information systems allow the manager to better capture and use information for their management responsibilities.
- Additional capacity has been planned for. The technical staff are attempting to get a terminal for everyone. Many functions (e.g., timesheets) can be filled out via terminals. The additional use of graphics and images may impact planned capacity.
- The facility is the regional competence center for MIS information systems and communications. Many external facilities make use of the MIS services. They are in the process of looking for additional corporate customers. They require a large customer base to achieve economies of scale.
- A centralized MIS center provides a unified approach to business, is less expensive to operate, and requires less training.

Level of Commitment in Business Plan

- Commitment is at a high corporate level, but at times this commitment is mixed.
- Senior Vice-Presidents are almost totally committed, with a few holdouts remaining.
- Support exists at a high corporate level, with funding available if it makes sense.

Short-Term Strategy

- Keep the current system running.
- Rebuild broadband "trouble spots."
- Move away from the point-to-point terminal network. It is a communication bottleneck that slows response time.
- Fill in the current voids. Put a terminal on everyone's desk and network all the system printers.
- Replace the PCS front ends. Current systems are twice as fast at a slightly lower cost than the installed systems.
- Provide support for communication growth to handle transmission of graphics and improve overall user response time.
- Need to handle three to four times more traffic for future growth.

Long-Term Strategy

- Reduce overall labor on network management and maintenance through the use of more computerized tools and automatic systems.
- Move toward fiber optics to handle the increased throughput and capacity projected in the future.
- Move toward standards and OSI. Projected benefits include lower prices, common application services, the ability to use any vendor rather than being locked into a specific vendor.

Case Study — Technology Planning Information

The following information is paraphrased from actual interview data. The focus of each question is in bold, with the answers as bullet points. Each question was phrased in the context of communication and information systems.

Problems with the Current System

- Accounting information in the plant is read off a report generated by an application on the VAX and manually entered into the IBM system.
- Management issues regarding the point-to-point terminal network. Each modem has to be set up manually; no automatic procedure exists. In addition, potential security violations could occur. No security against changing setups.
- Performance of the point-to-point terminal network is sluggish. Some people are dropped off the network for no reason.
- Scheduling of downtime to handle hardware and software upgrades.

Advantages of the Current System

- DECNET and Ethernet on broadband works well. No major or recurring problems. Handles load well.
- 75–80 percent of personnel have e-mail accounts.
- Excellent interconnection through LAT bridges and DECNET throughout the corporation. Terminal emulation is also available with DECNET through the SET HOST command.

Communications and Information Required for Improvements

- Better connections from the VAX Cluster to the IBM system or direct connections of the Process Control Systems to the IBM system.
- Distributed time services so all computer system clocks are synchronized.
- Standardization of PLC interfaces.
- Standardized distributed control systems. The current application systems are very expensive to maintain.
- Database consolidation and common access techniques through the network. Implementation of a distributed database system.

Local and Corporate Backing

- Technology planning occurs at the corporate technical center, with support from the facility staff.

How to Justify an OSI-Based Network   333

Measurement: WEIGHT Location:	MIS Dept.	Network Tech.	System Analyst	Product Engineer	Average SD	Weight
Cost	5	5	4	4	4.5/.6	4/5
Flexibility	6	8	8	5	6.75/1.5	7
Expandability	7	9	8	8	8/.8	8
Uptime/Reliability	8	10	7	9	8.5/1.3	8/9
Manageability	8	9	7	6	7.5/1.3	7/8
Integration	7	9	5	3	6/2.6	6
Risk Level	7	5	2	2	4/2.4	4
System Throughput	8	7	7	7	7.25/.5	7
Security	4	7	6	1	4.5/2.6	5
Accountability	NA	NA	NA	NA	NA	NA

Figure 12-12 Network Selection Goal Summary (Weight).

- Plant management has no idea of technology requirements, and the corporate committees do not provide a solid direction. The corporate committees do not issue edicts.
- Different groups working on the same or similar problems throughout the corporation cause conflict rather than support. There is not enough centralization of efforts.

Case Study — Network Selection Goal Scoring

The "Network Selection Goal Summary Worksheets" were passed out and explained to the interviewees. They were allowed to take these worksheets back to their office and complete them over a two-day period. This much time was required because scoring intangible benefits requires a lot of reflection. In addition to these worksheets, a "Network Selection Goals — Requirements and Constraints Scratchsheet" was provided to document any special criteria.

Network selection goal scores are documented in Figures 12-12 through 12-14.

The following transcribes requirement and constraint comments submitted in conjunction with the scoring of the network selection goals. *Note*: These comments were transcribed word for word.

334 Open Systems Interconnection Handbook

Measurement: RANK Location:	MIS Dept.	Network Tech.	System Analyst	Product Engineer	Average SD	Rank
Cost	8	3	8	6	6.25/2.4	7
Flexibility	7	6	6	5	6/.8	6
Expandability	5	5	4	2	4/1.4	4
Uptime/Reliability	3	1	7	1	3./2.8	1
Manageability	1	2	3	4	2.5/1.3	2
Integration	4	9	1	7	5.25/3.5	5
Risk Level	6	8	9	8	7.75/1.1	8
System Throughput	2	4	2	3	2.75/1	3
Security	9	7	5	9	7.5/1.9	9
Accountability	NA	NA	NA	NA	NA	NA

Figure 12-13 Network Selection Goal Summary (Rank).

Measurement: PRIORITY Location:	MIS Dept.	Network Tech.	System Analyst	Product Engineer	Average SD	Priority
Cost	4	NA	2	2	2.6/1.2	2
Flexibility	3	NA	1	2	2/1	2
Expandability	2	NA	1	1	1.3/.6	1
Uptime/Reliability	1	NA	3	1	1.6/1.2	1
Manageability	1	NA	1	2	1.3/.6	1
Integration	2	NA	2	2	2/0	2
Risk Level	2	NA	1	3	2/1	2
System Throughput	1	NA	1	1	1/0	1
Security	5	NA	1	3	3/2	3
Accountability	NA	NA	NA	NA	NA	NA

Figure 12-14 Network Selection Goal Summary (Priority).

Cost

- Project should have parts which could be funded in prices less than $1M. The lower the price, the easier it competes for funding.
- Cost is important, but cannot be considered first. After the network is designed, then find the best buy that meets your needs.
- Must meet standard three-year payback.

Flexibility

- Must live, grow, and conform to new construction and removal of buildings. Trunks must be expandable. Trunks must be capable of isolation for partial shutdowns of the network.
- Must be able to work on sections; affect as few people as possible.

Expandability

- Must be expandable both in capacity and in topography.
- Needs to have a minimum distance of 2.5 km.
- Easily expandable.

Uptime

- Total user uptime must be >99.99 percent. Individual user uptime must be >97.5 percent.
- We look for utility of 99.5 percent.
- 99.95 percent or greater utility.

Manageability

- Self-documenting would be ideal.
- Need to have some automated way of managing the network, as well as monitoring.

Integration

- Need to work with Moore Products, Bailey, Foxboro, DCS systems. PLC's and PCS systems.

Risk Level

- No life-support system will use the network.
- As risk increases, we *must* be able to balance it with in-house competence.

Performance

- Must be fast enough to keep terminal users from drifting <1 second.

Security

- Not critical. Plant is surrounded by fence. No data yet deemed worthy of encryption. Computer passwords and access control lists are currently sufficient.
- For the most part, security must be handled by the application, not the network.

Case Study — Comparison and Analysis

Case Study — CSP Definition

Two communication system profiles (CSP's) were defined for the HMD Tank Car project. The CSP documents a network architecture option and consists of information relating to the protocol and media for the backbone and subnetwork alternatives. The two CSP's defined for the HMD Tank Car project were:

- **MAP**
  — MAP 3.0
  — Broadband MAP Channel

- **PROPRIETARY LAN and POINT-TO-POINT**
  — Proprietary computer LAN
  — Broadband CSMA/CD Channel
  — Broadband Point-to-Point Channel

In the MAP 3.0 CSP, the PLC 5/15 is connected to the MAP backbone via a data gateway. The PLC appears to be a node on the MAP backbone to other MAP nodes. The operator uses a device manage-

How to Justify an OSI-Based Network 337

ment application to read and write information to the PLC. Reporting information is sent to the VAX Cluster via a MAP file server on a µVAX attached to the VAX Cluster. Both the PLC 5 and the operator workstation can access or be made to access other nodes on the MAP network (see Figure 12-15).

In the proprietary/point-to-point CSP, the PLC 5/15 is interfaced to the process control system residing on a PDP 11. The interface is through a point-to-point link, with a custom driver written for the PDP 11 to accommodate communications to the PLC 5. The operator communicates with the PLC through a workstation connected to the PLC by a point-to-point link. The filing information generated by the PLC is stored in a file on the process control system and transferred to the Vax Cluster via the proprietary computer LAN. Neither the PLC 5 nor the operator workstation can access any nodes on the proprietary network directly (see Figure 12-16).

Case Study — CSP Cost Estimates

CSP communication component costs and implementation time were computed. The initial implementation costs were:

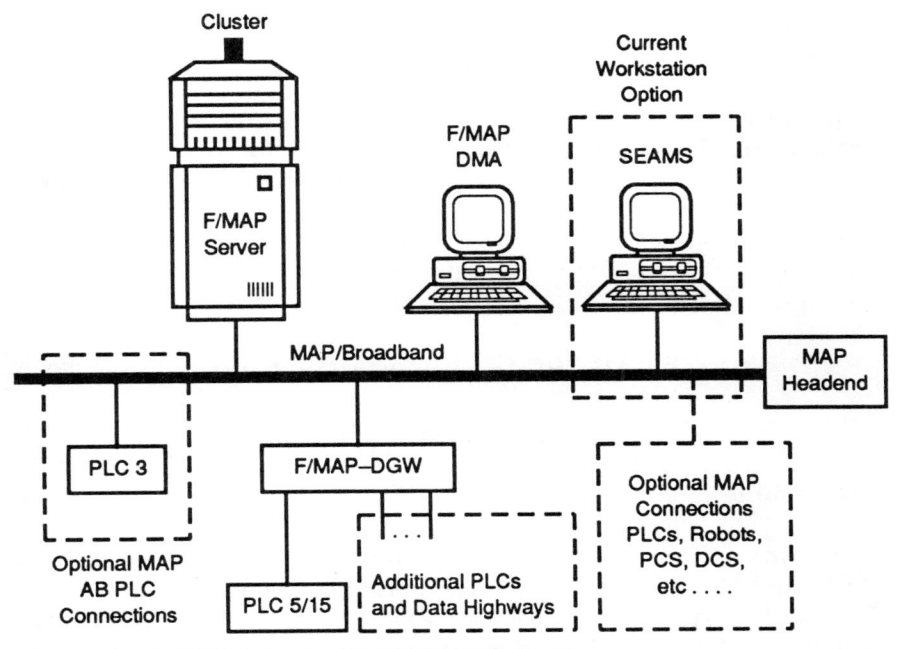

Figure 12-15 MAP Communication System Profile.

338 Open Systems Interconnection Handbook

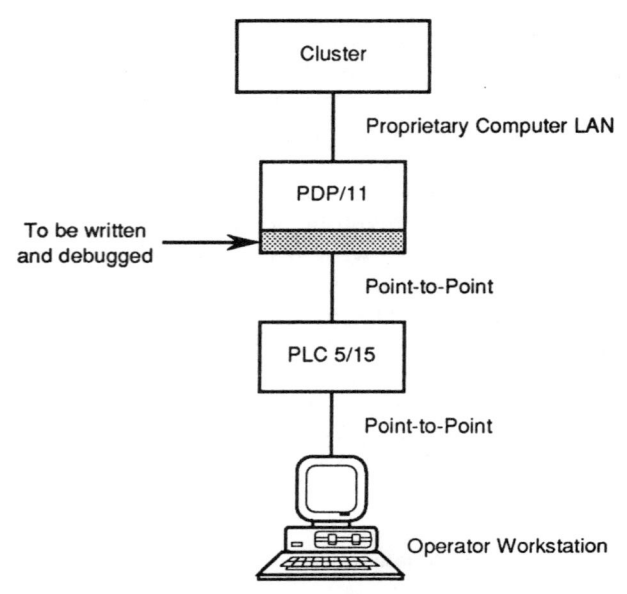

Figure 12-16 Proprietary/Point-to-Point CSP.

MAP 3.0

Component	Description	Cost
Communication H/W and S/W	(1) µVAX board and S/W	$6380
	(2) PC boards and S/W	$6800
	(1) PLC gateway S/W	$4000
	Head end remodulator	$8100
Application S/W	µVAX Server	$5000
	Operator Workstation	$3000
Configuration and Testing	5 days @ $750/day	$3750
MAP CSP Implementation Total		**$37030**

PROPRIETARY LAN/POINT-TO-POINT

Component	Description	Cost
Communication H/W and S/W	Pair of broadband Point-to-Point modems	$1000
Custom PDP/11 Driver and Application	2–8 weeks @ manpower burden of 100K/year (2K/week)	$4000–$16000

How to Justify an OSI-Based Network 339

Configuration and   1–4 weeks @ manpower $2000–$8000
Testing   burden of 100K/year

Proprietary/Pt–Pt CSP Implementation Total $7000–$25000

Note that the MAP CSP incurs communication hardware and software costs because MAP has not yet been implemented. If the MAP communication components were in place as with the proprietary/point-to-point CSP, or the communication components were provided by a technology transfer group from the corporate staff, the cost would be:

MAP 3.0

Component	Description	Cost
Application S/W	μVAX server	$5000
	Operator workstation	$3000
Configuration and Testing	5 days @ $750/day	$3750
MAP CSP Implementation Total		**$11750**

Note that the MAP CSP manpower costs are vendor rates. Due to project timing, a MAP vendor would have to be used due to the initial learning curve with new technology. If a vendor were contracted to implement the Proprietary/Pt-Pt CSP, the cost would increase to:

PROPRIETARY/PT-PT

Component	Description	Cost
Communication H/W and S/W	Pair of broadband Point-to-Point modems	$1000
Custom PDP/11 Driver and Application	2–8 weeks @ $3750/week	$7500–$30000
Configuration and Testing	1–4 weeks @ $3750/week	$3750–$15000

Proprietary/Pt–Pt CSP Implementation Total $12250–$46000

Note that the price differs depending on who implements the system and on the components that are already in place. These cost differences should be kept in mind for future projects, even though it may not be relevant to match the two CSP's on the same manpower costs and component availability used for the HMD project.

The initial installation costs and issues are a part of the overall life cycle of the project. Additional costs and issues arise throughout the planning, design, implementation, installation, debugging, operations, and changes of a network over time. The architecture defined for each CSP was reassessed across the life cycle of the project in order to define additional costs and issues. Life cycle issues for the CSP's are:

PROPRIETARY/POINT-TO-POINT CSP
LIFE CYCLE ISSUES

Implementation	• Software development of the custom driver
	• Test development for custom driver
	• Testing and debugging of driver and test software modules
Debugging	• Symptom categorization and problem identification with the custom driver
	• Fix verification times and costs
Installation	• Integration of custom driver with the PROSE system on the HMD PDP/11
Operations	• Unscheduled maintenance of the custom driver could become time consuming and expensive if the original author is not available
Changes	• Changing or adding communication functions of the driver will incur additional costs and could become time-consuming and expensive if the original author is not available

MAP CSP
LIFE CYCLE ISSUES

Implementation	• None; the use of off-the-shelf products based on communication standards minimizes these cost issues
Debugging	• Communication hardware and software has to be installed and configured
Installation	• Training is required for network configuration and management due to the lack of MAP experience

How to Justify an OSI-Based Network 341

Location:	Weight	Ranking	Priority
Cost	5	7	2
Flexibility	7	6	2
Expandability	8	4	1
Uptime/Reliability	9	1	1
Manageability	8	2	1
Integration	6	5	2
Risk Level	4	8	2
System Throughput	7	3	1
Security	5	9	3
Accountability	NA	NA	NA

Figure 12-17 Network Selection Goal Overall Summary Worksheet.

Operations
- A MAP spare parts inventory should be started and a MAP maintenance program initiated

Changes
- None; change, expandability, and flexibility are inherent qualities of MAP

Case Study — Prerequisite Information/ CSP Selection Parameter Comparison

Priority and weight information from the "Network Selection Goal Overall Summary Worksheet" (see Figure 12-17) is entered into the "Network Selection Goal Comparison Worksheet"; one worksheet is completed for each CSP. CSP weights are the measure of how closely the CSP architecture and CSP selection parameters meet the defined project needs that were documented in the prerequisite information and interview worksheets. CSP weights are documented in the corresponding worksheets (see Figure 12-18 for MAP 3.0, Figure 12-19 for Proprietary LAN/Point-to-Point).

The results from the MAP and proprietary goal comparison worksheets are as follows:

342 Open Systems Interconnection Handbook

Network Selection Goal	Priority	Ranking	CSP Weight	Goal Weight	Goal Score	Priority Level
Uptime/Reliability	1	1	8	9	−1	
Manageability	1	2	7	8	−1	
System Throughput	1	3	7	7	0	
Expandability	1	4	10	8	2	0
Integration	2	5	8	6	2	
Flexibility	2	6	9	7	2	
Cost	2	7	5	5	0	
Risk Level	2	8	5	4	1	5
Security	3	9	7	5	2	2
Accountability	NA	NA	NA	NA	NA	NA

Location: Raw Score 7
Communication Systems Profile: MAP 3.0

Figure 12-18 Network Goal Comparison Worksheet (MAP CSP).

Network Selection Goal	Priority	Ranking	CSP Weight	Goal Weight	Goal Score	Priority Level
Uptime/Reliability	1	1	9	9	0	
Manageability	1	2	8	8	0	
System Throughput	1	3	6	7	−1	
Expandability	1	4	3	8	−5	−6
Integration	2	5	3	6	−3	
Flexibility	2	6	1	7	−6	
Cost	2	7	8	5	3	
Risk Level	2	8	7	4	3	−3
Security	3	9	8	5	3	3
Accountability	NA	NA	NA	NA	NA	NA

Location: Raw Score −6
Communication Systems Profile: Proprietary & Pt. to Pt.

Figure 12-19 Network Goal Comparison Worksheet (Proprietary CSP).

How to Justify an OSI-Based Network 343

	MAP 3.0	PROPRIETARY/POINT-TO-POINT
Uptime/Reliability	−1	0
Manageability	−1	0
System Throughput	0	−1
Expandability	2	−5
Integration	2	−3
Flexibility	2	−6
Cost	0	3
Risk Level	1	3
Security	2	3

A negative score indicates that the CSP does not sufficiently meet the defined project needs. A positive score indicates that the CSP exceeds the project needs. A zero score indicates that the CSP closely meets the project needs.

COMMENTS ON CSP WEIGHTS FOR MAP 3.0

Uptime/Reliability: Uptime will be high once all the network configuration issues have been resolved.

Manageability: The information required to manage the system is available and accessible with vendor products. The only issue is the learning curve involved with managing the MAP network.

System Throughput: The PLC link is limited to 19.2 Kb. However, direct connections to the PLC 5 are possible through the MAP network. Data does not have to be "parked" on any intermediate devices.

Expandability: MAP on the broadband backbone has the capability and capacity to handle expansion. Expandability is an inherent benefit of MAP.

Integration: Not only does the MAP CSP meet current and future requirements, it also matches the corporate information access and integration direction.

Flexibility: The ability to change and move physical and logical components of a MAP network is an inherent benefit.

Cost: The cost for the MAP CSP is relatively high. Many of the initial components needed to get a MAP network operational have to be purchased and installed (e.g., head end remodulator, communication boards). Once the cost is burdened by an initial installation, the future CSP weight for cost will be higher.

Risk Level: MAP 3.0 products are relatively new in the networking product world. Additionally, facility personnel have little experience implementing MAP technology.

Security: All devices have the potential to be accessible on the network. It would take a significant amount of work to "crack" into a MAP node. Accidental access is very unlikely.

COMMENTS ON CSP WEIGHTS FOR PROPRIETARY LAN/POINT-TO-POINT

Uptime/Reliability: Due to the simplicity of the custom software and the reliability of the LAN, the system will be reliable once fully tested and debugged.

Manageability: Since this connection is "hard-wired" and will not be expanded, there are no management issues.

System Throughput: The PLC link is limited to 19.2 Kb, with no direct connection from the PLC to the VAX Cluster. The PDP 11 acts as a "file parking lot."

Expandability: The PLC 5 and the operator workstation are dedicated to the HMD project and cannot be expanded without custom software development.

Integration: This solution mirrors previous implementations. It does not follow the corporate or facility information access and integration direction.

Flexibility: The operator workstation is solely dedicated to the PLC 5 and cannot be used for other functions. Any changes may result in changes in the custom software.

Cost: The cost for this system is relatively low. Many of the components (e.g., communication boards) are already in place. The custom software development is the majority of the total cost.

Risk Level: The risk is low. Point-to-point and the proprietary computer LAN technology have been used at the facility for years.

Security: The only security risk is physical access to the operator workstation.

Case Study — Summary of Network Selection Goals

For each network selection goal, the average and standard deviation were computed for the weight, rank, and priority. While the average gives a mathematically correct score, one has to take into account the source of the information. For example, the process engineer's input may reflect a better view of the "total picture" than that of a user of a specific aspect of the entire process. Using information gathered through the interview process and the computed average and standard deviation, overall weight, rankings, and priority scores were determined for each network selection goal. (See Figure 12-17 for an overall summary of the scores.)

Case Study — Quantify the Intangible Benefits of Each CSP

The overall goal weights were accumulated at each priority level in order to compute a priority score. The raw score was computed by accumulating all the priority scores. As you can see in Figures 12-18 and 12-19, the CSP priority and raw scores are:

	MAP 3.0	PROPRIETARY/PT—PT
Priority 1	0	−6
Priority 2	5	−3
Priority 3	2	3
Raw Score	7	−6

A negative score indicates that the CSP does not sufficiently meet the defined project needs. A positive score indicates that the CSP exceeds the project needs. A zero score indicates that the CSP closely meets the project needs.

Case Study — Final Recommendations

Cost was not the major issue of the HMD project, as illustrated by the scoring of the network selection guidelines and comments from the "Network Selection Guidelines — Requirements and Constraints Scratchsheet." If it had been, the Proprietary LAN/point-to-point CSP would probably have been recommended for the project.

The CSP's scores were practically the same for the two most important selection goals, uptime/reliability and manageability. The following recommendation is based on information from the lower priority 1 goals (system throughput, expandability) and the two top priority 2 goals (integration, flexibility).

Note that the most important goals focused on operational considerations. The secondary goals where the two CSP's differed focused on future growth and the ability to handle additional capacity and capabilities.

The MAP CSP should be used for the HMD Tank Car project based upon the following information:

- The accumulated scores of the secondary goals for the MAP CSP are 6 (0 + 2 + 2 + 2).
- The accumulated scores of the secondary goals for the proprietary LAN/point-to-point CSP are −15 (−1 + −5 + −3 + −6).
- The MAP CSP fills a gap in the corporate architecture. SNA is used to link the IBM systems worldwide, and DECNET and LAT bridges are used to link the plants and office operations together. When it comes to providing a communication direction for the manufacturing-related processes at the facility level, the need for standards arises. MAP provides a flexible, expandable, standard communication system that can meet the future integration needs of manufacturing processes within the facility.

- Even though the MAP CSP costs 12K to 30K more to implement, it follows the level of commitment in the business plan because this "funding makes sense." 26K of the MAP CSP implementation cost was for communication hardware and software to get the MAP network operational. These costs decrease for future projects once the MAP network is operational.
- MAP provides the ability to use many vendors rather than being locked into a specific vendor.

Summary

For many years the selection and justification of an open system like an OSI-based network has been considered a "black art." I hope the guideline procedure described in this chapter provides insight into how network justifications have been performed so the black art becomes a hard science for you.

About the Author

Bill Andrews has worked for the past twelve years with Fortune 100 companies integrating components of CIM technology. As a consultant with the General Motors MAP group, he specialized in the integration of MAP and TOP to support the automation of the CAD/CAM cycle. His practical implementation experience at GM was later used at Eastman Kodak, where he designed and installed MAP-based DNC applications for the machine shop environment. His understanding of TOP is reflected in the highly regarded three-day "TOP Application Layer" training course he developed for Eastman Kodak. While at SISCO, the industry leader in MMS technology, he designed and implemented two of the first production MAP 3.0 networks for the continuous and discrete manufacturing environments.

Mr. Andrews is currently manager of CIM Services for Autoflex, Inc., a subsidiary of MIS International. His department performs network selection and implementation consulting, GOSIP training, and CIM system justification studies and implementation. He can be reached by phone at (313) 253-9500 or (800) 878-1118, by FAX at (313) 253-9506, or by mail care of AutoFlex, Inc., 445 Enterprise Court, Bloomfield Hills, MI 48302.

Chapter

13

OSI Transition Strategies: How to Get There from Here

by Carol Herbst, Rick A. Johnson and Clayton J. Morlok

Introduction

This chapter looks at OSI from the perspective of organizations that desire the advantages of OSI, but already have substantial investment in one or more proprietary network architectures. Is immediate cutover to pure OSI practical for these organizations? If not, can an evolutionary approach to OSI from proprietary networks be successful and beneficial? Can current proprietary networks be merged into a larger, organization-wide network based on OSI? This chapter examines these questions in five parts:

1. Historical Context — Examines the historical context driving and shaping the movement toward OSI among existing networks.
2. Benefits — Describes the benefits of the evolutionary approach of OSI transition that brings proprietary protocols and resources within a standards-based, open architecture network.
3. Transition Process Overview — Provides a brief overview of the process — from financial, managerial, as well as technical

viewpoints — of changing from proprietary to open architectures.
4. **Transition Strategies** — Outlines the transition strategies available to developers and managers who support this process.
5. **Case Study** — Describes how one U.S.-based multinational firm has begun its transition from proprietary networks to OSI.

For the purposes of this chapter, transition (sometimes referred to as "migration") is defined as the movement from a purely proprietary network environment toward one based upon open architecture standards, specifically, the Open Systems Interconnection (OSI) standard. The endpoint of the transition may be a purely open network environment ("pure" OSI) or it may be a more limited implementation of the open environment, which retains proprietary elements within an OSI-based architecture.

The Historical Context — Network Evolution

As with previous changes in networking, the changeover from proprietary to open will be evolutionary. For example, when true SNA networks came into being in the 1970s, the earlier emulation environments such as mainframe-based, point-to-point, and bisynchronous communications, weren't abandoned (see Figure 13-1). Instead, they were merged into the SNA environment. By the end of 1989, SNA became the dominant homogeneous architecture with more than 32,000 SNA networks in operations around the world, connecting thousands of mainframes and millions of terminals and PC's.

Since the early 1980s, hierarchical mainframe-centered networks expanded in a fairly orderly fashion under MIS control. At the same time, PC's, workstations, and UNIX processors appeared on desktops, often linked by Local Area Networks (LAN's) and servers. These devices were frequently under the control of various independent departments. Today, some organizations may have hundreds or thousands of computers using a variety of proprietary standards — each incompatible with the other. Yet the business objectives of the organization demand that these devices be integrated.

Achieving compatibility among the varied network resources requires solutions that will combine traditional proprietary networks, such as SNA, with open system solutions, such as OSI. In real terms, this means that SNA will continue to be the dominant organization-wide networking technology for several years. However, the new

OSI Transition Strategies 351

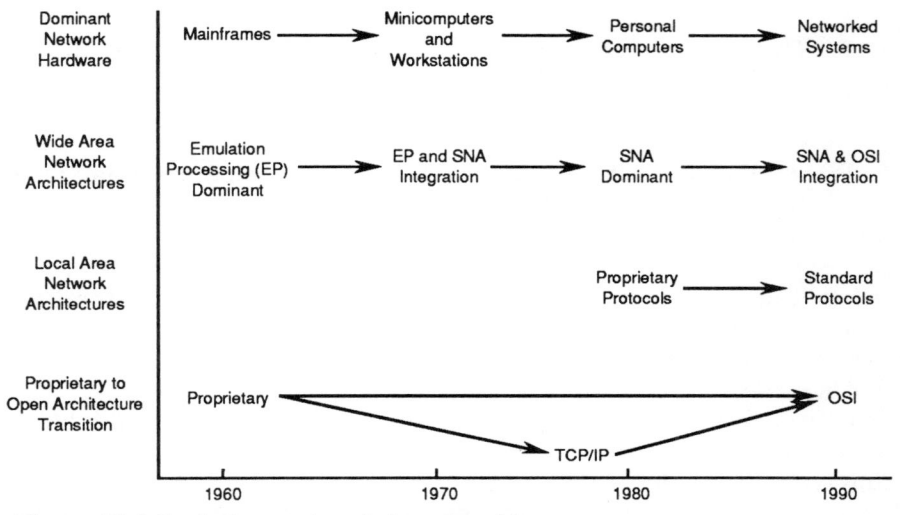

Figure 13-1 Evolutionary trends in networking.

network technology that will eventually replace SNA is an architecture designed for multivendor distributed processing. Today, the most likely technology to displace SNA is the International Standards Organization's Open System Interconnection (OSI) standard.

Based on the above hypothesis, open computing environments will not supplant, but rather will incorporate existing proprietary architectures as organizations make the transition to OSI. But from a practical standpoint, how can this transition be accomplished when many organizations today find themselves with an SNA network, a DECNET network, PC-based LAN's, and other pockets of proprietary computing?

Successful transition or co-existence requires a common organizing principle: a long-term, organization-wide plan aimed at a defined standard. This plan must do more than just link networks or nodes. It must give the user true interoperability — an overall network that allows each user to access, share, and process data anywhere within the overall organization. This total solution is often referred to as a *cooperative open network solution*.

Benefits — The Advantages of Evolving to OSI

Much of the interest in OSI transition is being driven by two requirements:

1. The need to create organization-wide networks based on different Local Area and Wide Area network technologies.
2. The ability to acquire equipment from multiple vendors.

When all aspects of communication and networking are considered in upgrading a corporate network, OSI can reduce the complexity and expense of the task, while providing a stable base for the future. It provides a high degree of choice in program and product selection as well as consistency across vendor product lines. With a standard OSI network as the backbone, gateway usage can be minimized, which, in turn, reduces conversion-caused transmission error rates, bottlenecks, and difficulties in network management.

OSI enables corporations to focus their resources on solving business problems instead of establishing and reestablishing methods of interconnection among computer systems. OSI provides a cohesive environment that can be expanded as needed for network growth and it can even reduce the time required to incorporate new technology. This consistent environment provides organization-wide access to information, as well as an open communications environment through which suppliers and customers can exchange information electronically.

To obtain these benefits, a variety of OSI transition strategies can be used. In fact, a combination of strategies may be appropriate, depending on the existing networks, the business and technical goals of the organization, or even the organization's "customers," for example, a commercial enterprise vs. a government agency.

The Transition Process — An Overview

The differences between proprietary and open architectures are, on a structural level, primarily differences of organization and distribution of functionality. For example, the proprietary SNA transaction services layer contains elements of both the application process and the OSI application layer. Other proprietary architectures exhibit varying similarity with open architectures. From the practical perspective of planning and implementing a transition to an open architecture, the differences are much more striking (see Table 13-1).

Given these differences between proprietary and open architectures, four general considerations are pertinent when selecting a strategy or group of strategies for transitioning to an open environment from existing proprietary network environments:

Table 13-1 Proprietary and Open Architectures Compared

Criteria	Proprietary	Open
Standards-based	No	Yes
Vendor options	Single vendor	Multivendor
Product choices	Limited	Flexible
Pricing	Vendor-set	Market-driven
Controls addition of features/services	Single vendor	Industry (vendors and users)

1. The process should be evolutionary, not revolutionary.
2. Integration must occur as part of a phased plan. This avoids costly and potentially catastrophic disruptions of network services. It also works to minimize unwanted interruption of daily operations and end users.
3. Investments in existing network infrastructure (hardware, software, human capital) should be leveraged and preserved whenever possible.
4. Transition strategies should allow sharing of network resources among disparate systems. This helps support efficient, properly paced management of further network expansion.

Selecting a strategy is just one phase of the overall process of moving from proprietary to open architectures. In addition to the technical considerations, there are numerous financial, managerial, and even political aspects of the process that must be considered to ensure the success of the transition. The following six steps provide a basic outline of the actions required:

1. Choose the interconnection standard, such as OSI, and express the goal of the new system in terms of its benefits to the organization or the system. Resist the temptation to formulate the system goal in terms of network performance or capabilities.
2. Train appropriate staff on the chosen standard so that they can perform the strategic planning of the network. Don't jump to specific implementation plans. Familiarize the developers with the capabilities and benefits of OSI as they can be applied to specific functional requirements. Also, identify those transition paths most likely to accomplish the system goals.

3. Develop a general plan for presentation to the executive level and other key decision makers. The objective is to get them truly committed to the plan. Without their commitment, the plan cannot succeed. Therefore, be realistic in discussing the time, effort, and cost involved. They are substantial. But so are the benefits. Include qualitative as well as quantitative benefits. Some benefits, such as organization-wide access to information, may be difficult to quantify, but the need for such access is clear.
4. Select vendors with products that fit the transition and integration strategies (defined in the next section) for the plan. Perform product training with internal staff and strategic planning staff — no end users yet. Overall OSI knowledge and expertise are important parameters to consider in selecting vendors. Be sure that vendors have a complete OSI plan to provide a total solution, not just a plan for the individual products they provide. In addition to the plan, the vendor needs to be willing to ensure interoperability with other vendors' equipment, as well as a transition plan for their own products. It is critical that vendors be able to give assistance throughout the process. They should be able to help with planning, selling management, training, documentation, and registration of OSI objects. Installation and implementation are not enough.
5. Test the hardware and software through pilot installations. Evaluate and analyze the test results to verify that the components meet the system goals and requirements. Find new vendors as needed and reevaluate.
6. As pilots are successfully completed, add additional network components or applications. For example, once an X.25 backbone is verified operational, begin to add X.400 pilots to test their utility in the network.

Transition Strategies

Six of the most common OSI transition strategies are:

Parallel networks
Bottom-up integration
Multiple protocol routing and bridging
Top-down integration
Application gateways
Hybrid networks

The strategies may be grouped by their degree of interoperability. The first strategy, parallel networks, is the method by which networks have grown in the past. It provides for an "island" of open architecture in parallel with other networks. It is especially well suited to pilot programs or other "lab" type implementations aimed at establishing the viability of open architectures before implementing other transition strategies.

The next three strategies, bottom-up integration, multiple protocol routing and bridging, and top-down integration, are most appropriate for networks whose end connections are "like to like." Such networks must allow varied network devices to share communications and other network resources, but true interoperability is not required.

The last two strategies, application gateways and hybrid networks, address the achievement of interoperability across the network. A brief discussion of the advantages and disadvantages of each strategy follows.

Parallel Networks This strategy involves the concurrent support of multiple autonomous networks (see Figure 13-2). Where selection of appropriate network speed is important, but interoperability is not, the parallel networks strategy is a good fit. Parallel networks also offer a quick means of meeting organization objectives. Instead of a single, consolidated network, the organization maintains separate infrastructures for each network desired, such as OSI, SNA, or others.

For example, a LAN router network may be built in parallel with an existing SNA WAN or X.25 network. This strategy works well when there are discrete user groups that don't need interconnection. It also allows organizations to establish pilot sites where OSI networks can be tested and enhanced without disrupting the entire organization.

Parallel networks allow each network to operate at optimum efficiency for specific applications rather than providing general purpose services for diverse applications. Users on existing networks are not disrupted by the addition of another network. The strategy allows an organization to implement OSI networks in isolated parts of the organization, where the greatest benefit from the open architecture can be quickly realized, and, if necessary, later expanded. The parallel networks strategy also permits organizations to physically isolate networks handling secure traffic.

The drawbacks of the parallel network strategy include high communication costs caused by duplicated network functions and redundant staffing for each network. It also requires multiple network management systems, with the accompanying costs for each system.

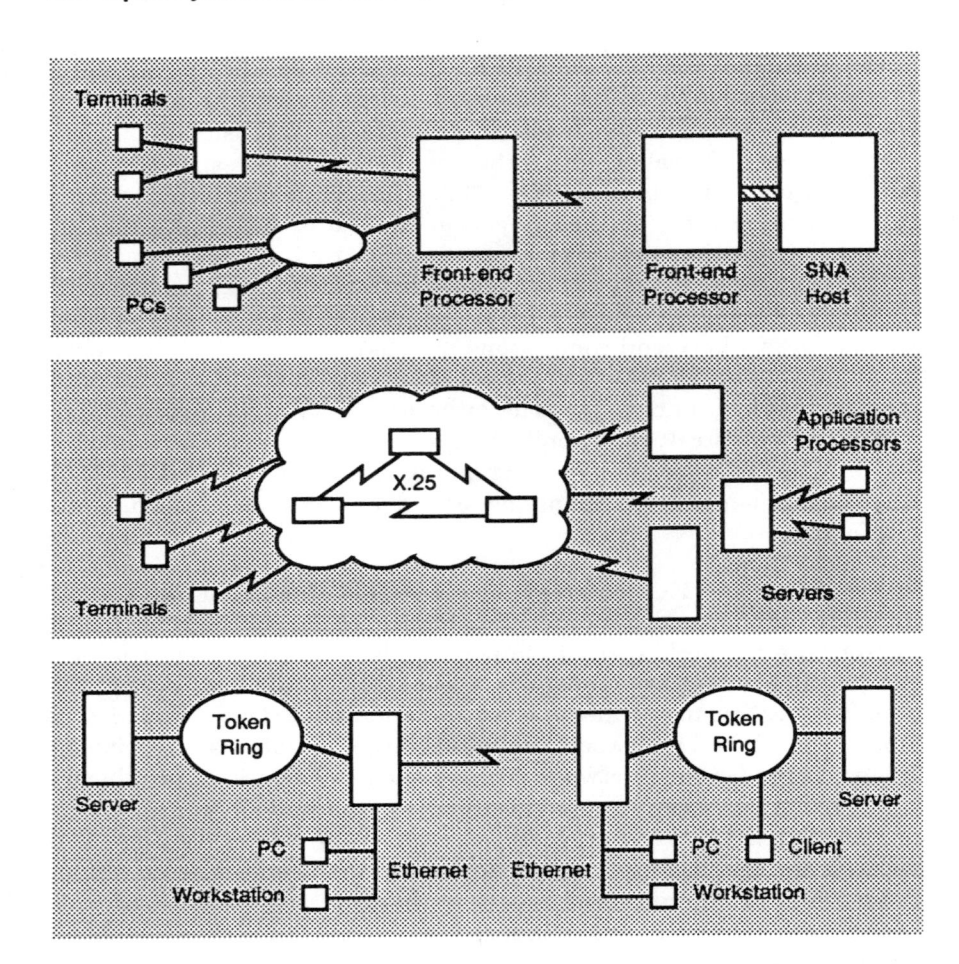

Figure 13-2 Parallel Networks.

Bottom-up Transition Bottom-up transition involves substituting OSI lower (transport) layer protocols, such as X.25 WAN's, for the proprietary networking protocols (see Figure 13-3). Bottom-up transition is particularly popular in Europe, where large numbers of X.25 networks are installed. Bottom-up transition provides connectivity between computing systems, not application interoperability. The bottom-up approach may be coupled with another strategy to address the interoperability issues. Since nearly all vendors support connections to X.25 networks, diverse multivendor equipment can be accommodated with this approach. In addition, the bottom-up approach

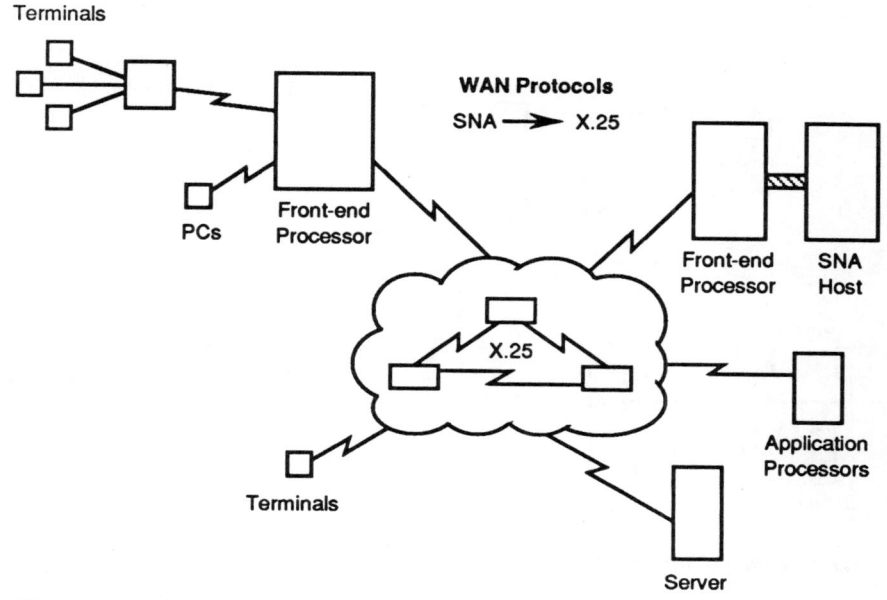

Figure 13-3 Bottom-up Network.

supports both hierarchical and peer-to-peer type connections, with each network retaining its own addressing scheme.

With the bottom-up approach, transition to OSI occurs in the lower layers of the model, so that the existing applications remain unchanged. Because users continue to access familiar applications, this type of transition is transparent to the users. Organizations using this method can expect to see line cost savings through the sharing of a common industry standard network for most applications. However, the change to a new network backbone may mean investing in additional network equipment as well as in personnel for installation, management, and optimization of the network.

Multiple Protocol Routing and Bridging This strategy consists of a single computing system concurrently supporting multiple, coexisting protocols (see Figure 13-4). For networks where it is impractical or impossible to standardize on a single protocol, the multiple protocol strategy offers a solution. Examples of multiple protocol stacks include LAN routers simultaneously supporting OSI, TCP/IP, and DECnet communications protocols or LAN bridges tying two or more physically different LAN's into one logical LAN. Essentially, this

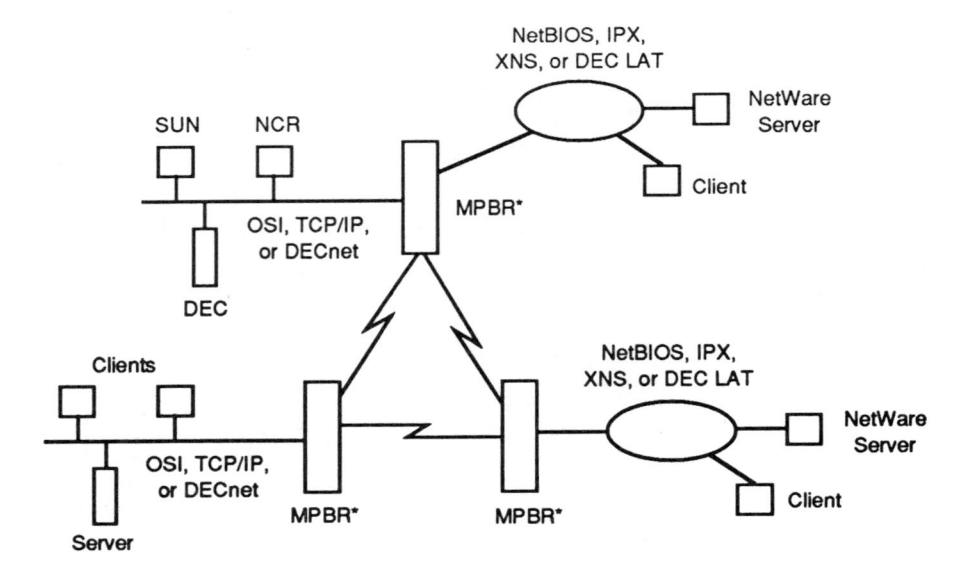

Figure 13-4 Multiple Protocol Bridging and Routing Network.

* MPBR = Multiple Protocol Bridging and Routing Products

method allows multiple types of peer-to-peer connections within a given backbone network: TCP/IP to TCP/IP, OSI to OSI, and peer-to-peer SNA connections.

This strategy is most commonly seen in LAN internetworking environments using routers from Cisco, Wellfleet, Proteon, and others. However, most of these backbone nodes use proprietary protocols between nodes and only speak to like equipment. OSI-based internetworking products, such as NCR's Open Network System™ (ONS™), are just beginning to come to market. As these routers and bridges begin to standardize on internodal protocols using OSI, equipment from multiple vendors can be used to build the backbone.

The multiple protocol routing and bridging strategy allows sharing of communications facilities and processing power among the multiple networks, thus reducing costs. As a result, an organization can continue to operate its existing LAN networks while introducing new OSI applications. By establishing OSI capabilities while preserving existing networks and applications, multiple protocol stacks support a gradual integration of OSI into an existing environment. However, these solutions can be limited to a small network configuration and may not be appropriate for a larger organization-wide solution. In addition, multiple protocol routing and bridging, similar to the previous two transitions, only provides like-to-like interoperability. Finally, this approach may incur higher maintenance and operating costs because the organization must maintain personnel skilled in several networks, as well as multiple network management systems.

Top-down Transition The top-down transition method implements OSI applications over an existing network, such as TCP/IP or SNA (see Figure 13-5). For example, the OSI File Transfer, Access, and Management (FTAM) application protocols can be transmitted over an existing TCP/IP network using a common transport layer interface (TLI) at the TCP layer. Another example is FTAM or X.400 transmitted over an existing SNA network.

Top-down transition leverages current proprietary network resources, including network control and management tools, such as TCP/IP Simple Network Management Protocol (SNMP), SNA host-based NetView, and NET/MASTER. The top-down method is most appropriate for OSI applications running over TCP/IP networks because the TCP/IP network services are closely related to OSI. Users get the advantage of the proven reliability of the TCP/IP network plus access to the growing number of increasingly robust OSI applications.

Top-down transition makes sense when OSI is a relatively small fraction of the total networking environment. However, as the number of OSI applications increases, the top-down approach may degrade network performance, especially when large graphics or image files are involved. Also, the centralized implementation of network management that goes along with the top-down approach tends to limit management choices.

Network "tuning" problems may arise from this approach, too. If a network is tuned for SNA applications, performance of OSI applications may be less than optimal. Furthermore, top-down transition does not provide interoperability between OSI and existing proprietary applications. In fact, even the same OSI application implemented in the TCP/IP environment and a pure OSI environment may not be interoperable because the protocols underlying the two environments differ. In these cases, special gateways are required for protocol conversion to allow OSI application exchanges between the mixed and pure OSI environments.

Gateways There are two types of gateways: application-mapped gateways and terminal-mapped gateways. Application-mapped gateways, as the name suggests, operate primarily at the OSI application

360 Open Systems Interconnection Handbook

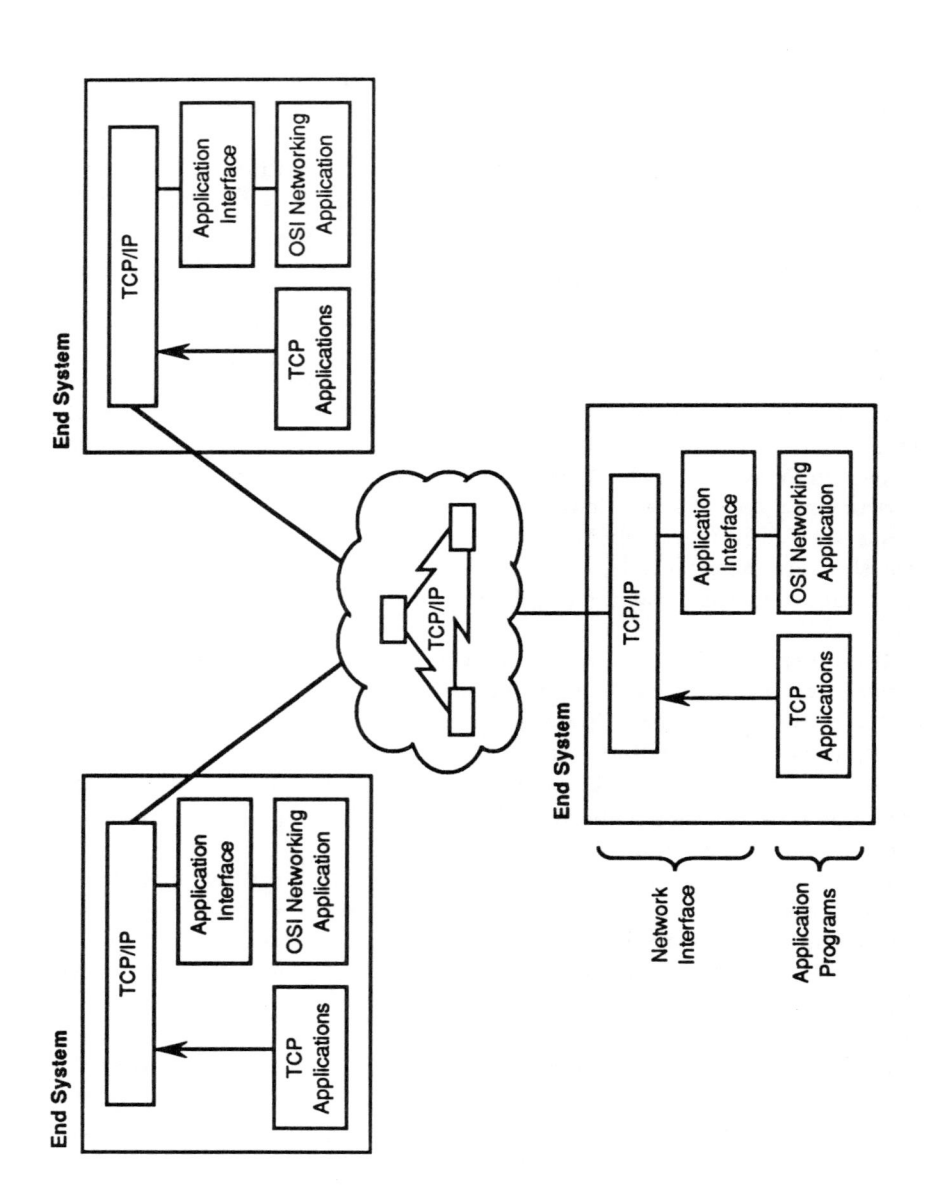

Figure 13-5 Top-down Network.

layer. These gateways typically use application level software to "map," or translate, proprietary applications (see Figure 13-6). For example, IBM's PROFs or DEC's All-in-One can be mapped to OSI's X.400 message handling system. The mapping process requires significant processing time and resources, so this approach is best suited to store-and-forward applications where response time is not critical. For interactive applications, terminal mapping is another type of application gateway.

The application-mapped gateway approach has merits, especially when OSI is being integrated into local environments in a phased process that minimizes communications disruptions. Because the proprietary application remains in place for the user, application-mapped gateways are considered "transparent" to users; the gateway handles format and protocol conversion, such as to X.400. This, in turn, maintains user productivity while leveraging existing hardware, software, and training investments. Application-mapped gateways also provide interoperability between varied applications, allowing them to be fully integrated into the overall network.

Application-mapped gateways, however, are ill-suited to bulk data transfer applications or to interactive applications such as file transfer because the processing overhead required to perform the necessary conversion may cause unacceptably slow transfer rates. Substantial degradation of user productivity may result.

Furthermore, gateways tend to proliferate since they are tied to individual proprietary applications. For example, a large network might have 20 different e-mail packages. That works out to as many as 400 (20 × 20) gateways. But converting to a single, consistent base, such as X.400, dramatically reduces the number of gateways needed. Regardless of the number of gateways, each gateway has its own acquisition, installation, maintenance, and processing overhead costs. What's more, upgrades or changes to either side of the gateway (proprietary application or OSI application) may jeopardize the gateway's ability to convert those features or capabilities. Gateways may only be able to operate on a "lowest common denominator" subset, which severely restricts the overall functionality of the network. Security is also a potential problem because gateways are a favorite entry point for illegal access into the network.

It is possible, however, to accentuate the positive attributes of gateways while minimizing their drawbacks. For example, gateways can be used primarily for access to systems such as LAN's, while proprietary environments predominate in the Wide Area Network (WAN). Another approach uses the gateway for conversion from proprietary application to an OSI protocol — but not an OSI application.

362 Open Systems Interconnection Handbook

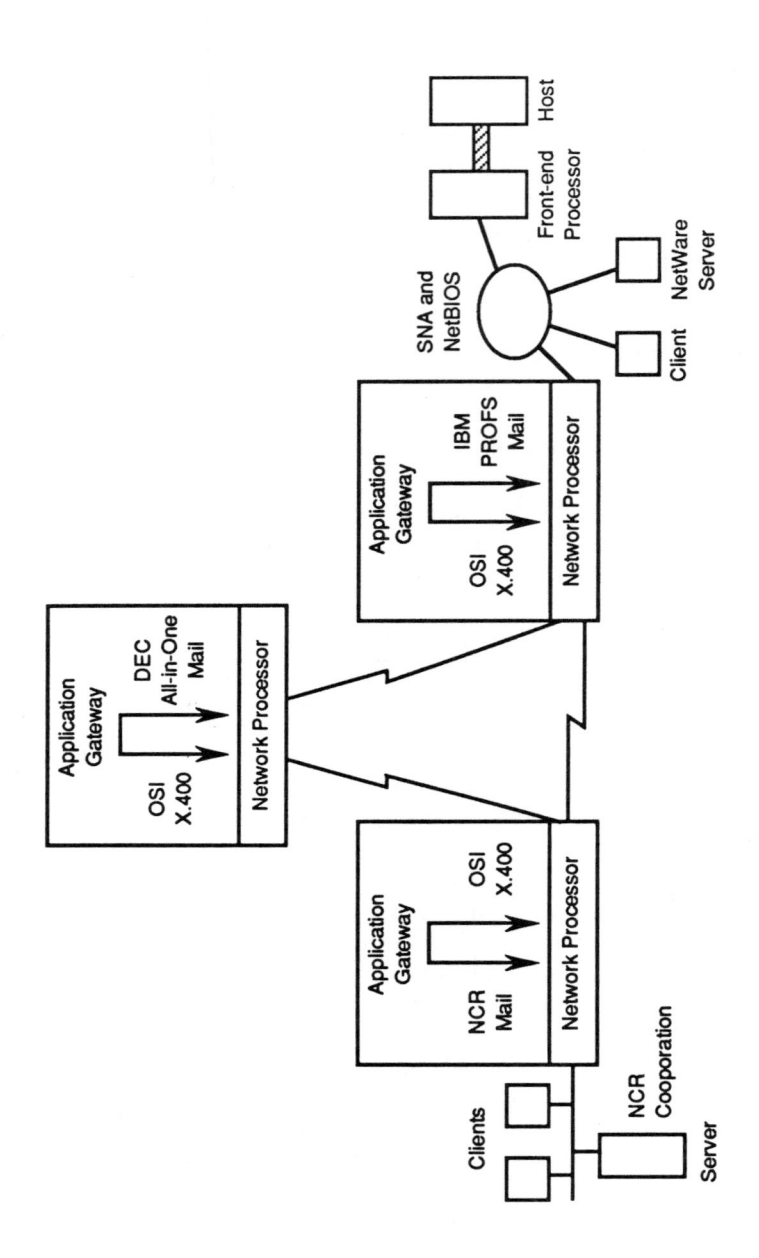

Figure 13-6 Mail Application Gateway example.

This approach takes DECnet All-In-One, SNA PROFs, and TCP/IP SMTP mail packages, uses proprietary-to-OSI gateways for each, and converts them to the X.400 protocol. The X.400 data can then be shared among the various proprietary applications via the gateways. By not mapping to X.400 applications, the number of gateways is limited to the number of proprietary applications, greatly reducing cost and network overhead. But the transition to OSI has still been accomplished in a way that is transparent to the end user.

Terminal-Mapped Gateways The second type of gateway consists of mapping real terminals to virtual terminals to mask differences between the terminals and the host system. Examples of terminal mapping include TCP/IP Telnet or TN3270, OSI Virtual Terminal (VT), and protocol conversion through free-standing protocol converters. Because a terminal's true "identity" is masked by the virtual terminal, this approach eliminates the need for multiple terminals to access host applications on systems from multiple vendors.

OSI VT allows terminals, regardless of model or design, access to local or remote host applications. With VT, a terminal can access an application program resident in a remote system without knowing the remote application's environment. This terminal-to-host connection is possible because the terminal and the host sides map the virtual terminal protocol to their own unique characteristics and control sequences. OSI VT's capabilities are defined broadly enough to provide terminal access to SNA and non-SNA host environments. This preserves an organization's investment in existing terminal equipment and applications, while providing a wide range of multivendor connectivity among terminal devices.

The most efficient way to access host applications is to use the protocols that the application is expecting directly from the terminal, for example, SNA protocols to SNA applications. Terminal mapping is less efficient than like-to-like proprietary communications. However, when the ability to access a range of different applications from a single terminal or PC is more important than efficiency, terminal mapping is a useful approach. Other gateway types might map to file transfers, databases, or network management programs.

Hybrid Networks In many cases, a single transition strategy will be inadequate to address the requirements and objectives of a given network. Therefore, hybrid networks consisting of the implementation of a combination of transition strategies may be the best solution. Hybrid networks may be particularly appropriate for networks that may require linking previously isolated islands of proprietary computing (see Figure 13-7) for the first time.

364 Open Systems Interconnection Handbook

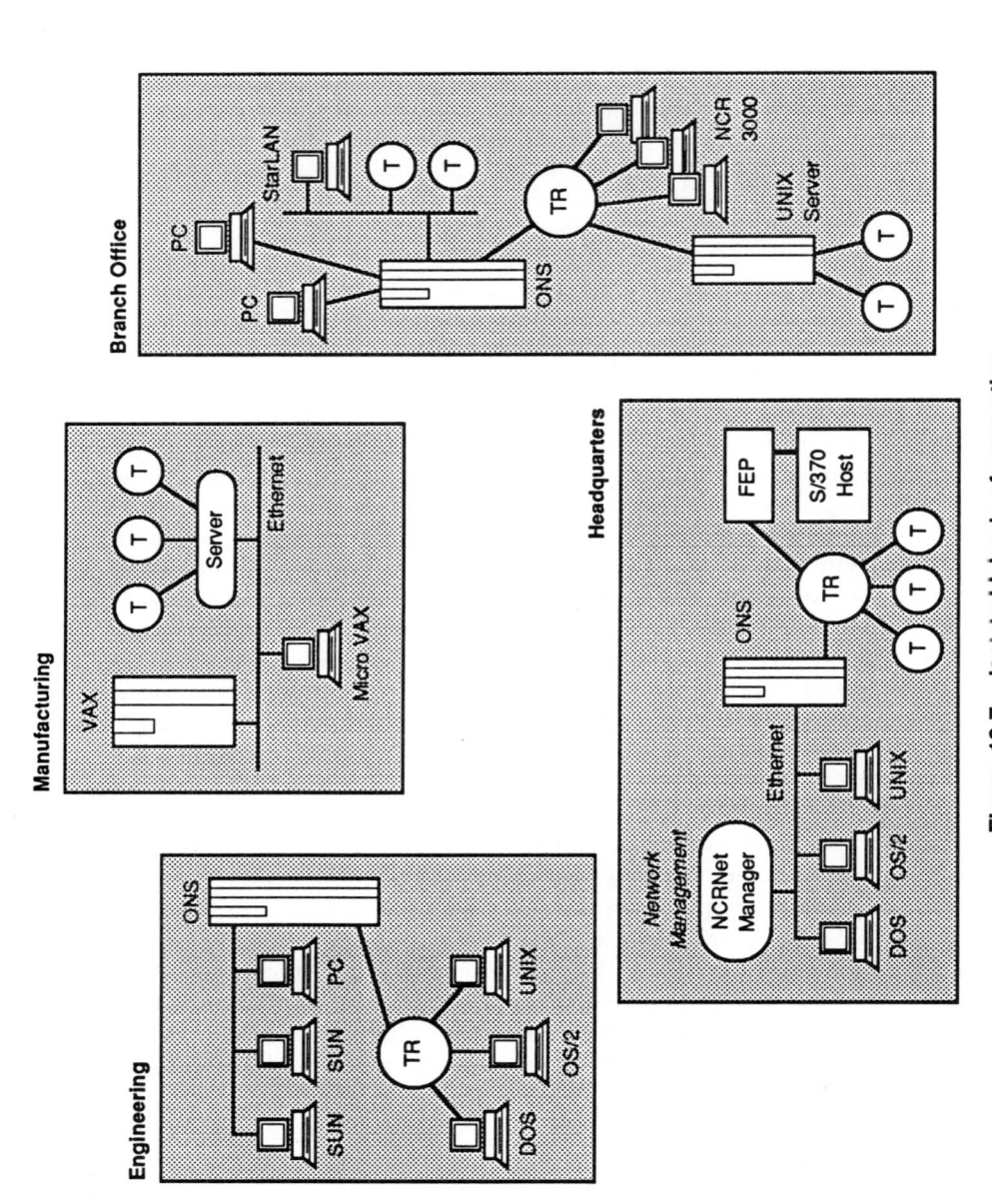

Figure 13-7 Isolated islands of computing.

A hybrid network solution to the problem posed in Figure 13-7 might contain, for example, elements of the bottom-up, multiple protocol routing and bridging, and application gateway strategies (see Figure 13-8). The bottom-up strategy provides OSI-based backbone networking and addressing capabilities. Multiple protocol routing and bridging strategies might be appropriate for continued operation of existing LAN networks and applications while allowing gradual insertion of OSI applications. Application gateways could be used to support network-wide applications such as electronic mail over the OSI backbone.

Indeed, it seems clear that many OSI-based network solutions, such as NCR's Open Network System and others, will have to provide support for a combination of transition strategies to adequately accommodate the varied proprietary networks frequently found within a single organization. The following case study gives a more detailed look at how one multinational organization is moving from proprietary to open architecture by integrating elements of existing proprietary networks within an organization-wide open architecture.

Case Study — Integrating Proprietary and Open Architectures

NCR Corporation's Worldwide Information Network (WIN) is an ongoing example of the process of transitioning to the OSI open architecture while retaining SNA and other proprietary network protocols within the network. Numerous corporate needs prompted this ambitious effort. First, the 56,000 NCR employees in 120 countries around the world needed a timely, cost-effective way to exchange information among themselves, with their customers, and with their suppliers. Competitive factors dictated that the only realistic, long-term solution had to be a cohesive, unified approach to the use of networks. As the scope of NCR's business becomes ever more global, the importance of these communications links will continue to grow. Unfortunately, NCR had no prescribed standard method of communication within the organization, between NCR and its suppliers, or between NCR and its customers.

The NCR computing environment included multiple networks supporting over nine protocols, many of them proprietary. There were multiple electronic mail systems including UNIX mail, public mail services, as well as "home grown" mail systems. As a result NCR found itself with worldwide communications systems that were hard to manage, inconsistent in quality of service, and less than acceptable in providing access to and from customers and suppliers. Conse-

Figure 13-8 Hybrid Transition Network.

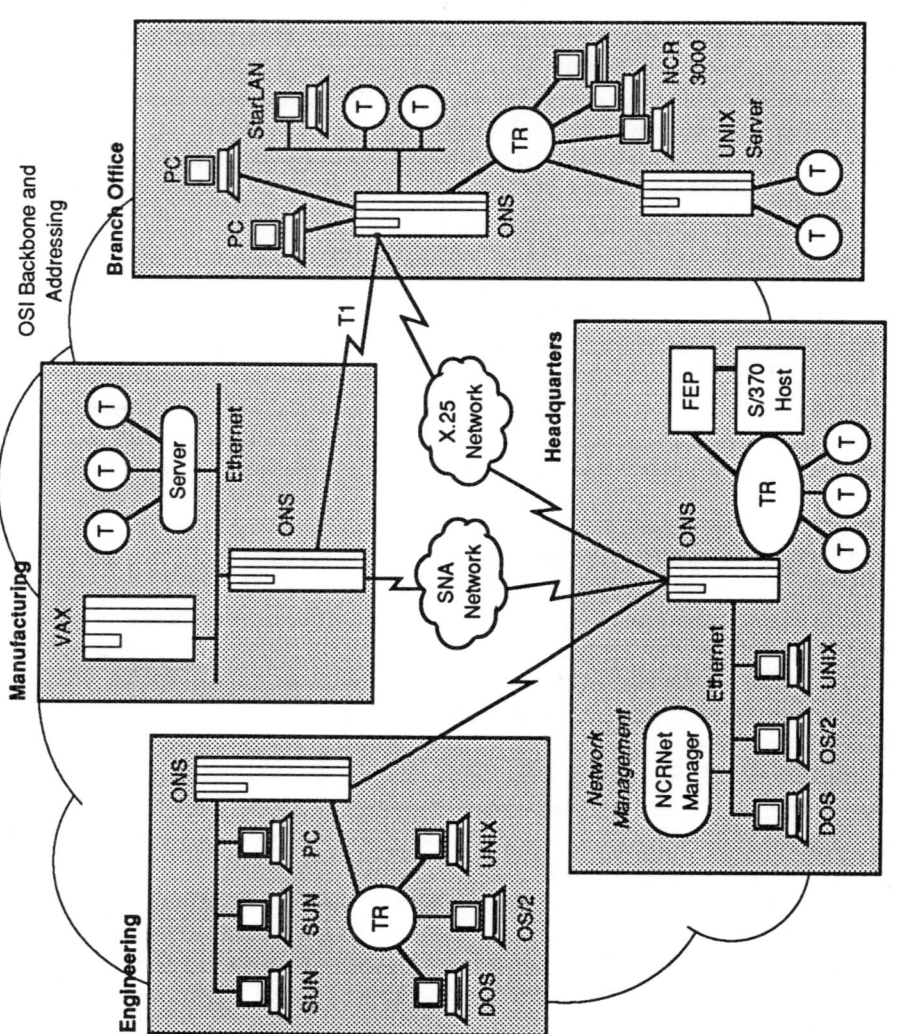

quently, NCR's developers of the Worldwide Information Network advocated a corporate goal: "Provide NCR with a consistent telecommunications and electronics messaging system to enable and facilitate the exchange of information transfer required for the support of NCR business processes throughout the world."

NCR recognized that it could continue to build proprietary gateways or it could adopt open standards as the guideline for integrating all its networks. NCR realized the best long-term approach was to pursue the use of open standards, with OSI as the backbone. This choice was partially dictated by worldwide presences and the need to interoperate with already established international PTT and OSI networks. But this was only the first step in a complex and demanding process.

Selling the Concept

Indeed, the first task was selling key people within NCR on the concept of pursuing the use of open standards for NCR networks. Because of the companywide nature of the project, top management had to be sold first. Their endorsement of the program was particularly important because later in the process, as problems occurred during the transition and implementation phases, those key people had to be called on for further support to maintain commitment to the program of an open standards-based network.

Since the concept would require new funds for hardware, software, and training, other groups within NCR needed to see that the benefits would justify the associated costs and effort. MIS staff had to be convinced that it would help them to become more productive and better able to address new business requirements. User groups and their management had to be convinced that the new systems and business techniques they desired would be achievable with the proposed networking approach.

Finally, NCR's strategic partners, business partners, suppliers, and customers also needed to sign-on to the concept. A case in point was an interest in Electronic Data Interchange (EDI), which is based upon OSI X.400 techniques. While NCR has been introducing EDI between the company and its business partners, NCR needed to further help them understand how it was going to help everyone reduce communication costs and improve productivity.

The amount of "sales effort" needed to provide a successful foundation for the actual implementation was and continues to be, substantial. For example, NCR's worldwide network planning staff visited each country that was a candidate for a major network node to sell the NCR WIN concept, its basis in OSI, and its ability to integrate their existing protocols into WIN. A number of techniques, such as internal news articles, videos, lapel buttons, posters, and face-to-face meetings, were used to convince these users of the benefits of moving to WIN.

Cost Justification

An important part of the sales effort was cost justification. Early on, NCR realized that an OSI transition and integration program was going to require significant capital and personnel resources. That made short-term cost justification very difficult. The financial and strategic benefits of WIN were clearly the long-term savings from integrating and consolidating networks. It was recognized that the most important benefits were difficult to quantify in financial terms: What is the volume of sales lost from not having information immediately accessible? How much productivity is lost when only certain employees are able to exchange data and others are not? What is the financial impact of waiting for information, even when other services are used? And what is the productivity cost impact from the labor and delay associated with exchanging data by paper instead of over electronic networks? The answers to these questions were important in cost justifying the transition to open architectures.

Planning

Once approval for WIN was given, the planning process had to resist the inclination to jump into implementation immediately. It was determined early on that integration of proprietary and open systems would be evolutionary and lengthy. It was recognized that it would not be possible to skip the transition and simply fit all existing networks with open systems and "pull the big switch."

A simple, one-time cutover approach would have been doomed for a variety of reasons. The most important reason concerned the need to change existing business procedures without interrupting business operations. Implementing WIN required new procedures within NCR, such as electronic mail for sales, sales support, product management, and marketing. The shift from paper-based to electronic transactions throughout a corporation the size of NCR is no small matter. Furthermore, since OSI is a peer-to-peer network, it forces the MIS staff to also modify its methods. The historic distinction between host operations and network operations is diminishing as MIS staffs become less centralized and more network oriented. The scope and magnitude of these changes argued for the evolutionary approach.

Selecting the Transition Strategy

NCR realized that of the major transition strategies outlined earlier in this chapter, no single strategy would meet WIN's needs. Many NCR offices are independently run, operating on a management concept called commercialization. This means that many departmental decisions are made with some independence from headquarters staff. Furthermore, some network transition strategies were more appropriate for one office than another.

The strategy selected for a particular part of the network was based on several criteria such as speed, overall network performance including impact on other applications, flexibility, and the need for specialized hardware and software. NCR also considered transparency to the user. However, this was done with the understanding that complete or total transparency was rarely achievable. Instead, functional transparency was the goal. Another consideration in selecting a strategy was network manageability. In other words, does the strategy increase or decrease the administrative burden on the network staff, MIS staff, or the end users?

By evaluating the relevant strategies against these criteria, NCR WIN selected a combination of a modified bottom-up strategy and a gateway approach. An OSI/X.25 backbone was installed (see Figure 13-9), allowing the other nine network protocols to use a standard backbone. Only select gateways between OSI and proprietary protocols (no proprietary-to-proprietary gateways) were developed. Any new applications, such as order management, on the network will be implemented in OSI.

Backbone and Gateways

The OSI backbone was structured so that all countries, country offices, and cities within a country are connected by an X.25 private network, or by a packet-switched X.25 public network when cost, usage, and regulatory considerations are factors. The backbone

370 Open Systems Interconnection Handbook

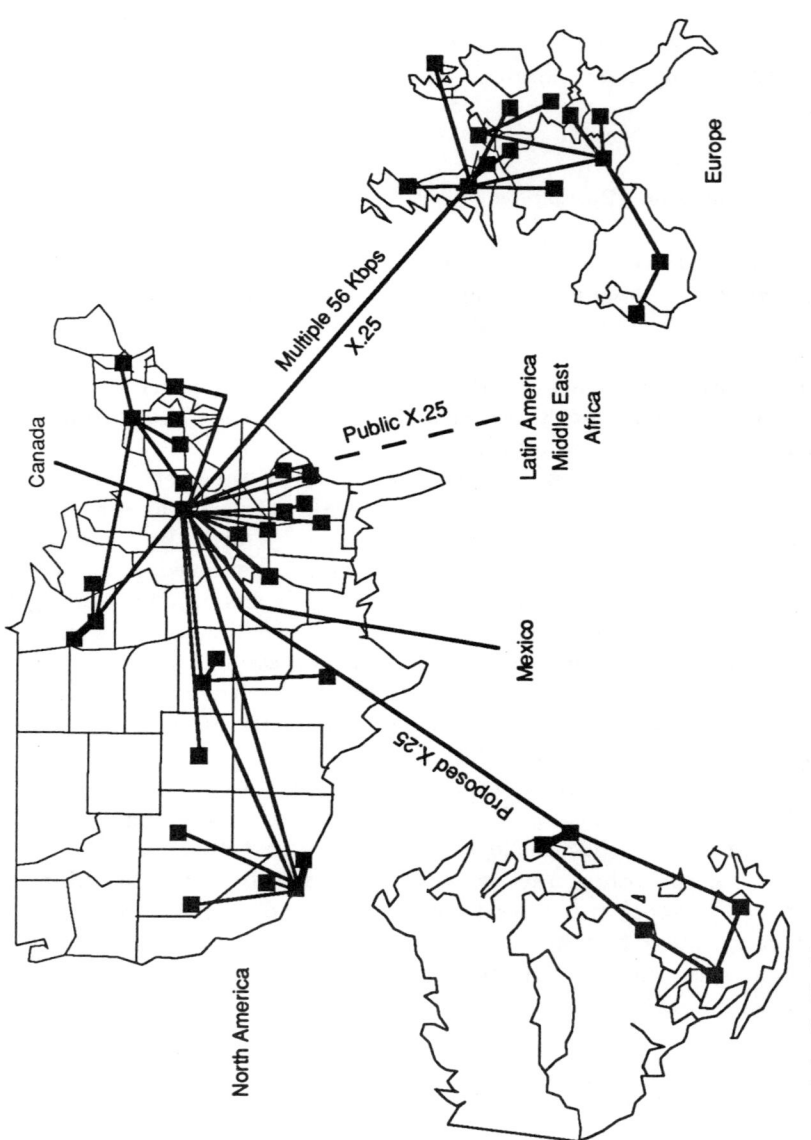

Figure 13-9 NCR Worldwide Information Network (WIN).

provides reliable connectivity that can guarantee a link, if not interoperability, between offices.

The limited use of gateways is best exemplified by NCR's headquarters in Dayton, Ohio, which occupies nearly 60 different locations throughout the city. Gateways are located in a single, city gateway (not in individual locations) that provides all gateway services such as X.400 to UNIX mail. While this is a somewhat hierarchical organization, it helps minimize the proliferation of gateways.

Lessons Learned

The combination of transition strategies for integrating proprietary networks and OSI taught NCR many lessons. For example, cost-benefit perceptions are crucial to maintaining user support for the network. Effectively selling the concept upfront and continually reinforcing the decision helps overcome resistance that may develop as actual costs begin to accrue.

Another lesson learned concerned vendor services. Most vendors did not provide the kind of training required to train end users and administrators. Even when training was available, it was directed at the wrong audience. Much of the training is aimed at implementors instead of end users and administrators. As a result, NCR developed a significant training program on its own.

The importance of documentation should also be underscored. Since OSI is still rather complex and dynamic, it's critical that the vendor provide useful documentation. As with training, documentation must aid the end user and manager as well as the implementor. In addition, vendor documentation can be very useful in persuading upper management and user management about the benefits of OSI.

It is a truism that an installed system doesn't always do the things expected of it. But NCR found this to be especially true for OSI because of the limited availability of conformance tests. Again, NCR had to conduct significant internal testing as pilot programs were implemented to make sure that the installed systems performed to specifications.

Installation of OSI products proved to be unexpectedly complex and time-consuming. In particular, NCR was caught off-guard by the need for OSI registered information. To achieve global OSI networks, the naming and addressing schemes used for individual networks must be unique, not just within that network, but globally unique. This requires registration of these schemes with the proper registration authority. Since the organization and responsibilities of these authorities are still evolving, this issue is a source of conflict and confusion.

Finally, the integration process takes time, not just for implementation and certification with user applications, but for user acceptance and the "learning curve." Allowances also had to be made for the fact that the functionality of some OSI products was not fully equivalent to their proprietary counterparts. This discrepancy in functionality between standards-based and proprietary applications can limit the system's ability to provide transparency to the end user. NCR found that documentation and training are keys to minimizing user dissatisfaction and maximizing productivity in instances where users must face changes in functionality caused by the change in protocols. Since OSI is still a maturing protocol, planning and patience will pay big dividends in smoothing the transition for implementors and users alike. NCR has plans for future OSI services in the NCR WIN network, such as OSI-based network management and client/server applications for LAN's interconnected locally and across wide areas.

Case Study Summary

The NCR Worldwide Information Network is committed to transitioning NCR corporate networks to the OSI standard. It is accomplishing that goal through a process of integration of existing networks with OSI using an X.25 backbone and a combination of transition strategies — a modified bottom-up and an application gateway.

The process of implementing WIN, the experience of planning and "selling" the system concept and goals, as well as beginning implementation of specific applications, has reinforced the original concept that integration of proprietary and open architectures is both desirable and achievable.

Conclusion — Making Transition Work

For organizations that wish to make the transition to OSI without abandoning their current investment in proprietary systems, the transition process should be viewed as evolutionary, rather than revolutionary. To accomplish this evolutionary transition, any of six strategies may be used alone or in combination.

However, a thorough understanding of the total transition process is just as important as selecting the proper strategies. The transition strategies must achieve an overall computing network objective that benefits the organization. As this chapter makes clear, network transition requires time, money, and dedication, so the transition to open architectures has significant financial and political elements, as well as purely technical ones. The NCR WIN Case Study shows that persuasive justification of network transition in terms of benefits such as productivity gains and long-term cost savings can win the firm backing of management at all levels. Without this support, the transition process becomes exponentially more difficult.

Properly planned and executed, the transition from proprietary to open architectures will mark another step forward in the continuing evolution of computer networks.

About the Authors

Carol Herbst

Carol Herbst is Product Manager in Advanced Systems within NCR Comten's Product Management organization. She has been active in data communications at NCR Comten for eight years and an active member of OSI standards committees for five years.

In her previous position, Ms. Herbst was a member of NCR Comten's Applied Communications department where she participated in various research and development projects including the design and implementation of OSI protocols.

Rick A. Johnson

Rick A. Johnson is a Senior Product Manager within NCR Comten's Product Management organization with responsibility for NCR Comten's OSI products. He has participated in the development of OSI standards through the NIST Lower Layer Special Interest Group, the OSINET Technical and Steering Committees, and the COS Network Management Subcommittee.

In previous positions, Mr. Johnson participated in various development projects involving the design and development of OSI, X.25, and LAN products for UNIX-based systems.

Mr. Johnson holds degrees in Business Administration and Computer Programming.

Clayton J. Morlok

Clayton J. Morlok is a director within NCR Comten's Product Management organization and is responsible for the company's OSI products. Morlok joined NCR Comten in 1973 and held several technical and management positions in Software Development.

In 1986 he received an Outstanding Technical Achievement Award from the NCR Research & Development Recognition Program for his work on the company's ACF/NCP product. He holds a Bachelor of Science degree.

Glossary

The majority of the terms in this glossary were contributed by Dr. James Doar, of Geibel Systems Integration Services, Inc.

Abstract Syntax — Refers to the syntax for data used in application-layer entities.

ANSI — American National Standards Institute; an industry-supported agency responsible for the coordination of all standards activity and the publishing and distribution of national and international standards within the United States. Also responsible for coordinating the American position on international standards. ANSI is the official representative from the United States to ISO and provides technical and administrative support to the U.S. State Department, the official representative to CCITT.

ARP — Address Resolution Protocol; a TCP/IP protocol that maps IP addresses to Ethernet addresses.

ARPA — Advanced Research Projects Agency; early sponsor of TCP/IP network development.

Asynchronous — Communication in which the time intervals between successive symbols may be unequal.

Bandwidth — The range of frequencies that can be transmitted by a communication system.

Baud — The per-second rate of signaling on a circuit.

bb — Baseband; a single-channel communications signaling technique, originally defined for coax cable, that does not use carrier frequency modulation. Data signals are imposed directly on the cable, typically at 10 Mbps. May be used with twisted-pair wiring with appropriate signal-balancing hardware. Specified by IS 8802/3 (IEEE 802.3).

BB — Broadband; a multichannel communications signaling technique used with coax cable at multiple (high) frequencies, generally ranging from 5.75 to 450 MHz (similar to cable TV, but providing for two-way communication). Typically, the frequency range is divided into 6-MHz-wide channels, each of which is independent of the others, allowing multiple communication systems to share the same cable plant. Data signals are frequency modulated onto each data channel at 10 Mbps. Specified by IS 8802/4 (IEEE 802.4).

Bus — A topology in which network nodes communicate through a common medium for transmission. The signals for control and data are signaled simultaneously.

CADD — Computer-Aided Design and Drafting.

CALS — Computer-Aided Acquisition and Logistics System; a DoD initiative to define the formats for delivery of data in electronic form for all DoD contracts. The CALS Specification requires all DoD contractors to deliver certain contractual data in standard formats, using CALS-defined profiles of national and international standards cited in appropriate MIL-STD documents. MAP/TOP 3.0 and CALS 1.0 use identical profiles for the standard interchange formats that both specify.

Carrier — A frequency in the transmission band of a medium that can be modulated to allow for the carrying of data.

CB — Carrierband; a single-channel communications cabling technique used with coax cable at high frequencies. Data is frequency modulated onto the (single) carrier frequency at 5 Mbps. Specified by IEEE 802.4 as an alternative to broadband.

CCITT — International Consultative Committee on Telephony and Telegraphy; one of the governing bodies for the adoption of international standards, particularly in the area of public voice and data networks. Most CCITT recommendations related to information technology are jointly published by ISO as International Standards.

Central Control — A common method for controlling the network. One central node, such as a mainframe computer, provides the routing tables for all other nodes.

CLNP — Connectionless Network Protocol; the international standard Internet Protocol for delivery of a connectionless (no permanent circuit) network service (CLNS), sometimes referred to as a "datagram" service.

Common Carrier — Used to denote a company/organization that provides communication services via its own communication backbone network. Common carriers are generally commercial organizations.

CONP — Connection-Oriented Network Protocol; the international standard Internet Protocol for delivery of a connection-oriented (virtual circuit) network service (CONS).

COS — Corporation for Open Systems; a consortium of communication and computer vendors and users chartered to promote the use of OSI-conformant protocols through the acceleration of the development of standard conformance tests. COS now provides conformance and interoperability testing services for some of the protocols required by the MAP/TOP/GOSIP specifications and has committed to providing the conformance tests and certification of the full range of MAP/TOP/GOSIP products.

CSMA/CD — Carrier Sense Multiple Access with Collision Detection; the media access method specified by the ISO 8802/3 (IEEE 802.3) international standard. When a station has a message to send, it waits for an idle state of the network before attempting to send. After sending a message, it listens to the network to verify that another station has not also sent a message. If a collision is detected, both stations recognize the collision and, after a (different) random interval, each tries again until no collision occurs.

DARPA — Defense Advanced Research Projects Agency; successor to ARPA.

DEE — Data Encryption Equipment; devices that provide encryption for a communications circuit.

DES — Data Encryption Standard; the federal government's encryption algorithm for sensitive information.

DNS — Domain Name Service; a TCP/IP protocol for matching object names and network addresses.

DXF — Drawing Exchange Format; a de facto standard for the exchange of CAD drawings between AutoCAD (the original developer) and several other CAD systems.

EDI — Electronic Data Interchange.

EIA — Electronics Industry Association.

FDDI — Fiber Distributed Data Interface; an IEEE 802 compatible physical and data-link control standard for a 100-Mbps fiber ring, currently being standardized by ANSI and ISO subcommitees.

FDM — Frequency-Division Multiplexing; a technique that provides for the dividing of the frequency bandwidth into smaller subbands to provide each user with the exclusive use of a subband.

FTAM — File Transfer, Access, and Management; an OSI IS for the protocols and services for file manipulations over a communication network. Specified by both MAP/TOP and GOSIP. Provides considerable enhancement over the TCP/IP FTP-based service.

Gateway — Computer software that provides for the translation of the network protocols of different vendors.

GOSIP — Government Open Systems Interconnect Profile; a Federal Information Processing Standard that specifies a well-defined set of OSI protocols for government communications systems procurement. Conformance to the GOSIP specifications became mandatory for all federal agencies in August 1990. GOSIP 1.0 is a proper subset of the MAP/TOP 3.0 specifications and is expected to remain so.

Heterogeneous — A network with host hardware and communications software from different vendors.

Homogeneous — A network with host hardware and communications software from the same or architecturally compatible vendors.

Host — A computer that supports users in storing and processing their data. For example, the host may serve as the central processor of a centrally controlled network.

ICA — International Communications Association.

ICMP — Internet Control Message Protocol.

IEEE — Institute of Electrical and Electronics Engineers; a professional association with long-term involvement in the development of standards. Assigned by ISO to lead the development of LAN standards in the physical and data-link layers of the OSI model (the IEEE 802 Project).

IGES — Initial Graphics Exchange Standard; an ANSI standard (ANSI Y14.26M, 1987) for the exchange of geometric information and part attributes in a neutral data format. Specified by both MAP/TOP and CALS.

Interoperability — The capability of computers from like or unlike vendors to work in tandem in the support of users.

IP — Internet Protocol; a Department of Defense protocol.

ISA — Instrument Society of America.

ISDN — Integrated Services Digital Network; a set of standards now being developed within ANSI, ISO, and CCITT for the delivery of various services over digital networks. MAP/TOP and GOSIP expect to incorporate appropriate ISDN standards into their specifications as alternate subnetwork building blocks after the ISDN Users Forum has developed the implementation agreements.

ISO — International Organization for Standardization; one of the governing bodies for the adoption of international standards, particularly in the area of Information Technology and Computer Communications.

ISODE — ISO Development Environment; a set of public domain software subroutines that provide an interface between the MAP/TOP/GOSIP-specified session layer (ISO) and the DoD-specified transport layer (TCP/IP). Allows the development of applications that will execute over both OSI and TCP/IP protocol stacks as a migration path from TCP/IP networks to MAP/TOP/GOSIP networks.

LAN — Local Area Network.

Layer — Within a reference model, such as OSI, a group of related communication functions is referred to as a layer.

LLC — Logical Link Control; a sublayer in the data-link layer of the OSI model. The LLC provides the basis for an unacknowledged connectionless service, or connection-oriented service, on the local area network.

MAP/TOP — Manufacturing Automation Protocol/Technical and Office Protocols; an internationally accepted set of specifications for open communication based on ISO/OSI standards. The current version, MAP/TOP 3.0, was produced by the North American MAP/TOP Users Group (with contributions from overseas) and has been officially endorsed by the Australian, European, and Japanese Users Groups, as well as the World Federation of MAP/TOP Users Groups.

MHS — Message Handling Service; the service provided by the CCITT X.400 series of standards, consisting of a user agent to allow users to create and read electronic mail, a message transfer agent to provide addressing, sending, and receiving services, and a reliable transfer agent to provide routing and delivery services. Specified by MAP/TOP and GOSIP.

MMFS — Manufacturing Message Format Standard; a precursor to MMS developed by a MAP Task Force Technical Committee for version 2.0 of MAP, later modified to produce the first draft of the MMS proposed standard.

MMS — Manufacturing Messaging Service; the ISO standard for provision of a messaging service between programmable devices, such as robots or programmable logic controllers, and a control system. The equivalent to human-oriented electronic mail services for computer-controlled devices. Specified by MAP/TOP.

NIST — National Institute for Standards and Technology; new name for the National Bureau of Standards, an organization that has been crucial to the success of OSI and the MAP/TOP/GOSIP effort in this country. The MAP/TOP/GOSIP and COS specifications are all based heavily on the OSI Implementation Agreements developed at the NIST-hosted OSI Implementors Workshops.

Node — A computer that is part of a network, passing data and performing other user-related functions.

NPDU — Network Protocol Data Unit; OSI terminology for a packet, a logical block of control symbols and data transmitted by the network layer protocol.

NVP — Network Voice Protocol; a TCP/IP protocol for handling voice information.

ODA/ODIF — Office Document Architecture/Office Document Interchange Format; a set of ISO standards defining compound document content and structure and interchange formats for both revisable and final form compound documents. Specified by MAP/TOP and GOSIP.

Open Architecture — Interoperability that is based on standard protocols adopted by multiple vendors.

OSI — Open Systems Interconnection; a set of national and international standards that conform to the ISO model for open systems communications, allowing the possibility of interoperability among multiple vendors' products.

Packet — A small unit of control information and data that is processed by the network protocol.

PDES — Product Data Exchange Standard; a developing international standard for the exchange of product and process data, also known internationally as STEP, Standard for the Exchange of Product Data.

PPDU — Presentation Protocol Data Unit; OSI terminology for logical blocks of control symbols and data transmitted at the presentation layer protocol.

PROFS — Professional Office System; an IBM proprietary product that provides a number of office-oriented services, such as electronic mail, calendaring, and scheduling.

RARP — Reverse Address Resolution Protocol; a TCP/IP protocol for mapping Ethernet addresses to IP addresses.

RF — Radio Frequency.

SAA — Systems Application Architecture; a strategic IBM application architecture intended to allow application portability across the entire IBM product line as IBM's computing architectures are enhanced to support it. The definitions have been made public so that third parties may supply applications that conform.

SAP — Service Access Point; the logical block of data and control symbols transmitted by the session layer protocol in the OSI model.

SDLC — Synchronous Data Link Control; a proprietary IBM protocol for data-link control, available from other vendors as well.

SGML — Standard Generalized Markup Language; a standard page description language, originally developed for interchange of page layouts in publishing applications. Specified by CALS.

SMTP — Simple Mail Transfer Protocol; a standard protocol for electronic mail used by the Department of Defense.

SNA — Systems Network Architecture; IBM's proprietary communication protocol, which many other vendors support to provide some form of connectivity to IBM mainframe systems, most commonly 2780/3780-type remote batch and 3270-type interactive terminal sessions.

SNADS — SNA Distribution Service; an IBM product.

STP — Shielded Twisted Pair.

TCP — Transmission Control Protocol; a Department of Defense data communications protocol.

TP — Transport Protocol; the OSI standard for providing a complete end-to-end data delivery service over an OSI network. Specified by MAP/TOP and GOSIP.

UTP — Unshielded Twisted Pair.

WAN — Wide Area Network.

X.21 — The CCITT standard for logical link control and media access control in X.25 networks.

X.25 — The CCITT standard for packet-switched network layer services, primarily in Public Data Networks, but now used in many private packet-switched networks.

X.400 — The CCITT (and ISO) set of standards for providing electronic mail services over an open network (see MHS). Includes the X.409 (ISO ASN.1) standard that is widely used for encoding binary data.

X.500 — The CCITT (and ISO) set of standards for providing directory services across an open network.

Index

Address, as name, 282
Addressing
   addresses used with CONS, 124-125
   network layer, 116-125
     NSAP addresses, 117-122
     OSINET NSAP address format, 122-123
     subnetwork point of attachment addresses, 125-126
     U.S. NSAP addresses, 123-124
Address mask parameter, 166-167, 174
Administrative domains, 176
Aliases, X.500 Directory Recommendations, 251
AmLink3 software, 76
Application layer, 13
Application protocols, networks, 99-100
Application Programming Interfaces, 46, 65
Architecture
   distributed architecture, 94
   open architecture, 93-94
   vision of network design, 104-6
Area address, 178
ARPANet, development of, 21-22
Attributes, X.500 Directory Recommendations, 249
Authentication, security, 253, 276-277
AUTOFACT, 16, 19

Basic rate service, Integrated Services Digital Network, 71
Binary coded decimal encoding rules, 121
Binding, 11
Bottom-up transition, of OSI, 356-357
Bus network structure, 99

Caching, namespaces, 266-267
CCITT Blue Book, 247
Cell
   advantages to concept of, 290
   illustration of, 291
   in OSF DCE, 289-290
Centralized systems
   versus distributed systems, 270-271
   nature of, 266
Clear request packet, 174-175
Clerk, 287
Computerized Acquisitions and Logistics Systems, 21
Configuration notification, 168-171
Confirm service primitive, 111
Connectionless network layer protocol
   mapping to X.25 subnetwork, 153-155
   mapping to 8802-2 subnetworks, 155
   OSI network layer, 139-155
   protocol for provision of, 139-135

385

Connectionless network service,
    OSI network layer, 111-113
Connection-oriented network service
    NSAP address format, 124-125
    OSI network layer, 113-115
    protocols of OSI network layer,
        128-138
Courier, 232

Data coherence, and global access,
    273
Data driven environment, components of, 95
Data link layer, 7-8
Data transfer services, OSI network layer, 108-111
Defense Data Network, 22
Delay metric, 183
Descriptive names, 282
Digital Equipment Corporation proprietary network, 28-30
    file transfer, 29
    MAILbus, 30
    network virtual terminal capability, 29
    program-to-program communication, 29
    remote command/batch file submission and execution, 29
    remote resources access, 29
Directed graphs, as naming structures, 283, 284
Direct mail, X.500 application, 260
Directories, 289
Directory access protocol, 287
Directory information base, 288
Directory Information Tree, 288
    X.500 Directory Recommendations, 249
Directory Schema, X.500 Directory Recommendations, 249-251
Directory service agents, 288
Directory service protocol, 288
Directory User Agent, X.500 Directory Recommendations, 254

Distance vector routing, 177
Distinguished name, 249
Distributed architecture, 94
Distributed computing environment
    advantages of, 268-270
    versus centralized systems, 270-271
    characteristics of, 267-268
    core services for, 275-277
        authentication service, 276-277
        distributed file system, 276
        global naming service, 275-276
        support for distribution of applications, 276
        synchronization of system time, 277
    evolution of, 266-267
    versus networked systems, 271
    Open Software Foundation, 278-279
    OSI and, 271-272
    pervasive properties of, 272-275
        global access, 273
        global availability, 274-275
        global management, 274
        global names, 273
        global security, 273-274
Distributed control system, 193
Distributed name services
    design criteria, 284-287
        caching, 286-287
        replication, 284-285
        scalability, 286
    versus distributed database, 280-281
    functional name service model, 287-288
    naming methods
        address, 282
        descriptive name, 282
        primitive name, 282
        route, 282
    network naming structures, 283-284

Index

directed graphs, 283
rooted graphs, 283-284
tree, 283, 284
unrooted graphs, 284
storage of namespace, 284
Distribution list, 224

EDIFACT, 64-65
8000 network systems, 226-227
development of, 226-227
8802-2 subnetworks, mapping CLNP to, 155
Electronic Data Interchange, 52
E-mail, X.500 application, 258
Encoding
binary, 121
preferred, 121
Enhanced Performance Architecture, 16
Error metric, 183
ES-IS protocols, 45-46
routing protocols, 159-167
for use with 8878/x.25, 167-175
Ethernet, 224-225
Ethernet address, 123
Europe
OSI profiles
Germany, 59-60
Sweden, 58-59
United Kingdom, 57-58
European Procurement Handbook for Open Systems, 54
Expense metric, 183
External mail gateway, 227-229

Fieldbus, 103-104
File transfer, access, and management, 101-102, 188, 199
File transfer program, Transmission Control Protocol/Internet Protocol, 24-25
Full-duplex, 11
Function placement, 94

Gateways
nature of, 203
terminal mapped gateways, 363
in transition to OSI, 357-359
General directories, X.500 application, 260
Germany, OSI profiles, 59-60
Global access
and data coherence, 273
and distributed systems, 273
Global availability, distributed systems, 274-275
Global management, distributed systems, 274
Global names
and distributed systems, 273
service, 275-276
Government OSI Profile
GOSIP 1.0, 20
GOSIP 2.0, 21
purpose of, 20
See also U.S. GOSIP
Grapevine system, 224-226

Half-duplex, 11
High order domain specific part, 181
Hybrid networks, in transition to OSI, 363-365
HYPERchannel network, 31-32

Inbasket Protocol, Xerox Network Systems Mail, 236-237
Indication service primitive, 110
Information resource dictionary system, 103
Integrated Services Digital Network
basic rate service, 71
classes of service, 71
as digital network, 69-70
as an environment, 70
equipment classification, 73
link layer, 75

nature of, 69-70
network layer, 75-76
network topography, 71-73
open standards issues, 80
physical layer, 74-75
primary rate service, 71
protocols, 74
R reference point, 73
software structure, 76-80
   layers 1 through 3, 76-79
   management entity, 79-80
S reference point, 73-74
terminal equipment/terminal adapters
   D channel-only terminals, 86
   adaptors for non-ISDN terminals, 84-86
   integrated voice/data terminal, 83-84
   LAN gateways, 87
   PC workstation ISDN boards, 81-83
   telephones, 81
T reference point, 74
U reference point, 74
voice/data integration, 87-88
Integration/integrated state
   nature of, 93-96
   prerequisites to, 96-99
Interconnection of systems
   case examples of, 212-219
   custom solution, 210
   de facto standard, 211
   implementation strategies
      added features, 220
      end-to-end solutions, 220
      OSI/X.400 as backbone, 219-220
      use of appropriate technology, 219
      use of existing applications, 220
   proprietary solution, 210-211
   reluctance to use OSI system, 211-212
Intermediate system hello, 160

Internal network layer architecture, OSI
   network layer, 126-127
International code designator, 121
International Consultative Committee on
   Telephony and Telegraphy, 4
International Standards Organization, CCITT OSI model, 3-6
Internet Protocol, 117
Internetwork datagram protocol, Xerox Network Systems Mail, 230
Interrogation operations, X.500 Directory Recommendations, 252
IS-IS routing protocols, 175-184

Knowledge information, X.500, 256

LAN gateways, ISDN, 87
Line termination, 73
Link state PDU, 181-182
Link state routing, 177
Logical address, 117

MAILbus, 30
MailTransport Protocol, Xerox Network Systems Mail, 234-236
Management information systems departments, use of OSI, 60-61
Manufacturing Automation Protocol, 53, 101
   history of, 14-15
   MAP 1.0, 15
   MAP 2.0, 15
   MAP 2.1, 15-16
   MAP 2.2, 16
   MAP 3.0, 16-17
   objective of, 14
   product certification, 18
   strategy of, 17-18
Manufacturing environment, use of OSI, 61

Manufacturing message specification, 102, 188, 199
Message handling services, 102
MILNET, 22
Modification user operations, X.500 Directory Recommendations, 252
Multicast, 288
Multiple protocol routing and bridging, in transition to OSI, 357-359

Name services. See Distributed name services; OSF DCE name services
Namespace, 289
N-CONNECT request service primitive, 113-114
N-DATA-ACKNOWLEDGE primitive, 114
N-DISCONNECT indication service primitive, 113-114
NETEX, 31-33
    HYPERchannel network, 31-32
    software for, 32-33
Network architecture
    analysis and non-ISO protocols, 203-204
    development of combine overall network architecture, 201-023
        identification of components of communication paths, 198-201
        identification of types of communication devices, 193-197
        showing required communication paths, 197-198
    rational for planning of, 188-190
Network entity titles, 109, 116
    OSI network layer, 125
Network layer, 8-9
Network protocol address information, 118
Network protocol control information, 109
Networks

architectural vision of design, 104-6
basic principles, 99-100
standards in support of, 100-104
Network service access point, 108, 109
Network service data unit, 108-109
Network systems, versus distributed systems, 271
Network termination, 73
N-EXPEDITED-DATA request, 114
NIST Implementor's Agreements, U.S. GOSIP, 38-39
NQuality of service parameterRESET service primitive, 115
NSAP addresses, 117-125

Objects, X.500 Directory Recommendations, 248
Office Document Architecture, 52
Open access/data transparency, 95
Open architecture, 93-94
Open Software Foundation, distributed computing environment, 278-279
Open Systems Interconnection model. See OSI
OSF DCE name service
    applications use of, 292-294
    cell in, 289-290
    name in, 291-292
    organization of namespace, 289
OSI
    benefits to use, 65-66
    deployment strategy, 62-63
    and distributed systems, 271-272
    increase in use of, 51-52
    layers, 52
        application layer, 13
        data link layer, 7-8
        network layer, 8-9
        physical layer, 7
        presentation layer, 12-13

session layer, 11-12
transport layer, 9-11
profiles
   creation of, 52-54
   German profile, 59-60
   Swedish profile, 58-59
   United Kingdom profile, 57-58
reference model, 6-7
reluctance towards use of, 211-212
subnetworks, 107
usefulness of, 63-65
use in government sector, 54-56
use in industry, 60-62
compared to XNS, 230-233
OSINET, NSAP address format, 122-123
OSI network layer
   addressing at, 116-117
   algorithmic determination of routing information, 158
   connectionless network layer protocol, 139-155
   connectionless network service, 111-113
   connection-oriented network service, 113-115
   connection-oriented network service protocols, 128-138
   data transfer services, 108-111
   internal network layer architecture, 126-127
   network addresses, 108
   network entity titles, 125
   network layer data transfer protocols, 127-128
   network layer routing, 156
   NSAP addresses, 117-125
   purpose of, 107
   routing protocols at network layer, 158-184
   routing/relaying, 116
   static configuration of routing information, 156-158
   subnetwork point of attachment addresses, 125-126
OSI selection process
   communication transaction requirements, 302-303
   comparison analysis, 313-322
      communication system profile cost estimates, 314-318
      communication system profile definition, 314
      communication system profile selection parameter comparison, 318-320
      quantification of intangible benefits, 320-322
      scoring network selection goals, 320
   cost justification, 368
   guideline prerequisites, 307
   hardware/software requirements, 301-302
   interview process, 307-313
      business planning questions, 308-309
      network selection goal scoring, 312-313
      project planning questions, 309-310
      technology planning questions, 310-312
   management report, 323-347
   network selection goals
      cost, 306
      expandability, 306
      flexibility, 306
      integration, 306
      manageability, 306
      performance/system thoroughput, 306
      risk level, 306
      security, 306
      uptime/reliability, 306
   network selection parameters
      application services, 305

architecture, 303
change, 304
changes to network, 304-305
maintenance, 304
media, 303-304
network management, 305
performance metrics, 305
protocol service support, 305
planning, 368-369
prerequisite information, 301-303
questions of project mission statement, 301
selling OSI concept, 367
OSI transition strategies
backbone and gateways, 369, 371
benefits of evolving to OSI, 351-352
bottom-up transition, 356-357
case example, 365-367, 372
gateways, 359-363
general considerations, 352-354
hybrid networks, 363-365
multiple protocol routing and bridging, 357-359
network evolution, 350-351
parallel networks, 355
strategy selection, 369
terminal-mapped gateways, 363
top-down transition, 359

Packet exchange protocol, Xerox Network Systems Mail, 232
Parallel networks, in transition to OSI, 355
PC workstation ISDN boards, 81-83
Physical address, 117
Physical layer, 7
Preferred encodings, 121
Presentation layer, 12-13
Primary rate service, Integrated Services Digital Network, 71
Primitive names, 282

Printing, Transmission Control Protocol/Internet Protocol, 27
PROFS system, examples of use, 212-218
Programmable logic controllers, 193, 197, 199, 200-201
Proprietary protocols
Digital Equipment Corporation proprietary network, 28-29
NETEX, 31-33
Systems Network Architecture, 30-31
Protection from unauthorized access parameterm, 112
Pseudonode, 182

Quality of service parameter, 112, 114-115
Query configuration PDU, 162

Referral, 288
Relative distinguished name, 249
Remote database access, 102-103
Remote procedure calls, 276
Replication, and name service, 284-285
Request service primitive, 110
Residual error probability, 113
Response service primitive, 111
Rooted graphs, as naming structures, 283-284
Route, as name, 282
Routing
algorithmic determination of, 158
default routing entry, 158
full destination NSAP address matching, 156-157
IS-IS routing protocols, 175-184
partial destination NSAP addresses, 157
protocols at network layer, 158-184

392 Open Systems Interconnection Handbook

ES-IS routing protocols, 159-167
ES-IS for use with 8878/x.25, 167-175
routing information base, 158
static configuration of information, 156-158
Routing domains, 176
Routing information protocol, Xerox Network Systems Mail, 232
R reference point, Integrated Services Digital Network, 73

Scalability
  and distributed systems, 270, 286
  and name service, 286
  nature of, 270
Security
  authentication in, 253, 276-277
  authorization in, 253
  distributed systems, 273-274, 276-277
  levels of, 112
Sequenced packet protocol, Xerox Network Systems Mail, 232
Servers, 224
Service primitives, 113-116
  types of, 111
Session layer, 11-12
  interface and Transmission Control Protocol/Internet Protocol, 28
Shortest path first algorithm, 183
Simple mail transfer protocol, Transmission Control Protocol/Internet Protocol, 27
Simplex, 11
S reference point, Integrated Services Digital Network, 73-74
Standardized Generalized Mark-up Language, 21
Star network structure, 99
Structured query language, 103
Subnetwork access protocol, 127

Subnetwork address resolution entity, 167-168, 174-175
Subnetwork dependent convergence protocol, 126-127
Subnetwork independent convergence protocol, 126
Subnetwork point of attachment, 116-117
  addresses, OSI network layer, 125-126
Subnetworks, OSI, 107
Sweden, OSI profiles, 58-59
Synchronization of time system, distributed systems, 277
Systems Network Architecture, 30-31
  data flow control, 31
  data link control, 30
  function management, 31
  path control, 30
  transmission control, 30

Technical and Office Protocol, 53, 101
  TOP 1.0, 19
  TOP 3.0, 19-20
Telemarketing, X.500 application, 260
Telephone directory, X.500 application, 258-260
Telephones, ISDN, 81
Telnet, 26-27
Terminal adaptor, ISDN, 84-86
Top-down transition, of OSI, 359
Transaction processing, 103
Transmission Control Protocol/Internet Protocol, 21
  file transfer program, 24-25
  network layer, 22-23
  printing, 27
  services of, 22, 24
  session layer interface, 28
  session/presentation/application layers, 23
  simple mail transfer protocol, 27

Index 393

transport layer, 23
usage, 23-24
virtual terminal protocol, 26-27
Transport layer, 9-11
Trees
and namespace, 289
as naming structures, 283, 284
T reference point, Integrated Services Digital Network, 74

United Kingdom, OSI profiles, 57-58
Unrooted graphs, as naming structures, 284
U reference point, Integrated Services Digital Network, 74
U.S. GOSIP
application layer, 42-43
conformance/interoperability testing, 43-44
data link layer, 40
development of, 37-38
information resources about, 50
limitations of, 44-48
network layer, 40-41
NIST Implementor's Agreements, 38-39
NSAP address format, 123-124
compared to other profiles, 44
physical layer, 40
presentation layer, 42
questions for vendors about, 48
reasons for creation of, 35-36
session layer, 41
transport layer, 41

VAX environment, 97
Virtual terminal protocol, 203
Transmission Control Protocol/Internet Protocol, 26-27
Voice/data terminal integration, ISDN, 83-84, 87-88

Xerox
8000 network systems, 226-227

Grapevine system, 224-226
influence on X.400, 229-230
Xerox Network Systems Mail
architecture of, 233-238
error/echo protocols, 232
Inbasket Protocol, 236-237
incorporation of X.400 gateway, 227-229
internetwork datagram protocol, 230
MailTransport Protocol, 234-236
compared to OSI stacks, 230-233
packet exchange protocol, 232
routing information protocol, 232
sequenced packet protocol, 232
XNS/X.400 mail gateway, 237-238